# Central Asia and the Caspian

*Open for Growth*

# Central Asia and the Caspian

## Open for Growth

Theodore J. Kim

Published by Euromoney Books

*in association with*

Commercial Bank Asaka
Ernst & Young
Halyk Savings Bank of Kazakhstan
International Bank of Azerbaijan
Kazkommertsbank
Kazkommerts Securities
White & Case L.L.P.

Published by
Euromoney Publications PLC
Nestor House, Playhouse Yard
London EC4V 5EX
Tel: +44 (0)171 779 8860
Fax: +44 (0)171 779 8541

The picture on page 155 (bottom) was supplied by Panos Pictures.
Typeset by JP Smith and Euromoney Books, England.
Printed in England by Clifford Press Ltd, Coventry.

# Acknowledgements

Additional reporting was by Carlotta Gall and Charles Piggot.

Theodore Joseph Kim was born in New York City and completed his secondary studies at Choate Rosemary Hall in Wallingford, Connecticut. After receiving a B.Sc. (Economics) Honours degree with a specialisation in International Relations from the London School of Economics and Political Science, he worked in Moscow for several years. Leaving Russia to pursue postgraduate studies in France, he was later awarded a Master of Science in International Economics with distinction at the University of Paris 1, Panthéon-Sorbonne. Afterwards, he returned to London to complete law school and was eventually called to the Bar of England and Wales as a Barrister-at-Law in 1995. His previous book, *Investing in the Baltic States: Estonia, Latvia, Lithuania*, was published by Euromoney Books in September 1998.

Mr Kim would like to thank Kazkommerts Securities, Kazakhstan, for their substantial input to the book as well as his Moscow-based assistant, Galia Oussenova, for her kind assistance in unearthing many obscure pages of Russian financial documentation.

Charles Piggot would like to thank the following for their help: Stephen Lewarne, Global Securities' Director of Research for the CIS; Stephen Shevoley and Libor Slechta, analysts at Thomson BankWatch, Cyprus; Julia Zilberman, press officer at the EBRD, London; Gavin Gray, economist at the EIU, London; and Madina Dushimova, head of research at Kazkommerts Securities, Kazakhstan.

Euromoney Books would like to thank the following: Ruben Lee and the OECD for the extracts from 'The development of capital markets in Central Asia' in Chapter 7, Banking and finance and Chapter 8, Azerbaijan; White and Case Kazakstan L.L.P. for the section on the legal environment in Chapter 9, Kazakhstan; and Ernst & Young for the sections on the fiscal environment in Chapter 8, Azerbaijan, Chapter 9, Kazakhstan, Chapter 12, Turkmenistan and Chapter 13, Uzbekistan.

The pictures in Chapter 11, Tajikistan were provided by Charles Piggot. All other pictures except the co-publishers' own were provided by Gregory Wrona.

The picture on pages vi–vii shows Balshoe Almatynskoe Lake in the Tian Sian Mountains, Kazakhstan.

# Contents

**Part II    MARKET PROFILES**

Co-publishers    163

ix

# CENTRAL ASIA &
# THE CASPIAN

N

RUSSIAN
FEDERATION

Samara

RUSSIAN
FEDERATION

Ku

Uralsk

Orenburg

Orsk

River Ural

Aktiubinsk

River Volga

Astrakhan

Atyrau

Aralsk

Aral Sea

Aktau

Muynak

Caspian
Sea

Nukus

GEORGIA

Kuba

Tashauz

Urgench

UZBE

ARMENIA

Gjandza

AZERBAIJAN

Sumgait

River Kura

Baku

Turkmenbashi

Darvaza

TURKEY

AZER-
BAIJAN

River Araz

Nebit-Dag

Buk

Kazandzhik

TURKMENISTAN

Astara

Chardzhou

Kizyl-
Atrek

Ashgabat

Beshky

Rasht

River Atrak

Tedzhen

Mary

Bābol

Serakhs

IRAQ

Tehrān

Mashad

Kushka

I R A N

RUSSIAN
FEDERATION

Omsk

Petropavlovsk

Kokchetav

*Lake Sileteniz*

Pavlodar

*River Irtysh*

Astana

Arkalyk

*Lake Tengiz*

Karaganda

Semipalatinsk

Ust-Kamenogorsk

MONGOLIA

AKHSTAN

*Lake Zaysan*

Zhezkazgan

*Lake Alakol*

*Lake Balkhash*

Ürümqi

Taldy-korgan

CHINA

rda

Almaty

*r Syr Darya*

Turkestan

XINJIANG

Taraz

Bishkek

*Lake Issyk-Kul*

Kara Kol

Talas

Kara-Balta

Balykchi

Barskaun

Shymkent

KYRGYZ REPUBLIC

Kara-Kul

Naryn

Tashkent

*Lake rdarkul*

Namangan

Dzhalal-Abad

Gulistan

Andijan

Osh

Jizzakh

Kokand

Fergana

nd

Khodzhent

Sary-Tash

CHINA

shi

TAJIKISTAN

Kashgar

Tursunzade

Dushanbe

Murgab

Termez

Kurgan-Tyube

Kulyab

Khorog

GHANISTAN

PAKISTAN

INDIA

# Introduction

The Central Asian and Caspian republics have only recently joined the investible emerging market universe. For over half a century, while under Soviet rule, Moscow did everything in its power to eliminate any cultural or economic differences between the republics. Instead, they were slowly developed into little more than commodity producing outlying colonies with little or no individual identity. Now, seven years after independence, the region's vast reserves of oil and gas will be the backbone of sustained growth.

## Continuing reform, remaining challenges

The financial crises, first in Asia, then in Russia, have dealt a severe blow to the region, but the downturn has not left it without hope. All the republics are reforming their economies, albeit at a different pace and with different economic policies. The Kyrgyz Republic has earned a reputation as a determined advocate of economic and structural reform. Azerbaijan shows new signs of reforming its economy outside energy and now offers opportunities to financial investors. Kazakhstan is pressing on with reforms despite the slide in commodity prices, and is also opening up to foreign banks. A peace deal has been reached in Tajikistan and the government has embarked on an ambitious reform programme in conjunction with an IMF programme. Uzbekistan and Turkmenistan are following a cautious, gradualist approach.

### Azerbaijan

Increased oil production should more than compensate for the deficit and export decline caused by the Russian crisis and low global commodity prices. Azerbaijan can also rely upon foreign direct investment (FDI) and multilateral loans to finance its growing trade and current account deficit, which, according to the IMF, was US$950 million in 1997, or 24.5 per cent of GDP. Relations between Azerbaijan and the IMF are excellent, and there have never been delays in disbursements. The government has attacked inflation, increased growth and has won large inflows of FDI.

Despite the windfall for international oil companies and a putative privatisation programme, there has so far been little to offer financial investors except for a thinly traded Treasury bill market. The only other traded instruments are privatisation vouchers and options on them. Investors have been waiting since mid-1997 for a stock exchange to be created.

The big investment opportunities in Azerbaijan apart from those in direct investment are still to come. Fund managers are eager to buy stakes in Aztelecom, Azerenergy and Azerigas. There is even a possibility that a 35 per cent stake in the State Oil Company of the Azerbaijan Republic (SOCAR) could come up for sale in 1999. SOCAR manages the country's entire oil and gas sector, and reports directly to the country's president, Heydar Aliyev. In the meantime, there are proposals pending for the privatisation of 50 major companies in the utilities, steel, chemicals, wine, tobacco, seafood and oil sectors, and the government is set to award advisory mandates to investment banks and audit firms to complete the transactions.

The biggest shake-up in Azerbaijan has probably taken place within the banking sector. Like other Former Soviet Union (FSU) countries, Azerbaijan inherited an over-banked, under-branched and undercapitalised system. This has been ruthlessly cut back, and of 240 private banks that existed at the peak, just 85 are left. This number should fall further to 20 or 30 by 2001, which is when all banks will have to have a minimum capital requirement of US$5 million (versus the current requirement of just US$1.25 million). All four of the state-owned banks have been placed under a restructuring programme backed by the IMF and the World Bank. With the exception of Savings Bank, each bank has linked up with a foreign adviser. For example, ABN AMRO should soon begin working with Prominvestbank, the third largest bank with assets of US$145 million.

The government's move to reform the banking sector was seen by most analysts as highly promising for the long run. For the first few years after independence, the overemphasis on oil worried the multilateral agencies, which worked with the government to ensure that the rest of the economy was not neglected. At present, oil and oil products account for roughly 70 per cent of exports. For Azerbaijan, the key question is what happens to the non-oil sector in the next five years; a timeframe that presents a crucial window of opportunity.

### Kazakhstan

President Nursultan Nazarbayev, took the courageous step of moving the capital from Almaty to Akmola, which in May

1998 was then renamed Astana. After this move, few analysts doubted at least his strong willingness to bring about substantial changes to the system. While portfolio investors in Kazakhstan (and elsewhere in the region) may remain frustrated, FDI to the country is flowing fast – an estimated US$1.2 billion in 1998 according to the European Bank for Reconstruction and Development (EBRD) – most of it into the oil and gas sectors. It is estimated that the Caspian Sea lies above huge oil and gas reserves, second only to those under the Persian Gulf. Recent surveys suggest that Kazakhstan's Caspian Sea shelf contains as much as 80 billion barrels of oil. The country also has annual production of over 100 million tonnes of major minerals and is the world's tenth largest producer of coal. So far, the government estimates that not even 1 per cent of total coal reserves have been mined.

In the Kazakh financial sector, which typically suffers if emerging capital markets are not buoyant, foreign banks are taking positions for the long term. Foreign institutions are prohibited from owning more than 25 per cent of the banking system's assets. Nonetheless, the likes of Citibank, Société Générale and HSBC have set up in the country, promising to provide stiff competition to others already established, such as Deutsche Bank and ABN AMRO (the dominant foreign bank for the past four years). Currently, foreign banks own about 10 per cent of the Kazakh banking sector. In February 1998, ING Bank also approached the Kazakh central bank to explore the possibility of buying a local bank. So far, foreign ownership of domestic banks has taken the form of joint ventures, 20 of which are in operation today. The government has given signs it might be willing to push the foreign ownership ceiling up to 50 per cent, which could be good news for a banking sector that comprises just 15 per cent of GDP, compared with an average of 40 per cent in OECD countries.

## Kyrgyz Republic

Although small, mountainous and land-locked, this country may yet prove to be the star performer in the region. The government is committed to privatisation and free enterprise and has followed a carefully planned programme of reform and transition to a market economy. Strict monetary and credit policies, major structural reforms, institutional and procedural reforms in the financial sector, and privatisation have contributed to the recent significant growth in GDP, a stable exchange for the local currency (the som), low inflation, a shrinking budget deficit and an improved fiscal environment. Because the Kyrgyz Republic has been among the most advanced of the newly independent states in moving to a market economy, it has attracted an enormous amount of foreign loans, credits and assistance. In 1997 GDP growth was spurred by a 20 per cent increase in industrial production, mainly attributable to output from the Kumtor gold mine, a

joint venture with Canada's Cameco. Agricultural production, a sector that generally barely manages to survive in the CIS, grew by 10.7 per cent in 1997.

Foreign investors enjoy a legal status at least equal to that of Kyrgyz citizens, and sometimes even enhanced status. For example, 51 per cent stock ownership triggers a profits tax holiday of from two to five years, with subsequent reduced taxation. PepsiCo, Coca-Cola (Turkish licensee), Cadbury Schweppes, André & Cie (Swiss, mineral water bottling) all have joint ventures with local partners. Korea's LG Electronics (GoldStar Corporation) in household appliances, leading Turkish firms such as Sabanci, Koç and Edjajibashi, and Japan's trading companies (Mitsui, Toyota and Kanematsu) have also established representative offices in Bishkek.

Whether via foreign or domestic sources, or international financing institutions, the Kyrgyz Republic must, in order to continue enjoying high rates of economic growth, invest in the public sectors of the economy. With its literate population and a plan to develop human resources, the country is hoping to expand its agricultural base and also to move directly into information technology. Thus, infrastructure reconstruction and development is inevitable to establish worldwide communications. Indeed, the country has the largest number of Internet users per capita in Central Asia, supported by an Asian Development Bank US$40-million loan for education and another US$10 million for computers.

## Tajikistan

The country is experiencing a slow transition from a command economy to a more market-oriented economy. The government has established an ambitious long-term plan for reform, focusing on agriculture, privatisation, fiscal policy, the national budget, reinvigorating moribund industrial sectors and attracting foreign investment. There appears to be significant political will backing implementation of the reforms, and progress, although slow, has been steady. Partially as a reward for the government's economic reforms implemented to date, and to encourage other international financial organisations, the IMF and the World Bank have begun an infusion of credit to Tajikistan. As a result of the civil war, the country has been relatively late in receiving the international monetary assistance and foreign investment already extended to other FSU republics.

The government appears to be ready to undertake the work necessary as a precondition for international donor support and to return the country to the standard of living experienced prior to the outbreak of the civil war. The government will need to implement new legislation to establish the legal basis for reform and to bring about faster privatisation, fiscal reform, price liberalisation and restructuring of the banking sector.

## Turkmenistan

Making any accurate analysis of Turkmenistan's prospects is difficult due to the poor quality of statistics and other available information. Despite being the least developed of the FSU republics, however, the potential of receiving world market prices for its gas and cotton exports improve its long-term economic prospects significantly. Turkmenistan has strong potential for growth if it can reform its system of economic management, reduce its complete dependence on Russia for market access and collect the debts owed to it by other members of the Commonwealth of Independent States (CIS).

The government recognises the need for infrastructure improvements, and in 1996 a new rail link between Iran and Turkmenistan officially opened. The 300-kilometre long railway between the Iranian city of Mashad and the Turkmen town of Serakhs connects Central Asia to the Indian Ocean. It should increase the country's international trade, especially aiding large volume shipments and transport of non-perishable goods. In late 1997 a gas pipeline linking Turkmenistan to the Persian Gulf through Iran was opened, giving the country its first direct access to the lucrative cash energy market outside the FSU. Because of the non-payment problem, gas shipped to destinations within the CIS was mostly, for all intents and purposes, given away for free.

For a nation of its size, Turkmenistan possesses formidable natural resources. Natural gas reserves are the fourth largest in the world, after Russia, the United States and Iran; according to analysis of Soviet data potential reserves could be as high as 14 trillion cubic metres. Oil resources may be as high as 6 billion barrels. The country is currently capable of producing more than 80 billion cubic metres of gas annually, most of which can be exported. Indeed, more than one-tenth of the FSU's gas exports came from Turkmenistan.

While Turkmenistan's oil and gas industry holds tremendous promise, major obstacles stand in the way of foreign investment, such as the lack of an adequate legal framework and the continuing problems of limited access to export markets through Iran. Turkmenistan's dependence on Russia's pipeline system has impeded development and foreign investment in the sector. Currently, Russia allows Turkmenistan to export gas and cotton only to Ukraine and the Transcaucasian nations. Nonetheless, foreign investment is bound to increase in Turkmenistan's energy projects. The government is actively courting large energy multinationals with promises of access to its reserves, although it remains unclear how much control the government plans to relinquish. Currently, the Turkmen administration is trying to develop eight major geological blocks with foreign participation.

## Uzbekistan

Uzbekistan's government presides over one of the most promising economic areas in the region. It has decided to follow its own model of transition to a market economy.

Uzbekistan (which, with a population of 28 million, is one of the most populous countries in Central Asia) is the world's fifth biggest exporter of cotton, seventh largest producer of gold, and fourth of uranium. These statistics help to account for the fact that several foreign banks, including Chase Manhattan, Deutsche Bank, Credit Suisse First Boston and, more recently, Commerzbank and Société Générale, have opened offices. They, along with a clutch of foreign companies – from Coca-Cola and Daewoo to small trading operations – are patiently waiting for reform. One of the main obstacles to reform is the country's dual currency system and an artificially overvalued local currency, which makes it extremely difficult for foreigners to repatriate profits. Foreign companies can obtain currency rations and licences that permit them to convert restricted sums of money, but the terms of these licences can change unexpectedly on a monthly basis.

# The challenges facing the region

Central Asia and the Caspian region is facing some tough challenges. The fallout from the Russian crisis has impacted adversely on indirect and direct flows into the region. Added to this, oil prices are at a nominal 10-year low; on an inflation-indexed yearly average basis, they are closer to a 25-year low. According to oil analysts there seems little hope of an improvement over the next two years. For the energy exporting republics, Azerbaijan and Kazakhstan in particular, this will have serious implications on the economies.

In addition, competition for foreign direct investors into the oil-producing countries is growing. For example, the Saudi Arabian government unexpectedly solicited US development partners in September 1998 for the first time in 20 years.

In the competitive global market for oil investment funds, Central Asia and the Caspian region will find it hard to compete with the low production costs, modern infrastructure and an investor-friendly stance of a country such as Saudi Arabia.

Infrastructure development, particularly transport and telecommunications, is an area which must be improved if more foreign investment is to be attracted to the region. Building intra-regional transport links as well as installing telephone lines was never an important issue during Soviet times. Since then, other than in a few cases directly related to the oil sector, there simply have not been the billions of dollars needed to improve the infrastructure.

While this may present an obstacle to many investment projects, it could also present a gold mine for infrastructure financiers and construction companies. As a case in point, the pipeline development plans in the region, already under way

*Mir-I-Arab
Madrassa,
Bukhara,
Uzbekistan*

to link the Caspian Sea with the Mediterranean and projected to eventually link Kazakhstan with the western energy markets, will be among the biggest civilian construction projects in the world. Central Asian and the Caspian infrastructure projects should prove to be on par in size with such construction projects such as the building of Eurotunnel, which links the United Kingdom to France. Whether foreign corporates are involved in shipping, construction, insurance, telecommunications, or project financing, they may eventually profit when the building of the region's infrastructure finally takes off.

The short-list of blue chip multinationals, such as in the tobacco, soft drinks and consumer goods industry, who are committed to being in every market in the world will certainly look to eventually expand their investment projects. If Marlboro cigarettes, Coca-Cola and Proctor and Gamble soap can generate billions of dollars in sales revenues from sub-Sahara Africa, the markets of Central Asia and the Caspian certainly present an unmissable long-term opportunity. Natural resource companies, whether involved in oil, gas or metals, make investments for the long term and are adept at thriving under adverse conditions. Although the short-term (one year) outlook for raw material prices may be gloomy, the medium-term (three to five years) looks decidedly more optimistic.

The wealth of human resources is a strength that the region has yet to fully develop. Even with a mass exodus of the Russian elite, who typically occupied prominent positions in industry and technology, the region has never suffered from any kind of massive 'brain drain'. The technical skills of local residents involved in banking, oil, metallurgy or agriculture are certainly well on par with Russian standards and, in many cases, equal to those in the West. Unlike the Middle East economies, which must import human resources in virtually every technically skilled profession from doctors and engineers to welders and mechanics, the region has a vast abundance of inexpensive, highly trained capable workers.

## The region's strategic position

Western policy experts have long argued that Central Asia and the Caspian region, because of its oil wealth, should become a new strategic centre of the CIS. An economically strong region supported by oil revenues, according to Washington policy analysts, would provide a buffer to Russia attempting to reassert its old Soviet-era domination. The Central Asian and Caspian republics themselves, desperate to distance themselves from Russia and bolster their political and economic independence, have been spurred on by western financial assistance and political support. The recent climax to this was the official visit by the US Energy Secretary Bill Richardson at a ceremony in Ankara to sign an agreement with five Caspian region republics including Turkey to build a 1,770-kilometre pipeline linking Azerbaijan with the Turkish Mediterranean port of Ceyhan completely by-passing Russian territory and thus depriving Russia of lucrative oil transit revenues.

The western alliance is not likely to abandon the development of an effective buffer to Russia nor allow the total economic collapse of the region. The United States, in particular, will continue to monitor the region and encourage US investment to thwart any long-term Iranian ambitions in the region or the resurgence of an Iranian-style Islamic fundamentalism. A clear example of this has been the United States' increased financial contribution to the Caspian pipeline project and polite pressure on US oil executives when their enthusiasm for the project noticeably started to wane in the face of the collapse in both oil prices and the Russian economy. The US government's push for continued investment by US companies in the region was triggered by the Iranian government's minor low key overtures to western corporates, particularly in the energy sector.

## Conclusion

The size of the region, its geographical significance as the bridge between Europe and Asia, as well as its vast quantities of readily marketable raw materials, albeit selling at depressed prices, are substantial strengths that cannot be ignored. The region possesses one of the world's oldest and most dynamic civilizations, which has endured everything from the invasion by Gengis Khan to mass collectivisation by Stalin. Given this history, the widening of yield curves on emerging market debt and the softening of prices on the International Petroleum Exchange may prove to be merely a minor setback along the path to one of the great economic transformations of the 21st century.

# 1 *Central Asia and the Caspian: A brief history*

## Central Asia

The first signs of an advanced, organised society in Central Asia date back to 1000 BC when nomadic cattle breeders inhabited both the highlands and river valleys. The first large-scale governmental structures were formed by the 7th century BC and the Silk Route was established, a trade network which allowed transcontinental communication.

In 334 BC Alexander the Great's armies crossed the Hindu Kush mountains and occupied Bactria, the ancient name of the territory now called Samarkand and Bukhara in Uzbekistan. Marching further south he encountered strong resistance from nomadic tribes, which took him nearly three years to suppress.

After Alexander's death in 323 BC, his empire fell apart and Central Asia moved closer towards political and economic connections with the Greek world. Greek colonists, merchants and philosophers exerted considerable influence in the spread of Greek culture. Later, a Graeco-Bactrian kingdom was formed, which was semi-independent from Athens for a time before it eventually collapsed, partly due to the invasion of Mongolian tribes, the Scythians, in 159 BC.

During the 1st century AD, a union of nomadic tribes was formed under the rule of the Kushan tribe. The principal seat of the Kushan was Bactria, and their power reached its peak at the end of the 2nd century. Kushan rule then started to decay and they lost more and more of their territory until, in the middle of the 5th century, a related tribe, the White Huns, formerly under the rule of the Kushans, conquered Bactria and ended Kushan rule in Central Asia. The White Huns themselves, however, did not last long, and their power was undermined by the attacks of the Tiurk tribes in the 7th century.

During the first half of the 7th century the Arabs succeeded in defeating the military forces of Byzantium and Sassanian Persia, the ancient regions of Turkey and Iran. In 646, they occupied Merv and by 651, the whole of Khorasan. In 670 they marched into the heart of Central Asia. At first, the Arab armies limited themselves to devastating the fertile valleys of the Amu Darya and looting the towns of Bukhara, Ferghana and other Central Asian territories. In 713 they finally seized Samarkand, making the Arab conquest of Central Asia complete. The Arabs stationed garrisons in important towns and settled their own people in Central Asia, but in most cases they ruled through the native chiefs. They also introduced the Islamic religion, which to a large extent was readily accepted by the native merchant and land-owning class who in turn were given many privileges, although the bulk of the population still remained true to their own cult of Zoroastrianism.

Under Arab occupation trade flourished, and many Central Asian towns became wealthy by serving as stopping-off points for well-laden caravans. In the last years of the 9th century Ismail-Ibn-Akhmed, founder of the Samanid dynasty, became the all-powerful ruler and made Bukhara the capital of all his domains. The Samanid formed a powerful state and carried on a determined struggle against the nomadic tribes who continued to attack the fertile oases and towns of Central Asia. At the end of the 10th century, the Samanid state was destroyed by Tiurk tribes and the Karakhanid dynasty then came to power.

Early in the 13th century the Mongols under Genghis Khan marched on Central Asia. In 1220, Genghis Khan's army pillaged Bukhara and Samarkand. The rule of the Mongols was extremely oppressive and lasted until 1370 when Timur the Lame (Tamerlane) came to power. After Timur's death in 1405, the empire collapsed under his successor, Ulug-Beg, as a result of violent in-fighting between Timur's sons, grandsons and the powerful emirs. Ulug-Beg attempted to preserve the crumbling empire, but was unsuccessful. He was assassinated by his own son in 1449.

Ulug-Beg's death was followed by further violent quarrels that provided the opportunity for the nomadic Uzbek tribe to conquer the region. The Uzbeks were a combination of Tiurks and Mongols who took their name from the Golden Horde, Khan-Uzbek. By the beginning of the 16th century the Uzbek's position was consolidated with the higher nobility seizing the land while the peasant class, mostly composed of Tadzhiks, were forced to become serfs. Progressively the Uzbeks intermingled with the Tadzhiks and other native tribes to form a single Uzbek nationality.

### Early Russian influence

In the middle of the 15th century a large group of Uzbeks moved to settle in the north-west region of Central Asia, in present-day Kazakhstan. This group called itself Kazakhs, which meant 'free people' in the Tiurk language. By the 16th century, diplomatic and trade connections had been established between Moscow and the Uzbeks as well as with the Kazakhs.

In 1717, when the entire territory between the Pacific and the Bering Sea was under Russian control, Peter the Great first attempted to take Central Asia by siding one feudal lord against another. It was not until the 1820s that the Kazakh Khanates, or feudal groups, were finally eliminated. The Kazakh territory was included in the Russian empire and redivided into new administrative areas.

After conquering Kazakhstan, the Tsar turned his attentions further south to Uzbekistan and despite heroic resistance the capital of Uzbekistan was taken in June 1865. The whole of Turkoman, as southern Central Asia was then known, was fully annexed into the Tsarist empire by 1884 with the invasion and fall of Merv, the ancient capital of Turkmenistan. By the end of 1885 the Russian conquest of Central Asia was complete. For the first time since Alexander the Great, European troops were stationed at the edge of Persia and China.

The Tsar's aim was to use the Central Asian colonies as a cheap source of foodstuffs and raw materials as well as a closed market for the sale of manufactured goods.

In 1916 the Russian armies engaged on the German–Austrian front in World War I. Although the Tsarist authorities did not extend conscription to Central Asians, they attempted to mobilise 250,000 men to work behind the lines in non-combative logistical supporting roles. Diverting a huge contingent of young men from the fields in the vital summer months could have been disastrous for the autumn harvest, leaving the rural population to starve. In response to the move, rage and defiance swept the region. The first to revolt were the tribesmen of Uzbekistan and Kazakhstan. Although Tsarist forces succeeded in temporarily suppressing the revolt – and eventually mobilised 120,000 Central Asians for the war effort in Europe – their control over the region was shortlived as in 1917 the October Revolution took place.

# Caspian region – Azerbaijan

Until early medieval times, present-day Azerbaijan was populated by eastern Persian speakers, such as nomadic Turkic tribes, Kurds and Caucasian Albanians. The first recorded political formation in Azerbaijan was the Manna Kingdom, in

around 800 BC. By the 4th century AD, many of these groups converted to Christianity and came under the cultural influence of the Armenians. After Arab incursions in the 7th century, Islam was first established under local rulers called shahanshah. After dissolution of the Arab caliphate in the 9th century, several tribal states emerged in the region.

The Seljuq invasions in the 11th century changed the composition of the local population and resulted in the dominance of Turkic dialects. Azerbaijan, unlike Turkey, continued to develop under Persian social and cultural influence. In fact, by the 16th century, practically the entire territory was united under the rule of the Persian Safavid dynasty.

### Early Russian influence

A new border between the Russian and Persian empires was established following a series of wars between the two powers. Russia acquired Baku, Shirvan, Ganja, Nakhichevan, and Yerevan. Azeris on both sides of the border remained largely rural, though a small merchant class and working class appeared in the second half of the 19th century. As Baku became the major source of oil for Russia, tens of thousands of Iranian, Armenian, and Russian workers migrated to the region in search of employment, and Russian economic and political influence could be felt in both parts of Azerbaijan. As the source of employment and the home of the nascent Azeri intelligentsia and revolutionary movement, Baku radiated its influence throughout the entire territory and into Persia. No specifically Azeri state existed before 1918. The ethnonym 'Azeri' or 'Azerbaijani' came into common use in the pre-Revolutionary decades at first among urban nationalist intellectuals. Only in the Soviet period did it become the official and widely accepted name for this people.

# Central Asia and the Caspian region within the USSR

In the years following the October Revolution, the Bolsheviks drew up the boundaries of Central Asia. Turkmenistan was created in 1924 out of the Tsarist province of Transcaspia. The creation of the Uzbek Soviet Socialist Republic (SSR) that same year was especially traumatic. The main social group was the Sart, urban dwellers who generally spoke Turkish or Persian. Those Sarts who only spoke Turkish were labelled Uzbeks and those who spoke Persian became Tajiks. Initially, the boundaries of the first Uzbek SSR included all of Tajikistan in what was then a self-governing region. However, in 1929, the Persian-speaking area was split off into a separate Tajik republic.

Azerbaijan briefly enjoyed a period of independence after the October Revolution, forming part of a Transcaucasian federa-

*Ruins on the Silk Route, Muyunkum Desert, Kazakhstan*

tion with Georgia and Armenia. In May 1918, the Democratic Republic of Azerbaijan was proclaimed. It existed until April 1920, when the Red Army invaded and, after a Bolshevik coup, a Soviet Republic of Azerbaijan was declared. With Georgia and Armenia it became part of the Transcaucasian Soviet Federative Socialist Republic in 1922, a political unit that lasted until 1936 when the three Transcaucasian states became separate Soviet republics in their own right.

Isolated by high mountains and divided by tribal loyalties, Kyrgyz communities had remained nomadic, pastoral peoples throughout the whole period of Tsarist rule. The Kyrgyz way of life remained largely untouched until Soviet occupation when the nomads were forced into the system of collectivisation. In 1924, when the Kyrgyz SSR was proclaimed, ethnic Russians were placed in all the leading positions and thus dominated the government. It was only in the late 1950s that ethnic Kyrgyz started to join the political elite.

After the collapse of Tsarist rule, the Kazakhs sought to become independent. In 1917, Kazakh nationalists declared an autonomous government in the east of the country. In 1920, however, the Bolsheviks took control and, by the mid-1920s, they had established an independent republic within the Russian Federation. In 1936, the Kazakh Autonomous Republic became a full union republic and was thereafter officially known as the Kazakh Soviet Socialist Republic.

## Exploitation of the region

During the Soviet era the region was left to stagnate as a satellite. Economic aid was concentrated on agriculture and commodities at the expense of other economic sectors and resulted in an unbalanced economy dependent on Russia as almost its only export market and its only source of manufactured consumer goods.

The USSR sought to exploit the agricultural potential of the region via large-scale irrigation projects. These projects were so successful that by the 1950s Central Asia had become a major agricultural producer for the USSR, particularly in sugar production and cotton. To provide a power base for the expansion of industry, to operate irrigation pumps and to provide for the electrification of rural areas, the hydroelectric potential of Central Asia was exploited at an increasing rate. By the 1960s, for example, 85 per cent of electricity in Uzbekistan was generated from hydroelectric stations.

However, despite huge capital investment in the region totalling R204.6 billion (at the time worth about US$200 billion), agricultural output in the 1980s only rose slightly faster than population growth. Kazakhstan became the third most important grain-growing republic behind Russia and the Ukraine. The major problem for agricultural development was the scarcity of machinery, significant transport problems and a grossly inefficient system of state farms.

One area of agriculture that did continue to flourish was cotton. Central Asia produced 90 per cent of the total Soviet cotton harvest, with output concentrated in Uzbekistan. Cotton was referred to as 'white gold' and there was continuous pressure from Moscow to increase production each year to fulfil the USSR's goal of becoming a cotton-rich country able to export throughout the socialist world. The official production figure for cotton averaged around 8 million tonnes per annum. The drive to increase cotton production was such that intensive irrigation projects led to the near destruction of the Aral Sea, once the world's fourth largest inland body of water. By the end of the Soviet era, over 30 per cent of the sea had been lost due to the years of diverting river water into cotton production.

A parallel goal of the USSR's economic plan was to develop the northern part of Central Asia as a supplier of metals to Russian factories. In fact, the whole of northern Kazakhstan was transformed into an appendage of the metallurgical complex of western Siberia and the Urals. Transport links tied Central Asian regions with cities in Russia, and the development of an extensive railway network in northern Kazakhstan made certain that the region would be economically linked to Russia as well as ensuring the reliable transport of non-ferrous metals, iron ore, pig iron and steel to Russian industrial centres. From the 1970s, the main Soviet rocket and space science complex was placed in Kazakhstan, with headquarters at Baykonur, 320 kilometres north-east of the Aral Sea.

In terms of infrastructure, one of the most significant accomplishments during this period was the development of an air transport network. All major cities and a large number of minor ones were linked through a scheduled, inexpensive airline system. The airport at Tashkent in Uzbekistan formed the hub for many routes within the region as well as for links to the Middle East and India.

# Post-1992: Independence, democracy, reform and restructuring

When the Soviet Union collapsed in 1992, the region was left devastated and, perhaps more so than any other of the Soviet regions. The region was immediately cut off from its supply of a large number of basic consumer goods, machinery, spare parts and equipment, and, as already mentioned, had heavily distorted economies dependent on producing only certain goods, such as cotton. All the countries were faced with a long, slow transition to market economies.

According to government statistics, by the end of 1992 the year-on-year slump in GDP averaged 30 per cent for the region. In Kazakhstan, where GDP fell by 40 per cent, about 65 per cent of the companies were effectively bankrupted, unable to produce or pay their bills due to the interruption of trade links with Russia. The collapse of the USSR also eliminated Russia as a transit corridor, preventing the delivery of products such as minerals and metals that were eventually destined for eastern Europe and the Ukraine. At the same time, whole industries were cut off from imports of badly needed machinery supplied by Russia and eastern Europe.

Ethnic conflicts and civil war also hit the region, notably in Tajikistan and in the Nagorno-Karabakh region of Azerbaijan.

Aside from ethnic conflict, transition to a market economy was also hampered by scarcity of capital investment or technology from either Russia or the West. While Moscow and the oil-producing regions of Russia (Azerbaijan included) may have enjoyed an influx of foreign investment following the collapse of communism, Central Asia was largely ignored.

The oil industry has formed the basis of Azeri economic restructuring since 1992 and will continue to do so well into the next century. In September 1994 a consortium of 11 international oil companies formed the Azerbaijan International Operating Company (AIOC) and it pumped its first shipment of crude in late 1997. A 30-year production sharing and tax agreement between the AIOC and the government is expected to yield net foreign exchange inflows of around US$100 million in the next few years and up to US$2 billion from 2006 onwards.

One of the key reasons behind the huge foreign direct investment (FDI) into Azerbaijan's oil industry is the government's firm commitment to the protection of foreign investment and to economic restructuring.

While Azerbaijan enjoys a wealth of natural resources, other countries have a painful dilemma to face in restructuring their economic sectors. For example, in the agricultural sector if the governments choose to retain the heavy dependence on cotton production, which has distorted economic development, further strains will be put on already depleting water resources and the health of the rural population, which has

*Top: Wedding party, Turkmenistan*
*Bottom: Young performers at Republic's Day celebrations, Kazakhstan*

been affected by the heavy use of chemical pesticides. On the other hand, reducing cotton production will lead to increasing rates of unemployment. Switching from cotton to grain, for example, may make sense in the free market, but because cotton employs six times as many workers, grain production will lead to massive job losses.

Although Central Asia and the Caspian is moving towards a western-style market economy, the region's full transition to this economy may still be more than a decade away. What is certain is that in the move to this transition there will be a substantial social cost to pay in terms of unemployment and in standards of living.

# 2 Geography and resources

## Central Asia

This is an arid region dominated by desert. It is bordered to the east and south by mountains and in the north by the plateaus and semi-deserts of Kazakhstan. Settlements are built mainly around oases along the two major rivers; the Amu Darya and the Syr Darya.

## Climate

Central Asia lies at the periphery of two important pressure systems. Winters are short but cold with January normally the coldest month. Typically, the lower course of the Syr Darya is frozen for four or five months, as is Lake Balkash. Lake Issyk-Kul, however, high in the ranges of the Tien Shan, does not freeze over due to locally mild winters, salinity and high water volume. The northern half of the desert lowland has a more severe winter, with monthly average temperatures below freezing from November to March. The southern half of the desert lowland has only two months that are truly wintry – January and February.

Spring is very short, lasting only a month (April in the north and March in the south). Within this short season, flooding is common as accumulated snowfall quickly melts and the majority of the year's precipitation falls in short torrential bursts.

The summer is long and dry. It begins in May and lasts until September. The lack of cloud cover contributes to the extraordinary heat for this latitude as well as the large temperature fluctuation. Average daily temperatures are above 15°C and can reach a daytime maximum of well over 50°C. This type of climate is excellent for the growing of cotton and other irrigation-intensive crops. The growing season is extensive, lasting between 204 and 288 days. Precipitation is practically non-existent in summer and the phenomenon of 'dry rain' is encountered in the Golodnaya Steppe, when the air and ground are so dry and hot that whatever rain does fall evaporates before it hits the ground. Humidity levels sometimes drop to below 50 per cent in Kazalinsk and 30 per cent in Bayram-Ali.

The transition from a hot summer to a cool autumn begins in the desert plains around the end of September or early October. The weather then is characterised by stable, dry and sunny days accompanied by increasingly cool nights. There is increasing cloud cover and, occasionally, precipitation or even snow as frosts begin to occur towards the end of October.

## Mountains

Central Asia begins in north-eastern Kazakhstan between the Tarbagatay Range and the Dzhungarskiy Alatau. This imaginary line – referred to as the Dzhungarian Gate – forms a break between the mountains associated with Inner Asia and those linked with Central Asia. This barren, narrow, gorge served as a pass through the mountains for nomadic pastoral animal breeders and caravans, and as a gateway for conquerors. It was also a cultural divide because further north the mountains give way to Siberian forests that supported hunter-gathers. In the south, sedentary, oasis-based cultures thrived.

The Tien Shan mountain system, named after the Chinese expression for 'Heavenly Gate', is an extensive, geologically complex group of high peaks. They extend west to east, half through former Soviet territory and the other half through China. Among the highest peaks are Khan Tengri (6,995 metres) and Pik Pobedy (7,439 metres). This latter, known as 'Victory Peak', is the second highest mountain in the Former Soviet Union (FSU) and is located near the junction of Kazakhstan, the Kyrgyz Republic and China. Between the Tien Shan peaks are basins that are generally flat and characterised by desert climatic conditions. The largest and economically most important is the Fergana Basin comprising one of the most densely populated areas of Central Asia. This basin stretches 300 kilometres north to south and 170 kilometres east to west. Other significant basins are the Ili Depression just north of the Tien Shan and Lake Issyk-Kul.

The Kopet Dag mountains in southern Turkmenistan are detached from the Central Asian mountain systems and are classified as part of the Near Eastern Highland Zone. They are an extension of the Iranian desert and run along the border

10

between Iran and the FSU. With peaks no higher than 2,700 metres, the range experiences subtropical weather with no permanent snowline.

## Deserts

More than three-quarters of the territory of Central Asia is desert lowland, which varies greatly in configuration. The greatest of these deserts is the Kara Kum, or, in Turkish, 'Black sands', extending to more than 350,000 square kilometres. It lies between the mountains and the Amu Darya river. To the west, it reaches the pre-Caspian lowlands and the desolate Ustyurt plateau and to the east it ends on the foothills of the Pamir–Alay mountains.

Between the Caspian and the Aral Sea lies the desert region covering the arid Ustyurt plateau in north-western Central Asia.

There have been some quite successful efforts made by local governments in the region to attract tourists for mountaineering and hunting expeditions; the Tien Shan, unlike the mountain regions of Nepal, have been effectively untouched by commercial tourism. Local administrations have been able to sell one-off hunting and climbing permits for around US$10,000. However, given the extreme remoteness of the region, the considerable expense of launching any expedition and the dearth of any tourist infrastructure such as hotels and restaurants, the commercial tourism industry is likely to remain a very tiny, niche business for some time to come.

## Ecology

As well as the damage caused by heavy industry during the Soviet era, Central Asia has inherited several serious environmental problems. For many years, Semipalatinsk in Kazakhstan was the Soviet Union's nuclear test site, and the area is still heavily contaminated by radioactivity. Although the cancer incidence is so far not above average for the region, the long-term impact on the environment and public health is still uncertain.

The Aral Sea, the shoreline of which Kazakhstan shares with Uzbekistan, is slowly drying up, causing major problems for water supply to agriculture and to the population. The sea appears to be vanishing because of the excessive use of the Syr Darya and Amu Darya rivers for cotton production in Central Asia, along with the overuse of fertilisers and pesticides, run-off from which is poisoning what water remains. The sea's average surface area has shrunk by over 50 per cent since the 1960s. Life expectancy near the Aral Sea is 59.5 years compared with a national average of 68.6 years. The Kazakh fishing industry based on the sea has collapsed. Kazakhstan, along with other Central Asian countries, is participating in a UN-sponsored project to save the Aral Sea, but there are no signs that its shrinkage is being arrested.

# The Caspian Sea

This lies to the east of the Caucasus Mountains and dominates the huge, flat expanses of western Central Asia. Its name derives from the ancient Kaspi peoples, who once lived in Transcaucasia to the west. The sea stretches 1,800 kilometres from north to south, although its average width is only 400 kilometres. It covers an area of about 386,400 square kilometres – larger than Japan – while its surface lies about 27 metres below sea level. The maximum depth, toward the south, is 1,025 metres. The sea is bordered in the north-east by Kazakstan, in the south-east by Turkmenistan, in the south by Iran, in the south-west by Azerbaijan, and in the north-west by Russia.

It is often stated that the Caspian is the greatest salt lake in the world. But this has not always been true. Scientific studies have shown that, until geologically quite recent times, it was linked, via the Sea of Azov, the Black Sea, and the Mediterranean, to the world ocean. The Caspian is of exceptional scientific interest since it offers clues as to the complex geologic and climatic evolution of the region. Man-made changes, notably those resulting from the construction of dams, reservoirs, and canals on the immense Volga River system (which drains into the Caspian from the north), have had their own devastating effect on its delicate environmental balance.

The sea possesses as many as 50 islands, mostly small. Chechen, in the north-west, is the largest, followed by Tyuleny, Morskoy, Kulaly, Zhiloy, and Ogurchin.

The shores of the northern Caspian are low and reflect the great accumulation of alluvial material washed down by the Ural and Volga rivers. The western shore of the middle Caspian is hilly. The foothills of the Greater Caucasus Mountains loom close by but are separated from the coast by a narrow marine plain. The Abseron Peninsula, on which the city of Baku is sited, juts out into the sea there, while just to its south the floodplain of the Kura and Aras rivers forms the Kura–Aras Lowland. The south-western and southern Caspian shores are formed of the sediments of the Länkäran and Gilan–Mazanderan lowlands, with the high peaks of the Talish and Elburz mountains rearing up close inland. The eastern shore of the southern Caspian is also low but is less steep, formed by sediments resulting from wave action; it is broken sharply by the low, hilly Cheleken and Turkmenbashi peninsulas. A most important feature of the eastern shore is the Garabogazkol, formerly a gulf of the Caspian but now a large lagoon separated from the sea by a man-made sandy embankment.

The major rivers — the Volga and Ural — empty into the northern Caspian, with their combined annual flow accounting for 88 per cent of all river water entering the sea. The

*Baku Port and oil field*

Sulak, Samur, Kura, and a number of smaller rivers flow in on the western littoral, contributing about 7 per cent of the flow, and the remainder comes in from the rivers of the Iranian shore. The eastern littoral is notable for a complete lack of permanent rivers.

The northern Caspian, with an area of 99,404 square kilometres, is the shallowest portion of the sea, with an average depth of 4 to 8 metres, reaching a maximum of 20 metres along the boundary with the middle Caspian. The middle Caspian, 137,917 square kilometres in area, forms an irregular depression with an abrupt western slope and a gentler eastern gradient. The Abseron Bank, a belt of shoals and islands rising from submerged elevations of older rocks, marks the transition to the southern Caspian, a depression covering about 149,106 square kilometres, which contains the Caspian's greatest depths.

The Caspian has long been famous for its sturgeon and sturgeon caviar, the sea accounting for about four-fifths of the

world catch. During the long period of water-level decline and consequent desiccation of the most favourable spawning grounds, the sturgeon population was reduced considerably. A number of measures, including prohibition of sturgeon fishing in the open sea and the introduction of aquaculture, have been undertaken to improve the situation. The seal industry also has been developed in northern regions.

# Azerbaijan

Part of Transcaucasia rather than Asia, Azerbaijan possesses a wide variety of landscapes. More than two-fifths of its territory is taken up by lowlands, about half lies at 400 to 1,500 metres and areas above 1,500 metres occupy a little more than one-tenth of the total area.

The highest peaks are Bazardyuzyu (4,466 metres), Shakhdag, and Tufan, all part of the Greater Caucasus range, the crest of which forms part of Azerbaijan's northern boundary.

The spurs of the Lesser Caucasus, in southwestern Azerbaijan, form the second important mountain system.

The south-eastern part of Azerbaijan is bordered by the Talish Mountains, consisting of three longitudinal ranges, with Mount Kyumyurkyoy as the highest peak (2,492 metres). The Länkäran Lowland lies along the Caspian coast and reaches the Iranian border near Astara.

A well-developed network of canals between the Kura and Araz rivers makes it possible to irrigate a major part of the lowland. The Upper Karabakh Canal, 172 kilometres long, provides a vital link between the Araz River and the Mingacevir Reservoir on the Kura River. The canal alone irrigates more than 250,000 acres of fertile land and in addition supplies the Araz River with water during dry summer periods. The 197-kilometre Upper Shirvan Canal also irrigates about 250,000 acres.

## Climate

The dry subtropical climate of central and eastern Azerbaijan is characterised by a mild winter and a long and very hot summer, with temperatures averaging about 27°C and maximum temperatures reaching 43°C.

South-eastern Azerbaijan is characterised by a humid subtropical climate with the highest precipitation in the country, some 1,193 to 1,397 millimetres a year, most of it falling in the cold months.

A dry continental climate, with a cold winter and a dry, hot summer, prevails in Naxcivan at altitudes of 700 to 1,000 metres. Moderately warm, dry, or humid types of climate are to be found in other parts of Azerbaijan. The mountain forest zone has a moderately cold climate, while an upland tundra climate characterises elevations of 300 metres and above.

Frosts and heavy snowfalls make the passes at such altitudes inaccessible for three or four months of the year.

## Settlement patterns.

More than half of Azerbaijan's population lives in urban areas. The most densely populated region is the Abseron Peninsula, on the western coast of the Caspian Sea. Baku, Azerbaijan's largest city and the most important industrial city in Transcaucasia, is located on this peninsula, as are other industrial towns, including Sumgait.

Other areas of dense population occur in certain lowland and foothill regions. Gjandza is the second largest town and the main urban centre of the interior.

The highest density of rural population is found in Lankaran and Masalli in the south-east. The Talysh, Iranian people who form the bulk of the local population, have preserved many of their old customs and traditions.

# Natural resources

## Water

The struggle for water has been a defining factor of Central Asian history throughout the Soviet era to the present day. Central Asia is a closed basin with no open sea or ocean outlet. Its cycle of rainfall is strongly affected by the desert climate. The very limited precipitation on the lowland plain, coupled with high temperatures, low humidity and high levels of sunlight make for a very high rate of evaporation. Water resources are thus mainly surface waters formed in the mountains and spent on the plains of Central Asia. Melt water from permanent snowfields is the main source of water for the rivers, with glaciers and seasonal snowfields contributing as well. The result is a fairly reliable river flow that deviates only slightly from year to year.

The most important rivers are the Amu Darya and Syr Darya. The Amu Darya is the largest river in Central Asia and is about 2,540 kilometres long. It begins in the Hindu Kush and is fed by the melt water from snow and glaciers. The cycle of melting snow produces two close but distinct flood seasons; spring (April and May) for snow thawing, and summer (June and July) for glacial melting. Both these flood seasons are highly beneficial to irrigation. At the Syr Darya's source in the region of permanent snow and glaciers in central Tien Shan, it is known as the River Naryn. Further downstream, merging with the Kara Darya, it becomes the Syr Darya and flows through the Fergana Valley and the lowland plain to the Aral Sea.

## Energy

The Caspian Sea's enormous oil and gas reserves are only now beginning to be fully developed. This has resulted in competi-

*Gold mining in the Tian Shan Mountains, Kyrgyz Republic*

tion both between western energy companies to win contracts to develop the potential, and between nations to determine the final export routes.

The Caspian Sea itself is so large (1,800 kilometres north to south) that six different hydrocarbon basins lie under its waters. The bordering countries also have additional substantial onshore basins. Uzbekistan does not directly border the Caspian Sea, but it is still considered to be in the Caspian region not only because it shares several of the region's hydrocarbon basins, but also because its proposed oil and gas export routes are shared with other Caspian countries.

Azerbaijan was the world's largest oil producing province in the early 1900s. However, the FSU did not have the technology to develop the Caspian's offshore oil and gas reserves, and once the onshore Azerbaijani oil was developed, the Soviet Union focused its resources elsewhere in onshore areas such as the Volga–Urals region and west Siberia. Most of the oil and gas reserves in the Caspian region have not been developed, and many areas of the Caspian remain unexplored. Most of Azerbaijan's oil resources (proven as well as possible reserves) are located offshore, and perhaps 30–40 per cent of the total oil resources of Kazakhstan and Turkmenistan are offshore as well. Proven oil reserves for the entire Caspian Sea region are estimated at 15–29 billion barrels, comparable with those in the United States (22 billion barrels) or the North Sea (17 billion).

13

Proven natural gas reserves are even larger, accounting for over two-thirds of the proven hydrocarbon reserves in the Caspian Sea region. Based upon proven reserves, Kazakhstan, Turkmenistan and Uzbekistan each rank among the world's 20 largest natural gas countries. Proven gas reserves in the Caspian region are estimated at 6.7–9.5 trillion cubic metres, comparable to North American reserves (8.5 trillion cubic metres). Most of the additional undiscovered hydrocarbons likely to be of commercial significance – the possible reserves – are oil, not gas. While this potential is not enough to create another Middle East, the region's possible reserves could yield another 163 billion barrels of oil if they become proven. This is roughly equivalent to a quarter of the Middle East's total proven reserves.

Possible gas reserves are as large as the proven reserves, and could yield another 9.3 trillion cubic metres if proven. However, these reserves are located far from potential markets in relatively remote Turkmenistan, Kazakhstan and Uzbekistan. The distance from potential markets and the relative lack of infrastructure to export this gas have tempered interest in the region's gas potential. The alternatives to exporting gas through the Russian pipeline system are exporting through war-torn Afghanistan, through Iran where investment is limited by sanctions, or by building some of the world's longest pipelines to markets in China and Europe.

## Minerals

Of the Central Asian states, Kazakhstan and Uzbekistan have the most diversified and substantial export potential in economically usable mineral resources. Among metal ore deposits, both have copper, lead, molybdenum, tungsten, uranium and zinc, with beryllium, chromite, iron ore, manganese, tantalum and titanium. Both states also have large resources of building materials, particularly cement, gypsum and marble, alunite, asbestos, barite, bauxite, bismuth, castorite, corundum, fluorspar, graphite, iodine-bromine, kaolin, ozocerite, quartz, soda and sulphur. Copper output, which is produced at competitive world prices, is annually around 260,000 tonnes in Kazakhstan and 80,000 tonnes in Uzbekistan. Kazakhstan's share of world output is also significant, exceeding 5 per cent in barite, beryllium, chromite, lead, manganese, silver, tantalum, titanium, tungsten, uranium and zinc. Kazakhstan has small but promising diamond pipes and a rich array of semi-precious stones.

The exploitation of precious metals has been long established in Kazakhstan, but has begun only recently in Uzbekistan. Kazakhstan has two major operating gold mines at Bakyrchik and Vasilovskoe, which currently comprise only 10 years' reserves. Sources of copper, lead, zinc, silver and gold are being developed in the same zone. Gold production in Kazakhstan has been officially announced at 14 tonnes. The

Ridder Sokol'noe and Tishinskoe mines, both operated by the Leninogorsk Polymetallic Combine, have been Kazakhstan's principal non-ferrous and gold suppliers.

Although gold ores were mined in the Angren river basin in Uzbekistan between 800 and 1,000 years ago, the region's modern industry dates from the opening of the Ridder mine in the Kazak Altai in 1794. Nevertheless, substantial gold production only began in 1958 after discovery of an important deposit at Muruntau in the Kyzyl Kum desert. In all, Uzbekistan has around 3,000 tonnes of gold deposits and its recent production levels, averaging 70 tonnes annually, placed it within the world's top 10 gold producing nations.

During peak production years, both Kazakhstan and Uzbekistan were among the world's leading exporters of Uranium. Kazakh output collapsed in the years following independence, but it is expected to increase production through two joint ventures with Canadian investors. Uzbekistan has significant uranium potential with more than 4,000 deposits containing an estimated 230,000 tonnes. The international concern aroused by the storage of radioactive waste from Kyrgyz uranium mines may be exacerbated as Kazakh and Uzbek production is stepped up.

Kazakhstan's steel production is based on domestically mined ore and coal. Ore production ran at 25 million tonnes a year in the 1980s but only 15 million tonnes in 1995. Production of coal fell from a high of 131 million tonnes in 1990 to 15 million tonnes in 1995, but has since recovered, reaching around 70 million tonnes in 1997. Production of metallurgic coke also fell between 1991 and 1995, from 4 million tonnes to 2 million. The Karmet steel plant at Karaganda is one of the world's largest steel mills and benefits from huge surrounding coal deposits measured at 1 billion tonnes. The whole operation, apart from open cast coal mining, has been taken over by a London-based private company, Ispat. With US$200 million in capital promised, Ispat aims to substantially increase productivity and output.

Uzbekistan has only small iron ore deposits measuring less than 60 million tonnes. Nonetheless, this did not inhibit the building of a steel works near Bekabad in the Fergana Valley in 1944 as part of the eastward evacuation of heavy industry by the Soviets during World War II. Output here expanded during the 1980s to over 1 million tonnes of steel and rolled products. Bekabad, which only produced 550,000 tonnes in 1995, is now being refurbished with German and Russian equipment.

## Human resources

During the Soviet era, the one resource shared by all the republics was the plentiful supply of cheap labour. (By con-

Exhibit 2.1
**Population data for the region, 1994–97**

| | | |
|---|---|---|
| Azerbaijan | Total population: 7.6 million | Ethnic composition: Azeri 82.7%; Russian 5.6%; Armenian 2.4% |
| Kazakhstan | Total population: 15.9 million | Ethnic composition: Kazakh 39.7%; Russian 37.8%; German 5.8%; Ukranian 5.4%; Uzbek 2% |
| Kyrgyz Republic | Total population: 4.6 million | Ethnic composition: Kyrgyz 52.4%; Russian 21.5%; Uzbek 12.9%; Ukranian 2.5%; German 2.4%; Tartar 1.6% |
| Tajikistan | Total population: 5.7 million | Ethnic composition: Tajik 62.3%; Uzbek 23.5%; Russian 7.6% |
| Turkmenistan | Total population: 4.4 million | Ethnic composition: Turkmen 77.0%; Uzbek 9.2%; Russian 6.7%; Kazakh 2.0%; Other 5.1% |
| Uzbekistan | Total population: 23.7 million | Ethnic composition: Uzbek 71.4%; Russian 8.4%; Tajik 4.7%; Kazakh 4.1%; Tartar 3.2% |

*Source:* Government statistics.

trast, oil and mineral producing regions in Russia were always hampered by severe manpower shortages owing to the extreme, inhospitable climate and difficulties involved with persuading urban workers to move.) The post-independence fall in output has not been accompanied by the massive labour shake out seen elsewhere in the Commonwealth of Independent States (CIS). Nonetheless, there has been an unemployment problem resulting from the gradual shift of the workforce out of agriculture and into light industry and the service sector. The decline in agricultural employment has been ongoing since the 1970s in line with industrial and economic development throughout the entire USSR. The key issue in comparing the region's workforce with that of Russia was that the rate of fall in agricultural employment was far slower in Central Asia and the Caspian region than elsewhere. Even today, job creation in the moribund industrial and service sectors in Russia is taking place at a far greater pace than in Central Asia and the Caspian region. This suggests that the region's economic development away from the Soviet welfare state system – where every able-bodied individual was guaranteed employment by the state regardless of market demand – is stagnating.

Apart from changes in agricultural employment, another key difference is the relatively less-developed professions of machine construction, metallurgy and engineering technology. In Russia, graduates with a technology-based education are relatively plentiful. In Central Asia and the Caspian, because the region's economies have for so long been agriculture- or natural resource-based, technical specialists have always been in far less demand. Whatever science technical skills the work-

force possessed were mainly directed towards the cotton production machinery.

Wage levels on a sector-by-sector basis have remained about 10 to 20 per cent lower in Central Asia and the Caspian region than in Russia. While volatile currency markets make it difficult to give accurate comparisons between the average earning power of a worker in, say, Turkmenistan with one in Siberia, the region is still considered to be low waged.

Labour productivity in the region is comparable with levels in developing countries. This is surprising given that the work force is much better educated and has enjoyed relatively free access to better healthcare than in most developing countries. Literacy is almost universal, with levels well above 95 per cent in most areas. Almost all children are enrolled in some sort of secondary education. By comparison, in Egypt, a developing economy with roughly similar per capita GDP levels, only 60 per cent of the population are literate and 79 per cent of children are enrolled in schools.

The growth in population in Central Asia and the Caspian region, particularly in urban areas, has been substantial, due to both an increased fertility rate and a decreased mortality rate owing to large-scale industrialisation and irrigation. Between 1951 and 1989 – the latter being the year of the most recent region-wide census – the population more than tripled, and the growth rate has been more than double the USSR average. Central Asia and the Caspian region's share of the total population of the USSR grew from 6 per cent in 1951 to 14 per cent by 1989.

Exhibit 2.1 shows the population data for the region.

*Caspian Sea, Turkmenbashi, Turkmenistan*

# Transport and telecommunications

The state of the region's telecommunications network may take a generation or more to fully remedy. During the Soviet era, investment in telecommunications was given little or no emphasis by the Moscow-based economic planners. After the collapse of the USSR, the region's telecommunication assets were broken up. International and domestic long-distance (ILD and DLD) operations were packaged into separate entities, creating huge, monopolistic service providers.

When looking at the possibility of establishing new joint ventures with a local operator in the region, the potential revenues figures are very thin. As recently as 1997, the entire CIS telecommunications industry generated only US$4.03 billion in revenues, which represented an average of US$104 per access line. By comparison, in the advanced US and German markets, per line revenues averaged over US$1,200. Even in Eastern European developing economies, such as Hungary, Poland and the Czech Republic, revenues per access line were on average five times greater than in Central Asia and the Caspian.

The major reason for low revenues relative to other markets is that tariffs for residential lines, comprising 80 per cent of all lines in the region, are fixed by regulators at artificially low levels to such an extent that business users heavily subsidise private residential users. Further, most local and DLD tariffs are regulated by regional authorities that are closely affiliated with local government. While the regulators are keen to see that the operators generate sufficient cash flow to improve service, make a profit, and pay taxes, politics have usually proved paramount. As a result, residential tariffs are currently fixed at very low levels relative to current operating costs and the expected future costs for crucially needed capital investment. Simply put, the local residential market cannot afford to pay the huge sums of money necessary so that investments can be made to bring the network up to even Hungarian standards. For many major foreign firms operating in the region, leasing a private satellite link operated outside the public network has become essential.

The transport infrastructure in the region is also thoroughly dilapidated and in need of major financing for refurbishment. While public transport and roads are reasonably well developed in major urban areas, this is not true in the more remote regions, particularly in the Kyrgyz Republic, Tajikistan, and Turkmenistan. In Kazakhstan, the vast open spaces were easily conquered during the Soviet era thanks to intensive maintenance of a huge rail and airway network. Today, those spaces – which have grown even larger with the breakdown of transport infrastructure – are proving to be an obstacle to the increased economic development and unity of the country.

The old Aeroflot network, with a hub in Tashkent in Uzbekistan, serves as a vital link for passengers and high-value freight. Regional airlines taking over from Aeroflot have experienced varying degrees of success.

## Azerbaijan

The country has had to rely on two international transport routes to the West since independence: through Georgia to the Black Sea, and south through Iran. These routes have been severely disrupted by political instability. Until recently, road and rail links into Russia were blocked by the closure of the Russian border and the state of disrepair of the rail network. The route to Yerevan in Armenia is sometimes blockaded. Travel between Azerbaijan proper and the detached enclave of Nachichevan is by air or by road through Iran.

Few of the rivers of Azerbaijan are navigable, and most freight – including that transported out of the country – is carried by rail and truck. Azerbaijan has 2,089 kilometres of roads that provide the main transport for freight. Road transport is also used extensively for passengers. Roads connect various parts of the country and are often the only means of land communication between remote mountain districts and the administrative centres and large cities.

Large stretches of the rail network are electrified. Nonetheless, some 700 kilometres of railway lines need to be rebuilt. Out of 800 rail cars in the country, about 350 are not functioning. There are no rail repair facilities in Azerbaijan, which was previously reliant on the Soviet rail system for equipment and maintenance. A major railway line traverses the Kura valley and connects Baku with Tbilisi and Batumi in Georgia. Another runs parallel to the Caspian Sea north of Baku.

Baku is a busy seaport, handling such goods as oil, timber,

*Tian Shan
Mountains,
Kyrgyz Republic*

grain, and cotton. The ferry link between Baku and Turkmenbashi augments considerably the amount of cargo passing through Azerbaijan. Air routes connect Baku with many European and Asian cities. Sea transport is particularly important to Azerbaijan given the uncertain relations with Russia. By sea, there are passenger and cargo links between Baku and Central Asia, Iran and Russia. Baku's port cargo handling capacity remains constrained due to the pressing need for port refurbishment and expansion.

The telecommunications infrastructure is slightly better than in neighbouring states although much of its inherited Soviet communications technology is outdated and unreliable. There are 780,000 phone subscribers, 85 per cent of whom are residential. Phone density in urban areas reaches 56 per 100 inhabitants, but is only 16.7 per 100 in rural areas. More than 200,000 people are wait-listed for telephone installations, and more than 700 villages have no phone service.

Telecommunications is a priority area for the Azerbaijan government. The Ministry of Telecommunications (MOC) has developed a programme to upgrade the communications network nationwide, and to create an industry for communications and transmission equipment production. The cost of this project is estimated at over US$25 million. Once parliament passes the new Law on Communications, the MOC will begin privatising some of its facilities. With privatisation, the MOC will become more of a regulatory agency than an operating company. The new law will allow private companies to develop and operate nationwide networks.

There are a number of existing telecommunications joint ventures with the MOC. Among them are: Baksell (GTIB, Israel), a cellular communications network in Baku, Sumgait and the Abseron Peninsula; Netash (Turkey), a DCM 100/200 type station developed in 1991 and a 150-channel satellite communications system between Baku and Ankara; IDB (United States), a 30-channel direct satellite communications system between Baku and New York; British Telecom (United Kingdom), a 15-channel direct satellite system between Baku and London; Telespazio (Italy), a 30-channel satellite communications system between Baku and Rome; Alcatel-Teletash (Turkey), a System-12 communication system in Sumgait developed in late 1993, allowing its 500 subscribers to have automatic access to international and inter-city communications lines; and Datacom (United Kingdom) and SWIFT Global (United States), a major telex and fax centre in Baku.

## Kazakhstan

Railways carry most of the long-distance freight. The Trans-Siberian, South Siberian, and Kazak trunk lines cross Kazakhstan east to west, and the Orenburg line extends as far as Tashkent, Uzbekistan in the south. Air transport carries the bulk of passenger traffic, both domestic and regional, since internal distances are so vast. The international airport at Almaty offers service to Frankfurt, Istanbul, London, and other cities. The republic has an extensive network of oil pipelines between Atyrau and Orsk and Shymkent and Tashkent, as well as the Uzen–Zhetibay–Aktau pipeline from the west. Nonetheless, the domestic energy transport system falls far short of meeting the country's enormous potential for gas and oil exports.

Kazakhstan is landlocked but has access to the Caspian Sea in the west, which in turn gives access to the Volga–Don Canal and then on to the Black Sea. Transport costs add significantly to the costs of selling exports on western markets. All Kazakhstan's oil and gas export pipelines currently end in Russia, giving it a control over the volume, pricing and direction of Kazakhstan's exports. The Kazakh government is extremely keen to reduce this vulnerability to Russia.

The Soviets neglected to develop the telepone network beyond urban centres. There were only 13.8 lines per 100 inhabitants in 1994, and breakdowns due to overload or equipment failure are common. Although the government has invited tenders from a number of foreign firms to develop the telecommunications system, the effort is piecemeal and poorly coordinated. An attempt to sell 49 per cent of the state telecommunications company, Kazakhtelekom, to Germany's Deutsche Telekom failed, as did a management contract arrangement with Australia's Telstra. In 1997, Daewoo purchased 40 per cent of Kazakhtelecom for US$1.37 billion, of which US$990 million will be invested in network improvement. However, Daewoo's own financial problems and the general recession in the Korean economy could mean that the investment is slow in coming. Telephone coverage is increasing but remains expensive.

## Kyrgyz Republic

This has 18,560 kilometres of roads, of which 140 kilometres are highways and 3,160 secondary roads. Plans are under way to expand the road network with some international support from Japan and the Asian Development Bank who have both expressed an interest in financing the Osh–Bishkek highway, a critical link between the north and south of the country. There are internal and external air connections, although reliability is extremely poor due to fuel shortages and administrative problems.

One main route climbs from Bishkek to Issyk-Kul (with extensions along the north and south shores of Lake Issyk-Kul), then swings south across difficult central terrain to Naryn and proceeds through the high Torugart Pass across the frontier with China and down to the city of Kashgar in China. The other major artery, the 'route beyond the clouds', from Bishkek to Osh, crosses the Kyrgyz–Alatau crest through a 3,200-metre tunnel. An important southern link is provided by the road joining Osh, via the Alay Pass, to the Pamir region of Tajikistan. An offshoot runs eastward through Irkeshtam to Kashgar.

There are 372 kilometres of railway track in the Kyrgyz Republic. A rail line from Bishkek through the Chu valley and over the border to Lugovoe in Kazakstan joins the north of the republic to the Turkestan–Siberian main railway line and, through it, to southern Kazakhstan and the entire railway network of the FSU. Another rail link extends the line up the valley from Bishkek to Issyk-Kul at the western tip of Lake Issyk-Kul. Southern lines reach the coal mines at Tash–Komur and Kyzyl–Kyya.

The state-owned telecom operator is now the subject of future privatisation, with the Vienna-based RZB investment bank having been appointed as official advisers. Initial reports suggest that RZB, after an extensive study, has valued the entire company at over US$500 million dollars. However, telecom analysts in other republics in the region have expressed serious doubts as to whether any major financial or strategic investors could be convinced that this is in any way a reasonable valuation. Ideally, the government hopes that a majority stake will be sold before the end of 1999.

## Tajikistan

This has a 13,600-kilometre road network. The main arterial road connects the city of Kokand in the north with the capital, Dushanbe. This road is closed over the winter when a 3,000-metre high pass is blocked by snow. During these times, road traffic takes a long diversion through southern Uzbekistan. Another key route links Dushanbe with the town of Khorog in the Badakhshan mountains, and then turns north to Osh in the south of the Kyrgyz Republic. There are plans to link the Tajik road network to the Karakorum highway that runs from Pakistan to western China.

Tajikistan has limited civil aviation connections, with two main airports in Dushanbe and Kokand. Air service from Ashgabat to Baku and Tashkent has been reduced since 1991.

The telephone network in Tajikistan is basic. Fewer than 10 per cent of inhabitants have access to a telephone and the entire system needs refurbishment. A small cellular exchange has operated since 1996.

## Turkmenistan

The country's main transport problem is that it is landlocked, forcing all oil and gas to be transported across competitor countries. The country's main export gas pipeline runs to Russia via Kazakhstan. However, the Russian state gas monopoly, Gazprom, restricts Turkmen gas exports and only permitted access to hard currency markets in 1994. Gazprom has made it clear that it strongly prefers Turkmen gas to be exported only to CIS countries. The first gas pipeline outside

the CIS was completed in September 1997 (with a capacity of 1.5 billion cubic metres per annum) linking Turkmenistan to Iran. These facilities provide the country with its first direct outlets for large-scale exporting to the Middle East and the West. It is planned that the pipeline will extend through Iran and Turkey all the way to the Mediterranean.

In 1991, the country had 13,400 kilometres of roads – 87 per cent of which were paved – and 1,120 kilometres of railway track. A slow rail line, opened in 1994, links Turkmenistan to Iran. In 1996, this connection was enhanced by a 300-kilometre railway line linking Tedzhen with Mashad in Iran.

The great dispersion of the towns in Turkmenistan requires extending rail lines to serve a scattered population efficiently, but the existing rail system falls far short of achieving that goal. A main trunk railway connects Turkmenbashi via Ashgabat and other towns with Tashkent in Uzbekistan, throwing off branch lines from Mary to Kushka and from Nebit-Dag to Vyshka. Another line extends from Chardzhou along the Amu Darya as far north as Qunghirot in Qoraqalpoghiston. However, trucks now carry most of the country's internal freight, and such traffic is developing more rapidly than rail transportation.

Water transport includes a merchant fleet and a ferry plying the Caspian Sea between Turkmenbashi and Baku in Azerbaijan. Air service from Ashgabat to Baku and Tashkent has been reduced since 1991.

The Turkmen telephone system network is also very basic, with only 6.71 lines per 100 inhabitants (the average for Eastern Europe is 15 lines). Exact data on car ownership is not available, but the number is thought to be less than five cars per 100 inhabitants.

## Uzbekistan

Uzbekistan is particularly reliant on bordering countries for transport links. It is so landlocked that goods often have to cross three other FSU republics before they reach a major seaport. The Russian Black Sea ports are 3,000 kilometres away. President Islam Karimov is cooperating with one of the EU's more ambitious ventures to create a transport corridor for Central Asia through the war-ravaged Transcaucasus to reduce dependence on transport links through Russia. Uzbekistan has 3,406 kilometres of railways (only 270 kilometres of which are electrified), equivalent to 7.7 kilometres per 1,000 square kilometres. There are 42,000 kilometres of main roads, of which 96 per cent are paved, with a further 90,000 kilometres of local roads, equivalent to a road density of 0.3 kilometres per square kilometre. Tashkent also has Central Asia's only metro network.

Car ownership is low, but is increasing as a result of selective government subsidies to public sector workers to buy

*Bishkek University, Kyrgyz Republic*

inexpensive Daewoo cars assembled in Uzbekistan.

The great obstacle to further development of markets for Uzbekistan's agricultural produce remains the antiquated transport infrastructure and means of distribution. Neither the existing surface nor air transport now available can efficiently or with adequate refrigeration handle the volume produced in Uzbekistan and needed by it's major agriculture export markets, such as the Baltic states, Russia, Belarus, and Ukraine.

Trucks transport most of the freight carried but the roads are in urgent need of repair. The Great Uzbek Tashkent–Termez Highway runs south almost to the border with Afghanistan. Termiz remains virtually a dead-end in terms of trade, especially since the Soviet intervention (1979–89) in the Afghan War. A second road, the Zeravshan Highway, connects Samarkand with Chardzhou, Turkmenistan, in the west. The Fergana Ring links the main settlements within the populous Fergana Valley.

Uzbekistan only recently established a domestic airline of its own. After independence in 1991, former Soviet Aeroflot

air planes and their pilots were chartered to fly rather infrequently from such cities as Samarkand and Tashkent to nearby cities. Air service now connects Tashkent with London, New York, and other foreign cities. The national carrier, Uzbek Khavo Yullan (Uzbekistan Airways), flies both within the FSU and earns hard currency on long-distance international routes. Improvements to air transport are a priority for the government. Airport modernisation projects are under way at Tashkent, Samarkand, Bukhara and Urgench airports.

Tashkent's analogue telephone switches date back to the 1920s, and being Soviet-built, are rudimentary by even that era's standards. Some other Uzbek cities had some telephone service installed at that time, but the rest of the country had no telephone network until the 1970s. Most maintenance of the network ceased in the late 1980s. Since the breakup of the Soviet Union, no replacements or spare parts have been available. By way of telephone density comparison, the Uzbek density figure of 7 lines per 100 people is roughly equivalent to those in Turkmenistan, the Kyrgyz Republic, and Mexico.

The national telephone company, and until recently, the sole local telephone provider, is Uzbekistan Telecom. This is a wholly owned entity of the Ministry of Communications. Foreign companies first came to Uzbekistan as equipment vendors. Beginning in 1996, some of these formed minority-share joint ventures with Uzbekistan Telecom to supply and operate regional telephone networks. Foreign companies have also set up joint ventures to provide niche market services.

In 1994, the government announced an overall renovation plan in three stages, 1994–2000, 2001–05, and 2006–10. The first stage calls for 400,000 telephone connections to be installed or replaced in Tashkent and most of the regional capitals. Forty per cent of all connections are to be digital by the end of this period. The plan calls for raising telephone density to 10 per 100. Also, the stretch of the Trans–Asia–Europe fibre optical line that will run through Uzbekistan is to be completed by 2000. In the second stage, new connections for the remaining regional centres and some rural areas are to be completed. In the third stage, all connections are to be digital, all rural areas are to be rewired, and density raised to 13 per 100.

In 1996, the government shifted its approach to telecommunciations modernisation and invited foreign companies to invest directly in the telephone network. Foreign companies are allowed up to 49 per cent ownership, with Uzbekistan Telecom remaining the majority owner.

Apart from supplying equipment, there is little immediate potential in direct investment into the network itself despite the government's offer to create joint ventures. The present foreign direct telecom investors mostly agree that the majority of the network will run at a loss for the foreseeable future with a substantial profit only perhaps a decade away. For example, Tashkent telephone subscribers pay a subscription fee of about

US$1 per month, which includes all local calling. Subscribers on the new digital systems pay about the same, which includes three hours' talking time.

The major foreign telecommunications companies active in Uzbekistan are Alcatel and Siemens from Germany, Daewoo Telecom from Korea, Mitsui/NEC from Japan, Italian Telecom and an Indonesian trading company, the Bakri Group. A British–Uzbek joint venture, Buzton, provides relatively expensive local telephone services with Inmarsat access. Its services are mostly used by foreign embassies and international organisations.

The German subsidiary of French Alcatel was the first major company into the Uzbek market in 1993. Alcatel has installed digital switching stations with a total capacity of 60,000 phone connections, with additional capacity of 18,000 connections still to be installed. This work has included upgrades in several urban centres, including Tashkent. Alcatel has also set up a joint venture maintenance facility with Uzbekistan Telecom.

German Siemens entered the Uzbek market in 1994 with a contract to install four switching stations with the capacity to handle 50,000 subscribers in Tashkent, and a further 20,000 in Samarkand. Siemens was also installing a 100-kilometre fibre optic cable to link 22 new digital switching stations in the Tashkent region. Siemens supplied its own financing of DM15 million for this project. The company also serves as an equipment supplier for other projects.

Korean Daewoo also came to the Uzbek market in 1993 and is now the largest telecom player in the country. Its first project was for switching stations capable of serving 50,000 subscribers in the Fergana region. To date, Daewoo has installed capacity for over 160,000 subscribers in the Fergana, Syrdaria, Andijon and Bukhara regions. Daewoo formed a joint venture with Uzbekistan Telecom to manufacture medium-scale switching stations. This joint venture, Aloka–Daewoo, plans that 70 per cent of production is to be installed in Uzbekistan and 30 per cent set aside for export.

In autumn 1996 Japan's Mitsui Trading Ltd was chosen to supply and install equipment with a capacity for 251,000 telephone subscribers in the western regions of Karakalpakstan, Urgench, Navoi, and Bukhara. The contract was worth about US$100 million dollars and was financed by Japan's Overseas Economic Cooperation Fund.

The Indonesian Bakri Group is another recent arrival. Bakri already owns a major hotel in Tashkent and now has formed a joint venture with Uzbekistan Telecom, called Uzbektelecom International. Bakri holds 49 per cent of this venture, which is estimated to be capitalised at US$330 million. As part of its capital contribution, Bakri assumed Uzbekistan Telecom's US$70 million debt to foreign equipment suppliers. The joint venture has contracts to install and modernise 385,000 tele-

*Varying styles of architecture Ashgabat, Turkmenistan*

phone connections in the Samarkand, Kashkadaria, Surkhandaria, Jizzakh and Tashkent regions. Bakri also plans to invest US$30 million in a maintenance facility, has invested US$7 million in an Uzbek cable factory for the production of fibre optic cable, and is negotiating with the Ministry of Communications to purchase, renovate, and then operate the pay phones in Tashkent.

Telecom Italia is another newcomer in Tashkent. This company has registered a joint venture that will build and operate Uzbekistan's stretch of the Trans–Asia–Europe fibre optic line. The new joint venture, to be called Udinet, is to be capitalised at US$300 million. Ownership will be 51 per cent for Uzbekistan Telecom, 41 per cent for Telecom Italia, which will provide the technical, marketing, and financial expertise, and 8 per cent for Siemens, which will provide the equipment.

The first cellular telephone company in Uzbekistan was an US–Uzbek joint venture, Uzdunrobita. Uzdunrobita's subscribers now number 14,000, but its period as sole service provider will soon end. The Ministry of Communications has already issued five additional licences for cellular operating companies.

## The Eurasian transport corridor and energy export routes

The development of the transport infrastructure, most notably oil and gas pipelines, is only the first step in building the much talked about greater Eurasian transport corridor, which will include development of road and rail links and allow regional trade to grow. Infrastructure development will grow in importance as the Central Asian and Caspian republics expand their ties to the countries beyond the FSU. As the economies of the republics begin to diversify, they will seek new export and import markets.

In fact, the Eurasian transport corridor has already taken shape in small ways. The volume of goods shipped via the intra-Central Asian transport corridor, despite its run-down state, has slowly increased. Oil produced at the Tengiz field in Kazakhstan is now shipped across the Caspian Sea on barges and transported by rail from Baku to Poti on Georgia's Black Sea Coast. This rail line is also used in the opposite direction, to ship goods and equipment from the Black Sea to Baku. A barge service also links Baku to Aktau in Kazakhstan, and to Turkmenistan. Uzbekistan now ships cotton by rail across Turkmenistan, by ferry across the Caspian Sea to Baku, and by rail to Poti in Georgia. Eventual development of a Chinese pipeline through Kazakhstan will serve as an additional catalyst for increased trade between the Central Asian and Caspian region republics and China, expanding the scope of the Eurasian Transport Corridor even further. The Chinese and Kazakh governments have already started cooperating on transport issues affecting their common border, helping to facilitate the flow of goods and people.

For the next decade, the most essential priority is for even more new energy transportation routes to be developed to carry Central Asian and Caspian oil and gas to world markets. The existing pipelines in the Central Asian and Caspian region were designed to link the Soviet Union internally, and were routed through Russia. Russia has commercial and political interests in continuing to be a major transshipment point for the region's energy resources. For this to happen, Russia must address commercial concerns regarding reliability, security, competitive tariffs, and access. While Russia has existing pipelines that are underutilised, these pipelines do not have the capacity to absorb all of the oil and gas the Central Asian and Caspian region could produce. An additional limitation is that most existing oil export pipelines terminate at the Russian Black Sea port of Novorossiisk, requiring tankers to transit the crowded and ecologically and politically sensitive Bosphorus to gain access to the Mediterranean and world markets.

Furthermore, there is some question as to whether the Mediterranean is the right place to send all of the forthcoming oil and gas from the region, as oil demand over the next 10-15 years in Europe is expected to grow by little more than 1 million barrels a day. However, oil exports eastward could serve Asian markets, where demand for oil is expected to grow by 10 million barrels a day over the next 10–15 years. Lastly, there are political and security questions as to whether the newly independent republics of the FSU should rely on Russia or any other country as its sole export outlet. As a result, multiple routes for the republics' oil and gas exports have been proposed. (A more detailed discussion of this complex, important issue affecting the entire region appears in Chapter 6: Energy transport and pipeline politics).

# 3 Economic and industrial overview

## Macroeconomic overview of the region

All the countries in the region share three key macroeconomic factors. First, being remote from the hard currency export markets for their commodities, they depend on other countries for transit. In the Soviet period their southern and eastern neighbours, such as Turkey and Iran, were all but closed to their trade because there was neither any political link nor any transport infrastructure in place. Only now are relations and transport routes to countries outside the former Soviet Union (FSU) being opened. Since 1991, goods for sale have, for the first time, been shipped east to China and the Pacific Ocean and south to Iran and the Indian Ocean. The Caspian Pipeline Consortium agreement, finally signed in November 1996, will allow Kazakh oil to reach the Black Sea, while Uzbek and Kazakh gas is fed into the Russian domestic and export network. Further export expansion for hydrocarbons demands heavy foreign investment and the maintenance of competitive costs of extraction and shipment. Comparative cost advantage is also demanded for exporting non-ferrous, rare and precious metals. All countries, especially Kazakhstan, are developing their metal export capability with foreign capital inflows and joint ventures.

The second characteristic common to the region is that the economies represent a mix of both high and low value-added production. The high value-added production results from the workforce being better educated than in developing economies with similar income levels. There exists a small but well-skilled core that facilitates the transfer of sophisticated technology from the West. In terms of technical ability, Kazakhstan has been harder hit than Uzbekistan by the collapse of the command economy, of military production and the ending of trade ties with Comecom and the USSR. But most governments in the region have avoided mass unemployment and poverty. Low value-added production results from the heavy reliance on agriculture and the underdevelopment of the potential of natural resources and heavy

industry. The Kazakh grain and Uzbek cotton crops have declined sharply since independence, mainly because of six decades of collective and state farming laws.

Third, heavy emigration of the upper and middle classes to Russia and the West has been a temporary hindrance to regional macroeconomic development by sharply reducing the size of the workforce with technical and professional qualifications. The most popular destinations for professionals who are part of this 'brain-drain' have been Moscow followed by Europe, Israel and the United States. However, replacements are being trained. Although capital investment in education has been slowed, current spending – such as wages and electricity bills for universities – has not. Furthermore, the creation of thousands of small private firms as well as newly privatised industries has created a whole new entrepreneurial class that previously was stifled under the Soviet system.

All the countries' economies are small enough to be able to adjust well within a generation to a competitive, free market western-style economy. Yet, at the same time, the countries are large enough to attract investment interest from most multinational corporations. Other FSU republics, such as the Baltics, Moldova and Georgia, are considered too small to be of any great interest to the Fortune 500 (list of large multinationals). At the central government level, the absorption of foreign direct investment (FDI) is being facilitated by the creation of market infrastructures, such as a financial sector, regulations on protection of investment and a commercial legal system. By 1996, the private sector in the region generated over 40 per cent of area GNP. Foreign majority partnerships now exist in many previously state-owned companies. However, a truly open, well-functioning economy is still years away.

Consumer-driven imports and a multitude of private individual shuttle traders have shifted the direction of trade away from the traditional Soviet partners – notably Russia and other Asian republics – and towards Turkey, India and China. In 1995, for the first time, Uzbekistan conducted over 50 per cent of its foreign trade away from the Commonwealth of

*Zhibek Zholi Street, Almaty, Kazakhstan*

Independent States (CIS) republics, while Kazakhstan's trade outside the CIS accounted for 44 per cent of its total and is steadily rising. Russia, however, will remain the number one trading partner for the region for some years to come.

Foreign investors and those involved in international trade have been attracted to the region because of its relative macroeconomic and political stability. After overcoming the 1992 shocks of price liberalisation, the loss of the massive subsidies from Moscow, and the withdrawal of the rouble trading zone within Central Asia and the Caspian, the republics have, with IMF assistance, successfully introduced new currencies. This enabled them to start building a new, viable economic trading zone, first within Asia and then further afield. The region's economy has also received substantial assistance from the EU, the European Bank for Reconstruction and Development (EBRD) and the United Nation's Development Programme (see Chapter 4).

## Regional economic development within the USSR and its impact today

Ever since incorporation within the USSR in the 1920s, Central Asia and the Caspian region was subjected to a classic form of economic colonialism. The region was used as a source of low-cost commodities; labour, energy, minerals and agriculture products. At the same time, the relatively large Central Asian and Caspian consumer market was an ideal dumping ground for Russian industry. The colonial system imposed by the Soviets was not without its merits. In return for supplying cheap commodities, the region benefited from the Soviet system of free universal healthcare, education and subsidised foodstuffs, transport and housing.

However, the economic colonialism of the Soviet era resulted in very unbalanced economies in the countries within the USSR. While the region is oversupplied with commodity producing firms, there is a relative scarcity of high value-added industry such as machinery, electronics or food processing. Mikhail Gorbachev's policy of glasnost, which began in the 1980s, highlighted the seriousness of the economic imbalance, including the over-concentration on cotton, oil and mineral production. Throughout the Soviet period, the region produced only a handful of products – albeit in massive quantities – and relied on Moscow for trade as well as access to capital and technology.

In all types of colonial relations, the requirements of the colonial centre rather than those of the colonised periphery determine the pattern of macroeconomic development. An example of this was given during a speech in 1994 at Kazakhstan's Ministry of Defence, when President Nazarbayev tried to explain the causes of the country's slow transition. He pointing out that during the Soviet period, 93 per cent of Kazakhstan's economy was managed from Moscow via Soviet ministries and 30 per cent of the republic's budget was allocated from central funds.

All Soviet leaders from Stalin to Gorbachev (pre-reforms) viewed the USSR as a single entity. They had a penchant for Union-wide economic autarky, and they pursued this in the context of a highly centralised system of economic planning. As a result, different republics in Central Asia and the Caspian were assigned specific production tasks and rigid output quotas. In deciding these tasks and quotas, little attention was paid to the development of at least a moderately diversified and self-sufficient regional economy, nor to the development of regional transport and communications networks, nor to environmental safety. What was important was meeting the production targets set by the central planning organisation, Gosplan.

Several characteristics of Soviet-era economics have left the Central Asian and Caspian republics burdened by problems. Since independence, these problems have exacerbated the region's economic woes and complicated the task of economic reform and reinvigoration.

### Reliance on agriculture

Despite 70 years of Soviet emphasis on industrial development, plus efforts at spreading industrial units across the Soviet Union as a means of reducing regional disparities, most republics in Central Asia and the Caspian still depend on agriculture as the mainstay of their economies and the principal source of national income and employment. Furthermore, the Soviet-era pattern of agricultural development was determined by the consumption and export needs of Moscow rather than by those of the individual republics, leading to over-reliance on a single commodity or crop.

In Uzbekistan, Turkmenistan and Tajikistan, cotton has been the major economic pillar. Even today, for Uzbekistan, which is one of the more industrially developed countries in the region, raw cotton exports constitute the principal source of foreign exchange. The difficulties of other single commodity economies, whether reliant on coffee, bananas or oil, and their extreme vulnerability to international commodity markets are well known. The overwhelming concentration on cotton production contributed to the Central Asian and Caspian states' inability to diversify their agricultural production according to their own consumption needs.

Methods of Soviet-era farming, such as the excessive use of fertilisers and pesticides, also adversely affected the environment and other potential forms of agricultural activity by eroding soil fertility and polluting water resources. The negative effects of these practices are today evident in the shrinking water resources of some countries, notably Uzbekistan. Environmental pollution, partly from the excessive use of fertilisers and pesticides, has made underground water resources unusable and crippled the ability of the republics to become self-sufficient in food.

## The workforce

Throughout the Soviet period, in Central Asia and the Caspian most skilled industrial workers and managers, especially at higher levels, were Russians, other Slavs, or, in places such as Kazakhstan and the Kyrgyz Republic, transplanted East Germans. For the Central Asian and Caspian republics, this situation resulted in an inadequately trained, unskilled native workforce and a higher percentage of low-income workers among the local population. As long as the Soviet Union lasted, this uneven pattern of skilled employment had the negative impact of creating a two-class society; the masses of poor indigenous workers mixed with a small minority of skilled Russian workers. The economic impact of this state of dependency on non-indigenous labour was most acutely felt immediately after independence when a sizeable proportion of the skilled workforce left the region. They left because of concerns about rising nationalism, inter-ethnic tensions, the declining standard of living or the simple belief that life would be better in their native land of Russia. After a few years, this exodus was more or less halted, primarily because conditions in Russia for native Russians were not substantially better than those in Central Asia and the Caspian.

## Transport and communication networks

In all colonial economic systems, the transport and communication infrastructure is based on moving goods and information from the centre to the periphery. At the time of the

*Baku, Azerbaijan*

region's independence, transport links and telephone lines to and from Russia were usually better than the links within any one country. The Soviet's largely self-contained and autarkic economic system intensified this colonial model of centre–periphery links. The Cold War, the use of the region as a strategic nuclear, military and space exploration site as well as the desire to contain any pan-Islamic movements all led to the isolation of Central Asia and the Caspian from the outside world. The adverse economic effects of this isolation were strongly felt after independence as the region attempted to create from scratch its own trading, transport and communications infrastructure.

The problem of isolation is especially acute in Kazakhstan where Russian territory is the only export outlet for oil produced in the western part of the country. Russia is also the only source of crude oil for Kazakh refineries in eastern Kazakhstan. In addition, there is only a very limited domestic gas pipeline distribution system within Kazakhstan, so the country is still dependent on imported gas from Uzbekistan. The vagaries of regional and international politics and Russia's desire to maintain influence in the region have so far hindered the development of the most cost-effective pipeline system.

## Trade and capital investment

The Soviet period left a legacy of inadequate trade relations within the Central Asia and Caspian region because the bulk of trade was concentrated to and from Russia. Since independence, the interruption of sources of supply from Russia have left factories idle or forced them to work at less than full capacity. At the same time, there was a pressing demand for certain finished goods, hyperinflation as a result of scarcity, and significant unemployment. In Kazakhstan, a number of oil refineries, such as the Pavlodar, remained idle from 1992 to 1993 because deliveries of Siberian crude were interrupted. Meanwhile, the decline of the Russian economy meant that there was a sharp fall in the demand for Central Asian and Caspian goods. Russia's trade network was also in a state of collapse. East European buyers, who previously were forced to purchase Soviet-produced goods, could seek out higher quality and lower prices from such producers as India and China. East European textile plants soon discovered that US-produced cotton was more reliably obtainable and of better quality than Central Asian output.

The artificial system of pricing and capital investment left over from the Soviet era also caused great problems in the post-independence republics. Under the Soviet system, money and prices performed a purely accounting function and were structured to facilitate Gosplan production quotas rather than to manage the efficient allocation of resources. Soviet prices bore little relation to world prices. After independence, the republics in Central Asia and the Caspian were thrust into the competitive world market and had to trade at real prices with real currencies. Given their weak and non-competitive economies, as well as their inclusion in the rouble economic sphere of influence, industry in the region found it nearly impossible to compete in international trade. In addition to these problems, there was a virtual halt to all subsidies and investment from Moscow. This investment shortfall has yet to be fully compensated for by new inward flows of foreign capital from outside the CIS.

## Legal and financial infrastructure

The self-contained isolated character of the Soviet economic system has left the FSU countries without the necessary legal and financial infrastructure as compared with the non-communist developing world. Protection of private property rights, an efficient and reliable banking system, adequate capital investment financing of newly privatised firms and effective debt collection never existed in the Soviet era and have only recently begun to take shape.

# Post-1992 pathways towards economic recovery

For the first few years after independence, all the countries in the region suffered from falling levels of economic activity and production in all sectors, high inflation, deteriorating trade balances and a drop in the standard of living (see Exhibit 3.1). The severity and extent of the economic decline varied from country to country. Economies like Uzbekistan, Kazakhstan and Azerbaijan that have moved towards privatisation and

Exhibit 3.1
**Macroeconomic indicators, 1991–95**

|  | 1991 | 1992 | 1993 | 1994 | 1995 |
|---|---|---|---|---|---|
| **GDP at constant prices (% change)** | | | | | |
| Azerbaijan | −0.7 | −22.6 | −23.1 | −19.7 | −11.8 |
| Kazakhstan | −13.0 | −2.9 | −9.2 | −12.6 | −8.2 |
| Krygz Republic | −5.0 | −19.0 | −16.0 | −20.0 | −5.4 |
| Tajikistan | −7.1 | −29.0 | −11.0 | −18.9 | −12.5 |
| Turkmenistan | −4.7 | −5.3 | −10.0 | −18.8 | −8.2 |
| Uzbekistan | −0.5 | −11.1 | −2.3 | −4.2 | −0.9 |
| **GDP per capita (US$)** | | | | | |
| Azerbaijan | na | 364 | 223 | 173 | 323 |
| Kazakhstan | na | 296 | 916 | 704 | 1,008 |
| Krygz Republic | na | na | 195.1 | 245.0 | 331.3 |
| Tajikistan | na | 52 | 133 | 141 | 82 |
| Turkmenistan | na | na | 1,191 | 552 | 562 |
| Uzbekistan | na | na | 232 | 251 | 442 |
| **Consumer prices (% change, annual average)** | | | | | |
| Azerbaijan | 107 | 912 | 1,129 | 1,664 | 411.7 |
| Kazakhstan | 79 | 1,381 | 1,662 | 1,892 | 176 |
| Krygz Republic | 85 | 855 | 772 | 228.7 | 52.5 |
| Tajikistan | 112 | 1,157 | 2,195 | 350 | 609 |
| Turkmenistan | 103 | 493 | 3,102 | 1,748 | 1,005 |
| Uzbekistan | 82 | 645 | 534 | 1,568 | 305 |
| **Trade balance (US$ million)** | | | | | |
| Azerbaijan | 60 | 489 | −5 | −163 | −275 |
| Kazakhstan | −3,200 | −1,100 | −400 | −920 | −222 |
| Krygz Republic | −41 | −74 | −166 | −199 | −179 |
| Tajikistan | na | −55 | −204 | −148 | −41 |
| Turkmenistan | 590 | 1,140 | 1.100 | 485 | 441 |
| Uzbekistan | 688 | −234 | −378 | 214 | 237 |

*Source:* EBRD.

sought to encourage foreign investment have declined far less sharply.

Reliable statistical data on countries in the region is not readily available. Figures published by the IMF and the EBRD are useful indicators of underlying trends. One trend is for certain; because of a combination of supply disruptions and falling demand between 1992 and 1995, all the countries in the region experienced a sharp drop in industrial and agricultural output causing negative economic growth rates. In Kazakhstan, GDP fell by 2.9 per cent in 1992, 9.2 per cent in 1993, and 12.6 per cent in 1994. By 1997, however, the trend had been fully reversed with GDP growing by around 2 per cent, although growth is forecast to only around 1 per cent in 1998. There have been significant positive changes in the structure of 1998 GDP, however: the share of agricultural and industrial output in Kazakh GDP have fallen, whereas the share of services and construction have grown. The expansion of construction in 1998 has largely been due to accelerated building work in the new capital, Astana.

In the Kyrgyz Republic, according to the EBRD, GDP fell by 5 per cent in 1991, 19 per cent in 1992, 16 per cent in 1993 and around 20 per cent in 1994. For 1994 the EU puts the decline in GDP at only 5.5 per cent, however, emphasising the problem of finding accurate statistics. An improvement followed between 1995 and 1998, and, according to the CIS Statistical Committee, the Kyrgyz Republic was the first country in the CIS to have positive GDP growth in 1995, (0.5 per cent). Growth rate in 1997 of 10.4 per cent assured the investor community of the potential for sustainable development. Further growth is expected in 1998.

The 1996 GDP recovery in the Kyrgyz Republic resulted from strong expansion in agricultural output, while 1997 growth was boosted by the start of production at the Kumtor gold mine. The country suffers from a low domestic savings rate and there are only a limited number of projects that are attractive to foreign investors. In the medium and long term, therefore, because of a lack of investment capital, much will depend on the willingness and ability of the government to attract significant flows of foreign investment, both direct and portfolio.

In Turkmenistan, GDP fell by 5 per cent in 1992 and 10 per cent in 1993, according to the EBRD. In 1993, according to some reports, the IMF had predicted that the economy would grow by 1.7 per cent. But difficulties, mostly arising from the non-payment by other CIS countries for imports of Turkmen gas, undermined this prediction. In Uzbekistan, the decline in GDP was the lowest among the Central Asian states. However, there are vast differences among estimates of the rate of decline of its GDP. For 1992, Uzbek government sources put the rate of decline in GDP at 2.5 per cent; the Economist Intelligence Unit, quoting IMF sources, propose 10 per cent; and the CIS Statistical Unit and the EBRD suggest 11.1 per cent. Real GDP grew by 1.5 per cent in 1996 and 2.4 per cent in 1997, according the the EBRD.

There are two main reasons for the outperformance of Uzbekistan's economy since 1992. First, its economic activity is concentrated in the agriculture and energy sectors, which both proved less vulnerable to the collapse of Russian industry. Second, Uzbekistan was much slower than other Central Asian countries in liberalising its economy and removing government purchase orders and subsidies. Uzbekistan's long tradition of entrepreneurs engaging in private small business and trade was another positive factor.

Because of widespread civil war and near total collapse of the economy in Tajikistan, its fall in GDP had been the highest. In fact, the size of the Tajik economy in 1993 was only 40 per cent of its 1988 level. Although from a low base, real GDP growth was 1.7 per cent in 1997 and is expected to reach 3 per cent in 1998, according to the EBRD.

## Inflation, unemployment and living standards

Despite the sharp economic contraction of the countries in the region, post-1992 inflation rates were initially high. For example, in 1993 the average annual inflation rate in Kazakhstan was 1,662 per cent, in the Kyrgyz Republic 772 per cent, in Uzbekistan 534 per cent and in Turkmenistan 3,102 per cent. Until mid-1993 (at which point all Central Asian countries were part of the rouble zone), because of the failing value of the rouble against major currencies and inflation in Russia, the rest of the CIS experienced a sharp rise in prices. Another factor was the immediate effects of certain economic reform measures, both in Russia and within individual republics, such as the removal of price controls and the reduction or elimination of subsidies. The high rates of inflation have also resulted in a steady fall in the level of real wages. The combination of these factors led to a significant decline in living standards. For example, the incidence of infectious disease has increased throughout the region. Across the region, inflation rates for 1997 and 1998 are under much closer control (see Chapters 8–13).

Accurate information on employment trends is not available, partly because statistics provided by countries in the region often do not account for hidden underemployment. In late 1994, for example, the Kyrgyz prime minister put the number of those officially unemployed at 11,000, or 0.6 per cent of the workforce, but he added that an additional 218,000 were unemployed in all but name (that is, either underemployed or on indefinite unpaid leave). If these figures are taken into account, the percentage of those unemployed in the Kyrgyz Republic was at least 12.5 per cent of the workforce. For 1995, the rate of unemployment was officially put at 20 per cent for Uzbekistan, 20 per cent for Kazakhstan and 6 per cent for Tajikistan.

## From rouble zone to national currencies

The dissolution of the Soviet Union as a political unit did not immediately lead to the disappearance of all economic institutions of the USSR, especially in the financial area. The Soviet rouble remained the common currency. Some or all of the republics in Central Asia and the Caspian region may have considered having their own national currencies sometime in the future, but leaving the rouble zone was not an early priority. Rather, most of the countries in the region preferred to maintain monetary union among the former Soviet states, or at least between themselves and Russia. They lacked adequate gold or hard currency assets that would be necessary to back up any new national currency. Their trade continued to be with Russia and other states of the FSU, and maintaining a common currency based on the rouble made sense, at least until they could become more integrated within the global economy and develop trade relations with other countries.

In the end it was Russia's economic and monetary policies, pursued without prior consultation, that forced the republics in the region to adopt their own national currencies. The process began when the Russian central bank decided to withdraw all pre-1993 Soviet roubles from circulation inside Russia and introduced a new rouble displaying the Russian flag and printed only in Russian. In fact Russia did propose the creation of a new rouble zone, but set conditions for inclusion in this zone that were so stringent that the Central Asian and Caspian republics were unable to meet them. For example, these conditions required the close coordination of budgetary, financial and monetary policies among all new member states. They also required the republics to make large deposits with the Russian central bank. Kazakhstan and Uzbekistan at first agreed to monetary union with Russia, but because of the harsh requirements and short deadline for creating a fundamentally restructured rouble zone, all Central Asian and Caspian republics except Tajikistan (which for all intents and purposes was a Russian protectorate), ended up adopting their own currencies. In spring 1995, Tajikistan finally followed suit and created its own currency.

The Kyrgyz Republic, the only republic that had opted for a national currency before Russia's decision to end the old rouble zone, consulted closely with the IMF and, with its financial backing, introduced a currency called the som in May 1993.

## Economic transformation versus maintenance of the welfare state

In the 1990s, the dominant method for bringing about economic reform and accelerating the pace of development has been privatisation and marketisation. Most government planners within the region argued that these twin processes distribute resources more logically within a given economy and, by intensifying competition, eliminate waste and other inefficiencies. The overall result, in theory, would be increased levels of GNP and improved living conditions for most people. In short, the idea was that the gains of the overall economy would in time 'trickle down'. In practice, the region's overly centralised system dependent on state subsidies, shielded from competition, and saddled with a large and inefficient bureaucracy, simply could not withstand rapid privatisation and an overnight move to a free market system.

International capital has played a vital role in post-Soviet development, but total dependence on the continued flow of external capital for economic development has serious pitfalls.

While foreign investors are seeking the highest returns with low or manageable risks, the region has had to contend with the massive social undertaking of removing the cradle-to-grave protection of their giant welfare state. The government's need to create jobs and improve the standard of living has proved to be in many cases incompatible with offering foreign corporates high returns and low risks.

The idea that privatisation alone will resolve the problems of economic disparity has not been supported by recent experience elsewhere in the CIS. So far, the Soviet experience of privatisation has shown that the process of trickle-down often does not take place, and that when it does, it is in a rather skewed manner. Out of the countless billions of dollars of foreign capital invested in the Soviet privatisation process, hardly any money at all has gone directly into developing industrial infrastructure, job creation or improving standards of living.

## Reform and privatisation

The pace of privatisation in the region has been uneven. The Kyrgyz Republic and Kazakhstan began the process early and moved ahead relatively rapidly. In the Kyrgyz Republic one-third of all state enterprises had been privatised by the end of 1994. The extent of privatisation was greatest in the trade and service sectors. Nonetheless, most of the privatised firms have been relatively small in size as well as in total contribution to GDP. Major firms and industrial sectors remain under the control of the ministries.

Efforts to privatise the Kyrgyz agricultural sector began in 1992, but were abandoned within a year. During this period, 165 state or collective farms were reorganised into 17,000 peasant enterprises. Also, the government has moved rather slowly to phase out non-viable enterprises, which continue to be a burden on the state. Similarly, the continued state monopoly in distribution and procurement, the prevalence of unfair practices in selling off assets and the lack of clarity in many laws has stifled the whole process.

Kazakhstan has also taken some important steps towards privatisation. Between 1991 and 1993 some 7,000 enterprises out of a total of 45,000 were formally sold off to workers, collectives and managers. In 1993, a new national privatisation programme was approved, but factors similar to those that affected the Kyrgyz Republic hampered the success of privatised industries. Kazakhstan had achieved limited success, but this is only because key industrial enterprises have become the property of private companies managed by officials from the respective ministries. This situation, which some Kazakh critics referred to as the process of 'Sovietised privatisation', has created another problem in the form of the unprecedented rise in corruption and embezzlement.

The privatisation of the Kazakh agricultural sector has proved more difficult, particularly in the northern part of the country where production is organised around huge, loss-making agro-processing firms. Nevertheless, some progress has been made, and 11 per cent of the land and a substantial proportion of the 1,720 agro-processing companies have been transferred to new cooperatives or small enterprises.

Until recently, Uzbekistan had been the least forthcoming of the Central Asian and Caspian region republics in terms of privatisation. Shortly after independence, President Islam Karimov maintained that Uzbekistan should not rush into a drastic privatisation programme, but would rather proceed slowly and try to find its own unique model for reform and development. In 1993, the government partially liberalised prices, imposed new taxes, and removed some import tariffs, and privatised small shops and residential housing. New laws on banking, property and foreign investment were enacted. Many observers, however, believe that during this period no real privatisation took place. Rather, privatisation amounted to little more than the appropriation of state property by communist bosses turned private businessmen.

Uzbekistan, similar to other republics in the region, was initially wary of borrowing from international institutions such as the IMF because it believed this would undermine its independence. This cautious course may have shielded the country from a huge debt default. Since 1994, mounting financial difficulties have led the Uzbek government to seek IMF credits and, in order to secure needed funds, the government has shown some limited willingness to accept IMF conditions for economic reform and restructuring. During a speech to mark the new session of the Uzbek Supreme Assembly in March 1995, President Karimov announced the government's commitment to enacting long-term economic reforms.

In Turkmenistan too, reform and privatisation have occurred very slowly. The process did not begin until December 1993. Even then, it was limited to small firms and involved the transfer of ownership to workers without any injection of new capital into the system. This strategy of limiting sell-offs to only small firms is likely to reduce the benefits of privatisation because the new owners, who are generally current employees, cannot by themselves meet the firms' often acute need for investment capital nor implement operating improvements necessary for functioning in a free market economy. In short, Turkmenistan still lacks a comprehensive privatisation strategy. The financial and banking systems also need fundamental reforms to transform them from institutions geared to meeting the state's financial and credit needs to ones that can mobilise resources and allocate them efficiently among various sectors.

Tajikistan has faced the worst economic problems since independence. Civil war has diverted attention away from economic reform. By the summer of 1995, however, a draft economic reform package was prepared, and Tajikistan began negotiations with the World Bank for assistance. World Bank delegations now frequently visit Dushnabe to determine the main directions of reform and to render concrete assistance to Tajikistan. The proposed reform package included a privatisation programme and price liberalisation.

In Azerbaijan, privatisation was adopted as early as February 1993 under the presidency of Abulfaz Elchibey. However, until 1995, only taxis and housing had been privatised by the successor administration of President Heydar Aliyev, who came under increasing criticism for the slow pace of reform. At the end of 1995, the private sector only amounted to about 20–25 per cent of GDP, one of the lowest figures in either the region or emerging Europe.

In July 1995, a privatisation programme for small and medium-sized firms was drawn up, to be implemented between 1995 and 1998. The implementation of the programme was delayed for a year, but between April and December 1996 about 6,200 small enterprises were privatised. In 1997 a mass voucher distribution programme was launched but by mid-year it was struggling to gain any momentum. At the end of 1997 small enterprise privatisation had all but been completed. By the end of 1999 it is intended that about 70 per cent of state enterprises will have been privatised.

The collapse of the Soviet economy brought about a spontaneous process of disintegration of Azeri agricultural cooperatives, and the informal seizure of lands. Failure to privatise land ownership meant that as late as 1995, rights of ownership and of transfer of land remained obscure. A new 1996 law on land reform distributed the land owned by the cooperatives and established private property rights over land, including the right to sell. These reforms laid the basis for foreign investment into Azerbaijan. In 1996, FDI inflows totalled US$455 million, some three times greater than in 1995. However, the bulk of this capital is in the oil sector.

# 4 *International relations and foreign investment*

## The region within the CIS

The key point to make at the outset is that there really is no functioning Commonwealth of Independent States (CIS) in existence today, at least in the form in which it was originally intended. By 1990, the USSR's economy was on the brink of collapse. Its leaders knew that the Union would have to be reinvented in a completely new structure if its essence was to be retained. In their search for this new structure, they studied many models and degrees of interstate integration. Some found the model of the British Commonwealth, membership of which comprises former British colonies, attractive. Thus, despite significant differences between the British Empire and the USSR, the revised structure was called the CIS.

The first result of this Soviet search for a new framework for intra-republic relations was President Gorbachev's New Union Treaty, unveiled in March 1991. Its reception within Central Asia differed widely from one republic to another. At this point, Boris Yeltsin's supporters were already in the ascendancy, and in their quest for power they kept promising more autonomy and even independence to the region. The Central Asian republics reacted positively to the treaty in line with their general loyalty towards Moscow. The fatal blow to the prospects of the New Union Treaty came, however, with the attempt by Russia to form a Slavic alliance with Belarus and Ukraine. The idea of a Slavic union, excluding Asians, was received with surprise, dismay and resentment. The Kazakh President, Nursultan Nazarbayev, for example, warned that the conclusion of a Slavic treaty would be seen as Moscow abandoning Central Asia. Following the move, therefore, the Central Asian countries tried to develop a unified stance towards Asian–CIS relations. The first step was a meeting of the Central Asian republics' heads of state in Ashgabat, the capital of Turkmenistan, on 12 December 1991.

Initially, there was some speculation that the Central Asian republics might form a counterbalance to the Slavic republics in the north. Some of the countries thought of adopting an indifferent posture toward the CIS, and indeed Turkmenistan initially opted for not joining and instead established bilateral ties with Russia and other individual CIS members. Similarly, the Kyrgyz Republic at first considered staying out of the CIS and remaining a neutral country, enjoying friendly relations with all states.

However, by early 1992, as the situation in Russia stabilised, all the Central Asian republics decided to join the CIS. But, even by the end of 1995, the CIS had still failed to transform itself into a well-integrated and efficient economic and trade organisation, despite the signing of innumerable accords on various aspects of intra-CIS relations, most of which have never been put into effect. Consequently, a range of issues facing the CIS have been dealt with at a bilateral level between Russia and individual Central Asian republics. Russia has signed various agreements with each country covering issues from economic cooperation and trade to military and security arrangements.

Effectively, the CIS has never developed into an EU-like, border-free trading bloc. Lack of clear purpose has been the CIS's most significant handicap. Without well-defined goals and structure, the CIS has mirrored the haphazard way in which it was created. No process of intra-Soviet Union discussion and consensus building had preceded the collapse of the USSR. Nor had any prior debate occurred on the wisdom of dismantling economic institutions of the Union, nor on the best way to go about forming successor organisations. As Boris Yeltsin admitted during a speech to the Russian Congress of People's Deputies, many issues concerning the legal succession to the USSR and the dividing up of joint property remained unresolved. These problems have continued to bedevil intra-CIS relations.

Russia had always wanted the CIS to be a closely knit, permanent institution, but without a supranational character that could limit its freedom of action in economic matters. Russia came to see the CIS as a convenient cover to legitimise its policy of reimposing its economic influence over oil and mineral rich Central Asia. Russia had also tried to gain international recognition for the CIS as a regional collective organisation, like the North Atlantic Treaty Organisation (NATO) or the EU. These attempts failed, and the possibility of developing Central Asian economies through increased intra-CIS cooperation and trade on the scale of the EU remains extremely remote.

Following Azerbaijan's initial reservations about joining the CIS, in September 1993 President Aliyev agreed to the country's membership. This membership partially helped in gaining Russian backing for the negotiated cease-fire in the disputed Nagorno-Karabakh region. However, after an initial warming, relations between Azerbaijan and the CIS became uneasy. First, in Azerbaijan, the CIS is seen primarily as a Russian-dominated infrastructure designed to extend and preserve Russia's influence over the FSU. Second, in part through the structure of the CIS, Russia has attempted to continue its economic and political involvement in Azerbaijan by pushing for involvement in Caspian oil transport as well as Azeri oil projects. As a result, Azerbaijan has actively sought to strengthen intraregional cooperation and trade. For instance, an agreement signed with the Georgian government in early 1996 laid the outlines of a strategic regional partnership between Azerbaijan and Georgia. Later in 1996, a four-way agreement on a Euro-Asian transport corridor was signed between Azerbaijan, Georgia, Turkmenistan and Iran.

# Internal and external relations

Foreign policy throughout the region revolves around Russia. All leaders, however, have been keen to show their political independence and autonomy from Russia. Russian foreign policy towards the region seems to be based on its desire to access vital raw materials and agricultural products, either through ownership or investment in projects by Russian companies, particularly in the energy and metals sector (for example, Lukoil, the Russian oil firm, has successfully gained membership of the AIOC consortium in Azerbaijan), and its wish to see stability in the region with strong political leadership.

While the republics assert their political independence from Russia, there is a willingness to promote further economic integration within the region. To this end, the Kazakh president, Nursultan Nazarbayev, called for the creation of a Eurasian Union. Although this Union was never formed, in January 1995 a CIS Customs Union was established between Kazakhstan, Russia and Belarus. The Kyrgyz Republic joined in 1996. Today, the administrative structures of the CIS barely function and the main effect of the Customs Union has been to restrict trade to within the region. In the absence of the Union, that same trade would have gone outside the CIS.

The primary goals of any intra-regional cooperation are to facilitate trade within the region and to provide strength in numbers against an increasingly politically volatile Russia. For more than 70 years of Soviet rule, the Central Asians depended heavily on free trade among themselves because commerce in Soviet Asia completely ignored the republics' borders. Now, this once economically integrated region uses separate currencies in addition to the Russian rouble, while the universally accepted US dollar is constantly in short supply. Although each state has entered into a bilateral security arrangement with Russia, the political situation is still volatile. Good diplomatic relations among Central Asian governments will lead to stronger security arrangements. Russia has no overt objections to such increased intra-regional cooperation as long as its own interests are protected.

In the case of oil-rich Azerbaijan, which provided the bulk of the energy needs for the rapid Soviet economic expansion after World War II, the relationship with Russia remains uneasy due to sovereignty disputes over the Caspian Sea and Russia's attempts to continue its economic and political involvement in the country. As a result, Azerbaijan is keen to strengthen intraregional cooperation and trade (see above).

## Re-emergence of links with Turkey

Turkey has been profoundly influenced by the political changes in Central Asia and the Caspian region. During the Soviet era, it followed a policy of excluding any territorial interest in the region despite the substantial linguistic and cultural links and the presence of a number of ethnic groups. Turkey enjoys certain advantages in developing diplomatic and commercial links with the region, notably the considerable degree of ethnic and linguistic affinity, a relatively well-developed industrial base, a vibrant private sector, and its position as the most western nation bordering the region. Turkey's image as a moderate Islamic, but secular and modern state has also been promoted by the West as an ideal model for Central Asia, and the United States and the World Bank have channelled some of their aid to Central Asian republics through Turkey. Also, the US Agency for International Development (USAID) has contracted various Turkish governmental and private institutions to train personnel from the Central Asian republics. From Turkey's point of view, the failure to gain EU membership and the end of the clear East–West delineation of the Cold War has given the region renewed importance. Many believe that if Turkey cannot prosper in the EU, the huge and untapped economies of Central Asia and the Caspian provide enormous potential and opportunity.

Relations between Turkey and Central Asia have also become institutionalised via regular Turkic summits. In addition, Turkey has taken it upon itself to train nearly 10,000 Central Asian students.

Turkey's principal handicaps have been its geographical remoteness and its economic and political problems, including the rise of Islamist tendencies, ethnic and sectarian strife, and a Kurdish insurgency. Although the advent of technology means that geographical proximity is no longer as important as it used to be, it is still significant given Central Asia's land-locked position. For example, because of its geographical remoteness, Turkey cannot provide a viable economic outlet for the Central Asian nations.

Russia is firmly committed to keeping the region well within the Russian sphere of influence, despite challenges from Turkey. Turkey took the lead in establishing the Black Sea Consortium that joins the region with the Ukraine, Russia and Europe. Its stated interest in creating a Turkish commonwealth of nations was an even more direct challenge to Russian interest because such an ethnic commonwealth would serve to further break up what little is left of the CIS as well as to move the region out of the rouble zone. Turkey's offer to provide military training and technical support also concerns Russia.

Since mid-1993, Russia has been expressing concern over what it has been describing as efforts to create a pan-Turkist alliance. These developments have fuelled a Russian–Turkish rivalry that creates certain dilemmas for the Central Asian countries. The emergence of a Turkic community could help reduce their dependence on Russia or on the CIS, and enhance their international weight. But increased links with Turkey could antagonise Russia, Iran, and China, which see pan-Turkism as a threat to their own security and territorial integrity. Kazakhstan, in particular, has been anxious to dispel any suspicions about its pan-Turkist aspirations, because of the sensitivity of its relations with both Russia and China. Turkmenistan, meanwhile, emphasises bilateral relations with Russia and is wary of close multilateral frameworks, whether these be the CIS or a potential Turkic commonwealth.

Turkey's private sector, which has been active in the region, has made significant progress, particularly in Turkmenistan. Some Russian observers have even expressed concern that Turkey may soon replace Russia as the dominant trading partner in the region. In Turkmenistan, for instance, Russia believes Turkish influence is being aggressively advanced through the Turkish Development and Cooperation Agency (TDCA). Besides its involvement in a series of activities in most areas of economic and social development, the TDCA has been showing special attention to the construction of a complex of mosques and Islamic religious schools. Similar activities by Turkey are under way in Kazakhstan and Uzbekistan, including the construction of a large mosque in Almaty.

Although the Central Asian countries favour close and multi-dimensional relations with Turkey, they do not want Turkey to become a new economic superpower. In fact, the initial Turkish attitude of wanting to play a so-called civilising role was resented by Central Asian republics. The regional aspirations of some Central Asian countries, notably Uzbekistan, make them reluctant to accept a leadership role for Turkey.

The future shape of the Central Asian republics' relations with Turkey will to a large extent be determined by the evolution of their ties with Russia and with the West. If Russia consolidates its position in Central Asia and if Russian–Turkish competition intensifies, Central Asian relations with Turkey will in all likelihood suffer. But if Russia fails in Central Asia, or if Russian–Turkish relations improve, Turkish–Central Asian relations will benefit.

Relations between Azerbaijan and Turkey have been affected by Baku's rapprochement with Iran (see below). The close ties between the two should have forced Turkey to distance itself from Azerbaijan as it has always been keen to show its staunchly western pro-NATO credentials. Particularly against any Islamic-inspired fundamentalism emerging from Iran or Iraq. Yet, Turkey, taking a long-term view of the region, has continued to be enthusiastic towards strengthening its ties with Azerbaijan, as it has with all neighbouring FSU states. Turkey remains a major strategic ally of Azerbaijan, although it has not been overly supportive of Azerbaijan in the Nagorno-Karabakh dispute. In 1996 Azerbaijan signed a long-term military cooperation treaty with Turkey.

## Iran

Historically, it was more often the Persian Empire that dominated the region rather than the Ottoman Empire. Iran, unlike secular Turkey, is a fervently Islamic state; a point not lost on the predominantly Muslim population of the region. Tajikistan, as a Persian-speaking state, is of especial interest to Iran, and this interest is strongly reciprocated by most Tajiks who see themselves surrounded by ethnic Turks. At the governmental level, relations between the two countries have steadily improved since 1992 when Dushanbe, the Tajik capital, accused Tehran of fomenting unrest among the Islamic opposition.

Turkmenistan has established particularly good relations with Iran. The country is strategically important for the export of Turkmen natural gas. US relations with Turkmenistan have been cool over this point of Iranian influence in the region.

From Iran's perspective, both Iran and Russia share the concern that Turkey will potentially be used as a western instrument of influence in their own back yard. Yet it is unlikely that there will be too much governmental collusion with Iran on the part of either Russia or Central Asia and the Caspian. For one thing, all the governments are keen to stamp out any signs of Islamic revolt within their rural regions, and for another, all the region's administrations are keen to attract investment from US corporates. The US government has shown that it will quickly exert its influence to prevent any US-led investment project that is linked to Iran.

Azerbaijan continues to support a generally friendly and open relationship with Iran. Their relationship began in 1994 when the Azeri president, Heydar Aliyev, made a state visit to

Iran as part of Azerbaijan's policy of investigating as many non-Russian transport and trading routes as possible. Iran has since sided with Azerbaijan against Armenia in the dispute over the Nagorno-Karabakh region.

## China

Sino–Soviet rivalries following the break-up of the Russia–China alliance in 1958, and Russia's propaganda against China, generated fear and suspicion in Central Asia towards China. For a long time, this suspicion inhibited expanding relations. By the mid-1980s, when Sino–Soviet tensions began to ease, the volume of Sino–Soviet trade – a portion of which was with Central Asia – also increased significantly.

China was ambivalent about the impact of the USSR's dissolution on its own national interests. Although the collapse of Soviet military might based in Central Asia was viewed as improving China's security environment, China worried about the increased risk of nuclear proliferation in its neighbourhood. During the Soviet era, the Chinese knew that at least some of the nuclear missiles based in Soviet Asia were aimed at them.

Despite mutual misgivings, China and the Central Asian republics have tried to remove, or at least mitigate, elements of discord and improve their relations.

A major turning point in Sino–Central Asian relations was the official tour of Central Asia by the Chinese prime minister in April 1994. The principal purpose of the tour was to reduce the hostility and the perceived threat from China in the region. China was also concerned about the future stability of the region, the potential rise of Islamic radicalism and Turkic (especially Uighur) nationalism, and the strengthening of Pan-Turkist tendencies in Central Asia. On the positive side, China's awareness of the potential of Central Asian markets prompted Prime Minister Li Peng to call for the renewal of the Silk Route. China's efforts to dispel Central Asian fears, along with its economic attraction to these countries, have improved the atmosphere between them and have increased the level of economic and trade interaction. Nevertheless, several unresolved issues continue to mar Sino–Central Asian relations.

It is still unclear as to the stance the republics' governments will take towards China. On the one hand, the governments want to foster good relations with China because of its importance as a foreign investor, particularly in Kazakhstan. On the other hand, it is unclear how the republics would respond should there be renewed hostilities between Russia and China. Historically, the region has been caught between the two countries. Moving too close to China may become a liability at some point in the future.

Azerbaijan, in keeping with its policies of exploring and developing as many non-Russian trading and transport areas anywhere near Central Asia, has also been keen to extend its nascent links with China. Relations are said to be open, friend-ly and growing closer. Unlike with Kazakhstan, Azerbaijan does not share any border with China so there is no chance of any territorial border dispute. The massive investment and interest by the Chinese National Petroleum Corporation in Kazakhstan's energy industry whose potential is less than Azerbaijan, has been closely followed by Baku. Although trade and investment between Azerbaijan and China are still limited, there is clearly very substantial room for major commerce between one of the region's great energy exporters and one of the world's great energy consumers.

## Ethnic and border issues

Added difficulties in Sino–Central Asian relations are caused by the significant numbers of Uighurs in Kazakhstan, the Kyrgyz Republic and Uzbekistan, and the 1.1 million Kazakhs living in Xinjiang province during the Soviet era. Because of Sino–Soviet tensions, the Uighurs were allowed a good deal of cultural autonomy by the Kazakh authorities. They used this freedom effectively and organised Uighur language newspapers, television and theatre. During the late 1980s and early 1990s, the Uighurs of Central Asia demanded autonomy for Xinjiang and greater religious and cultural freedoms for China's Uighur population. As pan-Turkist ideas re-emerged in Central Asia, Turkey and the Caucasus, there was also talk of creating an Uighurstan.

The Central Asian countries have tried to reassure the Chinese that they will not use the Uighurs to destabilise China. Yet for some Central Asian countries, especially Uzbekistan, the Uighur population remains a card that they can play if they decide to promote a Turkestani federation. The pressure from the 200,000 Uighur minority in Kazakhstan may have hampered the development of relations with China.

The presence of 1.1 million Kazakhs in the Kazakh Autonomous District of Xinjiang is potentially more destabilising. These Kazakhs enjoy better living standards than their kin in Kazakhstan, but complain about Chinese restrictions that prevent them from emigrating to Kazakhstan. They also complain that the steady stream of Chinese coming into Xinjiang is threatening the survival of the Kazakhs' pastoral and traditional lifestyle. The agreement reached between Kazakhstan and China during Prime Minister Li Peng's visit seems to have eased many of these concerns. The two countries agreed to eliminate all transport restrictions between them and affirmed the inviolability of their current borders. Yet, common ethnic groups settled on both sides of the Sino–Kazakh frontier remain a potentially serious source of tension.

There is also a small Tajik minority concentrated in the Tashgurgan Tajik Autonomous County, along the border with Tajikistan and Afghanistan. China's concern is the potential spread of radical Islam from Afghanistan and Tajikistan and the smuggling of weapons to the Uighurs. Some border problems with the Kyrgyz Republic remain unresolved.

## The nuclear problem

China's continued nuclear tests at Lopnor near the Chinese–Kazakh border strain relations with the Kazakhs.

Kazakhstan also fears that China might use its nuclear status to pressure it in other areas. To eliminate this concern, Kazakhstan requested from China a written commitment that it would not use or threaten to use nuclear weapons against Kazakhstan (a pledge similar to the one China previously made to Ukraine). The request was granted by China in February 1995. Nevertheless, in relations with Central Asia, because of nuclear weapons, the balance of power tilts heavily in China's favour, implying that the Central Asian countries must be sensitive rather than antagonistic to Chinese interests.

## Economic ties

By the mid-1980s and following the thaw in Sino–Soviet relations, trade relations between China and Central Asia expanded; a trend that continued during the period of reform in the Soviet Union and after its collapse. The bulk of the trade activity has been in the border areas and hence between China and Kazakhstan. In fact, China currently is Kazakhstan's biggest trading partner after Russia, although this situation is likely to change if Kazakhstan's relations with the West expand.

Indeed, the full potential of trade relations between Central Asia and China has not been realised. There has been talk of ambitious plans to construct a pipeline that would carry Turkmen and Kazakh gas to Japan through China, or a trans-Asian railway that would link the Persian Gulf to the Pacific Ocean. The economies of China and Central Asia are highly complementary and thus the potential for expanded economic and trade relations is very substantial. Progress has been hampered, however, by the lack of transport infrastructure, the high cost of development, the scarcity of and competition for investment funds, and foreign currency problems. Persisting political and security concerns, despite relatively successful efforts to defuse them, are also likely to have a dampening effect.

## China's investment in Central Asian energy

Although in the short run trade between China and Central Asia may be limited, in the long run few doubt that the energy links between the two will develop into a multi-billion dollar industry. In June 1997, the China National Petroleum Company (CNPC) bought 60 per cent of the Kazakhstan company, Aktobemunaigaz. The following September, China signed two major agreements with Kazakhstan for joint development in the Aktiubinsk and Uzen areas. The proposition was to build a 1,860-mile pipeline to China's western border and a shorter (155-mile) line south from Uzen to Iran's border.

Already China is the world's second-largest energy con-

sumer after the United States. Between 1995 and 2015, its oil consumption is projected to grow 4.9 per cent annually, fuelled by GDP growth of 7.3 per cent. China anticipates that in 1998 alone its demand for oil will grow by 7 to 8 per cent. Currently, two-thirds of this oil is imported from the Middle East. Other Asian states anticipate similar expansion in their energy needs in the long term despite the lingering effects of the financial crises of 1997. In fact, according to the US Department of Energy, while the oil demand in Europe over the next 10 to 15 years may grow by little more than a million barrels per day, the demand in Asian markets will increase by 10 million barrels per day.

# Foreign investment

Post-1992 foreign investment, especially foreign direct investment (FDI), in the region has so far been rather limited. The lack of adequate communications, legal and financial infrastructure, language difficulties, and problems involved in the transportation and export of natural resources and other products have tended to inhibit large-scale foreign investment.

Among the Central Asian countries, Kazakhstan with its oil and gas reserves has attracted the largest share of long-term foreign investment (see Exhibit 4.1). According to EBRD estimates, by 1998 it had received about US$5.7 billion, of which 40 per cent had been channelled into the oil and gas sectors.

Azerbaijan has also received large inflows (US$3.2 billion by 1998 according to EBRD estimates). Of this, over 60 per cent has gone to the oil industry.

Outside the oil industry, which has received the bulk of foreign funding, investment has mainly been directed into extraction industries, especially gold mining. The most successful project has been the Uzbek–American Zarafsjan–Newmont joint venture. The total value of the deal is estimated to be US$225 million, and the EBRD has provided a US$135 million loan. There have also been reports that the British company, Commonwealth and British Mineral, is negotiating with

---

Exhibit 4.1
**FDI (net), US$ million, 1993–98**

|  | 1993 | 1994 | 1995 | 1996 | 1997(e) | 1998(p) |
|---|---|---|---|---|---|---|
| Azerbaijan | 20 | 22 | 282 | 661 | 1,093 | 1,155 |
| Kazakhstan | 473 | 635 | 964 | 1,137 | 1,320 | 1,200 |
| Kyrgyz Republic | 10 | 45 | 96 | 46 | 83 | 29 |
| Tajikistan | 9 | 12 | 17 | 20 | 11 | 18 |
| Turkmenistan | 79 | 103 | 233 | 129 | 108 | 110 |
| Uzbekistan | 48 | 73 | -24 | 90 | 167 | 60 |

*Source:* EBRD.

Tajikistan for a joint gold mining project.

The tobacco industry has been another area of interest to foreign investors. This interest reflects the search by the industry for new markets as cigarette smoking in the western industrialised markets has declined. Philip Morris has invested US$300 million in Kazakhstan, and the British firm, BAT Industries, US$200 million in Uzbekistan over five years.

Uzbekistan has also managed to attract investment from the South Korean industrial group, Daewoo, which has put US$100 million into a car manufacturing factory and US$45million into a television parts factory.

German industrial concerns are also involved in Uzbekistan. According to some reports, 14 joint enterprises involving German capital are operating in Uzbekistan, and 13 German firms have established representative offices in Tashkent. Turkmenistan is another country where German investors have been active, and 10 German firms already operate there, including some as partners in joint ventures (see below).

In the region, Turkey has been the largest investor in Central Asia. The majority of Turkish investments has been in Turkmenistan, mostly in various construction projects, and in Kazakhstan in oil and gas. Turkey has also invested significantly in Uzbekistan. According to ITAR-TASS, more than 20 Turkish companies have offices in Tashkent, and a total of 172 joint projects operate in the republic's textile, food, building and automobile industries. Outside the oil and gas sectors, Turkey has also been a large investor in Azerbaijan.

## Western joint ventures

More than one-third of the FDI in the region is accounted for by inter-company transactions between foreign corporates and their local joint venture. This characteristic underlines the value to Central Asia and the Caspian of joint ventures.

Apart from FDI in the Azeri oil industry, the main western capital commitment is in Uzbekistan. One such example is the British American Tobacco (BAT), which purchased a 51 per cent share in the vertically integrated tobacco industry for US$60 million in 1994. An offer by BAT to purchase a further 46 per cent for US$54 million was deferred for five years. BAT plans to invest an additional US$232 million over five years in refurbishing two cigarette factories. The project, competing in the region with Philip Morris' similar purchase in Kazakhstan, has its export dimension. A cigarette sold under the brand name 'Hon' was launched in March 1996 for both domestic and export sale. BAT's Uzbek production was 14 billion cigarettes in 1996, but rebuilding a plant in Samarkand increased this to 20 billion. Uzbek law still does not allow private land ownership, but BAT negotiated a 99-year lease for its factory sites at a predetermined rent.

Also in Uzbekistan, the South Korean firm Daewoo has a joint venture involving US$100 million committed in Andijan

for the production of cars and minibuses. In addition, Daewoo purchased a textile plant in Tashlak for US$60 million and expects the re-equipped firm to reach US$25 million annual sales, of which some 90 per cent will be for export to other CIS states. Daewoo also established a television electronics joint venture for US$45 million.

An Uzbek–German joint venture with Mercedes Benz is making buses, while the French company Alcatel is re-equipping the national telecommunications network. Thomson is modernising Uzbekistan's air traffic control, Biomed is in pharmaceuticals and there are other French ventures in non-financial services. The Turkish group, Koç Holding, is building a bus and trailer factory near Samarkand. The Uzbek textiles sector, in particular, has attracted joint ventures. Silk ribbons are produced with an Italian firm in Namangan, cotton yarn and cloth is produced with a Korean firm in Tashkent, and shirts and bed-linen with a Turkish firm in Andijan. A Malaysian firm, Probadi, is redeveloping the Karaktai oil and gas deposit.

The official Uzbekistan Business Guide lists 166 offices of foreign firms which are mostly located in Tashkent, but also in Andijan. Namangan, Samarkand and Termez. IBM has set up in Tashkent to serve Azerbaijan, Tajikistan and Turkmenistan. Also established in Uzbekistan are a large number of medium and large German firms, including Schering, Hoechst, Siemens, and Deutsche Bank, plus nearly 20 French firms such as Louis Reihart, Olivier, Rhône-Poulenc and Delaplanque, as well as the Japanese Tomen Corporation.

Gold mining is currently the mainstay of the Uzbek economy. A number of joint ventures were established in mining even before independence, such as Newmont of Denver, Colorado, which has invested US$225 million and received a US$135 million EBRD loan. Newmont's Zarafshan joint venture with the local Navoi Mining and Metallurgical Combine is now a major open cast operation producing 55 tonnes of gold annually. Output is projected to reach 83 tonnes by 2000. Lonhro UK also established a joint venture with Navoi in 1995 in the Amantaytau gold mines with a loan commitment from the IFC. In total, US$100 million will be invested and projections put output at 145 tonnes after 1999.

At the end of 1996 a total of 2,397 joint ventures were operating in Uzbekistan, a significant increase from the 1,395 at the beginning of 1995.

The Kazakh government has had problems in seeking joint ventures for its gold mining. Reserves are estimated at 11 million troy ounces at Bakyrchik and 6.5 million ounces at Vasilovskoe. A new company, Bakyrchik Gold, which held 40 per cent of the state mining firm, was floated on the London Stock Exchange in August 1993. After an initial rise in the price of its shares, the company announced heavy losses and was rescued in 1995 by Robert Friedland, a Canadian billionaire. In December 1996 it became the first large gold mine in

*Norsel textile company, Turkmenistan – a Turkish investment*

the CIS to be wholly foreign owned.

The Kazakh chrome industry, developed by prison labour in the Stalin period, has experienced serious problems. However, in August 1996, a 55.2 per cent stake of Kazkhrom was purchased by the Japan Chromium Corporation with 32.8 per cent retained by the state, 10 per cent held by staff and 2 per cent by domestic investment funds. The new owner will invest US$5 million in reconstruction.

Foreign investment in Kazakh hydrocarbons is defined by two key characteristics; the vast potential of proven reserves and the need to ship exports through other CIS states. Although access to the undersea deposits remains in dispute, there are enough reserves in the north-west territory to have already attracted the major transnational oil and gas corporations, as well as a score of minor ones.

Operations are under way at 175 oil fields and 71 gas fields. The Karachaganak gas deposits, with huge export potential, were initially developed under contract with the government by a consortium of British Gas and Agip, now joined by Texaco and Russia's Gazprom. At Tengiz on the Caspian Sea, extracted gas is consumed within Kazakhstan. However, its 800 million tonnes of oil reserves are to be extracted for sale in Europe. Chevron was the first to enter into an agreement with the government and set up a subsidiary, called Tengizchevroil. Mobil subsequently purchased part of the government's share. Since the only existing evacuation route is through the Russian-owned Transneft network, and there have been numerous difficulties (such as the war in Chechnya) affecting Transneft , the crucial issue is transport. Other blocks of the Tengiz reserve have been promised to seven major companies: Agip, British Gas, Mobil, Total, Shell, BP and Statoil. Further oil corporations bidding for Kazak

reserves are Exxon, Texaco and Amoco.

Joint ventures in other Kazakh sectors include Philip Morris' investment of US$300 million in the Almaty Tobacco Combine, the Samsung Corporation's half share in the Zhezkazgan Copper Combine, which should produce 200,000 tonnes by 2000, and RJR Nabisco's purchase of the Chimkent Confectionery Factory. Some small joint ventures are in services, such as an agreement between Alexander Howden Reinsurance Brokers of London and the state-owned insurer Kazakinstrakh. The EBRD is participating in a number of infrastructure projects, of which the biggest is reconstruction of the Caspian port of Aktau (see below under 'Role of multilateral agencies').

# Role of multilateral agencies

Until recently, the flow of foreign aid to the region was slow and had fallen far short of the countries' early expectations. Moreover, the bulk of the assistance, especially during the first two years of independence, carried rather stringent conditions. This aid cannot be considered as official development assistance (ODA), which consists of aid in the form of grant, or soft loans with a high grant element.

The distribution of aid in the region has also been uneven. Major donors have included the principal international organisations, such as the World Bank and the EBRD, and the key industrial countries such as the United States, Japan and the EU.

## European Union

In December 1991 the EU established a credit line of ECU1,250 million (US$1,626 million) for all of the former Soviet Union (FSU) republics. The credit line's objective has been to provide the FSU republics with essential goods, especially food and medical products. Part of the EU credit is in the form of technical assistance to help restructure these republics' economic systems, as well as upgrade specific agricultural and industrial units.

The share of each type of assistance in the total aid programme has differed substantially depending on the needs of individual republics. For example, the bulk of EU assistance to Tajikistan has consisted of food, medicine and help for the refugees. Under the EU's credit, Tajikistan has received ECU55 million (US$71.5 million). In addition, between 1993 and 1995, it received ECU15.4 million (US$20.1 million) in food aid and other humanitarian assistance. Since 1994, as part of its Technical Assistance Programme to the FSU, the EU has also allocated ECU4 million (US$5.2 million) in grant form to Tajikistan. The assistance is used to improve food production, processing and distribution, human resource development, and energy production and distribution. Kazakhstan has been allocated ECU55 million (US$71.5 million) under the FSU credit line, of which ECU25 million (US$32.5 million) has been disbursed, plus ECU14 million (US$18.2 million) under the Technical Assistance Programme. In 1995, assistance under this programme was increased by ECU3 million (US$3.9 million), bringing the total to ECU17 million (US$22.1 million).

The Kyrgyz Republic was allocated ECU32 million (US$41.4 million) under the FSU credit line, but found conditions too stringent and decided not to use all of the loan. Since 1994, the Republic has been allocated ECU19 million (US$24.7 million) in humanitarian assistance plus ECU29 million (US$28.6 million) in technical assistance. Turkmenistan has received ECU45 million (US$58.5 million) from the credit line and ECU8 million (US$10.4 million) in technical assistance.

Uzbekistan did not sign an agreement with the EU to receive its share under the credit line until September 1994. At that time, it was allocated ECU59 million (US$76.7 million).

## World Bank

In April 1995, the Bank approved its first loan to Azerbaijan, a US$20.8 million credit approved by the International Development Association (IDA) to finance advisory services and create a framework to encourage foreign private investment in the petroleum sector. The credit will also help the government to improve the efficiency and reduce the pollution of Azerbaijan's oil fields by rebuilding infrastructure and directing drilling to the most productive areas. Another IDA project, approved in June 1995, provides a US$61 million credit to improve the water supply in Baku.

In 1996, two additional operations received approval. A US$18 million Institution Building Technical Assistance Project helped the government carry out privatisation and enterprise reforms, strengthen macroeconomic management, modernise the financial sector and improve the legal and regulatory framework. The US$65 million Rehabilitation Credit provided support for privatisation, enterprise restructuring, private sector development, development of competitive and anti-monopoly policies, and banking sector reforms. Support for reform continued in 1997, focusing on trade liberalisation, privatisation, legal and banking sector reforms.

A credit of US$20 million for Urgent Environment Improvement was approved on 30 June 1998 while a pilot reconstruction credit of US$20 million was approved on 2 July. As of late 1998, World Bank/IDA commitments in Azerbaijan totalled US$289.7 million for eight projects, of which US$130.9 million had been disbursed.

The World Bank has so far committed a total of US$89.5 million for three projects to Turkmenistan since it joined in September 1992. In recent years it has extended loans for an Urban Transport Project (totalling US$34.2 million) and a Water Supply and Sanitation Project (US$30.3 million). The loans were targeted to finance improvements in urban transport in Ashgabat, Mary, and Chardzhou and in water supply systems and sanitation in the Dashkhovuz Velayet, the region of Turkmenistan most severely affected by the environmental crisis of the Aral Sea basin. Both of these loans are repayable in 20 years, including a five-year grace period, at the Bank's standard rate for the Libor-based US dollar single currency loans.

In total, the World Bank has approved US$1.5 billion for 16 projects in Kazakhstan. These include five adjustment operations, three technical assistance loans and eight investment loans. Three of the adjustment operations have closed, while the other 13 projects remain active.

Recent World Bank loans include two adjustment loans of US$230 million loan for Public Sector Management Adjustment and US$300 million for Pension Reform Structural Adjustment; a US$10 million loan for Pilot Real Estate, and another US$7 million for Pilot Water Supply. In addition, there was a US$15.8 million loan for Treasury Modernisation; a US$109 million loan for Uzen Oil Fields Rehabilitation; and a US$15.0 million loan for Agricultural Post Privatisation Assistance.

The World Bank's Board of Directors approved in August 1997 a Country Assistance Strategy (CAS), which was jointly prepared by the Bank and the IFC. This CAS proposed a shift in Bank lending from adjustment and technical assistance loans to project lending, with an emphasis on private sector development, social protection, and social service delivery. The Bank has provided Kazakhstan with policy advice in the agriculture, financial and energy sectors, and is helping with petroleum legislation, taxation reform and legal reform and training. Five activities financed by the World Bank's Institutional Development Fund are providing training and technical support for coordination and management of external assistance to strengthen the country's statistical system, and to organise a study tour of industrial countries for government officials and managers of industrial enterprises.

Apart from financial structure reform, the World Bank is also coordinating with international efforts to reverse the severe environmental degradation of many areas of the country. More specifically, the Bank is supporting implementation of projects coming out of the recently approved National Environmental Action Plan.

As of late 1998, IDA commitments in Tajikistan totalled US$87 million for three projects, of which US$64.8 million was already disbursed. The World Bank has extended its support to the government's economic transformation efforts, poverty reduction and post conflict assistance. This has been achieved through a combination of policy advice, increased field presence, institutional capacity building, financing of post-conflict needs through rehabilitation and reconstruction operations, and by mobilising resources from other donors.

Within the post conflict framework of the World Bank, two conflict credits were approved in 1998 and 1999. A Post-Conflict Rehabilitation Credit and a Post Conflict Reconstruction Credit provided balance of payments and budgetary support, and direct support for reconstruction of war damaged infrastructure.

Given the extent of poverty in Tajikistan, the World Bank supports the government's agenda to achieve sustainable, employment intensive growth while, at the same time, addressing specific post conflict needs, revitalising the economy, fostering good governance and strengthening institutional capacity.

The recently approved CAS, prepared jointly with the government, provides a framework for World Bank assistance that started in 1998 and will last until 2000. It focuses on four main areas: privatisation through its Structural Adjustment Credit; farm restructuring and improvement of agricultural support services; and increasing coverage and quality of social services.

## International Finance Corporation

In Kazakhstan the IFC has provided assistance to the government in establishing the Almaty Stock Exchange. Through its Technical Assistance Trust Funds Programme, the IFC supported market and technical studies on medium-density fiberboard production for domestic and export markets and supported a technical and financial review of and provided advisory services to assist with the privatization of two government-operated mines producing complex copper/zinc ores.

The IFC's recent financing activities in Kazakhstan also include a US$65.7 million package for the Akshabulak Oil Field Development, and an oil and gas project costing US$266.9 million. The IFC's US$17.5 million financing package will help ABN AMRO Bank expand commercial banking operations for Kazakh enterprises and international joint ventures. Kazakhstan Guarantee Facility will enhance the credit risk of a group of banks by providing a five-year guarantee facility with the IFC's financing package of US$40 million.

The IFC has provided assistance to the Kyrgyz Republic in establishing a legal and regulatory framework for non-bank financial institutions and securities market development. The IFC also secured funding for a market and economic review and a project identification study for the wool sector through its Technical Assistance Trust Funds Programme.

Recent IFC financing activities also include a US$4.3 million loan to Demirbank Kyrgyzstan, which is the first major international joint-venture bank in the Kyrgyz Republic and will provide essential banking services to private Kyrgyz enterprises. The IFC also approved a US$40 million loan for Kumtor Gold Company, a gold mining project that would produce 480,000 ounces a year through a joint venture. The total cost of the project is US$335 million.

The IFC approved its first investment in Uzbekistan in fiscal 1994, and has made substantial progress on other investment proposals in the country. Through its Technical Assistance Trust Funds Programme, the IFC supported a study on completing facilities and defining the market for three hotels under construction and also funded a market and feasibility assessment for a proposed joint venture through the privatisation of a state-owned cotton-spinning mill. Recent IFC financing activities have included a US$5.6 million loan and equity financing to help Uzbekistan Leasing Company Limited write long-term leases in foreign currency for plant and equipment for joint ventures and local firms with export potential; a US$1 million loan to help ABN AMRO Bank Uzbekistan Limited establish the first major international joint-venture bank in the Republic of Uzbekistan providing essential banking services to the private sector; and a US$143.8 million financing to help Amantaytau Goldfields.

## EBRD

The EBRD has been a major source of financing to all of the Central Asian and Caspian republics, providing a combination of loans and equity to over 100 projects in both the public and private sectors. The financial assistance has been used in a variety of projects, including the development and upgrading of new and existing infrastructure, the preparation and carrying out of studies in energy efficiency improvement, and the development of the legal frameworks.

Uzbekistan has been the foremost recipient of EBRD financing of the six republics. At the end of June 1998 the EBRD had forwarded financing of ECU428.8 million (US$557.8 million) in the form of ECU376.7 million (US$490.01 million) in loans and ECU52.2 million (US$67.90 million) in equity to 14 signed private sector projects in mining, finance, energy, transport and natural resources. The largest project was the provision of a ECU82.2 million (US$106.9 million) loan for upgrading the Fergana Oil Refinery. Kazakhstan is the second principal recipient of EBRD financing. At the end of June 1998 the EBRD had approved financing of ECU307.5 million (US$399.8 million) in the form of ECU284.72 million (US$370.3 million) in loans and ECU22.7 million (US$29.5 million) in equity to six signed projects in the finance, transport and steel sectors. The largest project was a ECU123.3 million (US$160.4 million) loan to Ispat Karmet, the steel company. In Turkmenistan the EBRD had provided at the same date financing of ECU140 million (US$182 million) in loans and equity to 26 projects, of which ECU7 million (US$9 million) was forwarded under its Technical Cooperation Funds Programme. The largest project was the provision of a ECU45.7 million (US$59.4 million) loan for a road improvement project. The Kyrgyz Republic and Azerbaijan received ECU128.4 million (US$167.0 million) and ECU116.7 million (US$151.8 million), respectively as at 30 June 1998. Of the amount received in the Krygyz Republic, ECU120.2 million (US$156.4 million) was provided as loans and ECU8.2 million (US$10.6 million) as equity to eight projects. The largest project was the provision of a ECU34.7 million (US$45.1 million) loan to assist in the improvement of an energy network transmission project. In Azerbaijan the EBRD financing had been forwarded to five signed projects, 12 on-going projects and five completed projects. The two largest individual financings were for ECU1 million (US$1.3 million) each. The first of these projects was a twinning programme for the establishment of a small- and medium-sized enterprise (SME) credit line and preprivatisation of the International Bank of Azerbaijan, and the second was an Institutional Development Programme for a multi-bank SME framework financing facility. The EBRD has forwarded only ECU21.6 million (US$28.1 million) to Tajikistan, of which ECU5.4 million (US$7.0 million) was forwarded under the Technical Cooperation Funds Programme, ECU2.2 million (US$2.9 million) was in equity and ECU14.1 million (US$18.3 million) as straight financing. EBRD financing has been forwarded to 21 projects, of which the largest was the provision of ECU4.8 million (US$6.2 million) in financing and ECU1.6 million (US$2.0 million) in equity to the Obi-Zulol Water Bottling Plant.

## The Asian Development Bank (ADB)

The ADB is headquartered in Manila and is owned by 56 member countries, of which the United States and Japan are the largest shareholders. Central Asian members include Kazakhstan, Uzbekistan and the Kyrgyz Republic. ADB financing includes loans, equity investments and guarantees. Because the United States is a shareholder and contributor to the Bank, US companies are eligible to take part with NIS partners in ADB-funded projects.

The ADB's Central Asian strategy focuses on poverty reduction, improving the status of women, population planning and environmental protection. Going into the next century, the Bank wants to assume the role of a catalyst for Central Asian development.

The biggest project so far undertaken by the ADB in Central Asia is in Kazakhstan, where it approved US$100 million in loans to assist pension reform efforts, repayable in 15 years with a three-year grace period. The loan carries an interest rate based on the bank's variable lending rate system, currently at 6.82 per cent. In addition to the loan, the ADB will provide a US$680,000 technical assistance grant.

## Japan

The volume of Japanese assistance to Central Asia and the Caspian began to increase by early 1995. For example, during President Nazarbayev's visit to Japan in April 1995 a number of loan and other assistance agreements were signed. These included loans of US$l45 million and US$75 million from Japan's Export-Import Bank: the first loan was for 11 years with a five-year grace period and an interest rate of 4.75 per cent; the second was for 17 years with a five-year grace period at 7.5 per cent interest. The Export–Import Bank has also provided US$85 million in credit to Uzbekistan and a grant of approximately US$12 million to the Kyrgyz Republic.

# 5 Energy: the key to growth

## Oil

The region's energy potential has attracted much attention since the break-up of the Soviet Union. Azerbaijan, Kazakhstan, Turkmenistan and Uzbekistan are already major energy producers, and production will increase with additional investment, technology and the development of new export outlets. The Caspian Sea itself is so large (1,127 kilometres north to south) that six distinct hydrocarbon basins lie under its waters. Central Asian countries also have additional onshore basins. Uzbekistan, which does not directly border the Caspian Sea, shares several of the region's hydrocarbon basins and also will directly benefit from proposed oil and gas export routes that are also shared with other Caspian countries.

The prospect of potentially huge hydrocarbon reserves is one of the main investment opportunities of the region. Most of the additional undiscovered hydrocarbons likely to be of commercial significance – the possible reserves – are oil rather than natural gas. The region's possible reserves that have yet

*Oil rigs in the Caspian Sea*

40

Exhibit 5.1

**Proven oil and gas reserves in Central Asia and Caspian region (oil units = billions of barrels; gas units = trillion cubic metres), end-1997**

|  | *Proven oil reserves* | *Proven gas reserves* |
|---|---|---|
| Azerbaijan | 7.0 | 0.85 |
| Kazakhstan | 8.0 | 1.84 |
| Turkmenistan | na | 2.86 |
| Tajikistan | na | 0.03(e) |
| Uzbekistan | 0.6 | 1.88 |
| Russian Federation | 48.6 | 48.14 |
| Other FSU | 1.2 | 0.02 |

*(e)* estimate.

*Sources:* United States Department of Energy; *Petroleum Economist.*

Exhibit 5.2

**Central Asia and Caspian region oil production ('000 of barrels a day), end-1998**

|  | *Oil 1998 ('000 bpd)* |
|---|---|
| Azerbaijan | 241 |
| Kazakhstan | 571 |
| Turkmenistan | 140(p) |
| Uzbekistan | 165 |

*(p)* projected.

*Sources:* United States Department of Energy; *Petroleum Economist.*

to be proven could yield another 163 billion barrels of oil, which is roughly equivalent to a quarter of the Middle East's total proven reserves. Oil reserves that have already been proven for the entire Caspian Sea region are estimated at 15–29 billion barrels (see Exhibit 5.1), comparable with the

United States (22 billion barrels) or the North Sea (17 billion barrels).

## Azerbaijan

Azerbaijan, the oldest known oil producing region in the world, experienced an oil boom at the beginning of the 20th century and later served as a major refining centre in the Former Soviet Union (FSU). Oil production peaked at about 500,000 barrels a day during World War II, then fell significantly after the 1950s as the Soviet Union redirected energy exploration resources elsewhere. The Soviets also lacked the necessary technology to fully exploit Caspian reserves, and once the onshore Azeri oil was developed, the central government planners aimed their efforts to onshore areas such as the Volga-Urals region and western Siberia. Most reserves in the Caspian region have not been developed yet, and many of the potential reserves in the region remain unexplored. Most of Azerbaijan's oil resources are located offshore, as are perhaps 30–40 per cent of the total oil resources of Kazakhstan and Turkmenistan. One Azeri field – the Guneshli, located 97 kilometres off the coast – currently accounts for more than half of the country's oil production. Traditionally, all Azeri crude has been refined at the country's two domestic refineries in Baku, so that only petroleum products are exported.

Production has declined since Azerbaijan became independent in 1991, falling to an estimated 241,000 barrels a day in 1998 (see Exhibit 5.2). Development of new fields through joint ventures and production-sharing agreements (PSAs) in the Caspian will likely boost Azerbaijan's oil production well beyond its earlier peaks over the next 10–15 years. In what was described as 'the deal of the century', an international consortium – the Azerbaijan International Operating Company (AIOC) – signed an US$8 billion, 30-year contract in September 1994 to develop three fields at Azeri, Chirag and the deep-water portions of Guneshli, with total reserves estimated at between 3 and 5 billion barrels. For further details of Azeri oil consortia see Chapter 8.

## Kazakhstan

Kazakhstan produced 571,000 barrels of oil a day in 1998, and is the second largest oil producer among the FSU republics after Russia. KazakhOil, the state oil and gas company, is a partner in almost three-quarters of this production.

Kazakhstan has undertaken a number of reforms in its oil and gas sectors to further develop its potential. In 1995 the country adopted a new oil and gas law that was widely recognised as an important step in attracting foreign investment. Among other measures, the law contains a broad provision for competitive bidding on energy projects. Under the law, the Kazakh government may grant exploration rights by competitive tender or through independent, direct negotiations.

*Oil processing plant, Hurricane Investments JSC, Kazakhstan*

Contracts may be in the form of joint ventures, service agreements or production-sharing arrangements. As at July 1997, US$2 billion had already been invested in Kazakhstan's oil and gas sector.

Kazakhstan's reform process has included privatising a number of existing energy concerns. In November 1996, Hurricane Hydrocarbons (Canada) bought 89.5 per cent of Yuzneftegaz, an oil company with many peripheral businesses that accounts for 80 per cent of the economic activity in the Aral Sea region, and began restructuring the company to focus on its core oil and gas business. In April 1997, Kazakhstan sold a 60 per cent stake in its largest oil producer, Mangistaumunaigaz, to Central Asia Petroleum (Indonesia) for US$248 million. In mid-1998 the government transferred public stakes in its production and refining companies to state oil and gas company KazakhOil in preparation for possible privatisation.

Almost half of Kazakh production comes from three large onshore fields; Tengiz, Uzen and Karachaganak. By far the largest of these is the Tengiz field, estimated to contain some 6 to 9 billion barrels of oil. In April 1993, Chevron (United States) concluded a US$20 billion joint venture (Tengizchevroil) to develop the Tengiz oilfield, located in the North Caspian Basin. In April 1996, Mobil (United States) announced that it had purchased a 25 per cent share in Tengizchevroil, with Chevron (45 per cent), Kazakhoil (25 per cent), and LukArco (a 5 per cent, US/Russian joint venture between Arco and Lukoil) owning the remainder. Production had been constrained by lack of an export outlet, as well as by Russian complaints over the presence of mercaptans (corrosive, foul-smelling compounds of carbon, hydrogen and sulphur) in the oil. Tengizchevroil exports about 160,000 barrels a day of crude oil through the Russian pipeline system, by barge and rail to the Baltic, and by barge and rail to the Black Sea.

## Turkmenistan

Oil production declined sharply in the early 1990s but has been steadily increasing since 1995. For the first six months of 1998, oil production reached 130,000 barrels a day up from 88,000 in 1996, with plans to reach 140,000 by the end of the year. In March 1998, the Minister of Oil, Gas and Mineral Resources said that Turkmenistan planned to increase its energy output by inviting foreign investment in the country's offshore oil and gas deposits. In June 1998, President Niyazov signed a resolution providing for the creation of Turkmenistan's first national oil company. The new company, called Turkmen National Oil Company, will be made up of four oil and gas producing departments of Turkmenneft, the official government agency responsible for oil production. In July 1998, President Niyazov set out a programme for the development of Turkmenistan's oil resources until 2000, which will form the basis for an export strategy, decisions on pipeline use and construction, and control over prospecting, development, delivery and marketing of oil projects.

Although far behind Azerbaijan in successful deal making with foreign oil companies, Turkmenistan has nonetheless entered into a number of its own agreements with investors. In March 1998, the UK's Monument Oil reached an agreement with Iran's National Iranian Oil Company (NIOC) to provide oil from the offshore Burun field in western Turkmenistan to the northern border of Iran, and swap it for oil to be exported from the Persian Gulf. This swap deal would eliminate the need to tackle the problematic transport issue of shipping oil through Iran to the Persian Gulf. For the Iranians, the Turkmen oil is refined and distributed for use in the north of the country.

The Burun field in Turkmenistan currently produces approximately 14,000 barrels a day and is located in the Nebit Dag concession. A development agreement for the concession was signed in 1996 with Monument Oil (the operator) holding a 35 per cent interest, Mobil 40 per cent and Burren Energy 25 per cent. Production from Nebit Dag is expected to reach 20,000–30,000 barrels per day by the end of 1998. Monument began the oil swap in late July 1998, shipping its first cargo of Turkmen oil to the Iranian Caspian port of Neka. For its part, Mobil is barred by US law from trading with Iran; therefore, it is not part of the oil swap deal. However, in April 1998, Mobil submitted an application to the US Treasury Department's Office of Foreign Asset Control for a licence to swap Turkmen oil for Iranian oil. As of February 1999, a decision on the licence was still pending.

Another company, Dublin-based Dragon Oil, also initiated an oil swap deal with NIOC in April 1998. Dragon Oil is the operator and holds a 50 per cent stake in the offshore Block II fields in Turkmenistan. Production from Block II currently stood at 2,800 barrels a day in November 1998. The company carried out its first oil swap with Iran in July 1998. In October is made its first lift from the Iranian oil terminal at Kharg Island in the Persian Gulf. The shipment was about 400,000 barrels.

In July 1998, Turkmenneft, the Turkmenistan state oil company, signed two PSAs with Mobil and Monument Oil covering the Garashsyzlyk concession licence for onshore western Turkmenistan. The PSAs cover the exploration, development and production of oil and gas from a 1,855 square kilometre area adjacent to the Nebit Dag licence, and including the remaining onshore part of the Abseron Sill. Under the first PSA, Turkmenneft will be responsible for production and other development activities from existing mature fields in the agreement area. The second PSA covers undeveloped reservoirs discovered underneath the Kotor Tepe and Barsa Gelmes fields. Mobil will be the operator, holding a 52.4 per cent interest, followed by Monument Oil with 27.6 per cent and Turkmenneft with 20 per cent. Over the next three years Mobil and Monument Oil are expected to invest US$100 million in conducting seismic surveys and drilling appraisal wells. Monument Oil and Mobil estimate that development of the Garashsyzlyk area combined with expanding production from the Burun field could result in 500,000 barrels a day of oil production from western Turkmenistan by 2006–2007.

Three additional exploration deals were initiated in Turkmenistan in April 1998:

- Exxon signed an agreement to conduct a technical study of a 19,000 square kilometre undeveloped area on the banks of the Amu Darya River.
- Halliburton signed an agreement to study ways to optimise production from Turkmenistan's existing fields.
- Western Atlas signed a memorandum of cooperation to create a national, seismic database for Turkmenistan's oil and gas industry and technical initiatives to improve the country's exploration and development industry.

## Uzbekistan

This is the only former Soviet republic to have substantially increased its oil production since becoming independent, with total production (including natural gas liquids) increasing from 66,000 barrels a day in 1992 to about 165,000 in 1998. As a result, Uzbekistan is no longer a net importer of petroleum, although it has had to import some refined products because its oil has tended to be too sour (high in sulphur content) for its refineries.

Uzbekistan's long-term goals include becoming a net exporter of oil and gas and attracting foreign investors to help develop its resources and increase production via joint ventures and PSAs. Kayim Khakkulov, the president of the state oil and gas company, Uzbeneftegaz, estimated that 63 per cent of the country sits on hydrocarbon deposits. Uzbekistan has identified 32 new oil and gas fields to be developed, an additional 18 for rehabilitation, and nine more blocks for exploration. Uzbeneftegaz has been negotiating with Agip (Italy), Mobil (United States), Japan National Oil Corporation, Unocal Corporation (United States) and others on developing oil and gas projects. One promising region is the Fergana basin that Uzbekistan shares with Tajikistan and the Kyrgyz Republic. This basin is estimated to contain 4 billion barrels of discovered and undiscovered oil.

In November 1996 Uzbekistan signed a series of agreements with Unocal Corporation to evaluate the country's potential crude oil and natural gas resources, as well as to determine the feasibility of using part of Uzbekistan's pipeline network to tie into Unocal Corporation's proposed Central Asia Oil Pipeline (CAOP). If constructed, the CAOP would link Central Asian oil producers to a proposed new deep-water port on Pakistan's Arabian Sea coast. Completion of projects such as the CAOP would bolster Uzbekistan's ability to attract foreign investment and increase production.

Uzbekistan's goal of self-sufficiency in oil depends heavily on its refinery modernisation programme. Refinery upgrades will enable it to process increased oil production levels to avoid imports of costly oil products. In November 1997, Technip (France) commissioned the initial phase of the new US$400 million, 50,000 barrels per day Bukhara refinery, the first new refinery to be built in any FSU republic since independence. In addition, Japan's Mitsui signed a contract for a US$200 million upgrade, to be financed by the European Bank for Reconstruction and Development (EBRD) and Japan's Exim Bank, to expand desulphurisation capacity at the Fergana refinery by late 1999.

## Tajikistan

This country only produces about 2,000 barrels of oil a day. It therefore must import almost all oil and petroleum products from republics of the FSU.

# Gas

Natural gas reserves in the region may even be larger than oil reserves, accounting for over two-thirds of the proven hydrocarbon reserves in the Caspian Sea region. Based upon proven reserves, Kazakhstan, Turkmenistan and Uzbekistan each rank among the world's 20 largest natural gas countries. Proven gas reserves in the region are estimated at 6.7–9.5 trillion cubic metres (Tcm), comparable to North American reserves (8.5 Tcm). Possible gas reserves are as large as the proven reserves, and could yield another 9.3 Tcm if proven. However, these reserves are located far from potential markets in relatively remote regions.

Exhibit 5.3

**Caspian Sea region natural gas production (Bcm a year), 1997**

|  | *1997 production* |
| --- | --- |
| Azerbaijan | 5.97 |
| Kazakhstan | 6.10 |
| Turkmenistan | 17.29 |
| Uzbekistan | 51.17 |
| Russian Caspian region | 3.00 |
| Total | 83.53 |

*Source:* US Department of Energy.

## Azerbaijan

In Azerbaijan, gas production totalled 5.97 billion cubic metres (Bcm) in 1997 (see Exhibit 5.3). To meet domestic demand in the past, Azerbaijan had imported natural gas from Russia, Turkmenistan and Iran. However, state supplier, Azerigaz, announced in March 1996 that it did not intend to import any more gas and instead would develop its own new gas fields in the Caspian Sea to meet demand. Azerbaijan could be self-sufficient in gas within five years, following a complete overhaul of the gas supply system, including replacing worn-out compressors and upgrading gas pipelines. The EBRD is also studying a proposal for the Kalmas gas storage project.

Increased oil production in the Caspian Sea is also expected to increase gas production because most of Azerbaijan's natural gas production comes from offshore oilfields. Additional gas production could also come from the recently discovered offshore Nakhchivan field, with an estimated 25.5 Bcm of reserves. Azerbaijan is also boosting natural gas production by reducing flaring. As a result, gas production could increase by as much as 0.03 Tcm/year by the end of the next decade, and Azerbaijan could become a net exporter of natural gas to its neighbours.

## Kazakhstan

The country contains about 1.84 Tcm of proven gas reserves, and more than 40 per cent of this is located in the giant Karachaganak field (in north-west Kazakhstan), which is an extension of Russia's Orenburg field. In 1997, an international consortium consisting of Agip (32.5 per cent, Italy), BG (32.5 per cent, United Kingdom), Texaco (20 per cent, United States), and Lukoil (15 per cent, Russia) signed a US$7–8 billion final PSA to develop the field for 40 years. The Karachaganak field produced 50,000 barrels of oil a day and 1.9 Bcm of gas in 1996 (almost half of the country's total production of natural gas). However, production was only 50 per cent of what had been planned, and is far below the field's potential production of 200,000 barrels of oil a day and 20–25 Bcm per year of natural gas.

Development of the Karachaganak field in Kazakhstan has been hampered because the FSU intended for all gas to be processed at the nearby Orenburg field, and exported via pipelines from Russia. Although Russia's Gazprom had originally agreed to take a 15 per cent stake in the consortium in exchange for processing and exporting the gas, it has been unable to reach agreement on the terms of the deal with its partners, and has left the project. Even though a workable deal with Gazprom remains the best option for Karachaganak's development, President Nazarbayev has asked consortium members to develop interim solutions to process and dispose of the gas, as there is no large gas pipeline available other than the present Russian system to export the gas.

Kazakh fields other than Karachaganak do not have access to export pipelines at all. Kazakhstan's other significant producing areas are the Tengiz and Zhanazhol fields, with the Uritau field expected to eventually become the third largest gas producing field. Undeveloped offshore areas are also believed to hold large amounts of gas. While these fields are near the Russian gas pipeline system, they are not currently linked to it, and in the longer term, capacity in the Russian pipeline system may be insufficient. Either the existing Russian gas pipeline system must be expanded, or Kazakhstan will need to develop new routes, such as the proposed US$12 billion, 6,115-kilometre pipeline that would bring Central Asian

*Oil pumping station near Kyzyl-Orda, Kazakhstan*

*Oil rig, Baku, Azerbaijan – joint venture between BP and Statoil*

gas to China. In addition, the mostly sour Kazakh gas will require additional gas-processing equipment to be built.

In general, the Kazakh gas sector suffers from a lack of infrastructure, especially pipelines. Gas producing areas in the west of the country are not connected to consuming areas such as the populous south-east and industrial north and, as a result, Kazakhstan has two separate gas pipeline networks. Kazakhstan exported its gas production from the west to Russia, and imported three-quarters of its natural gas consumption needs in 1996 from Turkmenistan, Russia and Uzbekistan. Kazakgaz was responsible for distribution in the west, while Alaugaz had been responsible for distribution in the south-east.

In June 1997, Kazakhstan awarded Tractabel (Belgium) a 15-year contract to manage its natural gas network. Tractabel has pledged to spend US$600 million on investment, repair, construction and planning costs, as well as US$100 million to build a gas line in southern Kazakhstan to bypass the Kyrgyz

Republic. Other investment needs include capturing previously flared gas, field processing of natural gas, developing projects that support swap agreements with neighbouring states, appraisal work for gas fields located near consuming areas, meter installation at cross-border locations, and environmental rehabilitation and protection.

## Uzbekistan

This is the only other FSU republic (with Kazakhstan) to have substantially increased its natural gas production since becoming independent; production rose from 42 Bcm in 1992 to an estimated 51 Bcm in 1997 (see Exhibit 5.3), making Uzbekistan the eighth largest producer in the world. Most gas production is concentrated in south-east Uzbekistan in older fields such as Shurtan and Kokdumalak. Uzbekistan has taken short-term measures to increase gas production by upgrading facilities at existing fields. Longer-term measures involve finding new reserves with foreign help. Uzbekistan has negotiated with Enron (United States) and Gazprom (Russia), among others.

The republic has substantial reserves of natural gas (1.9 Tcm). As part of an effort to become self-sufficient in energy, Uzbekistan has been developing domestic uses for its plentiful gas. These uses include converting cars and trucks to run on compressed gas instead of gasoline, and using the gas for feedstock at a new US$1 billion gas chemicals plant at the Shurtan gas field. Rising domestic gas consumption has reduced the amount of gas Uzbekistan has to export. Exports have also been discouraged by the lack of export pipeline alternatives to the Central Asia–Central Russia pipeline that connected Uzbekistan to Russia and the other republics of the FSU. There is also a frequent non-payment problem shipping gas to destinations within the CIS.

Uzbekistan exported 2.6 Bcm of gas to southern Kazakhstan, the Kyrgyz Republic and Tajikistan in 1996. Exports to Kazakhstan were cut off for non-payment in 1996. As a result, some gas originally contracted by Kazakhstan was instead exported to Ukraine and Kazakhstan agreed to pay off its debt with Kazakh goods and with services, such as transporting Uzbek products through Kazakhstan to other markets.

## Tajikistan

The country has estimated natural gas reserves of 0.03 Tcm. However, gas production is low. Tajikistan thus relies heavily on imports of natural gas from neighbouring Uzbekistan and Turkmenistan. However, in June 1994 gas transmissions to Tajikistan from Uzbekistan were cut by 25 per cent for failure to pay an estimated US$46 million in outstanding gas bills. The Tajik government responded by immediately reducing gas supplies to municipal consumers.

# Electricity

## Azerbaijan

The Azeri power sector has a generating capacity of about 5 gigawatts consisting of eight thermal plants supplying over 80 per cent of generating capacity, and five hydroelectric plants. Mazut (residual fuel oil) powers two-thirds of the thermal generation, with natural gas as the secondary fuel. In addition to domestic power plants, Azerbaijan imports power from Georgia and Russia, and exports to these countries as well.

Economic conditions, high taxes, and non-payment by customers in Azerbaijan have left the power sector without sufficient working capital and investment funds. This has resulted in fewer repairs and less maintenance to ageing power generation facilities. Over half of the turbo-generators and boilers have been in use for over 40 years. In addition, the energy efficiency and environmental adequacy of the power sector must both be improved. The US Embassy in Baku has issued a report estimating that the large-scale upgrades needed by the power sector will cost US$2.5 billion.

President Aliyev issued a decree in 1996 to transform the state power company, Azerenergy, into a joint stock company. However, this will be delayed until it can generate sufficient revenues to pay its outstanding debts to the government. Although tariffs have been raised several times, rates are still low and bill collection is not adequate.

## Kazakhstan

The power sector has experienced numerous problems. As a legacy of being part of the FSU, its transmission and distribution networks are currently linked to two separate networks; the Russian network in the north and the Central Asian network in the south. Although it currently generates enough electricity to meet most of its demand, the separation of the networks has resulted in Kazakhstan becoming both an exporter (1.7 million kilowatt-hours) and importer (8.6 million kilowatt-hours) of electricity in accordance with regional needs. Imports from Russia, Uzbekistan, Turkmenistan and the Kyrgyz Republic have also been used to meet shortfalls; however, several regions were still left without power during the winter of 1996–97. Payment for imported power has been an issue, and Russian suppliers have often cut power to encourage payment of bills. Non-payment by domestic customers has also been a problem.

Kazakhstan's power sector has many obsolete power generation plants, and incurs large energy losses during transmission and distribution. In 1996, these losses reached over 10 billion kilowatt-hours, or over 15 per cent of power produced. Its generating equipment is mostly old, inefficient, and lacking in modern pollution controls. Some 80 per cent of its electricity is generated by coal-fired plants burning a dirty high-ash coal that visibly blankets the largest city, the former capital of Almaty. Kazakhstan has not taken full advantage of cleaner sources of power such as hydroelectricity, and only 10 per cent of the country's hydroelectric potential of 60 terawatt-hours has been developed. In addition, 94 per cent of gas turbines, 57 per cent of steam turbines and 33 per cent of steam boilers have been in place for 20 years or more.

In an effort to resolve its problems, the Kazakh electrical sector is undergoing major reforms, including a big push to privatise the entire system from generation to distribution. The government hopes to privatise all major power generating stations by 2000. Bidders are required to cover all debts and make investments in return for the option to buy up to 60 per cent of the companies. Kazakhstan's largest generating plant, the coal-fired 4,000 megawatt Ekibastuz No.1 plant, was purchased by AES in 1996, and AES has talked with the government about purchasing at least two distribution companies. Other big deals include the purchase of the 650 megawatt coal-fired Karaganda No. 2 plant by Kazakh Power Partners, a consortium comprising Independent Power (United Kingdom), Public Service Colorado (United States), and Samsung (South Korea), and the awarding of management rights for Almaty Power to Tractabel (Belgium). In addition, a subsidiary of ABB Brown Boveri (Sweden/Switzerland) was given a 25-year contract in 1997 to manage the national power grid.

## Kyrgyz Republic

The country's electric power industry is thought to be capable of fully meeting the country's domestic electricity needs while providing surplus electricity for export. Of the 20 electric power generating units in the Republic, 18 are hydropower. It is believed that only about 15 per cent of the mountainous country's potential hydroelectric resources are currently being tapped. Foreign investment will be needed to help harness this potential, but to date little progress has been made on this front due largely to the slow pace of privatisation in the energy sector.

The Kyrgyz Republic has two major electric power plants – a 1.2 gigawatt hydro plant at Toktogul, and a 0.76 gigawatt thermal plant at Bishkek – with plans for a major 6.8 gigawatt hydropower station to be built by 2010. Electricity is the Republic's major export, although it has had difficulty receiving world market prices from its main customer, Uzbekistan.

## Uzbekistan

This was the third largest exporter of electricity of the FSU republics in 1996 after Russia and the Kyrgyz Republic, exporting 5.6 billion kilowatt-hours to the Kyrgyz Republic, Tajikistan and Kazakhstan. However, Uzbekistan was an overall net importer of electricity in 1996, because its exports were exceeded by imports of 6.7 billion kilowatt-hours from Turkmenistan, the Kyrgyz Republic and Tajikistan.

Uzbekistan's electricity is generated mainly from natural gas-powered thermal plants, with smaller amounts coming from coal and hydroelectric facilities. Overall, Uzbekistan contains 11.8 gigawatts of electric generating capacity, with plans for an additional 4 gigawatts through rehabilitation of existing plants or construction of new facilities. The largest gas-fired plants are the Syr Darya and Navoi plants, which together account for about one-third of all generating capacity in the country. Coal-powered facilities consist primarily of two plants located near the Angren open pit mine near Tashkent. In addition, 25 hydroelectric plants supply almost 15 per cent of the country's electricity.

Uzbekistan's Energy Ministry hopes to increase the country's electric generating capacity through several projects, including an US$81 million renovation of the Syr Darya plant using funds from the EBRD. In addition, the Ministry has plans for renovation of the Angren and Tashkent coal plants, for construction of a thermal plant near Termez, and for construction of a 400 megawatt hydroelectric plant near Pskent.

## Tajikistan

The Pamir mountains, which divide the country, create ample rivers that could be used in producing hydroelectric energy. In an attempt to develop this energy source, Tajikistan has borrowed heavily from Russia. The terms of the loan require Tajikistan to pledge 50 per cent of the shares of the Nurek hydroelectric power station to Russia.

# Coal

## Kazakhstan

This is a major coal producer, consumer and exporter, with output centred in the Karaganda and Ekibastuz basins. Karaganda, located in north central Kazakhstan, has 13 mines that produce mostly high-quality coking coal. Ekibastuz, located in northern Kazakhstan, is the third largest coal basin in the FSU, and has three mines that produce mainly brown (sub-bituminous) coal for use in power plants.

Kazakh coal production has declined from 130 million tonnes in 1991 to 80 million tonnes in 1997 due to the collapse in demand for coal in its traditional market, the FSU. Although the Ukrainian steel industry had once been a major importer of coking coal from Kazakhstan, Kazakh exports to Ukraine ceased in 1996. This decline in markets resulted in the halving of both coal production and the number of mines in Karaganda from 1991 to 1996. Russian power stations also imported less coal from the Ekibastuz basin.

Despite the drop in exports, Russia remains the largest recipient of Kazakh coal, importing about 19 of the 25 million tonnes of coal exported by Kazakhstan. The major consumer of coal from the Ekibastuz basin is still the Russian utility, Sverdlovskenergo, which should continue to receive coal from Kazakhstan because it acquired two mines as payment for unpaid debts for power supplied to Kazakhstan.

## Kyrgyz Republic

The Republic is able to satisfy about two-thirds of its coal needs, although the country's coal industry has experienced difficulties in recent years due to lack of equipment and increasing extraction costs. In 1993 coal production totalled 2.8 million tonnes, down from 3.7 million tonnes in 1990.

## Uzbekistan

Coal reserves are concentrated primarily in the Angren, Baisun and Shargun deposits. Production at Angren, which contains mostly brown coal (lignite), accounted for 2.4 million tonnes, some 80 per cent of the country's total production in 1996. Modernisation of production facilities could significantly increase Angren's output, and Krupp Hoesch Stahlexport (Germany) signed an agreement at the end of 1996 to provide new equipment and upgrade the mining operation. The first contract is projected to increase production by more than 300,000 tonnes annually. The Angren mine also has underground coal gasification technology in place to produce 0.51 Bcm of gas for the Angren power station.

Uzbekistan also plans to upgrade mining operations at its other deposits. Additional investment at the Shargun deposit is expected to double or triple production of high-quality coal from current levels of 200,000 tonnes a year. Completion of a second mine at Baisun could quintuple the mine's production of 100,000 tonnes a year. Other planned investment projects include upgrading of mines, recovery of kaolin and other byproducts, and development of coal gasification projects. Foreign investment is expected to help Uzbekistan increase its coal exports from 1996's level of 100,000 tonnes.

# Caspian Sea legal issues

Legal problems have slowed development in the Caspian region. Issues surrounding the Caspian Sea's resources revolve around whether development rights are governed by treaties signed between the FSU and Iran in 1921 and 1940 (which did not establish sea-bed boundaries or discuss oil and gas exploration). In addition, there is the question of whether the Caspian is a body of water affected by the Law of the Sea Convention (inland lakes are not covered by this law).

Russia had argued that the Caspian was a sea and therefore subject to the Law of the Sea Convention and thereby common ownership of the waters and undersea resources beyond a 45 nautical mile limit applied. In December 1996, Russia called for joint navigation rights, joint management of fisheries and the establishment of an interstate committee of all boundary states. This committee would license exploration in a joint-use zone in the centre of the Caspian beyond the 45 nautical mile offshore limit.

Kazakhstan has called for partition of the Caspian Sea using a median line principle and recognising the de facto internal adminstrative boundaries between the republics established during the Soviet period. Azerbaijan and Turkmenistan broadly support this position. Final resolution of Caspian legal issues are a long way off.

However, in July 1998, Russia and Kazakhstan signed an accord dividing up oil and gas development in the north Caspian region using the median line principle, without any limits, giving each country full jurisdiction of its offshore oil resources.

Meanwhile, Iran has backed Russia's claim that regional treaties signed in 1921 and 1940 are valid, implying that all Caspian littoral states must approve any offshore oil developments. Iran's support of Russian proposals for joint development could pose a problem for US firms under Presidential Executive Orders that impose an embargo on trade and investment with Iran. Azerbaijan has rejected this view, believing that boundaries were formalised under the Soviet Union.

The United States supports the principle that the resolution of the legal status of the Caspian Sea must be decided among the regional states themselves. However, the United States would not favour any resolution that precludes US corporate involvement because of Iranian involvement.

# 6 Energy transport and pipeline politics

## The current picture

Much has been written about the complex geo-politics involved with selecting the pipeline network that will bring the huge oil reserves from the Caspian region to buyers in Europe and Asia. At stake in the decision is not only the awarding of billions of dollars of construction contracts, but also that the routes taken by the pipelines will determine the influence that each of the region's governments can exert on the Caspian oil industry.

The existing pipeline network, part of which is already being used as the Azerbaijan International Oil Company's (AIOC) main line from Baku to the Russian Black Sea port of Novorossiisk, was built during Soviet times and designed to serve chiefly Russian interests. The network remains under Russia's firm control and Russian oil companies have been quick to take full advantage of this ownership. At the same time, the efforts of the Central Asian and Caspian republics to increase the strength of their economies and become energy independent is frustrated by Russia's control of the energy flow and the perceived Russian intent to keep Central Asia and the Caspian weak and disunited.

Turkey, Iran, Pakistan and China are all seeking ways to take advantage of the desperate need for the region to build new pipelines. The United States is also keenly interested, partly to promote US corporate involvement in any new project as well as to eliminate or at least sharply curtail Iranian involvement.

Azerbaijan has so far been the most active player in the pipeline story. The only pipeline available to carry the first flow of Caspian oil extracted by the AIOC was the so-called 'Northern Route', which passes through the troubled region of Chechnya. When this pipeline was used the main advantage was clear: it was better than no pipeline at all. But Azerbaijan is concerned about security and even more concerned that Russia controls the conditions for use of the Northern Route.

Proposed alternative 'Western Routes' avoid Russia all together. One pipeline, which should be in full operation by early 1999, will take oil from Baku across Georgian territory to the Black Sea port of Supsa on Georgia's western coast. Turkey and western members of the AIOC have pressed strongly for the use of a pipeline from Baku through Georgia and Turkey to Ceyhan on Turkey's southern Mediterranean coast.

In response to concerns about the Northern Route passing through Chechnya, officials have been examining the possibility of bypassing this troubled region entirely by constructing a second pipeline through Dagestan to the north. Alternatively, oil could be shipped by Russian tankers from Baku to the Russian port of Astrakhan and then on by a new pipeline to Novorossiisk. Early in 1998, the former Russian Deputy Prime Minister, Boris Nemtsov, announced that a survey had been completed for this proposed US$313 million pipeline linking Astrakhan and Novorossiisk. While construction was reported to have begun, it is not entirely clear if and when the line will be finished, given Russia's severe financial difficulties.

In theory, Azerbaijan could choose a pipeline route that completely avoids Russian territory and thus Russian dominance. However, through a key member of the AIOC, the huge Russian oil company Lukoil, Russia has a strong and growing influence in the entire pipeline debate. Lukoil investments in Azerbaijan as at 1998 exceeded US$150 million. It has budgeted a further US$100 million and considers the Caspian one of its most important areas of expansion. Aside from a 10 per cent share in the AIOC, Lukoil also holds a 60 per cent share in the project which will develop the Shah Deniz field, a 60 per cent share in the D-22 Caspian project, and controlling shares in the companies developing the Karabakh project. Lukoil subsidiaries also run trading and insurance companies. In short, whether Azerbaijan likes it or not, Lukoil, with its close link to the Russian government, will play a significant role in the Azeri economy for a long time to come.

Exhibits 6.1 and 6.2 detail the status of the Caspian oil and gas export pipeline routes as at end-1998.

## Kazakhstan

Although so far not as successful as Azerbaijan at attracting

Exhibit 6.1
**Caspian oil export pipelines status report, as at end-1998**

| Pipeline | Route | Length | Cost | Status |
|---|---|---|---|---|
| AIOC main line | Baku to Ceyhan, Turkey | 1,770 km | US$3.3 billion | Agreement announced October 1998 |
| AIOC early oil 'Northern Route' | Baku to Novorossiisk, Russia | 1,400 km | US$2.4 million to repair Chechen section | In operation as of November 1997 |
| 'Northern Route' bypassing Chechnya | Through Dagestan, Russia | 283 km | US$313 million | Surveys completed 1998 |
| AIOC early oil 'Western Route' | Baku to Supsa, Georgia | 885 km | US$290 million | Planned operation in early 1999 |
| Caspian Pipeline Consortium | Tengiz, Kazakhstan to Novorossiisk, Russia | 1,500 km | US$2.2 billion | Planned operation in 2000 |
| Across the Caspian | Tengiz, Kazakhstan to Baku | 595 km underwater | US$2.2 billion | Planned operation in 1999 |
| Kazakhstan to China | Aktiubinsk to Xinjiang | 2,900 km | US$3.5 billion | Agreement signed |
| Turkmenistan to Pakistan via Afghanistan | Chardzhou to Gwadar | 1,609 km | US$2.5 billion | Partial agreement |
| Turkmenistan to Persian Gulf | Turkmenbashi to Kharg Island | 1,500 km | US$1.5 billion | Proposed |

*Source:* US Department of Energy.

investment into its oil industry, Kazakhstan is nonetheless the second largest oil producer in the Former Soviet Union (FSU) after Russia.

Despite abundant gas and oil resources and the capacity to produce surpluses well in excess of domestic needs, Kazakhstan's energy economy cannot prosper until sufficient export outlets are built. Annually, Kazakhstan now produces 25 million tonnes of oil, which is more than twice the amount needed to satisfy domestic demand. By 2012, the respective figures may grow to 170 million tonnes of oil exports, with 20 million tonnes needed internally. At present, Kazakhstan's Tengizchevroil (with a daily output of 160,000 barrels) reaches world markets via a Russian pipeline, with a Russian-imposed quota of 76,000 barrels a day.

Kazakhstan hopes to improve its transport infrastructure with the completion by 1999 of a 1,500-kilometre pipeline to be built by the multinational Caspian Pipeline Consortium (CPC). This new line will eventually be capable of carrying 1.34 million barrels a day from the Tengiz field through Russia to Novorossiisk. This will be the first direct link between Tengiz and European export markets. It is noteworthy that, as of February 1998, Kazakhstan and Russia had not yet agreed on transit fees. Nevertheless, in mid-1998 CPC director, Viktor Fedotov, reported that the necessary approvals from regional governors, whose territories the pipeline will cross, had been obtained. The pipeline is now expected to be completed by 2000. The project took a further step forward in April 1999 following the award of a US$360 million contract to a French construction group to build an oil export terminal 20 kilometres offshore from Novorossiisk. The first oil shipment is due in mid-2001 with mechanical completion of the terminal scheduled for later that year. Two Russian companies are also involved in the terminal's construction.

Meanwhile, Kazakhstan continues to look west, south and east for outlets to accommodate its growing energy extractions. To the south, a swap arrangement between Kazakhstan

Exhibit 6.2
**Existing and proposed natural gas export routes from the Caspian Sea region, as at October 1998**

| Line | Route | Gas capacity | Length | Investment | Status |
|---|---|---|---|---|---|
| Cross Caspian | Turkmenbashi, Turkmenistan to Baku | na | na | na | Proposed |
| Turkmenistan–Uzbekistan–Kazakhstan–Russia–Europe | Multiple routes under consideration from Turkmenbashi | na | na | na | Proposed expansion of existing system |
| Turkmenistan to Iran | Ekarem, Turkmenistan to Iranian border | 8 billion cubic metres (Bcm)/ year from 2005, up to 15 Bcm/ year by 2020 | 145 km | US$190 million | Exports currently under way |
| Turkmenistan–Uzbekistan–Kazakstan–China–Japan | Dauletad Gas Field, Turkmenistan to Xinjiang, China and then to Japan | 20 to 28 billion cubic metres (Bcm)/year | 7,9820 km through China and then to Japan | US$12 billion by China, US$23 billion by Japan | Preliminary feasibility studies under way |
| Turkmenistan–Iran–Turkey | Ekarem, Turkmenistan to Tabriz, Iran to Ankara, Turkey | 28 Bcm /year | 2,170 km | US$3.1 billion to US$3.8 billion | Signed agreement for exports |
| Turkmenistan–Afganistan–Pakistan (may extend to Uzbekistan) | Dauletad Gas Field or Yashlar Gas Field, Turkmenistan to Sui, Pakistan | 20Bcm/year | 1,450 km | US$2 billion to US$2.5 billion | Memorandum of under-standing signed with all four countries |

*Source:* US Department of Energy.

and Iran has so far yielded only limited success. Kazakhstan has agreed to supply Iran by tanker across the Caspian with 2 to 6 million tonnes of crude oil over a 10-year period. This oil will be refined and used by customers in northern Iran in exchange for Iran's commitment to supply Iranian crude via Persian Gulf terminals to the world market.

Discovery of oilfields in south-eastern Kazakhstan suggests new possibilities for sending oil eastward. Tengizchevroil has already tried to deliver oil from north-western Kazakhstan to China by rail. In June 1997, the China National Petroleum Company (CNPC) bought 60 per cent of the Kazakhstan oil producing company, Aktobemunaigaz. The following September, China signed two major agreements with Kazakhstan for joint development in the Aktiubinsk and Uzen areas. CNPC and Kazakoil are working on a feasibility study to build a 2,993-kilometre pipeline to China's western border and

a shorter (249-kilometre) line south from Uzen to Iran's border.

In October 1998, Kazakhstan, Azerbaijan, Georgia, Uzbekistan and Turkey backed the construction of an oil pipeline through Turkey to the port of Ceyhan (see previous section).

As for gas exports, Kazakhstan has been handicapped by its dependence on Soviet-era refinery and pipeline systems. In the north-west, gas from Karachaganak must still go north to Russia to be refined at Orenburg and is then exported by Russia to Europe. In the heavily populated south-east the demand for gas is great, but there is no pipeline to bring it from distant fields in Kazakhstan's north-west. As a result, 90 per cent of the gas consumed in the south-east is imported from Russia, Turkmenistan or Uzbekistan.

Kazakhstan's gas officials must negotiate with Russia's Gazprom to gain access to the world market. Because the cost of processing Kazakhstan's gas at Russia's Orenburg plant is so high, Kazakhstan receives only 16 or 17 cents for every dollar's worth of Karachaganak gas. Kazakhstan plans, therefore, to build its own gas plant at Karachaganak, although Gazprom chief, Rem Viakhirev, claims that Orenburg is actually more profitable for Kazakhstan. Most distressing to Kazakhstan's officials is Russia's refusal to allow Kazakhstan to use Russia's gas lines to reach world markets. In fact Russia even refused Kazakhstan permission for a one-off shipment of gas in order to repay its debts to East European nations; debts incurred under a treaty signed during the Soviet era.

In mid-August 1997, Viakhirev made clear that Gazprom will under no circumstances agree to give Kazakh gas an outlet to world markets where Russian gas could instead be sold. Stalemated, Kazakhstan's officials and energy industries welcome every offer by outside consortia and governments to help build the pipelines and supporting infrastructure they need.

## Turkmenistan

One reason Turkmenistan's economy cannot fulfil its full potential is that its energy sector, like those of its energy-rich Central Asian neighbours, lacks export pipelines. A second problem is that Turkmenistan's oil industry is largely on hold until the country's legal disputes with Azerbaijan over the ownership of several offshore fields in the Caspian Sea are settled. Development and operation of these fields cannot move forward, nor can investment funds be readily attracted, until their legal status is assured. In fact, until all the states bordering on the Caspian Sea reach agreement on ownership of offshore resources, legal uncertainties will continue to discourage foreign investment and hinder development (see Chapter 5, Energy: the key to growth).

Because Turkmenistan must use Russian pipelines to reach foreign buyers, its marketing strategies are drawn up in Moscow. One Russian strategy forces Turkmenistan to sell its gas to other Commonwealth of Independent States (CIS) members – that is, impoverished countries that consistently default on their payments. Turkmenistan would naturally prefer to sell to European customers who can pay world prices in hard currency. In spring 1997, in one of many efforts to raise prices and force payments, Turkmenistan cut off gas exports to Ukraine, which was then receiving 92 per cent of Turkmenistan gas exports. By September 1997, the collective debt of Ukraine, Georgia, Kazakhstan, Uzbekistan and Azerbaijan to Turkmenistan amounted to more than US$1 billion. To escape this non-payment trap, Turkmenistan has eagerly sought ways to bypass Russian pipelines, deliver its gas to cash customers, and strengthen its economy and political independence.

Muhammed Khatami's election in mid-1997 as President of Iran gave Turkmenistan an opening. In July 1997 Washington announced that it would not invoke the 1996 Iran/Libya Sanctions Act in relation to the building of a new pipeline across Iran to carry Turkmen gas. This law calls for sanctions against non-US companies concluding oil and gas business deals of more than US$20 million a year with Iran and Libya. Initially, a consortium of three European companies (Snamprogetti of Italy, Gaz de France and Royal Dutch Shell) that formed to build a pipeline across Iran from Turkmenistan to Turkey were under threat of possible sanctions. As a result, by the end of 1997 the Presidents of Turkmenistan and Iran were able to celebrate the opening of the first section of a Turkmenistan–Iran–Turkey–Europe gas pipeline. This 125-mile section – the Korpedzhe-Kurdkui pipeline – carried Turkmenistan gas on the first leg of its eventual journey to Europe. It was the first energy pipeline southward from Central Asia, and Turkmenistan's first step towards economic independence from Russia.

Foreign companies and nations have proposed multiple routes to circumvent Russia. Also in December 1997, Turkey's Prime Minister Mesut Yilmaz signed a memorandum of understanding with the Turkmen and Iranian presidents to build a gas pipeline from Turkmenistan westward, over the Caspian seabed, through Azerbaijan, Georgia, and Turkey to Europe. North-east corridors are possible through Uzbekistan and Kazakhstan into China. More problematic are proposals for pipelines south-eastward, through war-torn Afghanistan to Pakistan and India. In late January 1998, Pakistan's Oil and Gas Ministry announced that the US firm Unocal was completing an agreement with the Taliban leaders of Afghanistan to build a large capacity gas export pipeline, 1,400 kilometres long and costing US$2 billion, from Turkmenistan's largest gas field through Afghanistan and Pakistan to the Indian Ocean.

## Russian strategy

As heir to the vast Soviet energy infrastructure, Russia uses its multiple advantages to block Caspian basin oil and gas from entering the world market. The government's strategy is economic imperialism, and in the minds of Russia's energy executives, who prefer the term 'economic diplomacy', it is perfectly logical and justifiable to put Russia's interests first. It is also an economic imperative. Russia's energy sector was the country's main source of hard currency income in 1997. It supplied 40 per cent of budgetary revenues, accounted for more than 50 per cent of Russia's exports and paid 44 per cent of the taxes collected.

When the Caspian region countries devise plans for pipelines bypassing Russia, Russian authorities do their utmost to prevent

**Existing and potential oil and gas export routes from the Caspian Basin**

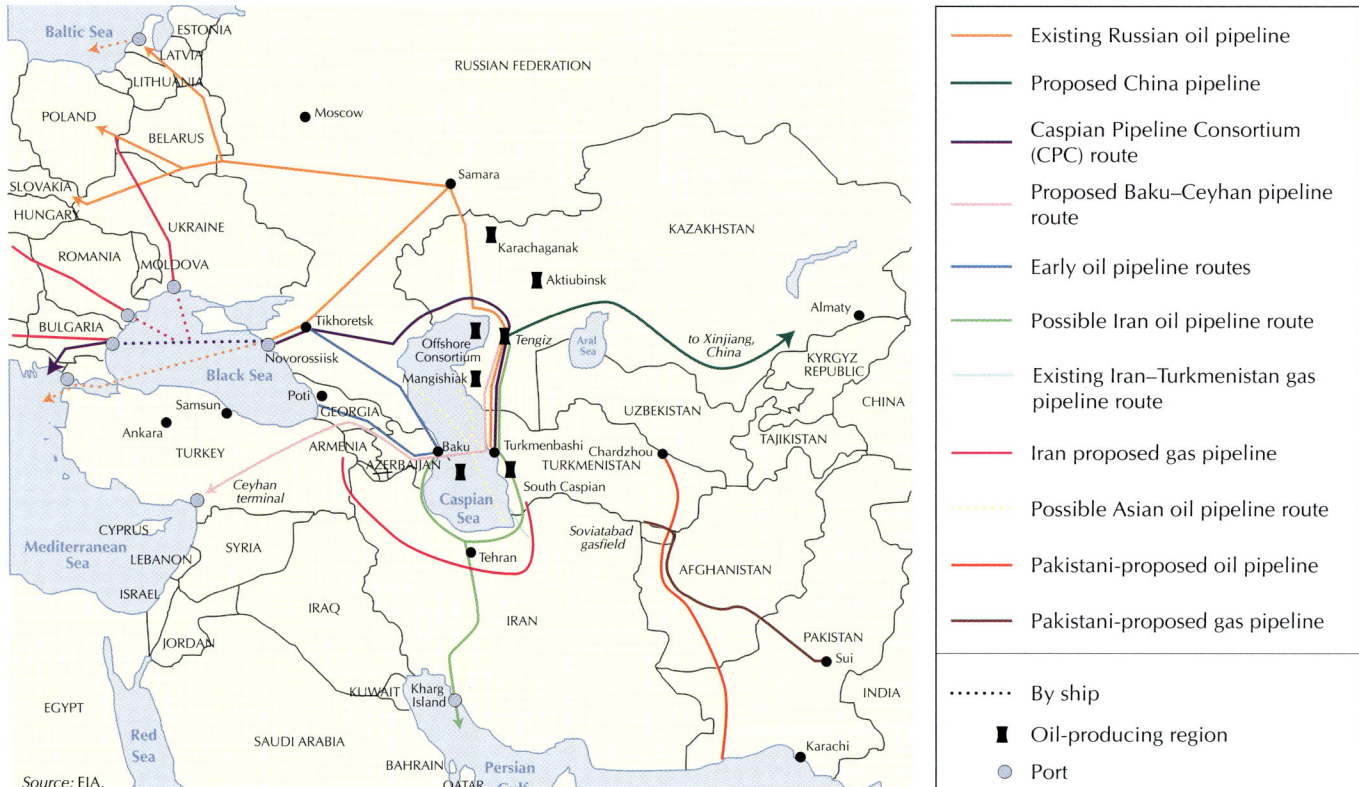

Source: EIA.

*Legend:*
- Existing Russian oil pipeline
- Proposed China pipeline
- Caspian Pipeline Consortium (CPC) route
- Proposed Baku–Ceyhan pipeline route
- Early oil pipeline routes
- Possible Iran oil pipeline route
- Existing Iran–Turkmenistan gas pipeline route
- Iran proposed gas pipeline
- Possible Asian oil pipeline route
- Pakistani-proposed oil pipeline
- Pakistani-proposed gas pipeline
- By ship
- Oil-producing region
- Port

or delay such construction. When these plans persist despite opposition, Russian companies, backed by the government, win equity positions in consortia allowing them to influence decisions, manage operations and share profits. Where these efforts are not successful, the Russians propose pipeline plans designed to supersede those of their competitors.

Gazprom, the world's largest gas company, epitomises Russia's tactics. Gazprom controls more than 95 per cent of Russia's gas production in the country's 100 largest fields, oversees eight production associations, owns and operates Russia's 140,000-kilometre gas pipeline grid, and runs 26 trading houses and marketing joint ventures in 13 European countries. Gazprom's chairman, Rem Viakhirev, has repeatedly made it clear that his goal is nothing short of total monopolisation of the CIS gas pipeline network.

In early, 1995, the company managed to join a consortium formed to develop Kazakhstan's mammoth Karachaganak field. Gazprom threatened that if it was not brought into the project, it would pay no more than 15 per cent of world prices for the field's output and would block the export of energy from Karachaganak. Russian officials further maintained that Gazprom should receive special profits because Soviet technology had originally developed the field.

In November 1995 when the Turkmen–Russian joint stock company, Turkmenrosgaz, was formed, Gazprom received a 44 per cent equity share, along with the right, as a member of the company, to explore further for natural gas in Turkmenistan. In return, Gazprom opened its gas pipeline for Turkmenistan's gas deliveries to Ukraine and the Caucasus countries, though few payments flowed back to Turkmenistan itself.

Apart from Gazprom, foreign investors have also targeted Transneft, the Russian company with a monopoly on the operation of Russia's oil pipelines for being greedy, not just for tariffs, but for control over the pipeline system it built up and managed for over four decades. When the CPC structure was revised in December 1996, Transneft lost out in a fierce power struggle with the foreign shareholders of the CPC, who refused to make Transneft a shareholder out of fear of its dictatorial ways. Under the eventual compromise, however, Transneft became the operator of the project, but was prevented from naming the director.

The Russian government lends strong support to Russia's energy companies. In September 1997, Gazprom, Lukoil, Yukos (Russia's second leading oil producer), and Slavneft (Russia's first truly international company, a merger of Belarussian and Russian firms) were attempting to acquire

**Selected oil infrastructure in the Caspian Sea region**

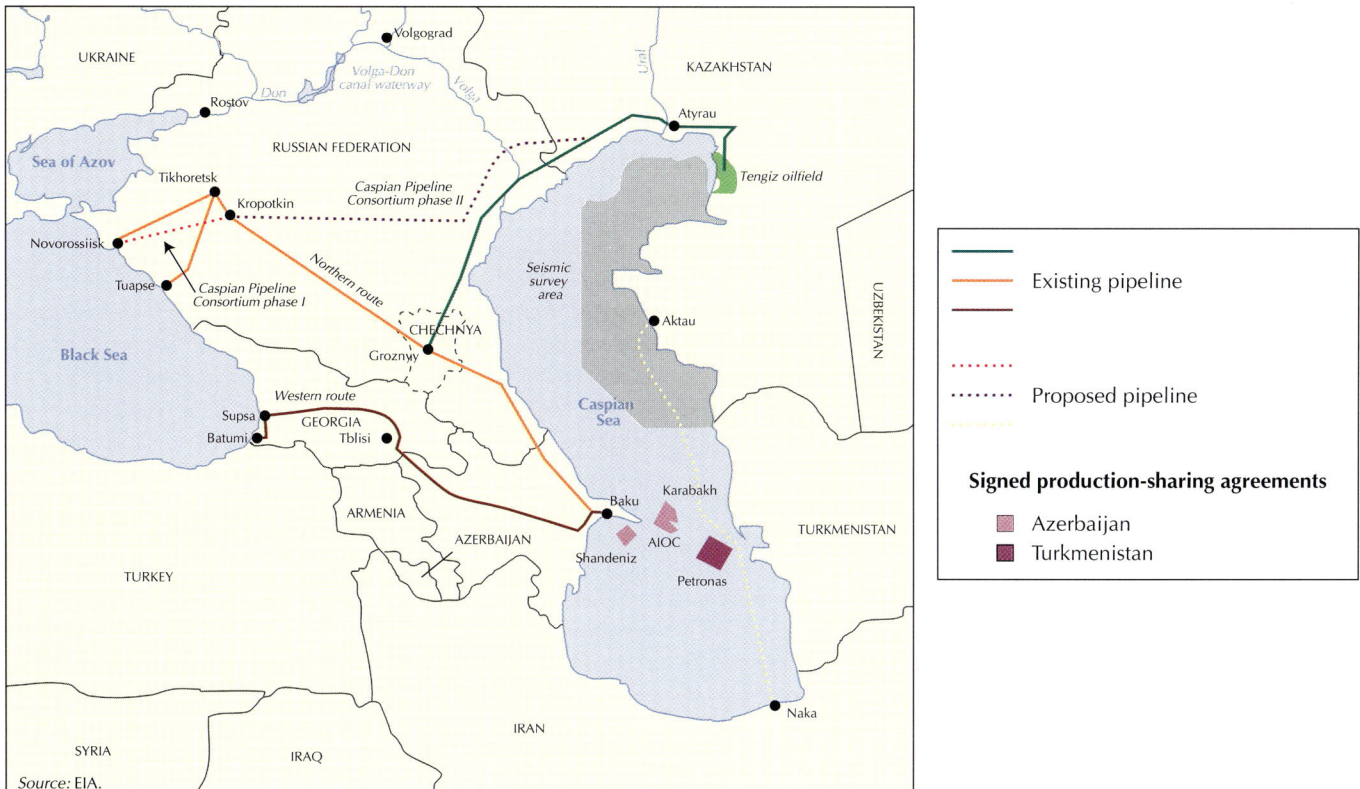

Source: EIA.

equity in Belarus oil and gas companies. However, they were opposed by Belarus President Aleksandr Lukashenko. Boris Nemtsov (then Russia's Minister of Fuel and Energy and first deputy Prime Minister) openly criticised Lukashenko for his opposition to the deal.

In October 1997, former Russian Prime Minister Viktor Chernomyrdin argued with Kazakhstan's President Nursultan Nazarbayev over how to select the energy companies allowed to develop Kazakhstan's offshore Caspian oilfields. Nazarbayev wanted to choose the companies making the best offers. Chernomyrdin insisted that Russian companies be given first priority. Failing to resolve this issue, the two leaders appointed an inter-governmental commission to continue the debate.

As the Caspian Basin states develop their own energy infrastructure and gain greater economic independence, some reduction of Russia's aggressive economic imperialism may occur. It is not in Russia's national interest to intensify the hostility of these countries along its southern periphery. Yet, Russia's self-serving policies have already created some animosity among some Central Asian states. A Central Asian coalition calling itself 'The Union of Five' has openly defied Russia. This union is an extension (with the inclusion of

Turkmenistan and Tajikistan) of the Central Asian Union formed earlier by Kazakhstan, the Kyrgyz Republic and Uzbekistan. At their first meeting in Ashgabat in January 1998, the five presidents focused much of their discussion on plans for a pipeline that would cross the Caspian Sea to the Caucasus and pass through Georgia and Turkey to the Mediterranean, thus bypassing Russia. Although Russia enjoys observer status in the Central Asian Union, no representatives were not invited to this meeting.

Subsequently, in January 1998, Chernomyrdin spent a working visit in the Turkmenistan capital trying to smooth feathers ruffled by Gazprom's policies. Turkmenistan's officials had accused Gazprom of unreasonableness because it still refused to allow Turkmen gas to be exported to Europe. Turkmenistan had responded by halting all operations of Turkmenrosgaz, the joint stock company that Viakhirev claimed was formed by Gazprom and Turkmenistan for the specific purpose of controlling all gas exports of Turkmen gas to CIS members.

Gazprom has been busy in Georgia and Armenia, forming two new joint companies – Gruzrosgazprom and Armrosgazprom – to distribute gas in the Caucasus and to encourage cooperation in the transit of gas deliveries across Georgia and Armenia to Turkey.

53

## Turkey's perspective

Istanbul wants increased supplies of oil and gas, both for its own development and for export to Europe. The Turkish State Petroleum Company (TPAO) is heavily involved in the development of Caspian oil projects in Azerbaijan and Kazakhstan. In Kazakhstan's Alibekmola oilfields, for example, Turkey plans to spend US$850 million along with Amoco Corporation for exploration and development.

Turkey is also vitally interested in planning pipeline systems to bring Caspian oil and gas to the West. Its preferred export route for Azeri oil from Baku is the proposed 1,770-kilometre pipeline that would cross Turkey to Ceyhan. It is also interested in the plan to transport Turkmenistan gas along the bed of the Caspian Sea from Turkmenistan to Azerbaijan, and then across Turkish territory to Europe, as first mooted in discussions in December 1997 between Turkey's Prime Minister Yilmaz and Azerbaijan's President Aliyev. In March 1999 Turkey stated that the pipeline route was a top priority for its energy policy and in April the country underlined its continuing support for the route by signing a pre-agreement accord to buy 18 Bcm of natural gas from Turkmenistan.

Although these plans suggest that Turkey may become the agent providing the Caspian Basin states with access to world markets, other pipeline scenarios challenge this prediction. Turkey is simultaneously locked into a relationship with Russia that promises immense future rewards for both countries. In November 1997, these two nations signed a major package of agreements to expand the volume of Russian gas deliveries to Turkey over the next decade. By 2010, deliveries are expected to reach 30 Bcm, a capacity that would largely satisfy Turkey's projected needs. Several corridors are planned: enlarged shipments through Bulgaria, new main lines through Georgia and Armenia, and a direct gas pipeline on the bottom of the Black Sea from Russia's coast to Turkey's Samsum and on to Ankara. This latter pipeline is called Blue Stream and is to be built and financed by Gazprom of Russia and Italy's Eni. Blue Stream may be completed before the Turkmen gas pipeline if it can overcome technical difficulties. Russia would then dominate Turkey's two main base load areas of Istanbul and Ankara, and other suppliers would be forced to share the remaining market.

This Russo–Turkish agreement promises Gazprom a large share of the expanding world gas market. It also indicates that Russia is still working effectively to block Turkmenistan's desperate efforts to reach European hard currency markets.

## China: The largest market for the 21st century

The Eurasian continental railway (10,914 kilometres long) links China's Yellow Sea port of Lianyungang with the Dutch port of Rotterdam. The entry point at Alataw on the border with Kazakhstan has become China's second largest railway portal, able to handle 3.5 million tonnes of freight annually. The significance of this economic corridor is well illustrated by the fact that from January to August 1996 it was used to ship more than 4,000 containers westward out of China.

Already China is the world's second largest energy consumer after the United States. Between 1995 and 2015, its oil consumption is projected to grow 4.9 per cent annually, fuelled by GDP growth of 7.3 per cent. China anticipates that in 1998 alone its demand for oil will grow by 7 to 8 per cent. Currently, two-thirds of this oil is imported from the Middle East. Other Asian states anticipate similar expansion in their energy needs in the long term, despite the after-effects of the financial crises of 1997. In fact, according to the US Department of Energy, while oil demand in Europe over the next 10 to 15 years may grow by little more than a million barrels a day, the demand in Asian markets will increase by 10 million barrels a day.

There is no doubt that the Chinese energy industry has a profound interest in the reserves of Central Asia. China has already explored the feasibility of building lengthy pipelines from Central Asia to the China coast. In 1992, Turkmenistan, the Mitsubishi Group of Japan and CNPC were seriously considering the feasibility of this gas pipeline out of Central Asia. In the summer of 1993, with China's consent, the Japanese government commissioned Mitsubishi to explore the possibilities of building a pipeline from China's north-western province of Xinjiang to the Pacific coast. In 1995, Exxon, Mitsubishi and CNPC announced a tentative agreement to build a gas pipeline from Turkmenistan through Uzbekistan, Kazakhstan and China to the Yellow Sea, with an underwater link to Japan. It would be 7,982 kilometres long – vaunted as the longest pipeline in the world – and would cost an estimated US$35 billion.

In September 1997, China's then Prime Minister, Li Peng, and the President of Kazakhstan signed an extensive package of agreements that promised important and tangible short-term results, and, by January 1998, draft contracts were being prepared between CNPC and Kazakhstan's Ministry of Energy and Natural Resources. The contracts call for the joint exploration of the Uzen oilfield and give China concessionary rights to develop deposits in the Aktiubinsk oilfields in western Kazakhstan.

In the long run, China will become a serious competitor to Europe in the market for Central Asian and Caspian oil and gas. Russia will be aggressively following this market, regardless of regional aspirations for economic independence from Moscow. One way or another, the struggle for Central Asia to develop its energy transport corridors will severely impact its relations with Russia and the West. The contracts for the construction and operation of the pipeline systems are so large, that there will definitely be a clear-cut list of winners among major construction firms, whether Japanese, European, Chinese or American. With the financial support of major construction and energy companies, the story of Central Asian and Caspian pipeline politics may eventually end with an economically stronger, more independent region.

Indeed, in the short term at least, some of the republics scored a minor victory following the October 1998 public confirmation by Azerbaijan, Turkey, Georgia, Kazakhstan and Uzbekistan of an agreement to develop a pipeline route from Baku to Ceyhan on Turkey's Mediterranean coast. The US Energy Secretary, Bill Richardson, pledged American backing for the proposed 1,730-kilometre pipeline, offering an initial, symbolic US Trade Development Agency aid package of US$823,000. Noticeably absent at the signing ceremony for the agreement was Turkmenistan, which did not give any official reasons for not attending.

## Iran: The 'wild card'

US legislation aimed at eliminating investment in Iran imposes sanctions on companies that invest more than US$40 million annually in the Iranian and Libyan oil and gas sectors. The maximum investment allowable was later lowered to US$20 million for countries not undertaking measures to inhibit Iran's actions in supporting international terrorism and pursuit of weapons of mass destruction. US laws require that sanctions be imposed for a minimum of two years. These prohibitions would likely apply to any joint-use arrangements in the Caspian Sea, including the Iranian sector of the Caspian Sea.

The US State Department decided in July 1997 that proposed exports of natural gas from Turkmenistan to Turkey via Iran do not technically violate the law. However, the US position could change if a memorandum of understanding to build an export pipeline across Iran results in a construction contract with more than US$20 million of outside investment.

Clearly, the United States is actively using its legislative heavy artillery to punish any company involved in a project linked with Iran. Yet, at the same time, Iran may develop into one of the most important investors in the region. Whatever Iran lacks in capital and technology is compensated for by its geographical importance, potential territorial claim on Caspian extraction rights, and its energy sector, which, although not as well developed as that in the West, is certainly more advanced than Central Asia and the Caspian's energy industry.

Iran possesses an immense energy infrastructure enabling it to offer the Caspian Basin countries the shortest and cheapest routes to the Persian Gulf, Europe and Asia. Politically isolated until the 1990s, Iran quickly took advantage of the fall of the Soviet Union to establish links with its neighbours. Border crossings with Turkmenistan were opened and, as early as November 1991, consulates were established in all the Central Asian republic capitals. The 1996 completion of an Iran–Turkmenistan railway, from Mashad to Tedzhen, neatly plugged Iran into the existing railway system linking all the Central Asian countries. Such rail connections have been key in expanding Iran's trade, joint ventures and bilateral relations with Central Asia.

Eager to use its strengths to profit from new pipelines and the transport of energy across its land, the Iranian government wisely financed 80 per cent of the US$190 million cost of the recently completed Korpedzhe–Kurdkui pipeline between Turkmenistan and Iran.

Recently there has been widespread condemnation of US policy and, despite the threat of sanctions, Russian and other foreign companies have been prepared to conclude lucrative oil and gas deals with Iran. The 28 September 1997 agreement between the Iran National Oil Company, France's Totale, Russia's Gazprom and Malaysia's Petronas to develop Iran's huge South Pars gas field came as a shock. When the United States objected, Russia's President, Boris Yeltsin, simply dismissed the objections as unnecessary interference in the affairs of sovereign nations. The French government also gave full support to the project. Since then, Lukoil has signed a US$3.8 billion agreement to develop another Iranian oilfield after the economic sanctions are lifted.

# 7 Banking and finance

## The inherited USSR financial system

As it operated a command economy, the Soviet Union ensured that the banking system was tightly controlled from Moscow. All payments leaving Central Asia and the Caspian to outside the USSR went through the Soviet central bank, known as Gosbank, while payments received were used for Union-wide needs – particularly Russian needs. Central Asian and Caspian exports, especially of energy, earned vast amounts of hard currency yet virtually none of these funds returned to the region. Thus, there was never any need to have any type of regional banking infrastructure other than merely administrative offices in each republic, responsible for disbursing currency, coins and subsidies from Moscow.

In November 1991, when the Commonwealth of Independent States (CIS) was officially established and the Soviet Union structures dissolved, the Supreme Soviet of the Russian Federation proclaimed the Central Bank of Russia (CBR) as the sole organ for monetary and foreign currency regulation in the Russian economy. The CBR was entrusted with the functions of the former State Bank of the USSR in issuing money and setting the exchange rate of the rouble. On 20 December 1991 the State Bank was officially dissolved and all its assets, technical facilities and property in Russia were transferred to the CBR. While this may have seemed to be a logical progression from the collapse of the USSR to the creation of a new Commonwealth, the practical result was that virtually all of the Soviet Union's hard currency and gold reserves ended up under Russian ownership. The banking system of Central Asia and the Caspian was more or less returned to its 1920s state of development.

## Commercial banking

As well as the crisis of confidence caused by pyramid schemes, banks also suffered as a result of assuming a portfolio of weak or non-performing loans. Inadequate credit analysis as well as the close link between the government and insolvent, loss-making subsidised industry meant that huge loans were granted with little or no hope of repayment.

Ill-informed lending decisions have been compounded by a lack of any understanding of customer service. Even in the major recognised banks, depositors often complain of officious clerks, obstructed access to withdrawals, unexplained levies on accounts, and unreliable transfer of funds and foreign exchange services. At times, central government pressure has been exerted on commercial banks to restrict state withdrawals as a crude disinflationary instrument.

### Azerbaijan

The country has made remarkable progress with macroeconomic stabilisation, and the pursuance of prudent monetary policies by the National Bank of Azerbaijan (NBA), the central bank, has helped reduce financial imbalances. Consequently, inflation has abated rapidly, interest rates are positive in real terms, and the exchange rate has appreciated steadily since mid-1995 (see Exhibit 7.1). As true market conditions take hold, weaknesses in the banking sector have been revealed (mainly in the form of liquidity problems, mismatches between funding costs and returns on lending, and large amounts of bad loans) which are only slowly being resolved. Resolution of these problems in the banking sector is slowing continued macroeconomic stabilisation and reform.

Beyond simple banking activity, development of other financial markets has been hampered by a combination of constraints by the authorities. Such constraints include favouring nationally owned banks over foreign-owned institutions, favouring banks rather than non-bank financial institutions, irregular timing of Treasury bill auctions, and the absence of the appropriate legislative framework.

Bottlenecks in the payment system still exist in key areas, in both domestic currency transactions and in the foreign exchange market. Delays and unconsolidated accounts require banks to hold large amounts of excess reserves. Overcoming these problems will require nothing short of a clear and determined effort by the authorities.

All of these problems have made it more difficult for the authorities to move towards their goal of being able to use

Exhibit 7.1
**Monetary indicators, Azerbaijan, 1994–98**

|  | 1994 | 1995 | 1996 | 1997(e) | 1998(p) |
|---|---|---|---|---|---|
| Broad money (end-year, % change) | 1,114 | 411.7 | 19.7 | 3.5 | 0.9 |
| Domestic credit (end-year, % change) | 841 | 61.0 | 33.2 | 11.1 | na |
| Broad money (% of GDP) | 55.9 | 12.2 | 11.3 | 13.4 | na |
| Interbank interest rate (% pa, end-year) | 406 | 144 | 336 | 22.9 | na |
| T-bill (3-month) rate (% pa, end-year) | na | na | 34 | 14.3 | na |
| Deposit rate (% pa, end-year) | 406 | 90 | 13 | 11.5 | na |
| Lending rate (% pa, end-year) | 406 | 107 | 33 | 21.5 | na |
| Consumer prices (% change, annual average) | 1,664 | 411.7 | 19.7 | 3.5 | 0.9 |
| Exchange rate (manat/US$, end-year) | 4,330 | 4,440 | 4,098 | 3,688 | na |
| Exchange rate (manat/US$, annual average) | 1,432 | 4,417 | 4,301 | 3,983 | na |

(e) estimate
(p) projected

*Source:* EBRD.

Exhibit 7.2
**Size and structure of the banking system, 1995–98**

|  | 1995 | 1996 | 1997 | 1998 |
|---|---|---|---|---|
| Total no. of banks | 210 | 180 | 136 | 99 |
| of which: state-owned | 4 | 4 | 4 | 4 |
| majority foreign-owned | 6 | 11 | 13 | 13 |

indirect instruments of monetary policy.

The number of banks has declined significantly in recent years (see Exhibit 7.2), but the structure of the system has changed little. The scale of activity by the state-owned banks has been limited by their need for restructuring, but they still continue to dominate the banking system although their share of bank business is declining (see Exhibit 7.3). Whereas they accounted for 97 per cent of manat deposits in 1997, they accounted for about 88 per cent in 1998, implying a fourfold increase in the business of private banks.

Similarly, private banks' credit extension doubled during this period, while only one of the state banks increased credit by any significant amount (about 20 per cent) and the others saw credit extension decline or stagnate. This growth by private banks is important at a time when banks continue to report difficulties in finding creditworthy lending opportunities and are reluctant to lend without sizeable collateral requirements. Banks' risks in lending remain high because of the absence until recently of a modern bankruptcy law, the absence of clear definitions and registration of collateral, and the legal preference given to paying enterprises' wage and tax arrears before dealing with overdue loans. Banks have also had to deal with other impediments that tend to sap public confidence and thus discourage deposits, such as sweeping powers given to the police and tax authorities with regard to access to bank assets and customer details.

Exhibit 7.3 shows the performance of the banking sectors between 1993 and 1997.

Exhibit 7.3
**Performance of the banking sector, 1993–97 (%, end-period)**

|  | 1993 | 1994 | 1995 | 1996 | 1997 |
|---|---|---|---|---|---|
| State-owned banks' share of total assets | 78 | 82 | 81 | 83 | 70 |
| Total assets as % of GDP | 15 | 90 | 20 | 26 | 24 |
| Total loans as % of GDP | 41 | 25 | 9 | 10 | 10 |
| Credit to private sector as % of GDP | 23 | 14 | 5 | 5 | 6 |
| Non-banks' deposits as % of GDP | 4 | 2 | 1 | 1 | 2 |
| Non-performing loans (as % of total loans) | 27 | 16 | 22 | 20 | 20 |
| Provisions for bad loans (as % of non-performing loans) | na | na | na | 2 | 5 |
| Average lending spread (deposit-lending rate) | 40 | 35 | 20 | 20 | 10 |

*Sources:* Azerbaijan National Bank; IMF.

*Private banks*

Many private banks are weak, partly because of earlier weak bank licensing rules. This led to a number of unsound institutions being granted banking licences. The problems caused by these banks have contributed to the low level of public confidence in the banking system. To overcome this lack of confidence, the NBA instituted new procedures in late 1996 requiring banks to prepare detailed documentation, including information regarding the financial position of the founders of the bank, as well as the professional skills of key management officials. Bank licensing regulations and procedures are now largely sound, but could still be improved. The IMF has suggested several key areas where changes should be implemented.

Many of the domestic private banks in Azerbaijan are essentially vehicles for financing particular enterprises and thus provide a limited banking service and do little to mobilise deposits. Nevertheless, these banks face a variety of institutional problems. The licensing regulations limit the number of branches a new bank may open based on its level of authorised capital, as follows:

| Authorised capital | Maximum number of branches |
| --- | --- |
| US$1.25 million | 15 |
| US$1.26–2.5 million | 30 |
| US$2.6–5 million | 50 |
| more than US$5 million | no limitation |

*Source*: NBA.

The authorities' rationale for this rule is to limit the risk for the customers if a bank goes bankrupt. However, this arrangement gives advantages to older, mainly state-owned, banks that were able to establish a large network before the regulation was implemented. Supervisory tools have been improved, and can now be used to manage these risks without the need for such restrictions. Since a network is an important way to channel financing and banking services beyond the capital, the removal of this restrictive regulation could invigorate banking activity.

Foreign-owned banks face additional obstacles. In particular, foreign-owned banks must seek approval for an increase in statutory capital, and the banking law allows the central bank (NBA) to set a limit (30 per cent) on foreign capital in the banking system. Once the limit is met, licensing of new banks with participation of foreign investment as well as branches of foreign banks is stopped. The ratio of such banks in the banking system as at 1998 was 20 per cent. Several foreign-owned banks have had their requests for capital increases denied or have had increases permitted at far below the amount requested. In addition, if neither the director nor one of the deputies

of a proposed bank is an Azeri citizen, the licence can be refused. Furthermore, the licensing regulation also requires that foreigners seek the NBA's permission to buy issues of the new share capital of banks.

The authorities argue that these restrictions protect domestic banks, which still suffer from a lack of banking skills, and from a generally poor financial situation. However, experience from other developing economies has shown that increasing foreign presence brings broad gains in terms of improved banking services, increased confidence in the banking system, more efficient mobilisation of savings, and probably improved returns on banking investment. These developments in turn could stimulate domestic growth, and help add resilience to the domestic economy. Furthermore, as has been revealed in many other countries, the strong and able domestic banks will find their niche and survive. The only price they will pay will be an enforced improvement in their efficiency and customer orientation.

*Restructuring the state-owned banks*

Some progress has been made with the restructuring of state-owned banks. This restructuring issue first came to light in late 1995 when a severe liquidity shortage for the Savings Bank exposed the general problem of a mismatch between these banks' funding costs and the returns on their lending activities. In response to this problem, the NBA initially developed rehabilitation plans for each of the state-owned banks, which were formalised in September 1996 and focused on loan recovery and measures to improve profitability. The plans foresaw liquidation if a bank could not establish profitability or failed to meet zero capital adequacy by mid-1997. Three of the four banks did not meet this test. However, the IMF agreed with the NBA that, in light of the progress made and the importance of these institutions in the payments system and for rural financing, liquidation would be premature. The rehabilitation plans were therefore reformulated, in collaboration with the World Bank, with specific targets to be monitored in the context of the Structural Adjustment Credit. The first phase of rehabilitation was an intensification of loan recovery, branch closures, and staff reduction. Once this phase was successfully completed, then consideration could be given to possible recapitalisation and privatisation.

Rehabilitation and privatization of the state-owned banks has not occurred as quickly as previously expected. All the state-owned banks have recently been audited by internationally reputable firms and their results have been mixed. The International Bank of Azerbaijan has developed well and was the first bank to be privatised in November 1998 (see Chapter 8, Azerbaijan). Savings Bank has made considerable progress in implementing its restructuring plan, and recorded only a small loss in 1997. The prospects looked good for the bank's privatisation by mid-1999.

Resolution of the liquidity problems at the state-owned banks also involved loans and guarantees from the Ministry of Finance and the NBA. The continued support of new guarantees have to be taken into consideration as the future strategies for these banks are developed, given the inadequate rates of loan collection, large losses, and administrative and management weaknesses that are still evident. In the near term, the operations of these banks may have to be reduced substantially while strategies for their future are developed, perhaps involving the help of foreign banks, and a more aggressive approach to dealing with bad loans.

*Banking supervision regime*

The NBA is in the process of creating better order in the banking sector by applying stricter bank supervision. It introduced new bank licensing regulations in November 1996. New prudential regulations were introduced in June 1997 that are largely in accordance with international best practices. However, during 1998, about one-third of banks were not complying with required capital adequacy ratios and most of these have had to face one of several sanctions, either fines (seven banks), higher required reserves (seven banks), or revocation of banking licence (10 banks).

The NBA can also revoke the licence of a bank if it fails to meet capital adequacy regulations for three consecutive months, or for not submitting its prudential reports for two consecutive months. During 1997, 13 banks had their licences withdrawn for violating prudential regulations.

The NBA also continues to exercise regulatory influence through the application of reserve requirements. Since February 1997, a single 12 per cent ratio has applied for manat and foreign currency deposits. Previously, the ratios were 8 per cent and 6 per cent, respectively.

While the bank supervision principles in Azerbaïjan are now good, implementation of them needs to be more forcefully and consistently applied. The NBA is improving its practices in this area by broadening staff training in on-site and off-site supervision and by giving management responsibility to a deputy governor.

## Kazakhstan

The banking system is two-tiered, with the National Bank of Kazakhstan (NBK) charged with overall supervision of all banks in the country, and the second-tier, commercial banks. The NBK performs standard central bank functions and acts as lender of last resort. The remaining banks consist of: nine large domestic banks with branches located throughout Kazakhstan; 13 foreign banks; five fully government-owned banks (the Kazakhstan Eximbank, the Housing Construction Bank, the Government Budget Bank, the Rehabilitation Bank, Turan-Alem Bank); one intergovernmental bank and approximately 35 small Almaty-based banks and 35 regional banks. Many larger banks offer personal banking services. Money transfers from the West can be completed in as little as 24 hours through the SWIFT network.

Kazakhstan Eximbank is now scheduled to be privatised. The Turan-Alem Bank was auctioned in April 1998 through a closed tender. (Bidders were required to be Kazakh banks meeting minimum share capital of 1.2 billion tenge, US$15.7 million, and without foreign participation). The buyer was Kazakh Investor, a consortium of local companies, which outbid Kazkommertsbank and a consortium of Kazagroprombank and Kazenergoprombank, with a price of US$72 million. Kazakh Investor was created solely to compete in the auction, and includes the following banks and companies: Temir Bank, Centercredit Bank, Kostanaiasbest, Araltuz, Melcombinat, Shymkent Makaronnaya Fabrica, Maktaapal, Semipalatinsk Flour and Feed Milling Combine, and Yassy. It is unclear whether Turan-Alem Bank will merge with another bank in the consortium or remain independent.

The largest Kazakh commercial banks in terms of assets, branch networks and national economic roles, are Kazkommertsbank (KKB) and Halyk Savings Bank, both graded B+/Stable/B in October 1997 by Standard & Poor's, and Turan-Alem Bank. All have headquarters in Almaty The largest of these, KKB, launched its first US$100 million, three-year Eurobond in April 1998, the proceeds to be lent to Kazakh industrial enterprises. The bonds have a three-year term, and the Dutch bank, ING Barings, is lead manager for the issue. The bank has a B2 long-term foreign currency deposit rating from Moody's, and its 1997 accounts are under audit by Deloitte Touche. The EBRD has been working with KKB through its loan department to finance a credit line for small and medium-sized enterprises. Through an EBRD-arranged twinning program, KKB is partnered with Credit Commercial de France. KKB has placed American and global depository receipts, has securities available in Frankfurt, Berlin and Istanbul, and is involved in the syndicated loan market with Germany's Commerzbank, with which it has a February 1998 framework agreement for financing projects in Kazakhstan.

Halyk Savings Bank, the local successor to the Soviet Union's Sberbank, holds over 40 per cent of individual savings in Kazakhstan, 63 per cent of Halyk's capitalisation. Halyk is the only Kazakh bank with a comprehensive branch network. Early in 1998, the first stage of a privatisation programme took place with the sale of 17.6 per cent in government shares worth 300 million tenge to bank depositors. Shareholders now total 49,000. This increased the bank's charter capital from US$1.8 million to US$2.2 million. According to bank chairman Karim Masimov, a second privatisation will leave the government with a 51 per cent stake. Halyk also plans a US$100 million Eurobond issue.

59

*Central Bank, Almaty, Kazakhstan*

In mid-March 1998, the NBK announced that Kazakhstan's banks had the right to hold pension deposits under Kazakhstan's pension reform programme: Kazkommertsbank, Temir Bank, Karaganda Territorial Bank, Gazprombank, Kazakhprombank, and Tsesna Bank. Turan-Alem Bank was on the list, but may no longer qualify since its sale in 1998. Pension fund managers may place up to 40 per cent of their client's pension savings in bank deposits, but no more than 10 per cent in any one bank. Other savings must be invested in securities issued by the government, international financial organisations (namely: the World Bank, EBRD, Asian Development Bank, African Bank for Reconstruction and Development, Bank of International Settlements, and IFC), and 'A'-listed companies on the Kazakhstan Stock Exchange. Kazakhstan now has nine pension savings funds, eight of which are private and one state-run.

*Foreign banks*

As at April 1998, there were 20 banks with foreign participation in Kazakhstan, representing a cumulative registered capital of 4 billion tenge – about US$50 billion. This leaves room for an increase in foreign bank capital, since the NBK has set a limit of 25 per cent on foreign ownership of the total capital of all banks in Kazakhstan. Twelve foreign banks have obtained full operating licences, but so far the only foreign bank actually operating in almost all areas is the Dutch ABN AMRO. The rest are joint ventures with foreign capital. Chinese and Russian banks have established 100 per cent-owned subsidiaries, and several Dutch and Turkish banks have established joint ventures. Citibank maintains a representative office in Almaty, with plans for expansion. Two Kazakstani-American banking joint ventures, Texaka Bank and Lariba Bank, offer small, community-based loans. Texaka Bank provides personal banking services. American investment in both banks is relatively small, approximately US$500,000 each. ABN AMRO serves corporate clients' cash management needs.

In March 1998, Société Générale Kazakhstan, a wholly owned subsidiary of France's Société Générale, received a licence to conduct banking operations in Kazakhstan. The initial authorised fund is US$6 million, expected to increase to US$25 million. Chairman Jean-Claude Valentin estimates total assets to be US$50–100 million at the end of 1998. Société Générale Kazakhstan will help place shares of KEGOC, the national grid company, and Kaztelecom, the national telecommunications company, on the stock market.

Exhibit 7.4
**Monetary indicators, Kazakhstan, 1994–98**

|  | 1994 | 1995 | 1996 | 1997(e) | 1998(p) |
|---|---|---|---|---|---|
| Broad money (end-year, % change) | 576 | 106 | 13.8 | 32.3 | na |
| Domestic credit (end-year, % change) | 745 | −23.6 | −12.4 | 33.5 | na |
| Broad money (% of GDP) | 13.4 | 11.6 | 9.5 | 10.4 | na |
| Refinancing rate (% pa, end-year) | 230 | 52.5 | 35.0 | 18.5 | na |
| T-bill (3-month) rate (% pa, end-year) | 354 | 58.8 | 32.6 | 16.1 | na |
| Deposit rate (% pa, end-year) | na | 44.4 | 30.0 | 12.6 | na |
| Lending rate (% pa, end-year) | na | 58.3 | 45.0 | 22.9 | na |
| Consumer prices (% change, annual average) | 1,892 | 176 | 39.1 | 17.4 | 10.0 |
| Exchange rate (tenge/US$, end-year) | 54.3 | 64.0 | 73.8 | 75.9 | na |
| Exchange rate (tenge/US$, annual average) | 36.0 | 61.0 | 68.2 | 75.6 | na |

*(e)* estimate
*(p)* projected

*Source:* EBRD.

*Foreign exchange controls*

The NBK allows the national currency, the tenge, to float. It is fully convertible with the US dollar. In July 1996, Kazakhstan joined Article VIII of the International Monetary Fund Charter, which envisages full convertibility of the tenge.

Kazakstani banks require that legal entities wishing to withdraw funds from hard currency accounts in local banks present an invoice for goods or services to be purchased to prove the currency is needed. Foreigners have complained that this requirement is burdensome, as businesses cannot predict future expenses in any given month.

*Credit*

The official NBK refinancing rate as of June 1997 was 24 per cent, down from a high of 300 per cent in March 1994. Tenge-based loans from Kazakstani banks carry a high interest rate, at times 20 per cent higher than the refinancing rate. These high rates are set partly because the rates lag behind falling inflation and partly because the banks are trying to compensate for losses due to bad loans of the past.

In the early 1990s, the government of Kazakhstan liberally issued sovereign government guarantees for loans from foreign creditors. In 1994–95, as government debt accumulated, Kazakhstan recalled as many as 30 guarantees. This move tarnished Kazakhstan's reputation in the international banking community. In an effort to regain its standing among international creditors, Kazakhstan paid US$87 million in arrears to foreign creditors by the end of 1995 (US Eximbank, one of these creditors, was paid its arrearages in April 1995). In late 1996, the government decided that it would limit its issuance of sovereign guarantees to a low US$50 million annually. International creditors will continue to approach Kazakhstan with caution and carefully monitor payments on outstanding loans.

In terms of payment systems, the safest method for an exporter to receive payment is through an irrevocable letter of credit (L/C) from a major western bank. In general, importers must deposit enough funds to cover the payment before applying for an L/C. Local companies may apply at any one of several local commercial banks to obtain an L/C, which in most cases, according to banking legislation, must be confirmed by a reputable western bank.

Kazakstani commercial banks are relatively inexperienced with regard to using L/Cs, and performance on L/Cs has been poor. Moreover, frequently Kazakstani companies are unable to pay for products and services obtained through them.

## Kyrgyz Republic

Considerable progress has been made in improving the soundness and stability of the Kyrgyz banking system. A substantial restructuring of banks was undertaken in 1996, supported by an International Development Association Financial Sector Adjustment Credit (FINSAC). In the spring of 1996, operations of Elbank and Agropombank, the last state and largest commercial banks, were shut down by the National Bank of the Kyrgyz Republic (NBKR). This move initially shook confidence in commercial banks as deposits fell, but eventually, the result was a financially sound banking system, which has enjoyed increasing public confidence. A Debt Resolution Agency (DEBRA) was set up in 1996 to help collect or write-off Agroprom's non-performing loans, and in 1997 was also given the task of liquidating Elbank's assets. A Settlements and Savings Corporation (SSC) was established to provide payments system services and a savings outlet, especially for rural areas, following the closure of Agrop
rombank branches. In April 1997, Promstroi Bank and AKB Bank, two other large former state-owned banks, were recapitalised without public finds. In March 1997, the Kyrgyz Agricultural Financial Corporation (KAFC) was launched to take over lending to the agricultural sector from the former Agroprombank and of lending from the budget.

The bulk of the liabilities of the liquidated banks consisted of directed credits that were financed through advances from the NBKR that acted upon government instructions. To compensate the NBKR for these advances, the government provided the NBKR with bonds totalling about 1 billion som, with a 30-year maturity and a 5 per cent interest rate. The NBKR also financially supported restructuring the sector. This mainly involved three operations that increased reserve money by 5 per cent. In two cases, the NBKR acquired buildings as collateral from illiquid banks that had overdue loans to the NBKR. In the third case, the NBKR provided funds to compensate Elbank depositors to secure the public's confidence in the system.

*Visa billboard, Bishkek, Kyrgyz Republic*

Exhibit 7.5
**Monetary indicators, Kyrgyz Republic, 1994–98**

| | 1994 | 1995 | 1996 | 1997(e) | 1998(p) |
|---|---|---|---|---|---|
| Broad money (end-year, % change) | 125.0 | 76.7 | 22.9 | 24.7 | na |
| Net domestic assets (end-year, % change) | 83.5 | 96.8 | 17.7 | 8.2 | na |
| Broad money (% of GDP) | 12.9 | 17.1 | 14.3 | 14.3 | na |
| Refinancing rate (% pa, end-year) | 89.5 | 45.8 | 45.9 | na | na |
| T-bill (3-month) rate (% pa, end-year) | 73.0 | 44.0 | 57.0 | 23.1 | na |
| Deposit rate (% pa, end-year) | na | na | 24.8 | 32.0 | na |
| Lending rate (% pa, end-year) | na | na | 58.3 | 50.1 | na |
| Consumer prices (% change, annual average) | 228.7 | 52.5 | 304 | 25.5 | 12.0 |
| Exchange rate (som/US$, end-year) | 10.7 | 11.0 | 16.7 | 17.4 | na |
| Exchange rate (som/US$, annual average) | 10.9 | 10.8 | 12.9 | 17.4 | na |

*(e)* estimate
*(p)* projected

*Source: EBRD.*

*Banking and finance regulation*

A number of key laws have been enacted, comprising the new Law on Banks and Banking Activity, the new Central Bank Law, and the Law on Pledges. Complementary legislation is being prepared for depositors' insurance, as well as for the non-bank financial sector to provide a modern legal and regulatory framework for insurance companies, private pension funds, and leasing companies, which should also boost the still largely dormant financial market activity. The NBKR also introduced a new chart of accounts for itself and for five commercial banks in April 1997. This chart was adopted by the remaining banks by the end of 1997. The NBKR is also in the process of modernising the payments system and has been strengthening bank supervision by issuing new regulations on insider lending, foreign exchange exposure, and loan provisioning. Under the old payments system, a payment from a customer in one bank to a customer in another bank could take up to one month to settle. In the new automated retail payment system, based on netting, settlement will take one to two days. A manual large-value gross payment system with same day settlement has already been established in the NBKR.

In addition, new minimum capital requirements in line with international standards are gradually being implemented. Seventeen out of the 18 operating banks are currently complying with all prudential regulations, and while non-observance of reserve requirements still occasionally occurs, only one bank has persistently failed to meet such requirements in 1997. Banks have also largely succeeded in writing off their non-performing loans, mainly by injecting new capital from their owners. This new capital has reduced the share of substandard or non-performing loans in the sector from 39 per cent in October 1996 to 7 per cent in June 1997. The proportion of bank loans classified as being under supervision has also fallen from 13 per cent to 4 per cent. Three new bank licences were granted in 1997, of which two were to banks with foreign participation.

These reforms managed to bring about a strengthening of the public's confidence in the banking system, as evidenced by the rising share of deposits in broad money and the decline of foreign currency deposits in total deposits. Nonetheless, some challenges remain. Banks have not yet become an effective vehicle for mobilising financial resources and allocating these to their most efficient uses. Private savings and financial intermediation remain low by international standards. Lending by commercial banks and credit programmes has so far met only a small part of the credit needs of large segments of the population and of the developing private sector. Banks generally also lack adequately trained staff in risk analysis and business plan evaluation. Moreover, foreign lenders, especially credit programmes, are having difficulty finding qualified investment projects. This difficulty is because risks of default are substantial, potential borrowers lack strong business plans, repayment culture is underdeveloped, the legal basis for collateral is still incomplete, and courts have yet to adopt adequate debt enforcement procedures. As a consequence, whatever foreign lending exists continues to be largely short term and often for trade purposes. Finally, the high returns on relatively risk-free T-bills may have discouraged lending.

*Tajikistan*

The Tajik banking sector is dominated by large specialised banks, a legacy of the state-owned banks of the Former Soviet Union. These banks – Agroprombank 'Shark', Tajikorienbank, and Tajikbankbusiness – account for over 96 per cent of bank lending. Sberbank remains the dominant institution in the individual savings market but has little role in lending. The

National Bank of Tajikistan (NBT) retains a significant role in the banking sector and the economy as a whole. The regulations it administers, the accounting system it uses and even the banks themselves remain squarely within the old Soviet system.

Cash is the dominant method of payment. Enterprises are not free to encash their bank deposits at will and must use payment orders for the majority of transactions. Cheques are rarely used.

In the transition to a market economy, the government's policies in the monetary and financial areas have generally hindered resource allocation. Credit, subject to a variety of controls, has been directed mostly toward sustaining industries and maintaining living standards. This has driven inflation to unprecedented levels. Deficit financing has allowed the government to avoid change in old activities and behaviours.

Interest rates that are subject to controls are severely negative in real terms (see Exhibit 7.6) and lower than Russian nominal interest rates. This contributed to an outflow of currency before the collapse of the rouble zone, as arbitrage between Russian and Tajik interest rates took place. The highly negative real rates have imposed a severe tax on household savings.

The skill base of the banking sector has been significantly eroded by the loss of Russian professional staff. This affects the NBT, the banks and the state insurance company. This exodus of skilled personnel has affected the NBT regulatory ability, banks' ability to manage their accounts and modernise, and the efficiency of the domestic payments system.

The government faces a large and growing contingent liability in terms of a future need to recapitalise the banking sector. A number of factors will weigh heavily on the recapitalisation needs of the sector. The government has encouraged the continuity of the banks' lending relationships with traditional clients, many of who are nearly insolvent. There is a lack of any arms' length relationship between banks and their shareholders; lack of effective NBT supervision, particularly in relation to large exposure lending; and the existence of long-term overdrafts in NBT settlement accounts. Further, hyperinflation has also severely affected the capital of solvent banks.

There are 13 banks in Tajikistan in addition to the NBT and Sberbank. Most are partially owned by state enterprises. In addition to these 13, there is a state insurance company and seven new insurance companies.

On 23 May 1995 the first hard currency auction took place since the introduction of the new Tajik currency, the Tajik rouble, on 10 May. The auction was held at the Tajik Interbank Currency Exchange, a closed-stock company established by eight commercial banks, including the NBT. According to the government decrees in support of the new currency, these auctions are to be held regularly, to establish the market exchange rate for the Tajik rouble. The auctions are carefully controlled by the government of Tajikistan, to ensure that the process does not get beyond the ideal limits imposed by the government and undermine the fragile confidence the people have in the new currency. While a person has the right to freely exchange money, in practice the exchange offices and the banks refuse to sell US dollars although they will eagerly buy them.

The laws regulating the banking sector are: Law on Banks and Banking Activities in the Republic of Tajikistan; Law of the Republic of Tajikistan on the National Bank of the Republic of Tajikistan 1991; Resolution No. 778 of the Supreme Soviet of the Republic of Tajikistan Concerning the Basic Thrusts of Monetary Policies for 1993; October 1991 Gosbank Rules Governing the Regulation of the Activities of Commercial and Cooperative Banks; Insurance Law (Draft); and Stock Exchange Law.

Exhibit 7.6
**Monetary indicators, Tajikistan, 1994–98**

|  | 1994 | 1995 | 1996 | 1997(e) | 1998(p) |
| --- | --- | --- | --- | --- | --- |
| Broad money (end-year, % change) | 159 | 413 | 143 | 117 | na |
| Domestic credit (end-year, % change) | 125 | 393 | 146 | 176 | na |
| Broad money (% of GDP) | 8.6 | 24.5 | 10.7 | 8.5 | na |
| Interbank interest rate, max 30-day (% pa, end-year) | na | 153 | 72 | 72 | na |
| Deposit rate, max 30-day (% pa, end-year) | 30 | 100 | 85 | 118 | na |
| Lending rate, max 30-day (% pa, end-year) | 30 | 500 | 124 | 136 | na |
| Consumer prices (% change, annual average) | 350 | 609 | 418 | 87.8 | 46.3 |
| Exchange rate (tajik rouble/US$, end-year) | 3,550 | 285 | 328 | 747 | na |
| Exchange rate (tajik rouble /US$, annual average) | 2,204 | 135 | 298 | 564 | na |

*(e)* estimate
*(p)* projected

*Source:* EBRD.

*National Bank of Azerbaijan, Baku, Azerbaijan*

*National Bank of Turkmenistan, Ashgabat, Turkmenistan*

There are several different legal types of banks: state; state-commercial; joint-stock commercial; commercial; and cooperative. The two state banks are Sberbank, which has a government guarantee on its deposits from households, and Khatlon Reconstruction and Development Bank. Khatlon Bank was recently established by the government as a vehicle to assist development in the Khatlon Region. Once this role is fulfilled, it will be dismantled. The difference between the joint-stock commercial, commercial, and cooperative banks relates more to their capital structure than to their functions. Joint-stock banks issue equities to attract capital, in addition to the capital provided by their founders. Commercial and cooperative banks have no ability to issue equity and must rely on their founders for capital.

Bank branches have their own correspondent accounts. They use the balances in these small accounts, rather than a group's entire net balance, in deciding whether they can extend credit. Branches are not effectively managed in terms of developing their loan portfolio due to a number of factors, including a lack of know-how and efficient information systems.

Although financing of industry in Tajikistan has broken away from the previous highly centralised allocation of resources, most credit allocation remains based on regulations, central funding, and past relationships. This greatly impairs the financial system's efficiency in allocating resources. To improve the situation, the government needs to reduce its role by eliminating credit directives and reducing deficit financing; the NBT should end its intermediation; and commercial bank skill levels should be raised. More broadly, a stable macroeconomic environment and realistic assessment of the viability of the larger enterprises in a market environment are also required.

*Agroprombank 'Shark'*
'Shark' is the successor to the previous Agroprombank. By far the largest bank, its lending is heavily concentrated in agriculture and agricultural industries. As the bank services the traditional priority in this area, it usually has a priority in obtaining loans from NBT. Agroprombank is the bank most dependent on NBT as a source of finance for its operations. It has suffered heavily from the loss of skilled staff, to the extent that some of this functioning is impaired.

*Tajikbankbusiness (TBB)*
TBB is the second largest bank, after Agroprombank, in terms of assets. TBB's clients are mainly in trade, light and local industries. TBB has two branches, which deal with entrepreneurs, lessees, and small enterprises. It plans to combine two branches into a large sub-bank to further develop its presence in this market.

*Tajikorienbank*
Tajikorienbank, based on the previous Promstroy Bank, mostly finances industry and construction, but also has some trading concerns and collective farms as clients. Most big industrial projects have been financed by Tajikorienbank, including the aluminium smelter and the hydroelectric plants.

*Tajikvnesheconombank*
Previously a subsidiary of Vnesheconombank of the USSR, this bank is the Agent of the Republic of Tajikistan in servicing external debt. In this role, its borrowing is guaranteed by the state. As a result, it is described as a state joint-stock commercial bank, although it is not in fact a state entity. The bank manages the existing foreign exchange reserves under the authority of the Ministry of Finance.

*Sberbank*
Sberbank reports to the Supreme Soviet, not to the NBT, and it is not included within the sphere of NBT's supervisory powers. Individual deposits at Sberbank are guaranteed by the state. With 1.5 million clients, Sberbank continues to dominate the market for individual savings, although other banks have been expanding their role. Individual accounts are freely available and have not been subject to restricted access. Sberbank is cautiously developing its lending capability, with a focus on smaller enterprises, private firms, and individuals; it sees its extensive branch network as a potential advantage in developing this market. Although the bank has been training its staff in lending since late 1992, a lack of trained staff limits its ability to make loans only from one branch in Dushanbe and one in Leninabad. Previously, Sberbank had no lending role.

The following banks all have foreign correspondent accounts and are permitted to open hard currency savings accounts: National Bank of the Republic of Tajikistan; Tajik Joint Stock Commercial Industrial and Construction Bank (Tajikorienbank); Tajik Joint Stock Commercial Bank of Social and Economic Development (Tajikbankbusiness); State-Commercial Bank for Foreign Economic Affairs of the Republic of Tajikistan; Shark Joint Stock Agroindustrial Bank; Savings Bank of the Republic of Tajikistan (Tajiksberbank); Somon Commercial Bank (Somonbank); Tajbank; Fonon Commercial Bank; and Central Asian Bank (Tajik–Cyprus Joint Venture).

## Turkmenistan

The country's financial system consists of the Central Bank of Turkmenistan (CBT) and 15 commercial banks. The CBT licenses and supervises the banks. Seven commercial banks are partially or mostly government-controlled; in addition, the government has a 50 per cent share in a joint venture with a foreign bank; and a minority share in another. Four banks are locally privately-owned, and two are branches of foreign banks. Twelve banks have general licences (two more than in 1996), allowing operations with non-residents and in foreign currencies, while two have a domestic licence only. Turkmenistan has no tradeable financial instruments and no non-bank financial institutions, although insurance companies are gradually developing.

The banking system remains heavily concentrated in the traditional public sector banks. Most banks engage in financing a specific economic sector or selected public enterprises, with competition only starting to emerge. The interbank market is small, due partly to delays in settlements. Three public sector banks accounted for 97 per cent of all commercial bank manat credit to the economy at the end of 1997, and most foreign currency transactions were channelled through the State Bank for Foreign Economic Affairs (Vneshekonombank). Reflecting the underdevelopment of the formal private sector in Turkmenistan, 96 per cent of all bank loans were held by public sector enterprises at the end of 1997.

The commercial banks play only a minor role in financial intermediation and continue to function more as administrators of public sector financial transactions. Public enterprises finance investments mainly by foreign borrowing. Manat credit is financed mainly by the CBT and is overwhelmingly (around 90 per cent) short-term (less than one year). There continues to be a general lack of confidence in domestic banks, due partly to continuing restrictions on cash withdrawals, and weakness in the currency. Savings and other deposits held by the private sector – excluding the blocked accounts of the cotton sector – increased to about 16 per cent of total manat deposits during 1997. However, this increase reflected changes brought by the agricultural sector reforms. Previously, most private sector deposits were held at the Savings Bank, but due

Exhibit 7.7
**Monetary indicators, Turkmenistan, 1994–98**

| | 1994 | 1995 | 1996 | 1997(e) | 1998(p) |
|---|---|---|---|---|---|
| Broad money M3 (end-year, % change) | 984 | 454 | 413 | 92 | na |
| Domestic credit (end-year, % change) | 915 | 405 | 1,391 | 88 | na |
| Broad money (% of GDP) | 15.6 | 11.3 | 8.2 | 11.8 | na |
| Interbank interest rate, max 30-day (% pa, end-year) | na | 55 | 121 | 39 | na |
| T-bill rate, 30-day (% pa, end-year) | 150 | 60 | 120 | 40 | na |
| Deposit rate, max 1 year (% pa, end-year) | 206 | 80 | 130 | 47 | na |
| Lending rate, max 1-year (% pa, end-year) | 300 | 70 | 200 | 48 | na |
| Consumer prices (% change, annual average) | 1,748 | 1,005 | 992 | 84 | 19 |
| Official exchange rate (manat/US$, end-year) | 75 | 200 | 4,070 | 4,165 | na |
| Official exchange rate (manat /US$, annual average) | 19 | 111 | 3,232 | 4,143 | na |
| Commercial exchange rate (manat/US$, end-year) | 75 | 2,400 | 5,055 | 5,090 | na |
| Commercial exchange rate (manat /US$, annual average) | 63 | 426 | 3,924 | 5,256 | na |

*(e)* estimate
*(p)* projected

*Source:* EBRD.

to increased competition and higher interest rates, almost 90 per cent of these are now held by other banks.

Exhibit 7.7 shows Turkmeni monetary indicators between 1994 and 1998.

## Uzbekistan

As of April 1998, there were 31 commercial banks in Uzbekistan: two state banks (fully owned by the government); three state-owned joint-stock banks; 17 joint-stock commercial banks with capital participation of the government and state-owned enterprises; four joint ventures with foreign capital participation; four private banks; and one subsidiary of a foreign bank. Twenty-eight banks were licensed to carry out foreign currency transactions, but the bulk of foreign exchange transactions were conducted by the National Bank of Uzbekistan (NBU).

The NBU, which is government owned and engages in a number of joint ventures with foreign banks, is the largest commercial banking institution in Uzbekistan. At the end of 1997, it accounted for nearly 70 per cent of total commercial bank loans and about 70–80 per cent of all transactions in foreign currency. Its dominant position is reinforced by the fact that Uzbekistan enterprises cannot hold more than one bank account nor can they operate with more than one bank. However, enterprises are allowed to keep sum-denominated accounts in one bank and foreign currency holdings in another bank. Indications are that a large proportion of balances denominated in foreign currency is held with the NBU.

Development of commercial banking has been affected in Uzbekistan by direct government intervention in foreign exchange and financial markets. In addition to the rule limiting enterprises to one account, which seriously limits competition among banks, enterprise deposits can be withdrawn only

for the payment of wages and travel expenses, in accordance with quarterly cash plans. The most important commercial banks are controlled by the government and follow the credit policies set by the Republican Monetary Policy Commission, which gives priority to sectors in line with the agricultural and industrial policies of the government. In some cases, commercial banks have assumed an equity participation in non-bank enterprises; for example, Pakhtabank established a quartz processing enterprise in 1997. Foreign trade finance is mostly a domain of the NBU, and foreign investment in the banking area not related to the NBU is limited. Although there is no formal deposit insurance system in Uzbekistan, it is implicit for state banks.

In December 1997, compulsory reserve requirements at the Central Bank of Uzbekistan (CBU) were reduced from 25 to 20 per cent of deposits. For deposits over three years, the reserve requirements were kept at 10 per cent. The liquidity impact of the measure was neutralised with the auctioning of Treasury bills (T-bills) yielding about 2 per cent higher than the rates ordinarily paid in T-bill auctions. This step resulted in an improvement in the income position of banks, since required reserves are not remunerated. Foreign currency deposits are not subjected to a reserve requirement at the CBU. During 1997, balances kept by commercial banks in correspondent accounts with the CBU exceeded by wide margins required reserves. This item includes free reserves, as well as balances deposited with the regional branches of the CBU to satisfy net liabilities that arise daily under the payments' settlement system.

In November 1996, the Board of the CBU adopted new charts of accounts for the CBU and the commercial banks. The new accounting system was introduced in March 1997 and has improved the quality of monetary statistics. However,

Exhibit 7.8
**Monetary indicators, Uzbekistan, 1994–98**

|  | 1994 | 1995 | 1996 | 1997(e) | 1998(p) |
|---|---|---|---|---|---|
| Broad money (end-year, % change | 680 | 144 | 113 | 36 | na |
| Domestic credit (end-year, % change) | na | 55.2 | 268.5 | 70.0 | na |
| Broad money (% of GDP) | 32.8 | 18.1 | 19.6 | 16.4 | na |
| T-bill rate, 3-month (% pa, end-year) | na | na | 36 | 26 | na |
| Deposit rate, 1 year (% pa, end-year) | 60 | 90 | 40 | 39 | na |
| Lending rate, 1-year (% pa, end-year) | 100 | 105 | 60 | 59 | na |
| Consumer prices (% change, annual average) | 1,281 | 117 | 64 | 50 | 33 |
| Exchange rate (sum/US$, end-year) | 25.0 | 36.0 | 55.0 | 80.2 | na |
| Exchange rate (sum/US$, annual average) | 11.4 | 30.2 | 41.1 | 66.7 | na |

*(e)* estimate
*(p)* projected

*Source:* EBRD.

commercial banks have experienced difficulty in using the new system, and only recently have the new classification of accounts been introduced in the People's Bank. In addition, risk assessment, and the corresponding classification of loans in commercial banks' balance sheets remains impaired by the fact that enterprises typically do not perform bookkeeping in accordance with internationally accepted accounting standards, and banks are inexperienced in risk assessment and risk management.

The Uzbek banking system is characterised by a small number of relatively sophisticated banks side by side with the successors of the former state banks. These former state banks are undercapitalised, have low-quality loan portfolios, and limited bank management skills. Problems for the former state banks are aggravated by the absence of adequate legal instruments, such as bankruptcy procedures, assets sequestering, as well as the method by which banking activity is taxed.

*Banking regulation and supervision*
In exercising banking supervision, the CBU relies on compulsory reserve requirements and a set of specified ratios, against which banks are evaluated once a month. Although banks broadly conform to the CBU ratios, there remain serious weaknesses that are not apparent by merely checking the required ratios.

The capital of Uzbek banks is likely to be seriously overvalued because risks and losses are underestimated, and thus the ratios are unreliable. Without a tradition of lending to small enterprises, banks tend to concentrate their loan portfolios in a limited number of large enterprises. This, together with the tradition of specialising the banking activity along sectoral lines, has prevented adequate risk diversification. Many commercial banks face serious solvency problems, being saddled with large numbers of non-performing loans and having low net worth.

A resolution adopted by the CBU in April 1997 established a timetable, with quarterly floors, for commercial banks to reach a minimum paid-in capital of Ecu2 million (Ecu1 million for rural and regional banks) by 2000. However, a presidential decree issued in August 1997 to stimulate the creation of private banks waived this minimum capital requirement for certain banks. Under this exemption, a number of small banks are in the process of restructuring.

In 1997, a regulatory framework was adopted by the CBU for the supervision of commercial banks, including procedures for the reorganisation of commercial banks; requirements for reporting to the CBU; procedures for registration, licensing, and liquidation of banks; and penalties for violation of banking regulations. A group of consultants started work in 1997 under the auspices of the World Bank and the Barents Group to advise the CBU on banking reform, with emphasis on banking supervision, rehabilitation, and banking legislation.

# The region in the international debt market

Of all the Central Asian and Caspian republics, Kazakhstan has been by far the most active in terms of tapping the international debt market. On top of two successful Eurobonds, the country has received a combination of syndicated loans, trade finance credit facilities and lending packages from the multilaterals. Total external debt, including all government and private borrowing, has increased significantly from US$1.9 billion in early 1994 to US$5.9 billion as at the beginning of 1998 (see Exhibit 7.9). Within this gross external debt, there was a significant increase in the private sector portion of debt not guaranteed by the government. This is mainly borrowing by second-tier banks and private companies. These types of legal entities only came into existence in late 1994. Debt arising out of foreign trade contracts, in particular, has increased dramatically since 1995. Exhibit 7.10 shows the structure of the country's external debt.

Compared with the CIS as a whole, Kazakhstan's ratio of external debt to GDP is moderate. Although in absolute terms Kazakh external debt is higher than that of most other CIS countries, this high absolute amount reflects the country's ability to attract foreign capital. Unlike Russia and Ukraine, Kazakhstan does not have the huge burden of financing repayment of old Soviet-era debt. Kazakhstan's external debt coverage ratio is realistic at 78 per cent of exports, as opposed to 640 per cent in Georgia or 147 per cent for Russia. Furthermore, since the beginning of 1998, the Kazakhstan government has not taken steps towards increasing its external debt. By comparison, Russia has received multi-billion dollar rescue packages from the IMF and other multilaterals, and saw a series of Eurobond issues by municipalities and corporations.

In December 1996, Kazakhstan became the first republic in the region to debut on the Eurobond market through a US$200-million issue that was well received by international investors. ABN AMRO acted as lead manager. The first tranche of Eurobonds is due in December 1999 and was placed with a 9.25 per cent annual coupon. The opening spread was 350 basis points (bps) over three-year US treasuries. Most of the buyers were specialised emerging market institutional investors from the United States (40 per cent), Europe (40 per cent) and Asia (20 per cent). During the period of this offering, the debt market for emerging Europe was especially buoyant given the success of an earlier Russian Eurobond.

In September 1997, Kazakhstan, advised by J.P. Morgan, successfully completed placement of its second tranche of sovereign Eurobonds. This tranche was US$350 million with a five-year maturity due in 2002. The annual coupon was set at 8.3 per cent. Reflecting increased optimism about Kazakhstan, the opening yield was 245 bps above US treasuries, a tightening of over 100 bps from nine months earlier.

Since the two Eurobond issues, the Russian financial crisis has caused Kazakh sovereign yields to increase significantly. However, despite the extreme caution among emerging market investors, in November 1998 a Kazakh private borrower, KKB, was able to negotiate a syndicated loan agreement worth US$20 million. KKB first tapped the external debt market with a US$100 million Eurobond issue in April 1998, just six months after the Asian financial crisis.

KKB's success in obtaining external private finance in the face of a virtual halt in investor lending to the CIS demonstrates Kazakhstan's ability to differentiate itself from the Russian economy. This differentiation is a substantial achievement given the tight correlation that most emerging Europe/CIS debt prices have demonstrated to the Russian sovereign Eurobond.

Exhibit 7.9

**Gross external debt of the CIS countries, as at January 1998**

|  | US$ billion | % of GDP | % of exports |
|---|---|---|---|
| Azerbaijan | 1.5 | 38 | 191 |
| Armenia | 0.7 | 44 | 320 |
| Belarus | 1.0 | 9 | 14 |
| Georgia | 1.6 | 32 | 640 |
| Kazakhstan | 5.9 | 27 | 78Kyrgyz |
| Republic | 1.1 | 63 | 190 |
| Moldova | 1.3 | 70 | 165 |
| Russia | 123.5 | 28 | 147 |
| Turkmenistan | 2.5 | 99 | 330 |
| Ukraine | 8.9 | 18 | 64 |
| Uzbekistan | 3.5 | 28 | 85 |

*Source:* Inter-governmental CIS Committee.

Exhibit 7.10

**Structure of Kazakhstan's external debt by type of borrower**

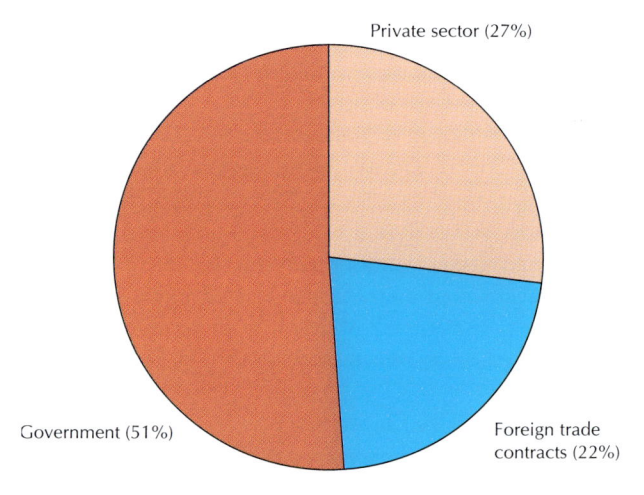

*Source:* NBK.

After Kazakhstan, Uzbekistan is the second most active player in the international debt market. However, the country has still not issued a debut sovereign Eurobond, primarily because of adverse market conditions. Although the Uzbek government has expressed interest in launching a debut issue, the Asian financial crisis in 1997, augmented by the Russian financial crisis in 1998, has created an extremely difficult climate for any CIS sovereign issue. The type of buyers who would normally take up much of any CIS bond offering – emerging market funds

*Baku skyline, Azerbaijan*

and banks with a substantial emerging market business – have suffered unprecedented losses in Russia. By the end of 1998, few of the buyers had any great enthusiasm, nor much extra cash, to place in any would-be Uzbek Eurobond.

The Kyrgyz Republic and Azerbaijan have been thought highly promising potential borrowers on the international debt market. The Kyrgyz Republic, in particular, has had opportunities to launch a debut Eurobond in the past, but instead decided to restrict borrowing to multilateral sources, which were significantly cheaper. For Azerbaijan, the collapse in oil prices and limited outlook for their recovery make it difficult and costly for the country to tap the Eurobond market in the near future. Multilateral lending and foreign direct investment in the country's oil sector, nonetheless, should provide the government with sufficient revenues for the foreseeable future.

As for Turkmenistan and Tajikistan, it may be some years before private sector institutional investors are willing to buy any external bonds. Until then, most of the lending will be in the form of multilateral programmes, project finance and secured trade finance.

# The development of the region's capital markets*

The stage of development of the region's capital markets varies from republic to republic. In some republics, such as Turkmenistan and Tajikistan, the markets are something of a formality with little or no day-to-day trading. In fact, most foreign investors are not aware of the existence of these markets. In Uzbekistan and the Kyrgyz Republic, capital market activity consists mainly of trading local T-bills. Kazakhstan

and Azerbaijan have the most developed markets.

The best all-around source of information on capital markets in the region is the Istanbul-based Federation of Euro-Asian Stock Exchanges (FEAS). It was established at the initiation of the Istanbul Stock Exchange on 16 May 1995 and reflects heightened levels of interest in Central Asia and the Caspian among Turkish investors. Currently, there are 22 FEAS member exchanges representing 6,919 traded companies with a combined market capitalisation of over US$160 billion; average daily traded value is US$350 million. In terms of seeking new investments absolutely unheard of in the main financial centres, FEAS also can provide leads on buying equities in Iraq, Iran and Albania.

Among all the nascent Central Asian and Caspian exchanges and FEAS members, the Kyrgyz Stock Exchange (KSE) may offer the most long-term potential. Although it is still undeveloped and highly illiquid, a series of proposed privatisation deals may begin to attract foreign investors, many of whom may have gained their first exposure to the Kyrgyz economy through local currency T-bills.

The number of companies traded on the KSE rose from 40 in 1997 to 47 in 1998, and KSE officials expected this number to exceed 50 by the end of 1999. In August 1998 the first foreign issuer, the International Business Bank, listed on the exchange. The KSE promotes itself to the investing public, potential issuers and to foreign fund managers, but the crisis in Russia has made this a difficult task. Nonetheless, negotiations have started concerning the establishment of exchange branch offices throughout the Kyrgyz Republic in an effort to provide local services to investors.

## Azerbaijan
### Treasury bills

The capital markets in Azerbaijan are in their infancy. The most developed instrument so far traded is T-bills, first launched in September 1996. The T-Bills are of the standard form, namely par value securities without coupons sold at a discount. The NBA acts as the agent for the Ministry of Finance in the market.

### Market mechanisms

T-Bills are sold in the primary market via auctions held on the Baku International Currency Exchange (BICEX). Only primary dealers can submit bids in the auctions, and only banks can be primary dealers. Bids are ranked from highest to lowest, and the Ministry of Finance chooses a cut-off point below which they do not accept bids. All bids above the cut off point are awarded bills at the prices at which they bid. Two types of bids may be submitted: competitive and non-competitive. Competitive bids are accepted at the price the banks bid, and may or may not get filled. Non-competitive bids are filled at the average price accepted. One or two days before each auction, the Ministry of Finance gives details about the intended issue to the NBA, which in turn gives them to BICEX, and it in turn gives this information to its members and the media. If any securities are unsold at an auction, the NBA may advertise these securities for sale in the secondary market in the days following the primary auction.

Currently, BICEX holds the depository for T-Bills, and it also settles trades of T-Bills. BICEX has an account at the NBA with a sub-account for each of the primary dealers. Each primary dealer also has an account at the NBA. At the start of the trading day, a bank will transfer the necessary funds from its account at the NBA to its BICEX sub-account. The funds in a BICEX sub-account can only be used for trading on BICEX. The auction system verifies whether a participant has sufficient funds to pay for any orders submitted. If there are insufficient funds, the orders are rejected as being invalid. In the depository, BICEX has an account for each member (called a 'sub-depository') which consists of two parts – the main section, and the trading section. Before the trading day, banks must block any T-bills they wish to trade by transferring them from the main section to the trading section. After trading, the depository informs dealers about their respective positions. BICEX forbids the short sale of securities.

The total amount of T-bills outstanding is about AZM35–40 billion (approximately US$10–12 million at the exchange rate of AZM3,500/US$1). As at mid-1998, there had been 11 auctions of one-month bills, and nine auctions of three-month bills. Generally speaking, there has been a limited issuance of T-bills given the low need for deficit financing as a result of the revenues the government has been receiving from oil-production contracts with foreign oil companies. The collapse in oil prices and expected fall in oil revenues may change this.

Initially, there were 28 primary dealers, but as at mid-1998 there were less than 10. If a bank proves inactive in the market, the NBA may retract its licence. Many banks do not find it worthwhile being a primary dealer for several reasons: the market is small; the secondary market is illiquid; yields are unattractive; and the number of auctions is small and irregular. Further, even for those auctions that do exist, the likelihood that a bid will be filled is uncertain, given the Ministry of Finance's previous desire to cap yields. In the past, yields were frequently set at 11.98 per cent or 12.02 per cent by the Ministry of Finance because it was unwilling to pay much more than the NBA's refinancing rate of 12 per cent.

Each transaction carries a stamp duty of 0.1 per cent paid by the buyer. There is also a commission paid to BICEX by both buyer and seller of 0.03 per cent. Thus, the total tax cost is 0.16 per cent of the value of a transaction. BICEX originally had a commission rate of 0.3 per cent, but this was reduced in early 1997 to 0.1 per cent, and then again in August 1997

to 0.03 per cent. Although it is tax-free for Azeri residents to invest in T-bills, foreigners have to pay a 15 per cent repatriation tax. The major purchasers of T-bills have been the Savings Bank, which has purchased up to 95 per cent of certain issues, followed by the International Bank of Azerbaijan, which has bought up to 40 per cent of some issues.

There have been concerns about the functioning of the market, notably the access permitted to foreign investors. Officially, non-residents were at first not allowed to hold the securities, although this rule was widely sidestepped. In addition, any institution applying to become a primary dealer had to have more than 50 per cent of its capital owned by Azeris. Since April 1998, however, non-residents have been allowed to purchase T-bills as a result of new government legislation. Further, any bank licensed to operate in Azerbaijan has also been allowed to become a primary dealer regardless of its ownership structure. The British Bank of the Middle East, a subsidiary of HSBC, has since signalled its desire to become a primary dealer. Previously, there was some concern within the Ministry of Finance that the huge funds available to foreign investors might allow them to determine market prices and crowd out all domestic institutions.

*Baku Interbank Currency Exchange (BICEX)*
Although Azerbaijan suffers from the lack of an independent stock market, the beginnings of an equity market can be seen in the country's currency exchange. BICEX is a non-profit organisation comprising a currency section, a credit section, and a securities department. The five largest state banks in Azerbaijan, including the ANB, established BICEX in 1993 and regular auctions for US dollars starting in late 1994. Although some stock exchanges were established before this, including the Baku Securities Exchange in 1991 and the Baku Goods and Stock Exchange in 1992, it is unclear whether any trading was ever conducted on these systems and they are not currently in operation.

The securities department at BICEX was founded in April 1996 and operates the primary and secondary market for T-bills. BICEX also operates the markets for both listed and pre-listed securities. The Exchange Council drafts BICEX regulations and has produced rules on exchange membership, securities trading, listing, and settlement procedures. In order not to slow the growth of trading on the exchange, the Exchange Council allows the shares of companies to be traded without satisfying the listing requirements. Membership of the securities department has been open since October 1996, and as at January 1997 it had 28 broker members. In April 1998 BICEX installed a computer system whereby banks can input prices directly onto screens in their offices. There are approximately 10–15 remote terminals in banks from which it is possible to deal in all the markets operated by BICEX.

Since December 1997, only two shares have been listed on BICEX: Azeri Gas Bank, and Respublica Bank. Each bank acts as the depository for its own shares, and both banks put offers of their shares for sale on the trading system. Most of the members of the BICEX stock department are banks, and they do not wish to buy shares of their competitors. All shares are dematerialised. The depository BICEX uses for T-bills is separate from the one used for shares.

In January 1998, registries of joint-stock companies were introduced, with registration of share transactions beginning in March 1998. However equity trading in Azerbaijan remains thin. The National Depository System was established by the State Property Committee (SPC) to facilitate clearing and settlement of share transactions. Currently, the SPC also licenses depository activities. So far, the most significant action taken by the National Depository System was the establishment of the National Depository Centre (NDC). The NDC is a joint stock company, 100 per cent owned by the SPC, which acts as the registrar and custodian for all privatised shares. There has only been a limited amount of trading in privatised shares through the NDC, with reportedly only 500 transactions recorded between November 1997 and May 1998.

Widespread ignorance and confusion about both the voucher trading and financial markets has restricted the development of the Azerbaijan securities market. This includes confusion regarding which authority supervises which markets, uncertainty about how privatisation vouchers will be disbursed, lack of transparent company accounts, accusations of insider activity, and abuse of minority shareholder rights.

There is a common perception that the privatisation process brought about a more unequal distribution of wealth than ever existed before (for more details on the privatisation process see Chapter 8, Azerbaijan).

## Uzbekistan

The state of development of the capital markets in Uzbekistan is mixed. On the one hand, in a relatively short period of time Uzbekistan has succeeded in creating most of the infrastructure necessary for the functioning of a capital market. Four main institutions have been established central to the operations of the securities market: the Goskomimushestvo (GKI – the State Property Committee); the Centre for the Control and Coordination of the Securities Markets (CSM); the Tashkent Republic Stock Exchange (TRSE); and the National Depository (ND).

However, on the other hand, the manner in which the Uzbek capital markets actually operate is so different from normally accepted procedures, that it is questionable whether a free market actually functions. Furthermore, the government's explicit desire to limit the speed of economic reform has meant that there is little willingness to cede control of

enterprises, or to allow share prices and trading volumes to be determined by a free market. The decision not to allow convertibility of the currency has also halted any further development of the market.

*Treasury bills*

The T-bill market trades par value securities without coupons sold in the primary market by auction at a discount. Primary dealers buy the T-bills from the central bank, which acts on behalf of the Ministry of Finance. All the auctions, trading, clearing, and settlement take place on the Republican Currency Exchange (RCE), which is co-owned by the CBU. There is an auction for three-month and six-month T-bills every month. The first three-month bill auction was held in March 1996, and the first six-month bill was sold a year later. Eventually, the government intends to issue bills of longer maturities of up to a year. Only local residents can buy T-bills.

Normally, the Ministry of Finance officially offers about UZS5.5 billion of T-bills at each auction (at the official rate of UZS210/US$1 this equals US$26 million). In practice, however, the ministry only accepts bids for an amount of securities significantly less than the total amount of securities on offer – at times as little as UZS3.5 billion. The balance of unsold securities are then sold in the secondary market the following day at prices higher than those at which bids in the primary market are accepted. The free auction process is thus essentially not used to determine yields as they are effectively pre-specified by the Ministry of Finance.

Even with this auction process, the lack of alternative investment vehicles in Uzbekistan make T-bills attractive. This is also despite the fact that they currently have a negative rate of return given the high inflation rate. Yields have fallen recently primarily because of increased demand. Enterprises do not have enough foreign currency to buy necessary supplies, and thus have an excess amount of spare sum.

The secondary market for T-bills is sporadically illiquid. There is an automated trading system on the RCE on which dealers can put bids or offers, but the amounts are frequently less than UZS10 million. Often, the market is so illiquid that it is not possible to sell at all. Non-bank participation in the market is small. In 1998, investors other than banks held only 25 per cent of outstanding T-bills. The lack of interest in the T-bill market is due to three factors: low yields as compared with the high returns possible by simply holding dollar bank notes; restrictions prohibiting banks from selling the bills to the public outside the auction; and the lack of T-bill based repurchase agreement operations between banks and the public.

*Privatisation investment funds (PIFs)*

A mass privatisation programme was started in June 1996 through the establishment of PIFs. The PIF programme had a series of goals: to accelerate the de-nationalisation of small and large industrial enterprises; to involve all sections of the population in the privatisation process using a process other than vouchers; to educate the public about the nature of markets; to facilitate the process of restructuring privatised companies via external pressure on corporate governance by the PIFs; to allow people to make capital gains; and to develop the securities market with a view to attracting foreign investors. Although the proportion of the value of the companies sold through the PIF programme compared with the total value of companies privatised has been small, the programme is important, not least because of its high political profile.

A PIF is a fund that may raise money by selling its shares (called Public Participation Shares) to the public, and then use this money to invest in privatised companies. Only individuals were initially allowed to buy the shares of PIFs. The investment strategy of each PIF must be publicly disclosed, and each PIF is required to retain a separate, independent management company to manage their investments. After establishment, PIFs were allowed to sell an unlimited number of shares during a period of six months. Following this initial subscription period, however, no further issues of shares were allowed.

## Kazakhstan

Kazakhstan is in the formative stage of defining and developing its securities market system and infrastructure. For the last few years the securities market has developed unevenly, due to insufficient legislation; lack of proper institutional infrastructure; a disconnection with mass and individual privatisation; lack of quality securities; and limited market liquidity. The professional participants of the securities market have taken several important steps to support the development of the market and intensify the activity of foreign and domestic investors.

At the start of 1997, the National Securities Commission (NSC) granted broker-dealer licences to 95 companies. Twenty-one banks were licensed as brokers. Banks can only deal with government securities and act as a corporate securities custodian. The major consolidation of the broker-dealer community occurred at the beginning of 1997, following the increase of minimum equity requirements from US$15,000 to US$130,000 in December 1996. In 1999 56 brokerage firms held a valid licence, and 24 (12 banks and 12 non-banks) of these worked as nominal holders for their clients. Deposit taking banks are allowed to hold up to 15 per cent of outstanding shares of listed companies. The NSC requires that broker-dealer activities be an exclusive operation of a licensed company. Some foreign brokerage firms have applied to the NSC to establish subsidiaries in Kazakhstan and to buy a seat at the stock exchange.

According to the NSC, in the near future three major groups will become prominent: broker-dealers owned or affiliated with local banks, foreign-owned subsidiaries/joint ventures, and independent brokers. Current brokerage firms are members of the national association of broker/dealers, the Kazakhstan Stock Exchange (KSE), and the central depository. Providing financial services in the course of the privatisation process generates significant revenues for brokerage firms. They also function as traders and financial consultants, each conducting market research.

The first independent registrar obtained its licence in 1996. In June 1997, there were 33 licensed registrars in 13 Kazakh cities. Under the law, joint-stock companies with shareholders exceeding 500 are to move their register to an independent registrar. Companies with less than 500 shareholders can run their internal registrar if they employ a licensed registrar manager. The NSC has licensed over 400 people to work as registrars.

In 1997, the government approved new regulations for licensing custodians. The NSC has received applications from some large local banks. ABN AMRO Kazakhstan, KKB, ATF bank, and Narodnyi Bank have received a custodian licence and, in the near future, may receive a global custody status. Custody licence requirements are strict. Banks functioning as custodians may also provide services for private pension funds or become involved in asset management. According to the NBK and the NSC, over seven large local banks may be able to receive the custodian licence.

The KSE was established as a closed joint-stock company in the middle of 1997. In the near future, the KSE will obtain a self-regulatory organisation licence. The government has compiled a list of 32 blue-chip enterprises, all of which will soon be listed.

The NSC is an executive regulatory body, which reports directly to the president of Kazakhstan. The NSC consists of a chairman and three executive directors – members of the commission, who have equal status and rights in making decisions in the field of securities market regulations. The NSC shares the registration of share issues with the Ministry of Justice, which is in charge of the registration of small and medium-size enterprises.

The Central Depository (CD) is a privately operated non-profit organisation. The CD settles securities transactions; functions as a safe- custody of nominee holder's securities; and performs the administration of securities held in its care. Securities are dematerialised and ownership is recorded by the records of the registrar. Settlement information is electronically transmitted from the KSE and is controlled by the CD. The NBK accepts cash payments through CD accounts. Settlement is done on a trade-for-trade basis. The CD settles corporate issues of various corporations; government T-bills issued by the Ministry of Finance; national savings bonds of the Ministry of Finance; and short-term bonds of the NBK.

To promote the issuance of corporate bonds, the NSC adopted a new regulation in December 1996. Under the existing regulations, a company's emission of bonds cannot exceed its paid-in share capital. The draft of a new company law has provisions for convertible bonds. When the law is implemented, convertible bond issuance should jump-start the corporate bond market in Kazakhstan.

The main issuers of securities in Kazakhstan are joint-stock companies privatised under the national programme of decentralisation and privatisation, newly founded joint-stock companies, and the central government. The bulk of equity securities traded on the securities market are shares of privatised state enterprises. No foreign securities are traded in Kazakhstan.

The majority of shares traded are blue-chip enterprises from oil and gas, metallurgy, mining, and banking sectors. Most of these enterprises began the privatisation process via management contracts, which were introduced in early 1995. Strategic investors now hold majority positions in the shares of most of these companies. Few of the remaining government shares have found their way to the local stock market.

Almost 170 PIFs have been registered. People were given coupons, which were not actually tradeable securities as they could only be invested in a PIF. Sixty-seven per cent of the Kazakhstan population invested their coupons in a PIF of their choice. The funds now hold shares in several thousand enterprises.

*The sections on Azerbaijan and Uzbekistan are extracts from 'The development of capital markets in Central Asia', from *Financial Market Trends*, No. 71, pp135–173, OECD, November 1998. © OECD.

# 8 Azerbaijan

## Introduction

Azerbaijan is fast becoming the business and transport hub of the Caspian. Its position on the western shore of the Caspian, poised between Central Asia and Europe, has made it an obvious conduit for crude oil heading for western markets. The capital, Baku, is subject to an influx of investment in new hotels, business centres and offices. Although the country is small, with a population of just 7.6 million, Azerbaijan is a leading player in the region.

The country's economy is forecast for continued rapid growth, high investment, low inflation and exchange rate stability in the next few years. Since achieving independence in 1991 and ending its war with Armenia in 1994, Azerbaijan has turned resolutely to the West and opened its doors to foreign investors, particularly international oil companies. The economy continues to depend disproportionately on oil: since 1995 the country has signed 14 contracts worth about US$40 billion with oil companies to exploit its reserves, but there is little prospect of balanced economic growth across all sectors of the economy. This means that the country is sensitive to oil price movements.

The country needs to make improvements in the legal environment. The European Bank for Reconstruction and Development (EBRD) has earmarked the court system, overlapping government jurisdictions and the accountability of the state bureaucracy as areas that need to be improved to sustain the privatisation process and promote the private sector. Despite the substantial oil-related revenues received by the government, the country needs to further open its infrastructure to the private sector and to investors.

## History, culture and politics

Azerbaijan gained independence on 18 October 1991 with the collapse of the Soviet Union, but many trace the country's modern day existence back to 28 May 1918 when the short-

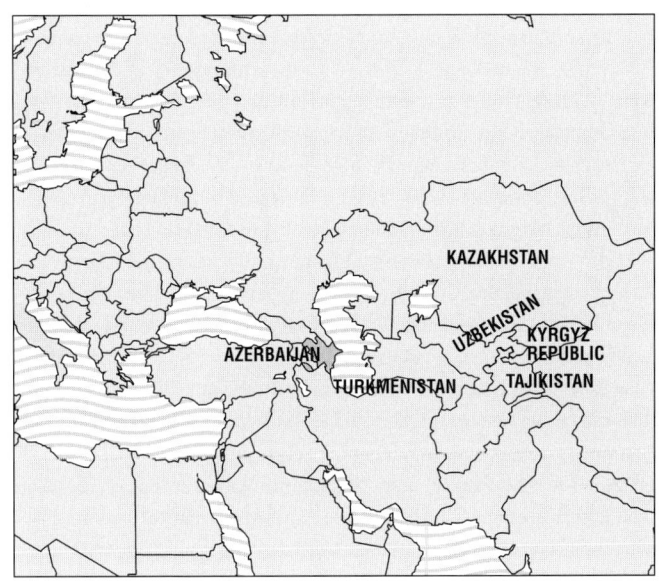

Exhibit 8.1
**Country facts**

| | |
|---|---|
| Area | 86,600 square kilometres |
| Population | 7.6 million |
| Capital | Baku |
| Other large cities | Sumgait, Gjandza |
| Currency | Manat (AZM) |
| GDP per capita (1999) | US$686 |
| Inflation, annual average (1998) | 0.9% |

Exhibit 8.2
**Political information**

| | |
|---|---|
| President | Heydar Aliyev (born 1923) |
| Elected | 11 October 1998 (for second term) |
| Term | 5 years |
| Percentage of vote | 76.11% (1993: 98.9 %) |
| Next election | 2003 |

lived Democratic Republic of Azerbaijan was established. It survived only two brief years of independence before the Red Army seized control of Baku and made Azerbaijan a republic of the Soviet Union. Today the founder of that independent state, Mamed Amin Rasulzade, is a source of national pride. Alone among the newly independent countries of the Caspian region, Azerbaijan has something of a democratic history.

Seventy years of communist rule brought the development of industry, in particular the oil and chemical industries. The break-up of the Soviet Union was, however, followed by war and instability in the Caucasus that has brought most of the country's factories and enterprises to a standstill. Azerbaijan fought a six-year war with Armenia over the region of Nagorno-Karabakh, an Armenian-populated territory within Azerbaijan that made a bid for independence in 1989. By the time a cease-fire was declared in May 1994, Azerbaijan had lost Nagorno-Karabakh and a large swathe of surrounding territory – 15.3 per cent of the country – to Armenia and was struggling to cope with nearly a million internal refugees. Negotiations on Nagorno-Karabakh have been slow.

The war led to severe political instability and Azerbaijan had three different presidents in as many years. The democratic government of Abulfaz Elchibey came to power after independence but was overthrown in a coup in 1993 after just one year in power after which Heydar Aliyev, the former communist party leader of Azerbaijan, assumed power. He was confirmed president unopposed in a referendum in October 1993 and in October 1998 was elected for another five-year term (see Exhibit 8.2), although there have been allegations of election irregularities. Aliyev has successfully led his country out of turmoil towards stability and statehood. He has repeatedly stated that his long-term aim is to create a market economy and a modern democracy in Azerbaijan. However, his opposition is getting stronger, increasingly united and determined to rule.

Azerbaijan lies at the crossroads of Europe and the Middle East, Iran and Russia and is party to the complex geo-politics of the Caucasus countries that have included separatist wars for much of the past decade. Azerbaijan is also linked to the Orient and Central Asia through its shared Caspian Basin. From the 19th century it was part of the Russian Empire before which it was ruled by Persian principalities. The people of Azerbaijan are overwhelmingly Muslim, mainly Shiite, and Turkic speaking, although some minority peoples speak languages closer to Farsi.

Azerbaijan has been an oil producer since the 10th century when, historians relate, oil bubbled out of the ground.

Since 1994 President Aliyev has capitalised on his country's oil resources and led a foreign policy of cooperation with his neighbours. He has included companies from neighbouring Iran and Russia, as well as from Europe, the United States and Japan in the international consortia that are exploring off-shore deposits, ensuring that all the major powers have an interest in the continued stability, and indeed survival, of Azerbaijan.

Azerbaijan is an energetic participant in NATO's Partnership-for-Peace programme and is pursuing membership of the Council of Europe. After ending the war with Armenia in 1994, Aliyev has stressed the need to resolve the conflict by peaceful means through the mediation of the Minsk Group of the Organisation for Security and Cooperation in Europe (OSCE). Peace talks have stalled, however.

Azerbaijan adopted a new constitution by referendum in November 1995. The cabinet of ministers and executive branch are directly subordinate to the president. The parliament, the Milli Majlis, is a single chamber of 125 deputies, but has little power without the backing of the president. It adopts the state budget but does not control its implementation. Azerbaijan has yet to hold municipal elections and regional governors are still appointed by the President.

There is a broad spectrum of political parties in opposition to President Aliyev. Key among them are the Popular Front led by former president, Abulfaz Elchibey, and Musavat led by former parliamentary speaker, Isa Gambar, which have until recently been suppressed. The two, in a coalition with several other parties, boycotted the 1998 presidential elections in protest at the lack of democratic conditions. Five candidates ran against Aliyev in the presidential elections, with Etibar Mamedov, leader of the National Independence Party, his closest rival, winning some 11 per cent of the vote. Political culture, in abeyance for five years, was once more raising its head in Azerbaijan in 1998 with the lifting of press censorship and reforms to the presidential election law.

The opposition parties are expected to gain strength over the coming years and intend to push for more political change. Their views do not differ greatly from the leadership on foreign policy and all support the broad welcome shown to western investors. They are growing more vociferous on internal issues however, in particular corruption and alleged crony capitalism that they say is creating a widening disparity between the rich and poor in the country.

# Macroeconomic profile

## Economic development

Since economic reform began after the end of the war, Azerbaijan's macroeconomic achievements have been impressive. The signing of the 'Contract of the Century', that is the first production sharing agreement with the oil consortium, the Azerbaijan International Oil Company (AIOC) in 1994 was a milestone for the country that heralded a new period of political and economic stabilisation.

Exhibit 8.3
**Inflation, (%), 1994–98**

| | 1994 | 1995 | 1996 | 1997 | 1998 |
|---|---|---|---|---|---|
| Inflation, annual average (%) | 1,664 | 411.7 | 19.7 | 3.5 | 0.9 |
| Inflation, end year (%) | 1,788 | 84.5 | 6.5 | 0.4 | 3.9 |

*Source:* EBRD.

## Inflation

Hyperinflation was brought under control with tough action to stop unsustainable budget deficits and uncontrolled extension of bank credit to state enterprises. From a high of about 1,800 per cent in 1994, the inflation rate was reduced to zero at the end of 1997 and has been close to zero in 1998 (See Exhibit 8.3). The depreciation of the national currency was reversed and, since 1995, the manat has begun to appreciate against the dollar.

## Price controls

Price controls are now limited to public utilities and rents following the liberalisation of producer prices in agriculture. However, the concentrated nature of industrial structures and the marketing of agricultural produce through a single state-owned entity have dampened price competition. In 1998, a new law on competition was being prepared with the help of the EU.

## The budget deficit

In November 1997, Azerbaijan introduced a Treasury (that is, a single government bank account) in order to achieve better control of government expenditure. The budget deficit in 1997 was less than 2 per cent of GDP, down from 10.3 per cent in 1994. However, it has since risen to a predicted 3.7 per cent of GDP for 1998. High oil investment proceeds have helped keep the deficit from rising still further.

Exhibit 8.4
**Government accounts, 1997–99**

| | 1997 | 1998 | 1999 |
|---|---|---|---|
| Current account (%) of GDP | −23.8 | −33.7 | 33.4 |
| Fiscal balance (%) of GDP | −2.9 | −4.0 | −3.0 |

*Source:* ABN AMRO.

## Fiscal policy and the social sector

The government has implemented a series of fiscal reforms to bring all government accounts into one Treasury account in line with recommendations from the IMF. According to the EBRD, tax administration has been strengthened but collection rates are as low as 50 per cent for some taxes and total revenues amounted to only 18 per cent of GDP in 1997. So that oil revenues do not lead to excessive appreciation of the currency, the government has committed itself to keeping oil-related revenues separate from its general expenditure.

Significant budgetary arrears are owed to public utilities. There are also serious social problems stemming from the war. Among these problems are 800,000 internally displaced persons and a high unemployment rate of 19 per cent, according to the EBRD. The World Bank is helping to finance the rehabilitation of areas worst affected by the war.

The charm of Baku's Old City and turn of the century architecture hides many basic problems in housing, water, sanitation and power. The EBRD and the World Bank are providing loans to help upgrade power stations and improve the water supply to 2.5 million people in the city and its suburbs, which has deteriorated sharply in the past decade. Much of the country experiences power shortages in the winter months, and even householders in Baku suffer power cuts daily. Some 40 per cent of Azerbaijan's power generating equipment is worn out and needs to be replaced. The government has also marked as a priority telecommunications, which are clearly inadequate for the country's growing needs.

## Government revenue from oil

The stabilisation process has been eased by payments from foreign oil companies to the government for exploration and production rights. From 1994 to 1997 the government received more than US$450 million. By November 1998, 14 production sharing agreements (PSAs) had been signed with foreign oil consortia worth some US$40 billion. The oil sector stands to benefit greatly from foreign investment and technology. The Azeri partner in each of the deals is the quasi-governmental State Oil Corporation of the Azerbaijan Republic (SOCAR).

## GDP

The sharp decline in production since the collapse of the Soviet Union and the wars in Nagorno-Karabakh and Chechnya has been arrested and the economy began to show growth in the second half of 1996. Real GDP growth reached

*Nizarmi Museum of Literature, Baku, Azerbaijan*

Exhibit 8.5
**Economic structure**

|  | 1997 | 1998 | 1999 |
|---|---|---|---|
| Nominal GDP (US$ billion) | 3.8 | 4.1 | 4.4 |
| Real GDP (% change) | 5.8 | 5.5 | 3.5 |
| Industrial output (% change) | 0.2 | 2.0 | 4.0 |

*Source:* ABN AMRO.

5.8 per cent in 1997 and 5.5 per cent in 1998. Growth for 1999 was estimated to be 3.5 per cent (see Exhibit 8.5). Wages and social benefits remain at low levels compared with other countries of the Former Soviet Union (FSU) but have begun to rise in real terms. More than 60 per cent of the population are estimated to live below the poverty line as defined by the World Bank.

The resumption in growth has been driven by the strong investment activity in the oil sector, which has also aided a recovery in the trade, construction and service sectors. Agriculture has finally shown the first signs of growth in 1998 after seven years of decline, with the elimination of price controls and the dissolution of state farms.

### Foreign exchange reserves

Gross foreign exchange reserves have increased from almost zero at the end of 1994 to US$570 million in 1998. Reserves for 1999 were estimated to be US$700 million, equivalent to import cover of 3.7 months (see Exhibit 8.6) At the time of independence Azerbaijan had almost no external debt. In 1999 its external debt was estimated to represent about 23 per cent of GDP. The IMF approved two credits for Azerbaijan for a term of 10 years in 1996; an Enhanced Structural Adjustment Facility (ESAF) of US$135 million and an Extended Fund Facility (EFF) of US$84 million. As of late 1998, World Bank/International Development Association Commitments in Azerbaijan totalled US$289.7 million for eight projects, of which US$130.9 million had been disbursed. As at 30 June 1998, the EBRD had agreed to forward US$145.2 million to finance five infrastructure projects.

Exhibit 8.6
**Foreign reserves, 1997–99**

|  | 1997 | 1998 | 1999 |
|---|---|---|---|
| Foreign reserves (US$ million) | 466 | 570 | 700 |
| Import cover (months) | 4.1 | 3.9 | 3.7 |
| Total debt/export ratio | 0.7 | 1.0 | 0.9 |

*Source:* ABN AMRO.

# Privatisation

Azerbaijan's government continues to debate how to privatise state-owned assets. The private sector was expected to account for around 60 per cent of GDP at the end of 1998 having accounted for just 24 per cent in 1993. The test for Azerbaijan in the next few years is to push further ahead with structural reforms and ensure that stabilisation is turned into balanced growth that benefits the private sector. The government has declared this a priority but there is a sense that the pace of reform slowed in 1998, perhaps because it was an election year or because impetus has been lost as the decisions become tougher.

Privatisation of small businesses has moved ahead rapidly with 80 per cent privatised by late 1998. By mid-year 2000, the government aims to have privatised 70 per cent of the 3,200 medium- and large-scale enterprises that have a book value of over US$12 billion. This will include all sectors, with the exception of natural resources and some infrastructure such as roads and railways. Voucher auctions for medium-scale enterprises are going ahead (see below) and tenders for larger-scale ones, including key companies in the telecommunications and oil industries, are being prepared, although they are behind schedule. The first auction was held in August 1997, and by June 1998 711 companies had been privatised.

A small number of strategic enterprises, such as the petrochemical industries, banking and infrastructure, are to be sold through investment tenders. These will be selected by the president. In November 1998, the government sold 20 per cent of the International Bank of Azerbaijan, the strongest bank in the country, to the EBRD. Another 25.2 per cent is now slated to be sold for cash in a tender open to all investors.

The government was also expected to announce its 1999 privatisation schedule in February with mounting speculation that SOCAR will be included in the list. SOCAR has signed oil deals worth US$40 billion in the past nine years. Azerbaijan's telecommunication operations are under consideration for privatisation, although they are still regulated in conjunction with the transport sector. The IMF has mentioned that its US$100 million credit facility will in part be tied to how the new privatisation programme is written and implemented.

According to Global Securities, the following enterprises are in the current draft schedule: Aztelecom; Azerigas SOCAR; Azerengergy; Caspar (Caspian Shipping Company); Azal (national airline); Azersigorta (national insurance company); and Azerbalik (national fishing company).

It is also likely that the four publicly owned banks will be sold, although some changes in the privatisation law for 1995–98 will be necessary before this can begin. A new law for 1999–2000 is due.

The government expects to raise substantial revenues from privatisation in 1999.

Despite the advances, the privatisation programme has been widely criticised for its lack of transparency. There have also been allegations that auctions have been fixed.

## Privatisation vouchers and the State Property Committee (SPC) [1]

The government clearly wants to retain voucher privatisation as an integral part of its programme. However, there is increasing pressure to raise cash to finance the budget deficit.

Although privatisation was first considered in Azerbaijan at the end of the Soviet era in 1991, the first implementation programme was not drawn up until 1995. This programme proposed a privatisation plan for 1995–98, and established the SPC as being the entity officially responsible for privatising state assets.

A mass privatisation voucher programme was initiated in March 1997 with the aim to distribute to every person in the country a book of four vouchers that could be used to purchase assets being sold. Voucher books were distributed primarily through the Savings Bank. A total of 8 million voucher books were issued, of which 7.2 million were claimed. The vouchers expire in August 2000.

Vouchers may be sold or presented for payment at privatisation auctions. There are three ways to sell vouchers: through the four major licensed broker-dealers; through the voucher shops; or on the black market. All four brokers act on an agency basis and do not actually make a market in vouchers. It is estimated that as of mid-1998, approximately US$300 million had been invested in vouchers from outside Azerbaijan – primarily from specialised institutional investors, who have bought about 5.5 million books.

At the start of the privatisation programme, the SPC optimistically estimated the total value of all state assets to be privatised at about US$6.5 billion. With 8 million books of vouchers outstanding, the SPC therefore valued each book at about US$800. The market, however, was far less generous with their valuation. In early 1997, the first traded price for each book was only US$100. By mid-1997, the price fell to US$10 and then rose to US$70 by mid-1998. The market remains highly illiquid.

## Enterprise reform

Corporate governance in the privatised sector is weak and there are claims that privatisation has played into the hands of enterprise insiders leaving companies with little control by outside shareholders. The EBRD points out that the lack of a securities market hampers the development of good corporate governance by limiting market discipline and the tradability of shares in privatised firms. Residual interference in large privatised enterprises remains a problem, as do arrears.

Inter-enterprise arrears of US$10.5 billion were more than double GDP of US$4.2 billion in 1998.

## The new bankruptcy law

Azerbaijan adopted a new law on bankruptcy in June 1997. However, this has so far had only limited affect. Bankruptcy procedures cannot be undertaken against companies that are to be privatised, while elsewhere in the sector industries are kept going by de facto subsidies from the public utilities. According to the EBRD, utility prices at least cover operational costs, but arrears on payments for electricity, gas and water are rising. These stood at 3.9 per cent of GDP by the end of 1997, up from 3 per cent a year earlier.

## Public sector reform, tax and regulation

There remains an urgent need for public sector reform and also reform of the regulatory and taxation frameworks. As in other FSU republics, corruption is impeding normal business activity and beginning to deter foreign investment, especially in the non-oil sector. The country is set to receive substantial capital inflows with the development of its oil sector over the next decade. The volume of money flowing into the country represents a danger to the economy. Economists warn that Azerbaijan is exhibiting symptoms of the 'Dutch disease' that has plagued many countries experiencing an oil boom. Large increases in investment and consumption, rapidly rising wages and an appreciating real exchange rate create difficult conditions for industries outside the oil sector, in particular export companies.

## Non-oil industries

In addition to oil- and mineral-based industries, Azerbaijan's main industries include chemicals, textiles and fishing. Azerbaijan's long-term economic success will depend not only on oil developments and good macroeconomic management, but also on substantial investment outside the oil sector. Non-oil-related investment has started to increase. In 1997–98, total foreign direct investment (FDI) was over US$1 billion, according to the EBRD. Of this, more than half went to non-oil related sectors such as textiles and food processing. Examples of investment outside the oil sector include several cotton factories that were sold by the government to Turkish investors and the Gjandza beer factory that was sold to French investors.

# Natural resources

Azerbaijan's estimated oil reserves of 30–50 billion barrels are the third largest in the world, but there are still difficulties in dividing up the oil wealth under the Caspian Sea with its

*Top: Baku Panorama*
*Bottom: Azpetrol, Baku*

neighbours. With 14 PSAs signed in the past four years and several more in preparation, Azerbaijan is hoping to boost its hydrocarbon production from 9 million tonnes in 1997 and 6 billion cubic metres (Bcm) of gas to about 50–60 million tonnes of oil and about 14–15 Bcm of gas a year by 2005. That would put the country into the league of North Sea oil producing countries.

The country has a long history of oil production. By 1901 Azerbaijan was producing nearly half of the world's oil (11 million tonnes a year, compared at the time with the United States' 9.1 million tonnes a year). In 1925 an oil pipeline from Baku to Batumi on Georgia's Black Sea coast was completed to take Caspian crude to Europe. The oil industry was nationalised

under the Soviet Union and after a sharp fall production reached its peak of 23 million tonnes a year during World War II.

Post-war development saw the building of the extraordinary Oily Rocks complex, a network of offshore platforms connected by kilometres of tarmac roadways, spanning out from a landfill area where 2,000 workers live in concrete apartment blocks on the sea. A feat of Soviet large-scale engineering and possible because of the abundance of Soviet steel, Oily Rocks produced 22,000 tonnes of oil a day during the 1960s and 1970s. Today Oily Rocks may look obsolete but it still lies over 30 million tonnes of oil. Likewise, Guneshli, a field lying in shallow water beyond Oily Rocks, is still producing 75 per cent of Azerbaijan's annual production after nearly 20 years in development.

Development of this sector is ongoing, but transportation remains a problem. The oldest field Bibi Eibat, where Baku's first gusher was discovered in 1873, is still operating today, dotted by nodding donkeys and old iron derricks. Much of the Abseron Peninsula, the curved hook of land that juts into the Caspian Sea around Baku, is covered with oilfields. There are 37 onshore and 17 offshore oil and gas fields still being worked, of the total of 67 discovered. Most are in an advanced stage of development, however, and show reduced output. Due to ageing equipment and lack of investment in latter years, Azerbaijan's oil and gas production has declined over the past decade.

Despite the long history of oil production here, there remain many more structures to be explored and tapped. Azerbaijan's current proven recoverable oil reserves are about 7 billion barrels. Estimates of total reserves are 30-50 billion barrels of oil. Most of that potential lies offshore in Azerbaijan's section of the Caspian Sea and has been the target of foreign oil companies' investment. SOCAR has identified 145 structures under the sea, only 17 of which are being developed so far. SOCAR is also intent on boosting onshore production and has said exploration of new onshore fields will be a priority in coming years.

In addition to oil and gas, Azerbaijan's mineral resources include iron, aluminium, zinc, copper, arsenic, molybdenum, marble and clay. Small reserves of gold lie in the occupied Kelbajar region and are currently being extracted by Armenia. A US consortium signed a contract in 1997 with the state-owned company, Azergyzyl, to mine nine other deposits of metal ores, among them gold, silver and copper. There are also large reserves of iron ore (estimated at 200–250 million tonnes) and aluminium ore in the Dashkesan range of mountains in western Azerbaijan, although extraction has been halted for several years.

## Formation of the AIOC

In 1994 after ending the war in Nagorno-Karabakh, Azerbaijan signed its first PSA with foreign oil companies to develop three offshore oilfields at Azeri, Chirag and deep-water Guneshli. Twelve companies from eight countries eventually formed the Azerbaijan International Operating Company (AIOC) to exploit the estimated 3–5 billion barrels of oil reserves. BP–Amoco now holds the largest share with 34 per cent, and the SOCAR holds 10 per cent. Other partners are US companies Unocal (10 per cent), Exxon (8 per cent), Pennzoil (4.8 per cent), Norway's Statoil (8.5 per cent), UK's Ramco (2 per cent), Lukoil of Russia (10 per cent), the Turkish Petroleum Company (6.75 per cent), Itochu of Japan (3.9 per cent), and Delta Oil Company of Saudi Arabia (1.7 per cent). The estimated total investment is US$8–US$10 billion.

The consortium produced its first oil in November 1997 and began exporting via the newly refurbished pipeline running from Baku through Russia to the Black Sea port of Novorossiisk. By mid-1998 production had reached 70,000 barrels a day, on its way to the goal of 800,000 barrels a day by 2005. However, in the light of the low price of oil, the consortium's plans for the next phase that will upgrade production to 300,000 barrels a day have been delayed. There are also issues raised by the merger of the AIOC's two largest shareholders, BP and Amoco.

Following the AIOC deal, came another signed in 1995 by the Caspian International Petrol Company (CIPCO) consortium led by Pennzoil, Lukoil and Agip, and which includes SOCAR, to explore and develop the Karabakh field. At the end of 1998, two attempts to find oil in the Caspian Sea's Karabakh oil field were disappointing. Two more agreements were signed in 1996: Shakh–Deniz led by the BP–Statoil alliance, which included Iran's Oil Industries and Engineering Company but no US presence; and the North Abseron Operating Company led by Amoco, Unocal and Itochu. SOCAR, which drafts and negotiates the terms of the agreements, stepped up the pace in 1997 and 1998, signing five more PSAs each year.

Exploratory results of the first two consortia to follow the AIOC have been disappointing. The agreements are designed for the development of oil, but the first wells have revealed mostly gas and some condensate, and at low volumes. There is some doubt that the fields will be declared commercial. All eyes in Baku are now on Shakh–Deniz, which commenced drilling its first exploratory well deep offshore in the autumn of 1998.

The production of natural gas is set to become more important in Azerbaijan. The associated gas from the offshore fields will be significant, with the AIOC expected to boost output beginning in 2005 to 13.4 Bcm. US company Exxon and SOCAR are also preparing to develop the Nakhchivan field, which has an estimated 25.5 Bcm of reserves. Gas production currently falls short of national demand.

*International Bank of Azerbaijan, Baku*

## Oil services and infrastructure

Lack of infrastructure could stall Azerbaijan's oil boom. The country's infrastructure needs to be upgraded or renewed to cope with the rapid development of the big oil investments. Although Baku was the centre of the Caspian Sea's oil industry, with the bulk of the machine and shipbuilding facilities, its facilities and machinery, including the rigs, supply ships and pipelines, are becoming obsolete and dangerous. The Caspian's landlocked location has meant bringing in rigs from outside is impractical so the foreign oil companies have started almost from scratch, stripping and rebuilding from the base Azerbaijan's old rigs, platforms and the shipyards to build them in.

The AIOC's Chirag-1 platform was completely rebuilt to western standards, as was the Dada Gorgud, an old Western Pacesetter rig, until recently the only working rig in Azerbaijan. Its use is shared by a rig-club of four consortia who are taking it in turns to drill their exploratory wells. The AIOC has also upgraded the crane ship Azerbaijan, the pipe-laying ship Israfil Guseinov, supply ships and mother ships, investing a total of US$1 billion. In October 1998, the Shakh-Deniz consortium completed a total rebuild of Shelf 5, a semi-submersible drilling rig, now renamed Istiglal and transformed into a world-class rig capable of drilling in 700 metres of water to a reservoir depth of 7,000 metres. The rebuilding cost about US$210 million and an additional US$15 million was spent on upgrading the shipyard. The completion of Istiglal is an important addition to the country's assets.

With the two rigs Dada Gorgud and Istiglal, Azerbaijan is by far the best equipped of the Caspian littoral countries. It has a further four jack-up rigs for shallow-water drilling, and another two semi-submersible rigs, all of which will need similar rebuilding to bring them up to western standards. Lukoil is meanwhile completing Shelf 7, a semi-submersible under construction in the Russian port of Astrakhan. Lukoil has also brought in another rig from Bahrain and is reassembling it in Astrakhan.

As with the country's rigs, there is a shortage of choice in virtually every other aspect of the oil industry. Caspian Geophysical, an Azerbaijan–US joint venture, was formed in 1993 to offer modern geophysical services to foreign oil companies and remains the only company in Azerbaijan providing seismic exploration services. The company owns two specialised vessels, including the flagship research ship, the Baki, now equipped to undertake 3-D seismic survey work.

Oil companies are building new facilities as they require them. The AIOC built a new terminal at Sangachal, south of Baku, where crude from Chirag arrives onshore. Pennzoil has installed a gas compressor station at Oily Rocks which is already handling associated gas from surrounding oilfields, including the AIOC's Chirag, before sending it to shore.

## Pipelines

Transportation of oil to the international market is one of the most consuming problems in Azerbaijan and for the whole Caspian region. Azerbaijan was already linked into the Soviet pipeline system and the first obvious option was to transport oil via Russia. The AIOC invested US$2.4 million in the repair of the so-called 'Northern Route', a pipeline running from Baku through the troubled region of Chechnya to the Russian port of Novorossiisk on the Black Sea (for maps of the pipelines see Chapter 6, Energy transport and pipeline politics). The AIOC is also constructing a second pipeline on the Northern Route that bypasses Chechnya altogether, and instead passes through Dagestan to the north. Surveys were completed in 1998 and constuction is reported to have begun. The AIOC is also building a 'Western Route', from Baku across Georgia to the Black Sea terminal of Supsa, again

bypassing Russia, at a total cost of US$290 million. The first oil was expected to flow along this pipeline in 1999. Together the three pipelines, with some expansion, should be able to pump 400,000–500,000 barrels a day. The volumes expected to flow from Azerbaijan are, however, likely to rise well above that within the next decade. The AIOC alone expects to be producing 800,000 barrels a day by 2005.

A fourth larger pipeline, known as the 'main line', is planned to carry the bulk of Azerbaijan's oil, and possibly also crude from Kazakhstan and Turkmenistan, out to the international market. The route has been the cause of much strategic and political manoeuvring as governments have lobbied for their preferred routes and oil companies have sought the most economically sensible. The eventual route is likely to shadow the Baku–Supsa line, hence avoiding both Russia and Iran, branching down into Turkey to the Mediterranean port of Ceyhan. The pipeline will be designed to carry one million barrels a day, and is costed at US$3.3 billion. It will take five years to build, with an estimated completion date of 2003. In October 1998 Turkey, Uzbekistan, Azerbaijan, Kazakhstan and Georgia signed the 'Ankara Declaration', pledging their support for the route. The United States has pledged US backing for the pipeline and has offered an aid package (see Chapter 6, Energy transport and pipeline politics).

An oil shipment terminal at Dyubendi on the outskirts of Baku has also been developed to handle Kazakh oil arriving across the Caspian by tanker and being shipped on to Georgia's Black Sea coast by rail. About 2.5 million tonnes were shipped this way in 1997 and Kazakhstan is negotiating with Azerbaijan to increase that figure to about 15 million tonnes in the future, adding volumes for Azerbaijan's pipelines.

With these projects under way, and its oil already reaching western markets, Azerbaijan has surmounted its biggest obstacle and proved it has an export system that works. But there have been painful lessons along the way. The Baku–Supsa line and Shelf 5 cost nearly twice as much as originally budgeted for. Azerbaijan is pushing for companies to upgrade much of the rest of its infrastructure and build all future rigs and platforms in the country, but so far does not have the shipyards and infrastructure to support a significant increase in work.

## Transport

Demands on transport infrastructure have severely stretched the country. Airports, port facilities, rail and road links and distribution facilities are all badly in need of investment and development. The railways are the main source of transport for freight and virtually doubled their freight-handling volumes between 1996 and 1997.

Baku airport, which now handles flights from all over the Commonwealth of Independent States (CIS), western Europe and the Middle East, is being modernised with western funding (arranged through Greenwich NatWest and HSBC) and should be completed by mid-1999. The port of Baku has also been singled out for development as a key element of the logistics corridor for trade moving westwards from the region.

# Finance

## Banking

### Foreign banks[2]

There are 12 banks with foreign capital, the most active of which are British Bank of the Middle East, a subsidiary of HSBC, Rossiyskiy Kredit Bank, Most Bank and Azer Turk Bank. The banking law allows the central bank, the National Bank of Azerbaijan (NBA), to set a limit of 30 per cent on foreign capital in the banking system. There is some speculation that this may change with the pending privatisation of domestic banks that need to be recapitalised. Foreign banks face restrictions in obtaining licences and cannot receive a licence for investment banking.

Foreign-owned banks face additional obstacles. In particular, they must seek approval to increase their statutory capital, which in total is limited to 30 per cent of capital in the system. The current ratio is close to 20 per cent. Several foreign-owned banks have had their requests for capital increases denied or have had increases permitted far below the amount requested. In addition, if neither the director nor one of the deputies of a proposed bank is an Azeri citizen, the licence can be refused. The licensing regulation also requires that foreigners seek NBA permission to buy issues of new share capital of banks in Azerbaijan.

The authorities argue that these restrictions protect domestic banks, which suffer from a lack of banking skills and a poor financial situation. However, a foreign presence could bring gains in terms of improved banking services, increased

confidence in the banking system and more efficient mobilization of savings. Strong and able domestic banks would find their niche and survive.

### Domestic banks

The four main state banks – Prominvest, Agroprom, Savings Bank and the International Bank of Azerbaijan (IBA) (formerly the Azerbaijan branch of the Soviet foreign trade bank, Vnesheconombank) – account for 85 per cent of total assets. The four are currently being reorganised and prepared for privatisation, and the state will take over unrecoverable loans in their portfolios. IBA, which dominates import and export operations in Azerbaijan, was the first to be privatised when the EBRD took a 20 per cent stake in November 1998. (For details of the restructuring of state-owned banks, see Chapter 7, Banking and Finance under the section 'Azerbaijan'.)

## The stock exchange

A Law on Securities and Stock Exchanges was passed in 1997, but the establishment of stock markets and security exchanges has barely begun. Securities are almost non-existent, except for a small amount of Treasury bills (T-bills). Reforms are needed to develop wider markets in foreign exchange, credit, government securities and eventually in corporate securities. There are no private pension, investment or mutual funds in Azerbaijan, although private foreign insurance companies are starting to operate.

## The Baku Interbank Currency Exchange (BICEX)

BICEX determines the official manat exchange rate, based on a weighted average of exchange rates quoted by those commercial banks that are authorised to deal in foreign exchange. In practice it is dominated by the NBA and IBA. In addition to BICEX, there are a multitude of exchange offices that deal in cash exchanges.

## Treasury bills[3]

The capital markets in Azerbaijan are in their infancy. The most developed instrument so far traded is T-bills, first launched in September 1996. The T-Bills are of the standard form, namely par value securities without coupons sold at a discount. The NBA acts as the agent for the Ministry of Finance in the market.

The total amount of T-bills outstanding at mid-1998 was about AZM35–40 billion (approximately US$10–12 million at the exchange rate of AZM3,500/US$1). There had been 11 auctions of one-month bills, and nine auctions of three-month bills. There has generally been a limited issuance of T-Bills given the low need for deficit financing as a result of oil revenue. The collapse in oil prices and expected fall in oil revenues may reverse this. (For details of market mechanisms see

---

Exhibit 8.7
**Top 10 banks by assets (US$ million), 1998**

| | |
|---|---|
| International Bank of Azerbaijan | 274 |
| Agroprombank | 182 |
| Prominvestbank | 145 |
| Savings Bank | 42 |
| BBME (*) | 35 |
| Post Bank | 17 |
| Azerdemiryolbank | 13 |
| Arkobank | 12 |
| Rabitabank | 9 |
| Most Bank(*) | 8 |
| * Foreign owned | |

*Source:* Thomson BankWatch.

---

Chapter 7, Banking and Finance, under the section 'Azerbaijan'.)

## Trade

Azerbaijan has reoriented its trade significantly since gaining independence, moving away from traditional trading partners in the FSU. Much of this was forced by the breakdown of the payments system and inter-enterprise arrears, but the real test for Azerbaijan came in 1994 when Russia closed its borders with the South Caucasus during the war in Chechnya. When the border reopened in 1996, the CIS accounted for only 46 per cent of Azerbaijan's exports and 35.4 per cent of its imports, compared with 94 per cent and 80 per cent respectively in 1991.

As of the end of 1997 Russia still accounted for 23 per cent of Azerbaijan's exports and fewer than 50 per cent went to FSU countries. Trade with Turkey and Iran have both become significant with exports to Iran overtaking exports to Russia in 1997.

Azerbaijan is moving towards the goals set for WTO membership. Most foreign trade restrictions have been removed and some of the state monopolies have been disbanded. In 1997, average tariffs were standardised at 15 per cent, 5 per cent and zero for consumer goods, intermediates, and most capital goods respectively. The country has liberalised its foreign exchange regime, has cancelled all restrictions on payments and money transfers in current transactions and, with the World Bank and IMF, has been working on a new foreign trade charter in line with WTO requirements. The NBA is expected to finalise its arrangements to comply with Article VIII of the IMF, which guarantees current account convertibility. A reorganised Ministry of Trade and Foreign Relations is in charge of enforcing trade policies and rules and is preparing Azerbaijan's application for membership of the WTO.

Azerbaijan's main exports are oil products, chemicals and textiles. Principal imports are food, machinery and equipment. Azerbaijan is largely self-sufficient in basic foodstuffs but is dependent on imports for grain and many processed foods.

Exhibit 8.8 shows Azerbaijan's trade balance between 1994 and 1999.

## Foreign investment

The overwhelming weight of foreign investment has been in the oil sector in the form of PSAs. These are individually ratified by parliament and have the force of law. The agreements allow for the free export and import of material resources, and machinery and equipment for operations, and assure free access to existing infrastructure. They also specify tax and customs rates and so protect the foreign partners from many bureaucratic obstacles that others encounter. The Law on Protecting Foreign Investment, passed in 1992, allows full repatriation of profits and guarantees compensation in case of expropriation equal to the amount of the foreign investment. Companies with more than 30 per cent of foreign capital do not require a licence to export their goods. The Law also includes certain tax incentives that reduce corporate taxes on foreign shares of profits and tax reductions for investment in productive capacity, research and development and environmental protection.

Foreign companies working in the non-oil sectors are, however, experiencing many difficulties from the heavy bureaucracy of regulatory bodies, complex tax laws and the inadequate legal system. Corruption is also deterring many businesses from expanding as fast as they might.

Over the four years from 1994 to 1998, 66.4 per cent of total investment has gone to the oil industry according to the Ministry of Economy. Other industry accounts for 13 per cent, the construction industry 10.3 per cent, businesses and services 5.8 per cent, and transport and communications 2.5 per cent. Outside the oil and gas sector the largest foreign investors in Azerbaijan are Turkey and Iran, followed by Israel. Exhibit 8.9 shows the net foreign direct investment (FDI) inflows between 1994 and 1999.

Foreign investors have bought 18.2 million share options during the privatisation process, acquiring a controlling interest in several cotton purification plants and food-processing enterprises and contributing US$13.4 million to the state budget.

The government welcomes FDI. One of the first legislative acts adopted in Azerbaijan after it became independent was the above-mentioned Law on Protection of Foreign Investments. The Law guarantees equal treatment to foreign

Exhibit 8.8
**Trade balance, 1994–99**

|  | 1994 | 1995 | 1996 | 1997 | 1998 | 1999 |
|---|---|---|---|---|---|---|
| Imports (US$ million) | 845 | 955 | 1,338 | 1,375 | 1,750 | 2,300 |
| Exports (US$ million) | 682 | 680 | 789 | 808 | 750 | 900 |
| Trade balance (US$ million) | −163 | −275 | −549 | −567 | −1,000 | 1,400 |

*Sources:* EBRD; ABN AMRO.

Exhibit 8.9
**Net FDI (US$ million), 1994–99**

|  | 1994 | 1995 | 1996 | 1997 | 1998 | 1999 |
|---|---|---|---|---|---|---|
| Net FDI | 22 | 282 | 661 | 1,093 | 1,155 | 1,528 |

*Sources:* EBRD; ABN AMRO.

and Azeri investors. Contract enforceability is also guaranteed and changes to legislation cannot be retroactive. Foreign participation is possible through joint ventures with local companies, wholly foreign owned enterprises, and representative offices. Participation of foreign investors in certain areas, such as the energy sector, requires prior approval of the cabinet of ministers, and in some cases, President Aliyev.

The US Department of Commerce recently published the following list of their estimate of the best sectors for foreign investment in terms of non-agricultural goods and services:

- Oil/gas field machinery: International consortia will invest as much as US$18 billion over the next 10 years to develop their offshore oil-field concessions. Much of this investment will be in the form of the purchase of machinery and oil exploration related services.
- Telecommunications equipment: After energy, this has been the leading foreign investment category. Significant opportunities continue to exist for foreign products and firms.
- Electrical power systems: Azerbaijan must upgrade and replace much of its electrical generation system over the next few years. These projects will cost about US$300–500 million and will require external financing, foreign equipment and know-how.
- Pumps, valves/compressors, and pipeline equipment: Work is under way on export pipelines. Feasibility studies to identify main oil export routes are also being carried out. The World Bank and the EBRD are financing a major project to upgrade the Baku water supply pipeline system.
- Telecommunications services: Rapidly expanding communications needs, including the development of internet access, offer good prospects for foreign companies.
- Oil, gas, mineral production/ exploration services: Seismic information is needed for much of the Azeri Caspian. Substantial interest in finding and developing additional offshore oil reserves is also growing. The World Bank is emphasizing support for rehabilitating Azerbaijan's onshore oil and gas fields.
- Food processing/packaging equipment: Azerbaijan has great potential as a supplier of fruits and vegetables, particularly in the CIS. The demand for this type of equipment will steadily increase as land reform and modernisation of

the agricultural sector takes place. The World Bank has instituted a credit line to improve Azerbaijan's agricultural productivity.
- Aircraft and parts: The Azerbaijan national airline (Azal) is in the market for new commercial aircraft and maintenance services for both its international and domestic services.
- Drugs/pharmaceuticals: Azerbaijan faces a serious shortage of basic drugs. In 1996 Azerbaijan pharmaceutical imports exceeded US$10 million. Humanitarian organisations, the government and private firms expected to increase imports dramatically.
- Water resource equipment: The World Bank and the EBRD are already upgrading the Baku water supply system. The market for water purifying equipment for this project as well as for several other regional projects will grow.

## Access to Europe

Azerbaijan is geographically and culturally the region's link between East and West. Its capital, Baku, represents the gateway to Europe for Central Asia. In the era of the Soviet Union all roads led to Moscow, as did rail and air links. With the break-up of the USSR and the collapse of much of the trade between the FSU republics, Central Asia and the Caucasus have looked to develop trade routes westwards to Europe. An east–west transport corridor is now seen as vital to the economic independence of these new republics. Thanks to the large-scale investment Baku is already attracting, it is set to become the trade and transport hub of the region.

In September 1998, Baku hosted the Silk Road Conference, which drew high-level interest from many neighbouring countries, including six state leaders. Twelve countries from Central Asia, the Caucasus and the Black Sea region signed a multilateral agreement to develop a transportation corridor along the ancient 'Silk Road' trade route from China to the Mediterranean. They agreed to harmonise customs and trade tariffs and create an inter-governmental secretariat, based in Baku. The idea has come from the EU which has already provided US$200 million to jump-start the transport corridor with several projects to build bridges and upgrade ports along the route.

Access to Europe, however, remains underdeveloped. By 1999 Baku should have a world class airport, capable of handling 5 million passengers a year, which should easily serve the needs of Azerbaijan for the next 20–25 years. But road and rail links represent even more of a challenge and will take longer to upgrade. Access to international routes are west through Georgia to the Black Sea and Turkey, and south through Iran. Azerbaijan and neighbouring Georgia are developing cooperation with the countries around the Black Sea,

Ukraine, Romania and Bulgaria, which provide their most direct link to Europe. The road and rail routes north to Russia are also a link to Belarus, Ukraine and Eastern Europe.

The unresolved conflict over the region of Nagorno-Karabakh and the Armenian-occupied territories around it are a large obstacle to Azerbaijan's developing links with Europe. The lack of a peace settlement or any progress towards disengagement of the two armies threatens the main road, railway and pipeline running westwards to Georgia and the development of trade. Armenia signed up to take part in the Silk Road project, but Azerbaijan refused to cooperate with Armenia in protest at its continued occupation of Azerbaijan's territory. Road and rail links between the two are cut, and the province of Nakhichevan is cut off from Azerbaijan proper. Turkey has also closed its border with Armenia in sympathy with Azerbaijan. The United States in turn still retains the Amendment 907 of the Freedom Support Act, which bans direct government aid to Azerbaijan because of its blockade of Armenia. The issues, seemingly intractable, will inevitably complicate regional development.

# Prospects

Azerbaijan has in the past few years secured its independence and its own survival as a republic. The level of investment already pledged for Azerbaijan will ensure its rapid development and the country has shown it can produce and export its oil to the international market. If Azerbaijan uses its oil wealth wisely, it will ensure the prosperity of future generations.

1 This section is an extract from 'The development of capital markets in Central Asia', from *Financial Market Trends*, No. 71, pp135–173, OECD, November 1998. © OECD.
2 Reasearch for banking section provided by Stephen Shevoley and Libor Slechta of Thomson Bankwatch.
3 This section is an extract from 'The development of capital markets in Central Asia', from *Financial Market Trends*, No. 71, pp135–173, OECD, November 1998. © OECD.

# Appendix: Fiscal environment

Ernst & Young

## Taxation

### Introduction

Azerbaijan's tax system has undergone a number of significant reforms in recent years and remains in a state of flux. Tax legislation in Azerbaijan changes frequently and often with retroactive effect. Although much of the new legislation has tried to emulate international and Russian practice and approaches, many of the concepts which are in use are derived from former Soviet models. Major changes are to be made to current tax legislation with the introduction of a consolidated Tax Code, which is expected to become effective from 1 January 2000.

The Azerbaijan State Tax Committee was created pursuant to the Law of the Azerbaijan Republic No. 223 'Concerning the State Tax System' of 23 June 1992 to monitor compliance, verify tax calculations and to issue instructions on the application of tax laws. The tax system has been amended on numerous occasions and remains one of the more complex and underdeveloped aspects of the Azerbaijan business environment.

There are currently two types of tax regimes that are applicable – the statutory tax regime and the oil consortia tax regime. The statutory tax regime applies to all foreign investors operating outside PSAs. The oil consortia regime applies to all foreign investors involved in PSAs, including foreign oil companies functioning as contractor parties and foreign service companies providing services to the contracting parties or the operating company.

In accordance with current legislation foreign investors may elect to carry out activities in Azerbaijan either by establishing an Azeri legal entity (an ALE) or a foreign legal entity (an FLE). Currently FLEs are allowed to carry out activities in Azerbaijan via two types of legal representation: a branch or representative office (RO). The concept of RO in Azerbaijan is different from many other countries as an RO is normally permitted to conduct commercial activities as opposed to preparatory and auxiliary ones. Both ROs and branches of FLEs are subject to the general statutory tax regime unless they are considered a foreign sub-contractor under a PSA and, therefore, taxed under the oil consortia tax regime (discussed below).

### Statutory tax regime

Each FLE engaging in activity through a 'permanent establishment' (ie, through an RO or a branch) is obliged to register separately with the tax authorities, irrespective of whether its activity will be subject to profits tax or not. Tax registration should take place within one month of the start of activities. Termination of an RO's activities should be reported to the authorities one month before the end of operations. Failure to complete tax registration is considered concealment of income and tax avoidance. The following major taxes are applicable under the statutory tax regime.

#### Profits tax

Effective from 1 January 1997, the new Profits Tax Law which was signed by the President of Azerbaijan on 18 January 1997 applies the same tax rate and principles of taxation (with the exception of some tax concessions) to all types of legal entities registered in Azerbaijan. Profits tax is payable by all legal entities (including FLEs) engaged in business activities in Azerbaijan.

Profits tax is computed on the basis of an enterprise's taxable profits. Taxable profits are generally determined based on gross sales revenue (sale receipts) less value-added tax (VAT), excise tax, and expenses included in the enterprise's cost of production and deducted for profits tax purposes. Deductibility of expenses is governed by the Cost of Production Statute and certain supporting regulations of the government and the Ministry of Finance. Many expenses such as insurance, interest, training and advertising that would normally be profits tax deductible in the West are either non-deductible or deductible within small limits. The taxable base for an RO or a branch of an FLE should include only profits derived from taxable activity conducted through that office or branch.

The profit an FLE receives from foreign trade operations is generally not subject to profits tax. In such situations, foreign trade operations should be performed exclusively on behalf of an FLE and the title should pass prior to the goods crossing the border of Azerbaijan. An RO's activities should be carefully monitored to ensure its activities do not impact the taxability of offshore sales.

The new Profits Tax Law establishes a uniform profits tax rate for all forms of doing business in Azerbaijan (including RO's and branches of FLEs) at 32 per cent of the taxable profit. Tax relief provided by the old Profits Tax Law for joint ventures and representative offices has been repealed.

In accordance with current legislation taxable profit should not include:

- Dividends and interests received from shares and other securities issued in Azerbaijan, as these are taxed at source (see discussion below);

- Income obtained from operations in retail trading, catering and social amenities as these are taxed based on a percentage of gross turnover.

The following tax concessions are available in accordance with the new Azerbaijan Profits Tax Law:

- Taxable profit may be reduced by amounts related to capital investments for production purposes and to repayment of bank loans obtained for these purposes. Production-related capital investments means capital construction in the form of the new objects, reconstruction, expansion and also purchase of fixed assets for these purposes;
- Taxable losses incurred at the end of the financial year may be carried forward for five years, and are used to offset future taxable profits;
- Contributions to various charitable bodies may be tax deductible as long as no more than 1 per cent of taxable profit is donated to such organisations.

It should be specifically noted that the above-mentioned deductions are not currently available to ROs and branches of FLEs.

## Dividend withholding tax

### Domestic corporate shareholders
They are liable to withholding tax at source of 15 per cent on income received from shares held in Azeri enterprises. The paying entity is responsible for remitting the tax to the Budget. Azeri recipients of dividend income are not obliged to include this income in their profits tax returns.

### Individual shareholders
They are liable to pay personal income tax on dividends received at the normal statutory personal income tax rates. An individual will be responsible for submitting their own personal income tax return to facilitate calculation of the final personal income tax liability. Credit is given for income tax on dividends withheld at the source of payment.

### Foreign shareholders
They are subject to dividend withholding tax at the rate of 15 per cent. This tax, however, only applies when the dividend payment is subsequently transferred outside Azerbaijan. Dividend payments posted to an Azerbaijan bank account or reinvested in the territory of Azerbaijan are not subject to the 15 per cent dividend tax.

Tax is always withheld and paid in the currency in which the dividend was originally paid out. Double taxation treaties may reduce the rate at which dividend payments are taxed. Azerbaijan does not currently recognise double taxation treaties of the FSU.

## Other withholding taxes
FLEs with no registered permanent establishment in Azerbaijan are subject to withholding tax on income derived from sources in Azerbaijan at the following rates: 6 per cent – freight income; 15 per cent – interest; 20 per cent – lease payments; 20 per cent – management fees; and 20 per cent – other income.

## Value-added tax (VAT)
Turnover from the sale of goods and services rendered in the territory of the Azerbaijan Republic is subject to VAT. This should also apply to goods imported at customs (see discussion of import VAT below). Normally, VAT paid on purchases (ie, input VAT) is recoverable against output VAT which is charged on the sale of goods manufactured or the provision of works and services in Azerbaijan. In the past, VAT paid on the purchase of fixed and intangible assets was not recoverable against output VAT but was required to be capitalised and depreciated. However, amendments introduced to the VAT Law effective from 1 January 1997 have changed this provision, and input VAT on fixed assets should now be recoverable in accordance with the general rule.

VAT is charged at 20 per cent and is calculated based on the gross sales price for goods or services. Enterprises engaged in trading activities must calculate VAT at 16.67 per cent based on the trade margin (difference between the purchase and sales price).

### Customs VAT
When goods are imported from abroad, VAT is payable at the customs point of entry based on the customs value of imported goods. Customs VAT is payable on the vast majority of goods that are imported for subsequent resale in trade operations. The Customs VAT is 20 per cent of the total customs value of imported goods.

VAT paid at customs should be recoverable as input VAT. Therefore, any Customs VAT incurred in connection with the import of goods into the territory of Azerbaijan should be indicated as input VAT on the VAT return.

Due to certain budgetary problems reimbursement of Customs VAT is not normally available in practice. However, the company may be able to offset Customs VAT due from the budget against its VAT liabilities. It is not currently clear if Customs VAT due from the budget may be offset against other tax liabilities. Thus, in the event that a decision to offset VAT against other taxes is made, it is recommended that the applicant draft and submit a letter of request to the tax authorities.

## Royalties
Legal entities and individuals involved in mineral exploration and mining in the territory of Azerbaijan, irrespective of the legal

form, are liable to pay royalties. These are calculated based on revenue from sales of the natural resources extracted in the territory of Azerbaijan, including certain areas of the Caspian Sea.

## Excise tax

Enterprises engaged in the production and sale of 'excisable' goods, products, and beverages are liable to excise duties. Excisable goods (work and services) sold and exported outside the CIS countries are not subject to excise duties. Enterprises which import goods or services for resale are required to pay excise tax on certain goods. It should be noted that excise taxes are applicable mainly to consumer goods and also to oil products.

## Customs duties

Decree No. 62 of the Cabinet of Ministers of 16 June 1997 stipulates that goods imported for resale through retail/trade outlets are subject to customs duties. The standard rate of import customs duty is 15 per cent of the declared value of imported goods. Certain goods may qualify for an exemption from customs duties or a reduced rate of 5 per cent or 0 per cent.

Importers of goods and products are also liable for the payment of a standard customs processing fee. This fee is assessed at 0.15 per cent of the declared customs value of imported goods, but not less than three minimum monthly salaries established in Azerbaijan at the respective date. The customs processing fee is payable even if goods are exempt from customs VAT and customs duties.

## Assets tax

All legal entities operating in Azerbaijan, including ROs of FLEs, are subject to assets tax. This is 0.5 per cent of the average annual balance sheet value of a company's fixed assets. The value for assets tax purposes should be based upon depreciated cost of the assets of the enterprise.

## Land tax

The new Land Tax Law was signed by the President on 18 January 1997 and became effective from 1 February 1997. Legal entities that own land plots in Azerbaijan are subject to land tax. The Cabinet of Ministers established new rates for land tax, which vary from AZM3,000–165,000 per hectare and other conditions (eg, quality of land, location of land, and purpose of use).

## Personal income tax

This is charged at progressive rates ranging from 12–40 per cent of gross income. An employee's income tax liability should be calculated according to the monthly tax rate table. The 40 per cent tier is reached at approximately US$315. The income tax liability of foreign employees and entrepreneurs (ie, persons who obtained permission to engage in entrepreneurial activities) should be calculated according to the annual tax rate table.

## Social Insurance Fund

Employers are required to pay the equivalent of 35 per cent of an employee's gross salary to the Social Insurance Fund. Employees are required to pay 1 per cent of their gross salary (this should be withheld from their salary).

## Employment Fund

Contributions are payable by employers at the rate of 2 per cent of employees' gross salaries. All payroll taxes and withholdings should be paid to the relevant budget bank accounts on the employees' pay day. A penalty of 0.2 per cent a day of the amount due to the State Budget or Payroll Funds is applied for late payment.

### Personal income tax for foreign individuals

Foreign employees employed by companies operating in Azerbaijan fall into one of two categories: tax resident or non-tax resident. A foreign employee who is in Azerbaijan for more than 183 days in a calendar year is considered a tax resident. An individual who works in Azerbaijan, but does not meet the residency test, is considered a non-resident. A resident is taxed on worldwide income. A non-resident is taxed on Azeri-sourced income.

Foreign employees who are paid from an overseas source such as a head office, are deemed to receive income from sources in Azerbaijan (as the cost of such salaries are attributable to the operations in Azerbaijan). The tax authorities are taking the view that if an FLE chooses to deduct the cost of the salaries paid to foreign employees, such salaries are deemed to be Azeri-sourced income.

This interpretation effectively means that foreign employees are subject to personal income tax from their first day of arrival in Azerbaijan, even if the employee is paid from offshore.

The taxable base should include the following: base salary and any overtime payments; hardship and cost of living allowances; other allowances; family member's travel expenses; and compensation/payment of Azeri income tax on behalf of the employee. It does not include: amounts paid by the employer for state or government social insurance or pensions; provision of living accommodation; provision of a company car; or business trip expenses.

Foreign currency income must be converted into manats using the official rate at the NBA on the date such income is received.

A foreigner expecting to be in Azerbaijan for at least 183 days during a calendar year should submit a preliminary tax declaration to the tax authorities within a month of his/her arrival in Azerbaijan. The preliminary tax declaration should reflect the total income expected to be earned in the current year.

An annual tax declaration should be filed by no later than 1 February of the year following the reporting year. This return should indicate the actual income earned during the previous year.

A final tax declaration should be filed in the year of departure when a foreigner has been in Azerbaijan for at least 183 days in such year. The tax declaration should be submitted one month before the foreigner's departure and should reflect income received until that date and anticipated income for the remainder of the year.

All income tax payments of a foreigner are made on the basis of tax assessments prepared by the designated tax inspectorate for the district or region of the taxpayer's place of residence or work. Advance payments should be made in three instalments on 15 May, 15 August and 15 November. Each payment should equal one-third of the estimated total tax liability for the year. A final tax payment should be determined by the tax inspectorate within two months of receiving the taxpayers final annual tax declaration.

Provisions of applicable double tax treaty (DTT) should override the provisions of the Personal Income Tax Law, provided the foreign individual files a formal claim for treaty protection. Azerbaijan does not recognise the treaties signed by the Soviet Union with the exception of the treaty with Germany. Azerbaijan currently has DTTs with Georgia, Kazakhstan, Norway, Pakistan, Turkey, the United Kingdom, Uzbekistan. Treaties have been negotiated with the Netherlands, Poland, China and Russia, but have not yet been ratified.

## Oil consortia tax regime

Companies operating under PSAs are subject to a special tax regime in Azerbaijan. Currently there are about 17 signed PSAs, each of which has a separate tax regime provided for by applicable tax regulations. Each PSA contains a tax article that outlines the applicable tax regime for that particular agreement. Additionally, tax protocols are negotiated with the main state tax inspectorate which provide specific guidance in relation to the payment of taxes and the filing of reports. In general, existing PSAs and tax protocols contain similar provisions, some of which are outlined below.

Each PSA normally provides tax regimes applicable to contractor parties to the PSA and to the operating company. Separate provisions are stipulated for subcontractors, in particular, foreign sub-contractors that tender for contracts in the petroleum industries. The comments outlined in this chapter are based on existing tax protocols and, consequently, are of a generic nature and cannot be directly applied to tax aspects of other PSAs which are currently under negotiation.

### Corporate tax

Tax rules for contractor parties and operating companies are set out in respective PSAs and profits tax protocols, but may generally be characterised as follows:

- The profits tax rate is fixed in the agreement and is based on the prevailing statutory rate that was applicable on the signing date of the agreement. Currently all PSAs provide for profits tax at either 25 per cent or 32 per cent depending on when the agreement was signed. Normally PSAs provide protection against future increases in the effective profits tax rate.

- Taxable income is calculated in accordance with internationally accepted accounting practices in the petroleum industry rather than in accordance with Azeri statutory accounting procedures. Losses incurred by contractor parties to a PSA during the period of preliminary exploration may be offset against future income.

- Activities which are not connected with hydrocarbon activities in and/or relevant contract areas are deemed to be outside the scope of a PSA and the related protocol tax regime. If a company is engaged in both hydrocarbon-related activities and non-related activities, separate accounting books in accordance with statutory rules must be maintained to reflect income and losses generated from non-PSA activities.

- Operating companies are deemed to be non-profitable entities which allocate both related income and expenses to contractor parties in accordance with their interest percentage of the PSA.

Similar to contractor parties (above), in the event that a foreign subcontractor is only engaged in hydrocarbon activities of an oil consortium, they are not required to maintain statutory books and records. A foreign subcontractor is understood to be an entity or organisation which is incorporated, legally created or organised outside Azerbaijan.

Foreign subcontractors are exempt from all forms of taxation at the corporate level other than the income tax withholding tax that applies under the circumstances set out below.

A foreign subcontractor that renders works or services in Azerbaijan in connection with hydrocarbon activities is subject to income tax withholding tax at source of 5 per cent, 6.25 per cent or 8 per cent of the gross contractual payment. The sale of goods or equipment and provision of services outside Azerbaijan are not subject to income tax withholding.

Foreign legal entities carrying out business activities outside the oil consortia regime are required to maintain statutory Azerbaijan books and records and comply with the statutory Azerbaijan tax regime as described above.

The tax regime applicable to Azeri legal entities (including Azeri subcontractors to various oil consortia) is the same as the statutory rules outlined above. No income tax withholding tax applies to payments to Azeri legal entities conducting PSA activities.

## VAT

Operating companies and contractor parties are subject to VAT at 0 per cent for all works, services and purchases of goods and equipment. The operating company or contractor party should provide its subcontractors with copies of their VAT certificate. These are obtained from the tax authorities in accordance with procedures outlined in appropriate VAT protocols. The certificates should be available to both local and foreign subcontractors to a PSA according to VAT protocols. VAT reports are required to be filed with the tax authorities on a quarterly basis.

## Import and export customs duties

The import of equipment, raw materials and other items to be used in connection with hydrocarbon activities for oil consortia are exempt from all import and export charges. However, an insignificant customs processing fee is normally payable at the rate of 0.15 per cent of the value of the imported goods. A PSA party must apply for a customs duty exemption certificate with respect to the relevant PSA exploration and development block. The procedure for obtaining these certificates is set out in the applicable protocol concerning import and export taxes.

## Expatriate employees' tax

All existing PSAs address the issue of expatriate employees' taxation. Normally, an expatriate employee working for an operating company, a contractor party, an affiliate of a contractor party or a foreign subcontractor will be subject to the following tax regime.

An expatriate employee who is based in Azerbaijan in connection with employment in Azerbaijan becomes a tax resident in the event that he/she spends more than 90 days in the country in a calendar year. Income related to the employment for the entire period spent in Azerbaijan (not only days in excess of 90) becomes taxable once this residence test has been triggered.

Business visitors, those employees whose visits to Baku are supplementary to their primary employment and responsibilities outside Azerbaijan, could become taxable in Azerbaijan if they spend more than 30 consecutive days in a calendar year in Azerbaijan. Taxable income would only include the income earned during the period in excess of the initial 30 days. In addition, with respect to business visitors, if more than 90 days are spent cumulatively in Azerbaijan, days in excess of

the initial 90 days become taxable.

# Accounting

Establishment, constant development, improvements and control of accounting principles is maintained by the Ministry of Finance. However, some instructions pertinent to accounting may be passed by the Audit Chamber.

Enterprises keep accounts according to standards and chart of accounts based on the Law Concerning Accounting of Azerbaijan. It establishes the detailed accounting requirements to be followed to record daily activities of the enterprises.

The law allows revenues to be reflected on a cash or an accrual basis. Expenses must be recognised on a modified accrual basis, which essentially is a provision for known costs. It requires all transactions to be recorded primarily in local currency (manats) with secondary ledgers to be maintained to reflect balances in their original currency. All foreign currency transactions must be recorded in manats using the exchange rate prevailing on the date of the transactions.

The financial report for an accounting period (month, quarter, year) is the concluding stage in the accounting process. All enterprises, with the exception of enterprises with foreign investment, must present quarterly and annual reports to the owners, state tax inspectorate, state statistical bodies, other state bodies as required by legislation (eg, banks to submit information to the NBA). Quarterly reports must be submitted within 30 days of the quarter end. Annual reports must be submitted within 90 days of the year end.

FLEs must submit an annual financial report in relation to their economic activity, budget and profits tax declaration by 15 March following the end of the accounting year to the local tax inspectorate in which they are registered. The profit tax declaration should be submitted together with a report of an independent auditor of the Azerbaijan Republic.

# Auditing

An auditing firm is required to obtain a licence issued by the Audit Chamber. The Audit Chamber also regulates format and requirements for the issue of audit reports.

Audit services in Azerbaijan usually integrate local requirements with international standards.

It is a requirement for companies with foreign investment and FLEs to submit statements audited by a registered and licensed auditing organisation to the tax inspectorate.

# 9 Kazakhstan

## Introduction

Kazakhstan is the most progressive and politically stable of the Central Asian republics. By 1997, macroeconomic stabilisation in Kazakhstan had been largely achieved, its domestic market had become liberalised and open to foreign competition, and the role of the state in the economy had been considerably reduced. The country now has a good reform programme administered by young technocrats in key positions under a strong president, Nursultan Nazarbayev, who was re-elected for another seven-year term in January 1999.

However, the country faces key challenges posed by low oil prices and high borrowing costs. Institutions like the European Bank for Reconstruction and Development (EBRD) have urged the country's leaders to push ahead with privatising blue-chip industries to ease the budgetary strains caused by such problems and those associated with the Russian economic collapse. Meanwhile the government is under pressure from its supranational advisers to deliver a realistic budget and encourage non-energy resource-based income. If it meets these challenges, Kazakhstan will emerge a powerhouse of the region.

## History, culture and politics

Kazakhstan is the largest country of Central Asia, stretching from Siberia to the deserts of Turkmenistan and Uzbekistan, and from China to the Caspian Sea. The country covers two time zones and five climactic zones and has one of the lowest population densities in the world at 6.2 persons per square kilometre. Its size defines the character of the nation: everything is large in scale, from the wealth of its resources, to the scale of mainly Soviet industrial and agricultural enterprises. But the size of the country also presents a problem in that the distances within Kazakhstan and beyond to its export markets remain a hurdle to economic activity.

Kazakh history begins with a civilisation that flourished on the Central Asian steppes in the first millennium BC and has

Exhibit 9.1
**Country facts**

| | |
| --- | --- |
| Area | 2,724,900 square kilometres |
| Population | 15.9 million |
| Capital | Astana |
| Other large cities | Almaty, Karaganda |
| Currency | Tenge (KZT) |
| Exchange rate, end 1998 | KZT85:US$1 |
| GDP per capita (1999) | US$1,580 |
| Inflation, annual average (1998) | 10.5% |

Exhibit 9.2
**Political information**

| | |
| --- | --- |
| President | Nursultan Nazarbayev (born 1940) |
| Re-elected | 10 January 1999 |
| Term | 7 years |

94

since been chequered with war. Invading hordes, including Attila the Hun, Genghis Khan and Timur the Lame (Tamerlane), conquered and ruled the region. It was the Turkic-speaking tribes that developed trade routes including the Silk Road flowing east to west and the Sable Road connecting central Kazakhstan to the Altai and south-west Siberia. Islam was introduced in the 11th century.

It was only in the late 15th century that the first Kazakh states were formed and a Kazakh people emerged, divided into hordes ruled by khans. Russian expansion reached Kazakh lands in the beginning of the 18th century. By 1848 the entire region was incorporated into the Tsarist empire and Russian settlers began arriving in large numbers.

The Soviet era brought forced collectivisation and terrible famine in the 1930s. By the time Kazakhstan became a republic of the Soviet Union in 1936, ethnic Kazakhs had become a minority in their own republic. Some 1.5 million had died and tens of thousands more migrated to China.

The Soviets imposed agricultural development and industrialisation on a massive scale and a particularly rapid development in mining. Industrial towns, railways and roads were built across the steppes as Kazakhstan became a major producer of coal, oil, ferrous and non-ferrous metals for the Soviet Union. Agriculture was developed in the 1950s under Nikita Krushchev's 'Virgin Lands' plan, which aimed to make the Soviet Union self-sufficient in food grains and meat.

Kazakhstan entered a new era in the 1990s, led throughout by Nazarbayev. A graduate from the Karaganda Iron and Steel Complex Technical Institute, he took over leadership of the Communist Party of Kazakhstan in March 1989. He soon became a close supporter and colleague of Mikhail Gorbachev and joined the politburo in 1990. During the coup of 1991, Nazarbayev came out in support of Boris Yeltsin. After the coup, Nazarbayev dissociated himself from the Communist Party of Kazakhstan, stepping down as leader and urging it to rename itself the Socialist Party.

Nazarbayev was popular at home among both the Russian and Kazakh populations and won Kazakhstan's first direct presidential elections in December 1991. Since Kazakhstan declared independence on 16 December 1991, there has been a large exodus of ethnic Russians and other non-Kazakhs. Kazakhs now represent 45 per cent of the population and Russians about 36 per cent.

Kazakhstan's new constitution, adopted in August 1995, established a presidential system under which the president has widespread power. He appoints the prime minister, the cabinet of ministers and the head of the supreme court. Kazakhstan has two houses of parliament: the Majlis, or lower house with 67 seats, and the Senate, the upper house comprising 47 seats. Members of the Majlis have extended their four-year term to five years. The next elections are scheduled for

December 1999. The senate is made up of presidential appointees. The houses of parliament rarely oppose the president's policies. Nazarbayev's term was extended in a 1995 referendum until 2000. On 10 January 1999 Nazarbayev was re-elected after parliament called early elections and extended the presidential term from four to seven years. Political parties exist but there is little real opposition or criticism in the press. Although the political climate is stable, some 50 per cent of the population live in poverty according to the United Nations Development Programme.

On 10 December 1997 the capital of Kazakhstan was moved from Almaty to Akmola, a town in the centre of the country, in an effort to unite the nation and bring the capital closer to the northern region. The capital was renamed Astana in 1998. However, Almaty remains Kazakhstan's business and banking centre.

## Macroeconomic profile

### GDP

GDP grew at 2.2 per cent in the first half of 1998 compared with the same period in 1997 and reached US$10.9 billion.

Exhibit 9.3
**Economic structure, 1997–99**

|  | 1997 | 1998 | 1999(p) |
| --- | --- | --- | --- |
| Nominal GDP (US$ billion) | 22.5 | 20.6 | 10.8 |
| Real GDP (% change) | 2.0 | 1.1 | −0.5 |
| Industrial output (% change) | 2.7 | 3.2 | 4.0 |

*Source:* ABN AMRO.

Exhibit 9.4
**Structure of GDP, 1997–98**

|  | 1H1997 | 1H1998 |
| --- | --- | --- |
| GDP |  |  |
| Production of goods | 33.5 | 30.8 |
| Agriculture | 4.8 | 3.8 |
| Industry | 25.6 | 23.4 |
| Construction | 3.1 | 3.6 |
| Services | 61.7 | 64.3 |
| Transport and communications | 11.3 | 11.2 |
| Other services | 32.3 | 34.9 |
| Gross value added | 95.2 | 95.1 |
| Net taxes on products and imports | 4.8 | 4.9 |

*Source:* Kazkommerts Securities.

95

Exhibit 9.5
**Consolidated budget deficit, 1997–98**

| 1997 | 1Q1997 | 2Q1997 | 1H1997 | 3Q1997 | 4Q1997 | 1Q1998 | 2Q1998 | 1H1998 |
|---|---|---|---|---|---|---|---|---|
| −772.9 | −1.4 | −84.3 | −85.7 | −123.0 | −561.5 | 30.5 | −318.3 | −287.8 |

*Source:* Kazkommerts Securities.

ABN AMRO figures put nominal GDP for the whole of 1998 at US$20.6 billion and real GDP growth at 1.1 per cent (see Exhibit 9.3). Kazakhstan's economy is heavily dependent on commodity prices. The fall in world prices for oil, metal and grain, which make up 75 per cent of the country's exports, has hit its resource-oriented economy hard. Since the Asian crisis began in mid-1997, failing Asian economies and the devaluation of their currencies have reduced demand for exports to these markets and reduced Kazakhstan's competitiveness against Asian producer countries.

Despite this, according to a report by Kazkommerts Securities there were significant positive changes in the structure of GDP in the first half of 1998. The share of agricultural and industrial output fell while the share of services and construction grew (see Exhibit 9.4).

After the drastic decline in output which caused the economy to shrink by 31 per cent between 1992 and 1995, the economy showed its first growth in 1996, resulting in 0.5 per cent expansion for that year and an estimated 2.0 per cent in 1997. Growth is estimated at around 1.1 per cent for 1998 and forecast at -0.5 per cent for 1999. Due to the financial turmoil of 1997 and 1998 and the slump in world energy prices, growth in Kazakhstan's economy has stalled. Until energy prices recover, the economy is unlikely to register GDP growth.

The sectors of the economy that are now performing the best are construction, trade and industry which have recently started to pick up. The growth in construction can largely be attributed to the preparation of Astana as the national capital. Industrial recovery is also under way as investment in certain sectors, particularly foreign investment in the energy sector, continues to grow.

However, the fall in the price of oil has adversely affected the country's budget revenues. In addition, heavy budget expenditure related to reforms in the pension system, spending on healthcare and the capital's move from Almaty to Astana, have added to the budget deficit, forecast at US$676 million for 1999 (see 'The 1999 budget', below). Under an agreement with the IMF, the government is committed to keeping its budget deficit to below 5.5 per cent of GDP by cutting its expenditure by 25 per cent and pushing ahead with privatisation.

Exhibit 9.5 shows the republic's consolidated budget deficit for 1997 and the first half of 1998.

Exhibit 9.6
**Gross external debt of CIS countries, as at January 1998**

| | US$ billion | % of GDP | % of exports |
|---|---|---|---|
| Azerbaijan | 1.5 | 38 | 191 |
| Armenia | 0.7 | 44 | 320 |
| Belarus | 1.0 | 9 | 14 |
| Georgia | 1.6 | 32 | 640 |
| Kazakhstan | 5.9 | 27 | 78 |
| Kyrgyz Republic | 1.1 | 63 | 190 |
| Moldova | 1.3 | 70 | 165 |
| Russia | 123.5 | 28 | 147 |
| Turkmenistan | 2.5 | 99 | 330 |
| Ukraine | 8.9 | 18 | 64 |
| Uzbekistan | 3.5 | 28 | 85 |

*Source: Kazkommerts Securities.*

## Debt

Kazakhstan's debt has increased significantly in the past five years although the ratio of external debt to GDP is modest compared with many of the Commonwealth of Independent States (CIS) countries (see Exhibit 9.6). In early 1994, the country's total external borrowing stood at US$1.9 billion, but had reached US$5.9 billion by the beginning of 1998. At the beginning of the fourth quarter of 1998, internal debt stood at about 4 per cent of GDP while external debt stood at around 15 per cent.

The IMF approved a three-year loan of US$86 million to support the government's economic programme for 1998–2000.

## The 1999 budget

This assumes that increased tax revenue will cover an increase in public spending. However, this in turn implies much better collection rates and tax administration by the newly created Ministry of Revenues. The government is unlikely to meet these targets if the economy contracts. Pressure on public spending is building considerably as there has been a deterioration in the economic and social infrastructure. There is an emergency situation building up with the spread of tuberculosis that cost the government US$6 million from May to December 1999. Exhibit 9.7 shows public expenditure for 1997 and 1999.

Exhibit 9.7
**Public expenditure (US$ billion/% of GDP)**

| 1997 | | 1998 | | 1999(p) | |
|---|---|---|---|---|---|
| US$ billion | % | US$ billion | % | US$ billion | % |
| 2.64 | 11.5 | 3.56 | 14.0 | 3.72 | 17.0 |

Source: Global Securities/1999 Government Budget.

The government expects to cover 68.8 per cent of its US$676 million deficit with domestic financing. The budget also assumes privatisation revenues of US$556 million. It remains to be seen whether investors' interest will match this figure.

## Inflation

This has been steadily declining. In 1993 Kazakhstan left the rouble zone and launched a national currency, the tenge which brought down inflation. Thanks to a tight monetary policy since 1994, inflation has been reduced from an annual average rate of 1,892 per cent in 1994, to an estimated 10 per cent in 1998 (see Exhibit 9.8).

## Current account

The external current account deficits have been fairly large in relation to GDP in recent years due, in particular, to imports of capital goods needed to develop Kazakhstan's vast natural resources. However, the financing of the deficits has not posed major problems as the country has benefited from large foreign direct investment (FDI) inflows, mainly into the oil and gas sectors (see below and Chapter 4, International relations and foreign investment and Chapter 5, Energy: the key to growth.

## Price liberalisation

Since consumer price liberalisation in 1995, consumer prices have largely been determined by market forces. The exceptions are regulated prices for utilities (gas, electricity, water), rents, transport and telephony. According to the EBRD, household rates for utilities are subsidised by the higher rates charged for business and government customers.

## The currency and central bank monetary policy

The tenge has been relatively stable. Foreign currency reserves have traditionally been higher than the monetary base and in addition to a US$440 million Extended Fund Facility (EFF) from the IMF, this has been enough to keep the currency stable. Towards the end of 1998, the foreign reserves of the National Bank of Kazakhstan (NBK), the central bank, stood at about US$1.77 billion, equal to three months of import cover (see Exhibit 9.9). In addition, there have been low levels of speculative investment and high levels of long-term investment which have helped to create a stable currency.

The tenge is fully convertible. The exchange rate is a managed float and commercial rates are determined by auction at the Almaty Financial Instruments Exchange. The NBK announces the depreciation corridor in advance, and it adopts adopts the assumptions implicit in the government budget. For example, the depreciation corridor for 1999 was made public in December 1998. This assumes a tenge/US dollar rate of 92.6 by the end of 1999. Using this forecast, the maximum depreciation for 1999 is 10.2 per cent.

The tenge, after plunging when first introduced, has held its value well over the past two years, with a volatility of 1 per cent in 1997. The Russian crisis increased the pressure on the tenge in the second half of 1998 leading the NBK to raise interest rates on two occasions. Approximately US$600 million of reserves (out of total reserves of US$1.45 billion) were spent on supporting the currency in the autumn of 1998.

Monetary and credit policy by the central bank have been tight. Broad money, currency in circulation and deposits have increased roughly at a rate of about 6 per cent per annum in recent years. The increases in the net international reserves associated with government receipts from privatisation have not had a monetary impact as the fiscal position remained strong and central bank credit to government has declined substantially. In support of its tight credit policies, the central bank has maintained its refinance rate at 35 per cent during most of 1998.

The stability of the tenge has also increased confidence in the country and decreased fears about the health of the banking sector. Currency stability contributed to an increase in deposits of almost 12 per cent and an increase in currency in circulation of about 37 per cent during the second half of 1997.

Exhibit 9.8
**Inflation (%), 1994–98**

| | 1994 | 1995 | 1996 | 1997 | 1998 |
|---|---|---|---|---|---|
| Inflation, annual average (%) | 1,892 | 176 | 39.1 | 17.4 | 10.0 |
| Inflation, year end (%) | 1,160 | 60.4 | 28.6 | 11.3 | 9.0 |

Source: EBRD.

## Other economic developments

Tax reform remains weak. The government still needs to improve tax collection, as tax revenue represents only 15 per cent of GDP. This is important because the 1999 budget assumes improved collection rates. The government has recently created a new department, the Ministry of Revenues, to improve the efficiency of tax collection.

Kazakhstan became a member of the World Bank and International Development Association in 1992 and of the International Finance Corporation in 1993. By late 1998 the World Bank had approved US$1.5 billion for 16 projects of which US$900 million has been disbursed, mostly in the form of structural adjustment loans. Kazakhstan is the second principal recipient of EBRD financing in the region after Uzbekistan. By late June 1998, US$400 million of financing had been approved, concentrating mainly on the private sector. Kazakhstan has a three-year EFF with the IMF worth US$440 million, agreed in 1996 (for further details see Chapter 4, International relations and foreign investment).

The government hopes to meet the obligations necessary for joining the WTO in 1999.

# Privatisation

Although the government launched a speedy privatisation programme in 1993 and by 1997 had privatised all small- and medium-sized enterprises, plans for privatising large enterprises stalled. However, with falling budgetary revenue and increased public spending (see above), the government has committed to additional sales of government assets. Recent deals include US$500 million invested by Phillips Petroleum and a US$1 billion soft loan from Japan in return for a stake in the Offshore Kazakhstan International Operating Company (OKIOC) international oil and gas consortium.

Despite the fact that rapid progress has been made in the privatisation of small- and medium-sized enterprises, one-third of the Kazakh economy is still in government hands. Small-scale privatisation was officially completed in 1997, by which time more than 13,000 enterprises had been sold

Exhibit 9.9
**Foreign reserves, 1997–99**

|  | 1997 | 1998 | 1999(p) |
|---|---|---|---|
| Foreign reserves (US$ million) | 1,727 | 1,770 | 2,000 |
| Import cover (months) | 2.9 | 3.0 | 3.1 |
| Total debt/export ratio | 0.4 | 0.6 | 0.7 |

*Source:* ABN AMRO.

through cash auctions and voucher privatisation. After an early focus on voucher privatisation, the government concentrated on cash sales for large-scale enterprises. By mid-1998, 1,600 such enterprises had been sold in this way with about 400 remaining to be sold. The government has retained some ownership in the health, education and social service sectors.

Foreign investors have been active in the case-by-case sale of strategic enterprises. In 1997, the government sold two oil companies, a copper plant, a manganese plant and a 40 per cent stake in Kazakhtelecom to strategic foreign investors. Although the government has sold an estimated 70 per cent of its original assets, only 30 per cent of large enterprises are held by majority private ownership. According to the EBRD the government still has 100 per cent ownership of 330 large enterprises that account for 35 per cent of GDP. Despite its active approach to privatisation, there is still considerable scope for further sales, which would help relieve the pressure on Kazakhstan's budget.

A change in government in October 1997 signalled, however, a pause in and reassessment of the privatisation process. Since then the sales of five 'blue chip' companies (two metal plants, two oil and gas companies, and Kazakhtelecom) which have been valued at US$1.7 billion have been repeatedly postponed. A decline in investor interest and the contraction of Kazakhstan's securities market since the Russian crisis in autumn 1998, are likely to postpone the sales further. Oil remains attractive as shown by the government's sale of its 7 per cent share in the Kashagan reservoir for US$500 million to US company Phillips Petroleum and Inpex Nord of Japan in September 1998.

The next stage of privatisation is likely to focus on the floatation of seven of Kazakhstan's 13 blue-chip companies not previously included in the privatisation programme through initial public offerings. Although the government had already begun to market these issues with investors in major financial centres such as London and New York, plans for floatation have been delayed mainly because of the adverse financial climate in 1998.

In March 1998, Turan-Alem Bank, the third largest bank by assets, was privatised.

The case-by-case approach has so far been effective. Power, utility and telecommunications companies, as well as those dealing in natural resources, have succeeded in attracting buyers and raising substantial revenue for the government. Kazakhstan remains the furthest ahead with privatisation in these sectors in the region.

# Agriculture

Despite a decline in agricultural production, Kazakhstan remains a major producer and exporter of grain, wool and

*Presidential Palace (left) and Parliament (right), Astana*

meat. The Soviet 'Virgin Lands' plan, which converted Kazakhstan's grasslands to cultivation and reduced livestock herds, has distorted the land use. The land is marginal with low yields, and in recognition of that, about 2.5 million hectares have been let go and returned to grassland over the past 5 years. The severe climactic conditions make for extreme variations in annual harvests. Grain production in the 1980s would vary from 5–20 million tonnes a year and reached 25 million tonnes in 1990. The 1997 grain harvest was 11–12 million tonnes. The 1998 harvest was poor at only 7.5 million tonnes. Domestic demand is 4–5 million tonnes. Export of grain is hampered by the remoteness of Kazakhstan and high transport costs.

Privatisation of farms has occurred and farmers now hold the land on 99-year leases. In the south of the country privatisation has improved production, and irrigation and draining projects have had some success. But in the north of the country the huge state farms, around 50,000 hectares, have been corporatised but otherwise remain unchanged, with the same Soviet directors and structure. They are burdened with huge debts and ageing equipment. Kazakhstan shares with other countries in the region the enormous environmental hazard of the drying up of the Aral Sea created by massive Soviet irrigation and engineering projects. The Syr Darya river, which runs from the Fergana Valley in Uzbekistan through Kazakhstan to the Aral Sea, peters out before reaching the sea.

## Natural resources

Approximately 90 minerals have been discovered in Kazakhstan, 60 of which are being actively exploited. The country has some of the world's largest reserves of zinc, molybdenum, lead, chrome, copper and silver, among many other metals and minerals. Kazakhstan also has some of the largest reserves of oil and gas in the world. Oil was discovered at the beginning of the century. Kazakhstan sits astride one of the world's biggest oilfields, the Tengiz field in western Kazakhstan, and has more potential reserves offshore under the Caspian Sea. There is also the giant gas condensate field at Karachaganak, part of the formation that straddles the border with Russia around Orenburg. Oil currently accounts for 22 per cent of Kazakhstan's total export revenues, and non-ferrous and ferrous metals together account for 31 per cent.

99

## Mining and minerals

Soviet exploitation of mining was extensive from World War II onwards when the Soviet Union began to develop regions beyond the Urals. Vast deposits of iron ore, some of the largest in the world, were discovered in the 1950s in the Kustanai Basin in the north-west of the republic and an enormous iron and steel industry was set up to exploit these deposits. Kazakhstan became a major producer of coal and metals. By 1991 the country was producing 70 per cent of the Soviet Union's lead, zinc, titanium and magnesium, 90 per cent of its phosphorus and chrome and more than 60 per cent of its silver and molybdenum. It also produced about 25 per cent of the USSR's coal with 135 million tonnes coming from the Karaganda and Ekibastuz basins in northern Kazakhstan .

Production from Kazakhstan's mines went into severe decline after 1991. The decline has more or less been stopped, with a turnaround in zinc and lead production. Copper production has also shown signs of recovery. Metals accounted for 14 per cent of total industrial output and 30 per cent of Kazakhstan's exports in 1997. Coal production was 72.6 million tonnes in 1997. Foreign management of several key mines has contributed to the turnaround.

The Kazakh government has encountered problems in seeking joint ventures for its gold mining. Reserves are estimated at 11 million troy ounces at Bakyrchik and 6.5 million ounces at Vasilovskoe. A new company, Bakyrchik Gold, which held 40 per cent of the state mining firm, was floated on the London Stock Exchange in August 1993. After an initial and considerable rise in the price of its shares, it announced heavy losses and was rescued by Robert Friedland, a Canadian billionaire, in 1995. In December 1996 it became the first large gold mine in the CIS to be wholly foreign owned.

The chrome industry, developed in the Stalin period, has also experienced serious problems. At one point, the Russian electricity supply was cut for non-payment of bills and was resumed only after settlement and a tripling of the electricity tariff. As world demand was slack at the time, mainly because of an excess supply of stainless steel scrap, the firm Kazkhrom found itself in difficulty. In August 1996, however, a 55.2 per cent stake was purchased by the Japan Chromium Corporation with 32.8 per cent retained by the state, 10 per cent held by staff and 2 per cent by domestic investment funds. The new owner will invest US$5 million in reconstruction.

## Energy

Kazakhstan is the largest oil producer among the FSU countries after Russia. The country's oil reserves are the most important feature of the economy and are estimated as high as 80 billion barrels of oil equivalent, although proven oil reserves are calculated to be 8 billion barrels. Almost half of Kazakh production comes from three large onshore fields –

Tengiz, Uzen, and Karachaganak. By far the largest of these is the Tengiz field. About 12 miles wide and 13 miles long, the reservoir is enormous. It has yet to be fully defined, but is estimated to hold 25 billion barrels of oil, of which 6-9 billion are thought to be recoverable. An international consortium, Tengizchevroil, was set up in April 1993 to develop the field (see below). Production had been constrained by lack of an export outlet, as well as by Russian complaints over the presence of mercaptans – corrosive, foul-smelling compounds of carbon, hydrogen and sulfur – in the oil. Tengizchevroil exports about 160,000 barrels a day of crude oil through the Russian pipeline system, by barge and rail to the Baltic, and by barge and rail to the Black Sea. The company plans to expand production to 700,000 barrels a day by 2010.

There is thought to be more oil in Kazakhstan's sector of the Caspian Sea. An agreement with Russia signed in the summer of 1998 agreed a boundary which allowed Kazakhstan crucial access to offshore oil and gas resources.

The international oil consortium OKIOC has begun prospecting in the Kashagan formation, offshore in the north Caspian, which may prove to be another giant oilfield of the size of Tengiz.

The big gas condensate field at Karachaganak in north Kazakhstan holds reserves of about 1.33 trillion cubic metres of gas, 4.7 billion barrels of condensate and 1.4 billion barrels of oil. It is being developed by British Gas, Italy's Agip, Russia's Lukoil and Texaco of the US, based on a production sharing agreement with the Kazakh government negotiated in 1997. This has given a boost to the project which has been hampered by reliance on Russia for an export system and the fact that most of its customers are Russian enterprises that have payment difficulties.

Kazakhoil, the state oil and gas company, dominates the sector. It is a partner in almost three-quarters of all production. Kazakhstan has undertaken a number of reforms in its oil and gas sectors to further develop its potential.

Kazakhstan's total oil production in 1997 was a record 26 million tonnes and natural gas production was 6.1 billion cubic metres, an increase of 24 per cent from 1996. But production levels dipped in the first half of 1998, complicated by low oil prices and continued export problems.

Kazakhstan is a major producer, consumer, and exporter of coal, with output centered in the Karaganda and Ekibastuz basins. Karaganda, located in north central Kazakhstan, has 13 mines that produce mostly high quality coking coal. Ekibastuz, located in northern Kazakhstan, is the third largest coal basin in the FSU, and has three mines that produce mainly brown (sub-bituminous) coal for use in power plants.

Kazakh coal production has declined from 130 million tonnes in 1991 to 77 million tonnes in 1996 due to the collapse in demand for coal in its traditional market – the FSU.

Although the Ukrainian steel industry had once been a major importer of coking coal from Kazakhstan, Kazakh exports to Ukraine ceased in 1996. This decline in markets resulted in the halving of both coal production and the number of mines in Karaganda from 1991 to 1996. Russian power stations also imported less coal from the Ekibastuz basin.

Despite the drop in exports to Russia, it remains the largest recipient of Kazakh coal, importing 19 of the 25 million tonnes of coal exported by Kazakhstan. The major consumer of coal from the Ekibastuz basin is still the Russian utility Sverdlovskenergo. Sverdlovskenergo should continue to receive coal from Kazakhstan, as it acquired two mines as payment for unpaid debts for power supplied to Kazakhstan.

Although the government has tried to diversify the economy away from dependence on energy resources, this has not been a success.

## Export routes for oil and gas

Kazakhstan has a vast potential of 2 billion tonnes of proven reserves, but its energy sector cannot prosper until sufficient export outlets are built. Kazakhstan now produces 25 million tonnes of oil a year, more than twice the amount needed to satisfy domestic demand. By 2012, the respective figures may grow to 170 million tonnes of oil exports, with 20 million tonnes needed internally. At present, Tengizchevroil (with a daily output of 160,000 barrels) reaches world markets via a Russian pipeline with a Russian-imposed quota of 76,000 barrels a day.

Kazakhstan desperately needs outlets in the west, south, and east to accommodate its growing energy sector. To the south, a swap arrangement between Kazakhstan and Iran has yielded only limited success so far (see Chapter 6, Transport and pipeline politics).

Discovery of oil fields in south-eastern Kazakhstan suggests new possibilities for sending oil eastward. Tengizchevroil has already tried to deliver oil from north-western Kazakhstan to China by rail. And in early 1998, the China National Petroleum Company (CNPC) advanced its own plans to build export pipelines out of Kazakhstan.

As for gas exports, Kazakhstan has been handicapped by its dependence on Soviet-era refinery and pipeline systems. In the north-west, gas from Karachaganak must still go north to Russia to be refined at Orenburg and then exported by Russia to Europe. In the heavily populated south-east the demand for gas is great, but there is no pipeline to bring it from distant fields in Kazakhstan's north-west. As a result, 90 per cent of the gas consumed in the south-east is imported from Russia, Turkmenistan, or Uzbekistan.

Gas officials must negotiate with Russia's Gazprom to gain access to the world market. Because the high cost of processing Kazakhstan's gas at Russia's Orenburg plant, Kazakhstan receives only 16 or 17 cents for every dollar's worth of Karachaganak gas. Kazakhstan plans, therefore, to build its own gas plant at Karachaganak, although Gazprom chief Rem Viakhirev claims that Orenburg is actually more profitable for Kazakhstan. Most distressing to Kazakhstan's officials is Russia's refusal to allow Kazakhstan to use Russia's gas lines to reach world markets. In fact, Russia even refused Kazakhstan permission for a one-time shipment of gas in order to repay its debts to East European nations, debts which were incurred under a treaty signed during the Soviet era.

In mid-August 1997, Viakhirev made clear that Gazprom would under no circumstances agree to give Kazakh gas an outlet to world markets where Russian gas could instead be sold. Stalemated, Kazakhstan's officials and energy industries welcome every offer by outside consortia and governments to build the pipelines and supporting infrastructure they need. The oil and gas export routes for the region are discussed in detail in Chapter 6, Energy transport and pipeline politics but they can be summarised as follows: Caspian Pipeline Consortium (CPC) (connecting the Tengiz field to the Russian port of Novorossiisk on the Black Sea); across the Caspian Sea (one option to build an underwater pipeline to Baku from the Tengiz field, the other a barging system); Baku–Supsa pipeline; Azerbaijan International Oil Company's Baku–Ceyhan pipeline; Turkmenistan–Iran; CNPC pipeline (Aktiubinsk–China). The plan for this last project is to pump Kazakh oil to the fast-developing regions of western China. It is ambitious both technically and financially and could take a decade to complete, but China could prove a major customer for Kazakh oil.

## Foreign participation in the oil and gas sectors

In 1995, Kazakhstan adopted a new oil and gas law, which is widely recognised as an important step in attracting foreign investment. Among other measures, the law contains a broad provision for competitive bidding on energy projects. Under the law, the Kazakh government may grant exploration rights by competitive tender or through independent, direct negotiations. Contracts may be in the form of joint ventures, service agreements, or production-sharing arrangements. As at July 1997, US$2 billion had already been invested in Kazakhstan's oil and gas sectors. Kazakhstan's reform process has included a number of significant foreign investments (see Chapter 5, Energy: the key to growth).

# Structural reform

The government has made substantial progress towards reducing the government's role in economic production while at the same time defining its regulatory functions.

*Advertising for mobile telecommunications, Almaty*

government grant.

Kazakhstan has also made progress in restructuring its other remaining industries. One of the greatest problems has been the build up of arrears between suppliers, workers and to the state budget. At first the government experimented with management contracts, but it has moved to direct government intervention in the restructuring process. In 1997, 46 enterprises were transferred to the Rehabilitation Bank which works in conjunction with the State Property Committee. By the middle of 1998, 26 companies had been either liquidated or offered for sale. Meanwhile a new bankruptcy law for agricultural enterprises was amended in early 1998 to speed restructuring of this sector.

The first sector to arrest the decline in production has been heavy industry, which by 1995 accounted for 85 per cent of total industrial production. Most of that is early stage processing of oil and raw materials, driven largely by foreign investment. Light industry, by contrast, accounted for only 2.4 per cent of total industrial production in 1996. Food processing, production of consumer goods, construction and power generation were largely left behind but in 1997, began to show first growth. Construction has started to boom with the creation of the new capital.

The reform of the energy resource sectors has focused on the privatisation of viable enterprises and the closure of those that were unprofitable. The government has pursued oil enterprise restructuring and privatisation with public participation and strategic private investors. During 1997, the government closed eight unprofitable coal mines in the Karaganda basin. The oil and gas sectors drew the first major foreign investment in the country, attracting over 40 per cent of total foreign investment between 1993 and 1997. The government is currently reassessing its strategy concerning the further privatisation of the oil and gas sectors.

New management contracts and injections of foreign capital have helped turn several companies around. Ispat Karmet is one example, nearly doubling steel production in two years, and supplying 12 per cent of Kazakhstan's exports (see below). The production of copper has increased since Korea's Samsung invested in the Zhezkazgan Copper Combine in central Kazakhstan, which should produce 200,000 tonnes by 2000. Overall, non-ferrous metals account for approximately 30 per cent of foreign investment.

Government statistics showed growth in the mining sector in the first half of 1998 after 3.6 per cent growth in the previous year.

However, some plants are close to bankruptcy. The phosphorus industry, despite some foreign investment, has not revived. Declining output in machine-building has continued with some enterprises at a standstill.

Before independence, Kazakhstan was an important provider of raw materials and metals to Russia and other Soviet republics, and its industry has developed around natural resources, particularly in metallurgy, production of heavy machinery, industrial equipment and chemicals. Many of the plants were part of the cold war military-industrial complex which quickly became redundant in the post-Soviet era. Although Kazakhstan has lost its nuclear weapons and a space programme that employed tens of thousands of workers and included the historic flights of Yury Gagarin, and Soviet Union's main nuclear testing base, other industries have attracted large flows of FDI, particularly in the natural resources sector. There have also been some successful conversions of military industrial plants. One example is Byelkamit, a joint venture between the government of Kazakhstan and US-based Byelocorp Scientific, that has converted a nuclear torpedo factory in Almaty to make pressure cylinders for the oil and gas industry with the help of a US

*Zenkov
Cathedral,
Almaty*

103

# Finance

Kazakhstan has been a front runner in the CIS as far as financial sector reform is concerned. The establishment of a stock exchange, a banking sector that is strong in comparison with those of other republics in the region and wide reaching legislation have positioned Kazakhstan well for further development once the current crisis in emerging markets subsides. Banking in Kazakhstan is the most developed in the region and has been driven forward by some far-reaching reforms introduced by the NBK and the Ministry of Finance.

## The central bank

The NBK is widely regarded as one of the best managed in the region, and is respected for its anti-inflationary and stabilising policies. It has been in the forefront of introducing financial and economic reforms in Kazakhstan, which have concentrated on raising revenues from government securities, privatisation and taxes. It established a market in Treasury bills in 1994 and in 1996 successfully launched its first Eurobond, with a three-year maturity, to raise US$200 million. A second Eurobond with a five-year maturity followed in 1997. Plans for a further issue in 1998 were postponed, however.

There is some concern that the government is covering the budget deficit through the issuing of short-term T-bills. The overall issuance remains low, however, at US$125 million at mid-1998. But the government has reacted boldly to the fall in export revenues due to low oil prices and the Asian and Russian crises, announcing it was slashing expenditure in the second half of 1998 by US$500 million. Medium- and long-term public debt amounts to 20 per cent of GDP, and private debt 10 per cent of GDP.

## Treasury bills

Trading in government securities, which are predominantly short term (three, six and 12 months) began in 1994 and is now well developed. Yields, which are capped by the government, have steadily declined from 60 per cent in 1994 to 12 per cent in 1997. However the knock-on effect of the Russian crisis pushed yields up to 20 per cent in late 1998 at which point the government suspended sales.

## The stock exchange

The Kazakhstan Stock Exchange (KSE) was established as a closed joint-stock company in mid-1997. In the near future, the KSE will obtain a self-regulatory organisation licence. The government has compiled a list of 32 blue-chip enterprises, all of which will soon be listed.

The KSE has a fully functional infrastructure and regulatory regime that conforms with international standards. It has four tiers: blue chip companies have an 'A' listing, while other companies can list under the less stringent 'B' listing require-

ments. There is also a pre-listing board and an over-the-counter (OTC) market.

The National Securities Commission (NSC), formed in 1996, has announced the floatation of five blue chip companies on the stock exchange, although their launch has been repeatedly postponed. Trading on the KSE is still thin while the OTC market is more active, but lacks transparency. The majority of shares traded are blue-chip enterprises from the oil and gas, metallurgy, mining, and banking sectors.

In anticipation of further privatisation listings and with the reforms in the pension sector, several new brokerages and pension funds have recently been licensed. (For details of the KSE's regulation and trading mechanisms, see Chapter 7, Banking and finance.)

## Corporate bonds

To promote corporate bond issuance, the NSC adopted a new regulation in December 1996. Under the existing regulations, a company's issuance of bonds cannot exceed its paid-in share capital. The draft of a new company law has provisions for convertible bonds. When the law is implemented, convertible bond issuance should jump-start the corporate bond market in Kazakhstan.

The main issuers of securities in Kazakhstan are: joint-stock companies privatised under the national programme of decentralisation and privatisation; newly founded joint stock companies; and the central government. The bulk of equity securities traded on the securities market are shares of privatised state enterprises. No foreign securities are traded in Kazakhstan.

## Pension fund reform

The World Bank has extended a US$300 million loan to help finance pension fund reform. Domestic pension funds and insurance companies have already started to develop. A law on pension system reform was adopted in May 1996, under which voluntary pension funds (independent from the government's pension system), can be launched. According to the Kazakh National Securities Commission (NSC) which regulates the sector, non-government pension funds should accumulate about US$400 million by 2000, although so far about 90 per cent of the population prefer to deal with the State Pension Fund only and are reluctant to make pension contributions to non-government funds.

As at December 1997, the NSC had registered four private pension funds and one portfolio management company. The NSC has set a minimum capitalisation level of US$1 million for private pension funds, which are required to invest at least 50 per cent of their portfolios in domestic government securities, and can invest a maximum of 10 per cent in the securities of international financial institutions and 10 per cent in the corporate securities of blue-chip companies. During the next five years, rapid growth is expected in the pension funds industry due to the accumulation of significant personal savings.

Almost 170 Privatisation Investment Funds (PIFs) have been registered. People were given coupons, which were not actually tradeable securities as they could only be invested in PIFs. Sixty-seven per cent of the population invested their coupons in a PIF of their choice. The funds now hold shares in several thousand enterprises.

The government began a programme of fundamental pension reform in January 1998 that is the most forward-looking reform being conducted anywhere in the FSU. The reforms are aimed at converting the pension system from a pay-as-you-go basis to a fully funded pension system. To tackle a growing difficulty in meeting pension payments, and with an eye on Kazakhstan's demographics (a young population but a slowing birth rate), the government has created a system of private pension funds that will invest 25 per cent of their funds in securities on the KSE. Employees make mandatory payments of 10 per cent of their wages into a personal retirement fund in addition to existing contributions from a 15 per cent payroll tax that will be reduced to 5 per cent over the next 10 years. Contributions will remain mandatory but the State Pension Fund will be phased out gradually over 40 years. Mandatory contributions can go either to private or state funds and employees have the option to make additional voluntary payments.

The plan is expected to boost the fledgling stock market as well as solve pressing problems with pension payments. As at mid-1998, there were 12 private pension funds, three asset management companies and five custodial banks. In the absence of the launch of the blue-chip companies, the funds are investing in government paper.

## Banking

Kazakhstan's two largest banks account for about 50 per cent of all deposits and 40 per cent of outstanding loans as at the end of the third quarter of 1998. Although credit assessment techniques have improved, a legacy of bad loans has restricted lending to the private sector economy.

Kazakhstan has brought in stricter controls, creating a system based on international norms, instituted by the central bank. Capital requirements of banks have been raised and the number of banks has subsequently been reduced from over 200 to about 70 in late 1998. Further consolidation should occur over the coming years.

Banking is concentrated in the hands of the five major Kazakh commercial banks. The second largest in terms of assets (US$467 million as at end-1998) and the largest financial institution in terms of total retail deposits (60 per cent of

the total market share at end-1998) is the state-owned Halyk Savings Bank, formerly the Kazakh branch of Sberbank. Privatisation of the bank began in 1998 with the sale through auction of 17.6 per cent of Halyk to the bank's depositors and 10 per cent to private investors. Another 10–15 per cent will be sold during 1999–2001. Other banks are Kazkommertsbank, the largest private bank in Kazakhstan, Turan-Alem Bank, Almaty Merchant Bank and ABN AMRO Bank Kazakhstan.

KazKommertsbank has emerged as a leader in Kazakhstan. It is the largest private sector bank in terms of assets (US$638.2 million at end-1998) and the largest bank in terms of equity after completing an international share offering in 1997, raising US$50 million and doubling its capital. In April 1998, it was the first Kazakh bank to launch a Eurobond issue, with a US$100 million, three-year offer. Its subsidiary, KazKommerts International Securities recently listed on the KSE.

Turan-Alem Bank was created in early 1997 when two state banks – Turan and Alem – were merged because of bad loans in their portfolio. The bank was then recapitalised by the government and privatised in April 1998. Turan was formed from the Soviet industrial bank, Promstroibank, and Alem was the foreign trade bank, Vnesheconombank.

For further details on the bankings sector see Chapter 7, Banking and finance.

### Foreign banks

There are about 20 foreign banks that comprise about 22 per cent of the banking sector's capital. ABN AMRO Kazakhstan was the first foreign bank to begin operations in Kazakhstan. The bank is 51 per cent owned by ABN AMRO, 29 per cent by Kazkommertsbank and 20 per cent by the World Bank's financial arm, International Finance Corporation (IFC). Foreign banks are allowed to operate subsidiaries in Kazakhstan after a two-year period to allow local banks to prepare for competition. In 1998 Citibank, Société Générale and HSBC opened wholly foreign owned subsidiaries. Lending nevertheless remains low in Kazakhstan, at just 5 per cent of GDP.

## Foreign trade

Low oil prices and the Asian and Russian economic crises have affected Kazakhstan's exports. Growth in 1998, originally predicted to reach 3 per cent, is likely to be around zero. Forecasts for 1999 do not predict an improvement either.

Since independence, Kazakhstan has diverted just over half of its trade away from the FSU republics, but at the beginning of 1998 Russia still remained its largest trading partner, accounting for approximately 30 per cent of exports and 40 per cent of imports, according to Kazkommerts Securities.

*Kazakhstan is the largest country in Central Asia; the country covers two time zones and five climactic zones*

Exhibit 9.10
**Trade balance, 1994–99**

| | 1994 | 1995 | 1996 | 1997 | 1998 | 1999(p) |
|---|---|---|---|---|---|---|
| Imports (US$ million) | 4,205 | 5,387 | 6,618 | 7,154 | 7,400 | 7,700 |
| Exports (US$ million) | 3,285 | 5,164 | 6,292 | 6,760 | 6,300 | 6,700 |
| Trade balance (US$ million) | −920 | −222 | −326 | −385 | −1,100 | −1,000 |

*Sources:* EBRD; ABN AMRO.

The country has a liberal foreign trade regime and is in the advanced stages of negotiations to join the WTO. However, its membership of the CIS Customs Union with Belarus, the Kyrgyz Republic and Russia may complicate further tariff reductions as there is pressure to maintain a unified tariff structure within this union.

Exhibit 9.10 shows Kazakhstan's trade balance between 1994 and 1999.

# Foreign investment

Kazakhstan has been successful in attracting FDI (see Exhibit 9.11). To date it has received about US$5.7 billion, of which around 40 per cent has been channelled into the oil and gas sectors. According to the EBRD, cumulative per capita FDI has exceeded US$300 during the period 1989 to 1998. Probably the most successful foreign investments have been those where a foreign partner has purchased a controlling share or even the entire enterprise.

A number of institutions have been created to stimulate investment. The most important of these are the State Committee on Investment, which is authorised to provide tax and other incentives, the new stock market, and a foreign investment advisory council which was set up in 1998.

Even so, Kazakhstan has still had difficulty attracting the enormous amounts of investment required to significantly boost economic growth and there is still much to be done to improve the legal and regulatory environment governing foreign investment. Kazakhstan's vast mineral and energy resources have attracted investment despite the legal environment.

Nevertheless, the government has acted to spur greater for-

Exhibit 9.11
**Net foreign direct investment (US$ million), 1994–98**

| | 1994 | 1995 | 1996 | 1997 | 1998 |
|---|---|---|---|---|---|
| Net FDI | 635 | 964 | 1,137 | 1,320 | 1,200 |

*Source:* EBRD.

eign investment through legal reform in areas such as demonopolisation, privatisation, debt restructuring, banking reform, price liberalisation and the establishment of a new securities and exchange commission, the NSC (see below).

Although the government has promised that tendering of contracts will be done in an open and fair manner, there continues to be concerns about its operation. The government is in the process of overhauling its system of procurement from the private sector to include both open and closed tenders. In theory, tenders will be open to international competitive bidding. Kazakhstan has declared its intention to join the WTO's Agreement on Government Procurement. This should provide foreign bidders with better access to tenders and international standards of transparency.

*Selected investments*

- Tengizchevroil, a joint venture founded between Kazakhstanmunaigaz and Chevron, was formed as part of a 40-year, US$20 billion agreement signed in 1993. By January 1997, Chevron had invested over US$800 million in TCO. Mobil obtained a 25 per cent share in the joint venture in 1996. In March 1997, Chevron sold a 5 per cent share to the Russian company Lukoil (see below).

- Philip Morris signed an agreement with Almaty Tobacco Combine in 1993, under which Philip Morris pledged to invest US$300 million. The project is considered to be one of the largest privatisation efforts in the FSU. Philip Morris has been producing cigarettes in Kazakhstan for domestic consumption since 1994, and hopes to export large quantities of cigarettes to other CIS markets (see below).

- The CPC first explored, and now has the contract to develop, offshore reserves in the northern section of the Caspian Sea. Members are the government of Kazakhstan, BP/Statoil, British Gas, Royal Dutch Shell, Mobil, AGIP, and Total. Consortium members jointly paid approximately US$350 million for a seismic study and a bonus to the Kazakh government for the rights to prospect for oil in the Caspian Sea. Seismic work was completed in August 1996. Under a subsequent PSA, the CPC is now restructured for drilling exploration.

- AGIP and British Gas, now joined by the Russian company

Lukoil, and the US company Texaco, are developing the Karachaganak gas field in western Kazakhstan.

- In August 1996, the US company AES bought the Ekibastuz No. 1 power plant for US$5 million, and committed to invest more than US$500 million over the next six years to renovate and improve the facility. The power plant currently generates only 10 per cent of its potential capacity of 4,000 megawatts.

- In October 1996, the US company Access Industries bought the Bogatyr coal mine and 66 per cent of the neighboring Stepnoy coal mine (both part of the giant Ekibastuz colliery) for more than US$40 million. Access pledged to invest US$550 million toward upgrading the coalmines over the next five years.

- In August 1996 the UK-registered company Japan Chromium purchased 55.2 per cent of Kazkhrom (a chromium plant) and associated mine for US$67 million. It has pledged to invest US$5 million in reconstruction.

- In May 1996 the South Korean company Samsung purchased a half share in the Zhez Kazgan Copper Combine.

- In November 1995 the UK company Ispat purchased the Kermet Steelworks. It has pledged to invest US$200 million (see below).

- In November 1996 the Canadian corporation Hurricane Hydrocarbons' purchased Yuzhneftigas (a state oil company) for US$120 million. It pledged to invest US$280 million.

- In April 1997 Daewoo Corporation of South Korea purchased 40 per cent of the shares of Kaztelecom for US$1.37 billion. It is reported to have sold its holdings to an undisclosed investor.

- In June 1997 CNPC purchased 65 per cent of Aktiubinsk for US$325 million. It pledged to invest US$4 billion.

## Investment profiles

### Ispat Karmet

Ispat Karmet provides an example of how a large and ailing Soviet enterprise can be turned around with a relatively small investment but with a good marketing and management strategy. In 1995 the London-based steel maker Ispat International now part of the LNM group, bought 100 per cent of the Kermet Steelworks in northern Kazakhstan. Based in the town of Temirtau, near Karaganda, the steelworks included over a dozen coal mines that produce mostly high-quality coking coal, and a power plant that provides electricity and steam for the plant. The company employs 70,000 people, virtually supporting the entire local population and making it the largest single employer in the country.

The collapse of the Soviet Union caused the breakdown of the steelworks' traditional markets in Russia and other FSU republics. These had previously taken 70 per cent of the steel-works' production. Those customers that still existed could only pay by barter. This had caused a cash crisis so that by 1995 workers at the steelworks had not been paid for six months. The new management stopped all barter transactions and looked elsewhere for markets. It began supplying China, among others, which by 1996 accounted for 43 per cent of Ispat Karmet's exports. Production rose from 2 million tonnes in 1995 to 3.8 million in 1997, accounting for 12 per cent of Kazakhstan's exports. The EBRD arranged a syndicated loan in 1997, the first of its kind in Central Asia. It agreed a loan of US$285 million and the IFC a loan of US$165 million for the company to streamline the production process, increase output to 6 million tonnes of steel and improve quality to achieve international certification. The plant's short-term challenge will be to ride the shock of falling demand in Asia, and the subsequent fall in prices.

### Philip Morris

Philip Morris, the US tobacco company, acquired the Almaty Tobacco Combine, Kazakhstan's main cigarette factory, in 1993. It was the first cash privatisation in Kazakhstan and Philip Morris holds virtually all the shares. It is investing US$300 million to re-equip and modernise the factory and develop tobacco growing, build a model farm, invest in infrastructure and assist farmers. The company produced 17 billion cigarettes in 1998 up from 9 billion in 1992, mostly for sale on the domestic market, with some exports going to the Kyrgyz Republic and Russia.

Privatisation has changed tobacco growing with the break-up of the collective farms. In 1993 the company had contracts with 28 state suppliers of tobacco. By 1998, the company had signed 7,500 contracts involving 21,000 individual farmers. High-quality tobacco yields have tripled since the programme began. With investment in tractors, barns and buying points, the harvest in 1998 was expected to exceed the company's requirements. Plans are going ahead to expand with the building of a new US$170-million greenfield factory and headquarters on the edge of Almaty, which will produce 25 billion cigarettes a year by 2000.

Philip Morris attributes it sales success to close collaboration with the government of Kazakhstan, in particular on excise tax which has been kept low and so prevented contraband cigarettes flooding the market.

### Tengizchevroil

The Tengiz oil field is the flagship oil project of independent Kazakhstan and Tengizchevroil the first international consortium formed to develop the country's oil reserves. It began as a Chevron-Kazakh joint venture, and is still dominated by Chevron of the United States, which has a stake of 45 per cent. Mobil holds a 25 per cent share, Lukoil and LukArco (a

*Astana Airport*

US/Russian joint venture between Arco and Lukoil) both have 5 per cent and the national oil company KazakhOil retains 25 per cent. The company employs 3,100 people.

Tengizchevroil has already invested US$1 billion in the Tengiz oilfield and by 1997 was producing 28 per cent of Kazakhstan's oil, up from 5 per cent in 1993. Exports have been limited however by the lack of a direct export pipeline from Kazakhstan to international markets. In 1997 Tengizchevroil was limited to transporting 60,000 barrels a day through the Russian pipeline system, with the rest being exported through expensive alternatives by rail through Russia to Finland and by tanker across the Caspian Sea to Azerbaijan, and again by rail across Georgia to the Black Sea. Kazakhstan is also exporting via swaps with Iran, an opportunity that is denied to US companies because of US sanctions against Iran. Tengizchevroil is relying on the CPC's pipeline that will link Tengiz directly to the Russian Black Sea port of Novorossiisk. The project is expected to be completed by 2000. (For further details, see Chapter 6, Energy transport and pipeline politics.)

# Legal environment[1]

Kazakhstan is a civil law country. Kazakhstan's Civil Code came into force in 1995 and is the main law governing commercial activities. In addition, specific laws govern banking, privatisation, companies, partnerships, natural resources, securities, security interests, and so on. These laws, however, must not contradict the Civil Code.

## Foreign investment law

The law 'On Foreign Investments' (FIL) became effective in January 1995. There are no restrictions, generally, under the FIL on non-residents investing in Kazakhstan nor are there specific registration requirements for non-residents investing in Kazakhstan. The FIL establishes the principle that foreign investors have rights 'no less favourable' than those granted in a similar situation to Kazakhstan citizens or juridical persons.

The FIL guarantees 'prompt, adequate and effective compensation' in the event of the expropriation of foreign investments (such expropriation is permissible in limited circumstances). In addition, the FIL contains a 'grandfather clause' which states that 'in the event of a worsening of the position of a foreign investor as a result of changes in legislation and (or) the entry into force and (or) a change of conditions of international treaties, the legislation prevailing at the time of making the investments shall apply to the foreign investments for 10 years ...' The FIL also contains a number of other guarantees, including those against illegal actions of state agencies and for the repatriation of profits.

## Establishing a presence in Kazakhstan

There are essentially three different forms through which a foreign company may operate in Kazakhstan:

- Representative Office, which is mainly used for purposes of local support and marketing rather than for engaging in revenue generating activities.
- The Branch, which may be used for actual business but does not create a legal personality separate from a foreign entity.
- The Enterprise with foreign participation (subsidiary).

An enterprise with foreign participation can either be a joint venture or wholly owned by a foreign investor. The two corporate forms most commonly used by foreign investors setting up a local entity are the limited liability partnership and the joint-stock company (open or closed). Either form offers limited liability to a foreign investor.

## Foreign exchange

In 1996, Kazakhstan accepted the conditions of Article VIII of the IMF Charter. As a result, Kazakhstan has agreed not to introduce or increase any exchange rate restrictions, introduce any practice of multiple exchange rates, enter into any bilateral agreements violating Article VIII or impose any import restrictions. Accordingly, tenge may be freely bought and sold based on market forces at banks and other exchange offices.

Currency rules adopted by the NBK require registration and licensing of certain transactions involving non-residents. Kazakhstan residents must register with the NBK transactions involving the movement of capital (eg, investments, transfers of property, credits for a period exceeding 180 days) from non-residents to residents if the amount exceeds US$100,000 (or the equivalent). Where the transactions involve the transfer of currency from residents to non-residents, a licence from the NBK must be obtained before the transfer may legally take place.

## Capital markets

The Law on the Registration of Securities Transactions and the Law on the Securities Market were adopted in March 1997 to govern the issuance of securities, operation of organised securities markets, and registration of transactions. Trading on Kazakhstan's organised securities markets must be conducted through licensed professional participants (ie, custodians, broker-dealers, registrars and depositories).

One of the principal objectives of the NSC is establishing transparent and efficient securities markets and protecting the interests of investors. Its functions include registering the issuance of securities, issuing licences for professional participants in the securities markets, and overseeing compliance with Kazakh securities laws.

## Prospects

If Kazakhstan can avoid the worst effects of the Russian crisis, then it will remain the leading country in the region. Low oil and commodity prices, plus a drop in demand for its exports in Asia and Russia, are damaging the economy. There is no doubt that Kazakhstan faces a difficult few years but so far the government is reacting to the economic environment with impressive firmness and caution. Pressing ahead with economic reforms will be crucial in attracting the necessary foreign investment to help the government achieve its budgetary goals and help the country achieve sustained growth. Foreign investment is essential for further development and Kazakhstan must speed up the pace of privatisation

Key developments expected in oil exploration and pipeline construction in 1999 (that is, the results of drilling in the Kashagan reservoir and advances in the construction of the CPC pipeline project) will be vitally important in defining investor confidence for the years ahead. In the short term, the government will have to work hard to attract foreign investors who have grown wary of both the FSU and emerging markets.

There are signs that the government, with a mixture of young energetic technocrats and more experienced figures, and a president who has consistently supported reforms, will maintain its present course. With presidential elections over, the government can also expect a further period of political stability in which to push ahead with the necessary structural reforms. Kazakhstan's economic activity in the past eight years has been among the most impressive of all the FSU republics. If it can continue to match this track record, it should be an example to the region for the next decade.

1. This section was prepared by White & Case Kazakstan L.L.P.

# Appendix: Fiscal environment
Ernst & Young

## Taxation

The Law Concerning Taxes and Other Obligatory Payments to the Budget (Tax Code) was introduced in July, 1995. The Tax Code, international treaties, acts of the president and acts of the Tax Committee define and regulate all taxes in Kazakhstan. The tax system consists of nationwide and local taxes, including income tax on individuals and legal entities, value-added tax (VAT), special payments and taxes on mineral resource users, land tax, property tax, and vehicle tax. Other taxes and obligatory payments to the budget include customs duties, social taxes, pension fund contributions and the road fund tax.

The Tax Committee is a division of the Ministry of State Income and is responsible for the application and enforcement of tax law. All legal entities and persons registered as business agents are required to register with the local tax committee within 10 days of legal registration. Foreign legal entities operating through a permanent establishment must complete tax registration within 10 days of beginning activities in Kazakhstan.

Representative offices of foreign legal entities that do not create permanent establishments are also required to register with the tax committee. Although they will not be subject to profits tax, registration of the representation is necessary for the payment of other taxes, for example, income tax withheld from the salaries of the employees of the representative office. Regardless of the form they take, all foreign legal entities must complete legal registration with the Ministry of Justice before they can register for tax purposes.

The tax year is the calendar year. Kazakhstan's tax system operates on the principle of self assessment. The tax service is responsible solely for verifying the accuracy of the calculation and the timeliness of the payment of taxes. Taxpayers are required to submit annual returns and to make periodic payments of tax, the frequency of which depends on the level and type of tax concerned.

### Resident corporations

Most resident legal entities (Kazakh legal entities) are subject to profits tax on worldwide income at a rate of 30 per cent. Legal entities operating in the territory of a special economic zone are subject to a lower rate of profits tax at 20 per cent. Legal entities for which land is the main means of production are taxed at 10 per cent. Foreign legal entities (non-resident legal entities) are subject to tax on profits received from Kazakh sources.

Income received through a general partnership or a consortium is distributed between its partners and will be taxed as part of the income of each of them. A limited liability partnership is subject to tax separately from its partners.

The taxable base consists of income received from the business activities of the legal entity less any expenses incurred in connection with the receipt of that income. Deductions include labour costs, obligatory payments to pension funds, social taxes, various local taxes, and business trip and hospitality expenses within the specified norms for such expenses, which are relatively low.

Dividends and interest paid to legal entities are subject to income tax withholding at the source of payment at a rate of 15 per cent. Legal entities are entitled to an income tax credit provided there are documents to certify the payment of these taxes at source.

A capital gain is recognised on the sale of an asset and is determined as the difference between the sale price and the book value of the asset, adjusted for inflation. A sale is deemed to include the sale, exchange or other transfer of the asset. Capital gains are included in taxable profits and are therefore subject to profits tax at a rate of 30 per cent.

A foreign tax credit is available for foreign tax paid on income earned abroad. The amount of the credit may not exceed the amount of profits tax that would have been calculated on that income.

### Non-resident companies

Non-resident legal entities (foreign legal entities) operating through a permanent establishment are subject to profits tax at a rate of 30 per cent. Foreign legal entities are also subject to an additional tax on their net income after profits tax at a rate of 15 per cent. Foreign legal entities receiving income from sources in Kazakhstan without establishing a permanent establishment are subject to income tax withholding.

A foreign company may be considered to have created a permanent establishment on the basis of activities ranging from providing services to establishing potential business and government contacts.

### Taxation of individuals

For tax purposes, an individual is a resident of Kazakhstan if he/she is present in Kazakhstan for 183 days or more in any consecutive 12-month period. Residents are taxed on their worldwide income. Non-residents are taxed on Kazakh-sourced income only. This is income earned for services provided in Kazakhstan regardless of where the payment for services is made. In addition, Kazakh-sourced income includes income for any work, regardless of where it is performed, if the payment of the income is claimed by the payer as a tax deduction in Kazakhstan. If an individual receives income in Kazakhstan, the employer is responsible for calculating withholding income tax.

The taxable base for individuals is broad and includes:

- Wages, bonuses, allowances (such as hardship and housing allowances).
- Reimbursement of business expenses above the statutory norms.
- Value of benefits, such as payment for children's education, kindergarten care and medical care.
- Income tax paid by the employer on behalf of the employee.
- Employers' expenditure on premiums for life and health insurance.
- Personal transportation.
- Generally, all other monetary and in-kind benefits provided by the employer.
- Any gain from the sale of capital assets, such as land, securities, precious stones and jewellery.

However, dividends received by individuals that were taxed at source are exempt from income tax.

A personal allowance, equal to the stipulated annual specified index, is allowed for each individual and each dependent. No other deductions are permitted unless the individual is registered as an individual entrepreneur.

Tax is levied on employment income, self-employment and business income and other types of income of citizens and resident aliens at varying rates dependent on the amount of income received. Income received in a foreign currency is converted into tenge at the NBK's exchange rate prevailing on the date on which the income is received. Married persons are taxed separately, not jointly, on all types of income.

## Withholding tax

Tax on dividends or interest is withheld at source at a rate of 15 per cent. Legal entities receiving payments already taxed at source will receive a tax credit, provided there is documentation to show payment of the tax at source.

Income derived from a Kazakh source by foreign legal entities without a permanent establishment in Kazakhstan is subject to tax withheld at source. The tax is assessed on the whole sum paid without any deduction for expenses incurred by the foreign legal entity, at the following rates:

| | |
|---|---|
| Dividends and interest | 15% |
| Insurance premiums | 5% |
| International telecommunications or international transport services | 5% |
| Royalties, income from services rendered, rental income and other types of income | 20% |

These rates may be reduced or eliminated by current double tax treaties to which Kazakhstan is a party.

## Indirect taxes

The standard rate of VAT is 20 per cent, though certain foodstuffs are subject to VAT at 10 per cent. Legal entities and individuals engaging in commercial activities are subject to VAT. Legal entities and individuals importing goods are also liable for VAT on those goods.

The taxable base is the turnover from the sale of goods, work and services in Kazakhstan. Turnover is defined as the value of goods, works and services sold, as determined on the basis of established prices exclusive of VAT but inclusive of excise duties. The taxable base on imports includes the customs value of the goods, the import duties, the amount of excise duty in the case of excisable goods, and customs levies.

The amount of VAT payable to the budget is the difference between the amount of VAT assessed on goods sold, works or services carried out (output tax) and the amounts of VAT payable for goods acquired, work performed or services rendered (input tax).

Several types of turnover are exempt from VAT. Input VAT incurred in the course of the supply of exempt goods is not reclaimable. Some of the major exemptions include:

- The lease and sale of land or buildings, with the exception of the first sale of such property.
- Financial services, including the maintenance of bank accounts, operations with securities, cheques, debentures, deposits and certificates.
- Transactions related to the privatisation of state-owned property.
- Geological exploration and geological prospecting work.

Excise duties are payable on certain goods produced in or imported into Kazakhstan that are deemed to be luxury items or goods used in gambling businesses. Goods exported outside the CIS are not subject to VAT and excise duties if the producer provides proof of their export. Depending on the particular goods, duty rates vary from 5–100 per cent of the value of the goods or a flat rate per volume or quantity of the goods.

## Other taxes

There are no customs duties on exports with the exception of various types of wheat. Imports are subject to customs duties, ranging from 0–100 per cent of the customs value, depending on the nature of the import. In addition to the customs duties, the importer must pay a customs processing fee, which is currently 0.2 per cent of the total customs value of the goods.

Certain categories of goods imported on a temporary basis for a period of up to one year are exempt from customs duties. This period may be extended for an additional year, but the importer will have to pay partial duty of 3 per cent of the standard duty for each month the goods remain in Kazakhstan beyond one year.

Employers in Kazakhstan must pay a social tax, contributions to the Pension Fund and a fee for social welfare on behalf of all employees who are citizens of Kazakhstan. The amounts are based on gross salaries paid to employees. They are paid by the employer and not withheld from the employee's salary. For 1999, employers pay 31.5 per cent of gross salaries in aggregate payroll taxes.

Special tax provisions impose bonuses, royalties and excess profits taxes on mineral resource users. Bonuses typically include a subscription bonus and a discovery bonus. The amount of the bonuses and the determination of excess profits are issues currently subject to negotiation between the taxpayer, the Ministry of Finance and the ministry issuing the licence for the mineral rights.

## Local taxes

Land tax is payable on inhabited land and land used for agricultural, industrial, transportation, communication, defence or other purposes. Land areas of high security and land of the forestry fund or water fund is also subject to the land tax. The tax is imposed on legal entities or individuals who either own or have the right to the permanent use of the land. The amount of tax levied depends on the quality, location and water supply of the land and not on economic results from the use of the land. The rate of land tax varies depending on the designated use of the land and the quality score of the land.

The Road Fund payment is levied on all legal entities regardless of road use. The tax is assessed at a rate of 0.2 per cent of total revenues. Payment is due regardless of the net financial results of the company. The road fund payments may be deducted from income when determining profit tax.

Payments are made to the Environmental Protection Fund by certain tax payers as compensation for polluting the environment. The payments are assessed at rates set by regional administrations. Payments include compensation for polluting the environment within established norms, for polluting the environment in excess of allowed limits and for environmental damage caused by violating environmental legislation.

## Taxation treaties

Kazakhstan has entered into a number of double taxation treaties with countries including the United Kingdom and the United States, which may provide relief from taxation in Kazakhstan. Under most of these treaties, including the UK treaty, an individual will not be taxed on income earned in Kazakhstan if: he/she is present in Kazakhstan for 183 days or less in any period of 12 consecutive months; his/her salary is paid by or on behalf of an employer who is not resident in Kazakhstan; or the salary is not borne by a taxpayer in Kazakhstan.

Foreign legal entities that do not form a permanent establishment may be able to eliminate or reduce income tax withholding, by securing relief under a taxation treaty. In addition, treaties may provide a different definition of permanent establishment than that of Kazakh domestic legislation and exempt a company from Kazakh profits tax.

# Accounting and auditing
## Statutory requirements
### Books and records
Kazakhstan accounting laws mandate that all legal entities keep books of account and records of all accounting transactions. The Kazakh Accounting Standards (KAS) require that books of account be maintained in Kazakhstan and include a general ledger organised by financial statement classifications and a journal organised by the transaction date. The books and records for all transactions must be retained for at least five years after the last entry.

### Method of accounting
Financial accounting is based on the principals of the accrual method. Income is recognised and recorded when earned, while expenses and losses are recognised and recorded when incurred.

### Financial statements
The managing director of a legal entity is responsible for issuing financial statements within four months after the end of the entity's financial year. Financial statements must include a balance sheet, an income statement, a cash flow statement denominated in tenge, and notes to the financial statements.

### Sources of accounting principles
The National Commission of the Republic of Kazakhstan for Accounting was formed in May 1996. The Commission establishes the main principles and general rules for accounting as well as the requirements for the internal control and independent audit of legal entities in Kazakhstan.

The Commission has developed and approved the General Chart of Accounts, a set of guidelines for recording the financial and economic activities of legal entities. While the specific forms are not mandatory, a company must record its financial activities in a way that allows them to be classified in accordance with the KAS.

The major provisions of the KAS are:

- The standard format to be used in preparing annual financial statements.
- The required books and records of transactions, as well as the period of time they must be retained.
- General accounting principles to be followed in preparing the annual financial statements.

The Tax Code imposes additional tax accounting requirements, including the method of tax depreciation and the rule that certain deductions may be accrued for tax purposes only if they are recorded in the financial statements.

## Accounting principles and practices
### Fundamental concepts
Under the KAS, the fundamental accounting concepts are fair statement of accounts, going concern presumption, consistency of accounting principles, relevance, materiality, reliability, neutrality, completeness, comparability and prudence.

### Significant accounting principles and practices
#### Assets
These are the tangible and intangible property of a legal entity, expressed in terms of value.

### Liabilities
These are defined as an obligation of an entity (debtor) to carry out a certain action in favour of another entity (creditor).

#### Shareholder capital
This is defined as the assets of an entity after its liabilities have been deducted.

#### Current assets
In general, current assets must be carried at the lower of cost and market value. Accounts receivable and certain other current assets, such as cash and investments in shares, are carried at their nominal values less any related valuation provisions.

#### Fixed assets
These must be stated at cost less accumulated depreciation. They may be revalued under certain conditions. General revaluation for inflation is permitted.

Depreciation must be charged systematically over the period of use. The original acquisition cost of fixed assets, as well as the annual and accumulated depreciation of these assets, must be disclosed in the notes to the financial statements.

#### Inventory
Inventories are accounted for at the lower of cost and market value. Cost is the purchase cost or production cost. Overhead costs must be allocated on the basis of normal production capacity.

#### Intangible assets
Goodwill and intangible assets are recorded only if they are purchased. If recorded, they are stated at cost. Purchased goodwill may be amortised under the straight-line method over a reasonable period of time.

#### Financial Investments
When investments are acquired, they are recorded at the purchase value, including expenses that are directly connected with the purchase, such as broker fees and banking fees.

The difference between the purchase value and the value at maturity of an investment in securities (a discount or premium, which arises on the purchase) is amortised by the investor during the period of its ownership.

#### Reserves for losses and expenses
The Tax Code requires that reserves be reported in the financial statements. Provisions have been established for reporting probable losses or well-defined expenses for which the amount is not certain. Examples of these expenses are tax expenses for the fiscal year and expenses for future pension and severance payments to employees. Deferred tax expenses may also be recorded as provisions. Provisions must be disclosed in notes to the financial statements. The notes must show the provisions balances at the beginning of the fiscal year, use during the year, additions during the year and their values at the end of the fiscal year.

#### Organisation costs
Costs incurred during the formation of a company and similar expenses may be capitalised.

#### Leases
Leased property is recorded on the accounting balance sheet of a lessee as an asset, and lease payments due are recorded as liabilities. At the inception of a lease, lease payment liabilities are recorded at the sale price or at the discounted value of lease payments if they are lower than the sale price. When calculating the discounted value of lease payments the discount factor is the interest rate implicit in the lease. If it is impossible to determine the rate, the lessee's incremental borrowing rate of interest is used.

Lease payments consist of payments for financing (expenses for the payment of interest) and a payment that decreases the balance sheet value of the lease liability (payment of the principle liability). Payment for financing is recognised throughout the total period of the lease on the basis of permanent interest rates which are applied to the balance sheet value of the lease liability for each reporting period.

### Long-term contracts

Profits on long-term contracts may be recognised only on completion of the contract or when partial deliveries may be billed under the contract.

## Accounting for income tax

A tax payment for a reporting period is recorded on the basis of the accounting for the tax effect under the liability method, pursuant to which income tax is regarded as an expense incurred by a legal entity in connection with the receipt of income, and is accrued in the same period in which the corresponding income arose. The tax effects of the timing differences in a reporting period are included in a tax payment and recorded on an accounting balance sheet under the deferred taxes section. The deferred taxes account may have a debit or credit balance. A debit balance represents an early payment of future taxes, and a credit balance represents a liability for future taxes.

Tax legislation allows for losses to be carried forward for a certain length of time for application against future taxable income. This loss represents a potential savings in the form of a reduced future tax payment.

## Consolidated financial statements

Under the KAS, companies must publish annual consolidated financial statements if they control another company and hold (directly or indirectly) a majority of the voting rights of the subsidiary. The permissible consolidation methods are the full integration method, the equity method and the proportional integration method. The notes to the consolidated financial statements must explain the method of consolidation, the accounting principles used and the method of foreign-currency translation.

Under the full integration method, in the consolidated balance sheet, the parent company's investment in subsidiaries is replaced by the subsidiaries' balance sheet items, unless other regulations provide differently.

The equity method, a simplified type of consolidation, may be used by enterprises not required to use the full integration method. The equity method is required if a company holds at least a 20 per cent controlling interest in another enterprise. The controlling interest is disclosed in the consolidated balance sheet either at book value or at the value corresponding to the parent company's proportional share of the affiliated enterprise's net worth.

The proportional integration (pooling-of-interest) method of accounting is permitted if a parent or subsidiary company included in the consolidated financial statements manages another enterprise jointly with one or more enterprises not included in the consolidated statements. This type of consolidation is used primarily for joint undertakings in which none of the partners has a controlling influence. Under this method, the consolidated financial statements include a percentage of the affiliated enterprise's assets, liabilities, income and expenses equal to the percentage of the parent company's interest in the affiliated enterprise's net worth.

## Related-party disclosures

Related-party disclosures and receivables from and payables to affiliated and associated companies must be shown separately on the balance sheets of corporations. A corporation must disclose the name of other enterprises that individually hold more than 25 per cent of its shares. A limited liability company must disclose receivables from and payables to owners. Loans to members of the company's management or its supervisory board must be disclosed in its notes, together with a description of the terms of such loans. Interest charges to and from affiliated enterprises must be disclosed on the income statement.

## Foreign-currency transactions

Economic transactions should be recorded in the financial statements in tenge. Transactions made in foreign currency are converted to tenge by applying the exchange rate established by the NBK on the transaction date.

## Financial reporting

### Disclosure requirements

Generally, financial reporting consists of an accounting balance sheet, a statement of financial results of economic activities, a report of the movement of monetary funds, an explanatory note to it and other additional information, such as tables and diagrams. The aim of financial reporting is to provide users with useful, relevant and reliable information concerning the financial position of a legal entity, the results of activities and changes to its financial position for the reporting period.

### Reporting period

The reporting period for annual financial statements is the calendar year. The first reporting year for a legal entity begins on its registration by the state up to 31 December of the same year.

Legal entities must submit their annual financial statements no later than 30 April of the following year to:

- Shareholders as stated in foundation documents.
- State statistical bodies in the region of registration.
- State supervisory bodies in accordance with their jurisdiction.

*General information disclosed in financial statements*

All material information should be disclosed in such a manner that the financial statements are clear and understandable for the users. The classification of items in explanatory notes and monetary sums indicated in financial statements should be supplemented with explanatory information. Specifically, the notes must also provide information concerning fixed assets, provisions, reserves, short-term and long-term liabilities, capital and decreases in capital caused by losses.

Financial statements should indicate the name of the legal entity, location, reporting date and reporting period. The following should also be attached: a short description of the type of activity conducted by the organisation; its legal form; and the unit of measurement in which the financial statements are presented.

Accounting policies and supplementary information must be disclosed in the notes to the financial statements. The notes must provide sufficient information to ensure that the financial statements present a true and fair view of the results of the company's operations and of its financial position. The effects of changes in accounting policies must be quantified and the reasons for the change must be explained.

## Audit requirements

The Law Concerning Audit Activities was passed in November 1998. Audits may be classified as either obligatory or voluntary. Obligatory audits are stipulated by the legislation of Kazakhstan. Voluntary audits are carried out at the initiative of the legal entity.

## Accounting profession

Auditors must be members of the Kazakh Chamber of Auditors. To qualify as an auditor, an individual must have five years' experience and have passed the qualifying examinations. Only persons with higher education and work experience in economic, financial, accounting and analytical, control and revision or legal fields are permitted to apply for qualification.

A qualified auditor can apply to the authorised state body (Ministry of Finance) for an audit licence. To conduct audits of financial institutions in Kazakhstan a qualified auditor must apply for a separate Banking Audit Licence which is issued by the NBK.

# 10 *Kyrgyz Republic*

## History, culture and politics

The Kyrgyz Republic is a mainly mountainous region that also extends into the fertile Fergana Valley. The Kyrgyz people have the same Mongol origins as their neighbours, the Kazakhs, and speak a Turkic language. Six hundred years before Genghis Khan, the Kyrgyz were a formidable force in Central Asia.

The Kyrgyz call their land Altyn Beshik, the Golden Cradle or Homeland. Approximately 93 per cent of the country is made up of mountains including some of the highest ranges in the world. The Kyrgyz are Sunni Muslims with strong pre-Islamic animist customs.

The Russians annexed Kyrgyzstan in the 1860s after punitive raids sent thousands of Kyrgyz fleeing to Chinese Turkestan. Russian and Cossack settlers arrived to farm the land.

The Kyrgyz capital reverted to its pre-Soviet name, Bishkek, in 1991 with the country's independence. By 1991, Kyrgyz barely made up 50 per cent of the population, the rest comprising Russians, Uzbeks and other nationalities. Ethnic tension has flared, most notably in the Fergana Valley when violent riots broke out between Uzbeks and Kyrgyz in Osh in 1990.

Askar Akayev was elected president of the republic in 1990 and became the first non-communist leader in Central Asia. He immediately declared independence after the attempted coup against Mikhail Gorbachev in 1991 and was re-elected unopposed in December 1991 after the breakup of the Soviet Union.

Akayev has become known as an enlightened reformer, yet in his determination to push through reforms he has built up the power of the presidency at the expense of parliament and used referendums to push through key legislation.

The next presidential elections are scheduled for 2000 and Akayev is in a strong position to win. In July 1998, the Constitutional Court ruled that the constitutional ban on serving more than two terms in office will not bar Akayev from standing again because he was elected to his first term under the old Soviet Constitution.

Exhibit 10.1
**Country facts**

| | |
|---|---|
| Area | 198,500 square kilometres |
| Population | 4.6 million |
| Capital | Bishkek |
| Other large cities | Osh, Karakol |
| Currency | Som (KGS) |
| Exchange rate, February 1999 | KGS30.58:US$1 |
| GDP per capita (1996) | US$366 |
| Inflation, annual average (1998) | 12% |

Exhibit 10.2
**Political information**

| | |
|---|---|
| President | Askar Akayev (born 1944) |
| Elected | 24 December 1995 |
| Term | 5 years |
| Percentage of vote | 71.6% (1991: elected unopposed) |
| Next election | December 2000 |

# Macroeconomic profile

## Economic development

The Kyrgyz Republic has established a reputation as a determined advocate of economic and structural reform. During the first stage of transformation, the government freed most prices, created a national currency, introduced a liberal trade regime and eliminated most capital controls. Structural reform has included privatisation of small-scale enterprises and housing, the establishment of a two-tiered banking system, the introduction of a valu-added tax system and market-friendly legislation.

Even so, widespread unemployment and poverty remain and the government will need to keep up the momentum of reforms to see it through the effects of the Russian and Asian crises.

The country's economy is small and relies on trade, having few high-value natural resources. It was one of the poorest areas of the Former Soviet Union (FSU). After the breakup of the Soviet Union, trade almost stopped and industry, which was mostly tied into the Soviet military-industrial complex, collapsed. The country plunged into five years of economic decline, with GDP falling by 51 per cent and inflation soaring to triple digits. By 1997 half the population were living below the poverty line.

## Reform

The government acted quicker than most and launched a stabilisation programme with the IMF and World Bank as early as 1993. It successfully completed a three-year Enhanced Structural Adjustment Fund (ESAF) arrangement with the IMF in 1997 and embarked on a second programme worth US$86 million. It was the first country of the Commonwealth

of Independent States (CIS) to introduce its own currency, the som, in May 1993. The exchange rate is determined by a managed float and in 1995 the country formally accepted the obligations under Article VIII of the IMF Charter for currency convertibility. Of the currencies in the region, the som has held its value the most successfully, although the effects of the Russian crisis have placed it under pressure.

In 1999 the government announced that it intended to adopt an economic cooperation programme with Austria to develop the energy sector, light industry and tourism. This followed President Aliyev's visit to Austria in January.

## Economic recovery

After five years of decline, a broad-based recovery in output began in late 1995, with real GDP growing by 7.1 per cent in 1996 and 6.5 per cent during 1997 (see Exhibit 10.3). Even in the aftermath of the Asian and Russian crises, growth in 1998 was estimated at 2 per cent and growth was also forecast for 1999, if at a reduced level. Long-term growth will be modest, however. Unlike some of the other republics in the region, an oil boom would not affect the Kyrgyz Republic and with low gold prices, the government has had to revise its forecasted income downwards.

Economic growth has been chiefly driven by agriculture and the start of production in January 1997 of the Kumtor gold mine, which contributed 30 per cent of exports and 11 per cent of GDP in that year. There has also been growth to a lesser extent in manufacturing and trade. Structural reforms, especially privatisation and restructuring of public enterprises and agriculture, banking and the legal framework have also helped spur economic growth. The rebound in real GDP starting from late 1995 helped the government's revenues and the budget deficit was halved during 1995 and 1996, declining further in 1997.

There are widespread signs that private sector activity is expanding with the emergence of individual farming, small-scale enterprises and a variety of trading activities. Even though it remains inadequately measured in the official statistics, data suggest that the share of private sector activity in gross value added rose from 13 per cent in 1994 to 35 per cent in 1997.

The agricultural share of GDP has expanded to about 50 per cent in 1997 while the share of manufacturing dropped

Exhibit 10.3
**Economic structure**

|  | 1996 | 1997 | 1998 |
|---|---|---|---|
| GDP at constant prices (% change) | 7.1 | 6.5 | 2.0 |
| Industrial gross output (% change) | 3.9 | 20.0 | na |
| Argriculture gross output (% change) | 13 | 10.7 | na |

*Sources:* EBRD; Kazkommerts Securities.

Exhibit 10.4
**Inflation, 1994–98**

|  | 1994 | 1995 | 1996 | 1997 | 1998 |
|---|---|---|---|---|---|
| Inflation, annual average (%) | 228.7 | 52.5 | 30.4 | 25.5 | 18.4 |
| Inflation, end-year (%) | 95.7 | 31.9 | 35.0 | 14.7 | 12.0 |

*Source:* EBRD.

*Gold mine, Kumtor*

Exhibit 10.5
**Gross reserves (US$ million), 1994–98**

|  | 1995 | 1996 | 1997 |
| --- | --- | --- | --- |
| Gross reserves (end year) inc. gold | 123 | 129 | 200 |

*Source:* EBRD.

sharply. Construction activity rebounded in 1995 and 1996 because of construction at the Kumtor mine, which is the eighth largest gold mine in the world. Investment increased sharply as a result of the Kumtor mine project and a public investment programme. Saving rates continued to remain at low levels, with negative public sector saving.

## Price and exchange rate stabilisation

Significant progress has been achieved in establishing price stability. Inflation fell sharply between 1992 and 1997, although the projected 12 per cent was not met and instead inflation for the year recorded 18.4 per cent (see Exhibit 10.4). Substantial financial aid was provided through the multilateral development agencies and, with their help, the exchange rate stabilised in 1997 while international reserves steadily increased (see Exhibit 10.5).

## The current account

The current account balance, which was dominated in 1995 and 1996 by imports related to the construction of the Kumtor gold mine, improved in 1997 with the beginning of gold exports (see Exhibit 10.6). The country's competitiveness was maintained as wages in US-dollar terms remained at low levels and the real effective exchange rate depreciated during 1995 and 1996. Figures for 1998 were not expected to be as healthy because of the effects of the Russian crisis.

## Unemployment and wages

Despite low official figures, unemployment is likely to have been high in 1996 and 1997. After having peaked at 4.4 per cent (about 80,000 unemployed) in mid-1996, the official unemployment rate fell to 3.2 per cent (55,000 unemployed)

in August 1997. However, unemployment and underemployment are hard to measure. The World Bank estimates that unemployment is 18 per cent in rural areas and 21 per cent in urban areas. There are an estimated 1 million workers outside the official employment statistics, consisting of 350,000 agricultural workers, 300,000 workers in the informal private sector, and 350,000 subsistence farmers.

Wages have kept pace with inflation in recent years. In 1997, the average real wage was broadly unchanged from the previous year, thereby remaining at about 80 per cent of the 1992 level. In US dollar terms, the average monthly nominal wage rose from US$22 in 1994 to US$38 in 1996, but fell to US$32 in the first half of 1997. The monthly minimum wage, to which government wages are linked, was kept unchanged at KGS75 from November 1995 to June 1997. It was increased by 20 per cent to KGS90 as of mid-1997.

Wage statistics should be interpreted cautiously as an indicator of the standard of living, as many workers have more than one job. Furthermore, workers often receive extensive supplemental income flow from their primary employer, such as free goods and services. This type of compensation is difficult to quantify but may add an extra 20 per cent to the basic wage.

## Structural reforms

The liquidation of large, loss making enterprises under the Enterprise Reform and Resolution Agency is nearing completion. Much has already been achieved, but the country's full potential has yet to be reached. The government is gradually eliminating subsidies and liquidating enterprises with substantial arrears. Significant progress has also been achieved in tax reform, budgetary reform, financial sector reform, completion of the privatisation of small firms and enactment of new legislation. The 1997 bankruptcy law is slowly being implemented.

The private sector is still at an early stage of development. Private investment is constrained by low private saving rates and remaining obstacles in the legal and regulatory framework. A sound banking system has been established but has not yet taken over the role as a provider of medium- to long-term loans and other financial services. In agriculture, while significant progress has been made to lay the foundation for private farming, further reforms are needed to improve the

Exhibit 10.6
**Current account balance (US$ million), 1995–98**

|  | 1995 | 1996 | 1997 | 1998 |
|---|---|---|---|---|
| Current account balance (US$ million) | –242 | –425 | –139 | –165 |
| Trade balance (US$ million) | –179 | –252 | –15 | –40 |

*Source:* EBRD.

legal foundation of land registration, access to finance and the de-monopolisation of the agro-industries.

## Fiscal deficit

The government significantly reduced the fiscal deficit, down to 9 per cent of GDP in 1997. The deficit is largely covered by concessionary loans from the IMF and World Bank, totalling US$600 million, US$360 million of which was earmarked for 1998. Privatisation, intended to alleviate the deficit, has slowed. Tax collection has also remained low, accounting for about 13 per cent of GDP in 1997. In November 1998 the government announced further restrictions on spending, clamping down on soft loans to state enterprises and promising to enforce bankruptcies if necessary.

## Privatisation

The Kyrgyz Republic has made the most progress in privatisation of all the region's republics. Many small businesses were privatised in the two years from 1991–93. The next stage of privatising medium and large businesses was also achieved rapidly. Some 69 per cent of total industrial assets were privatised by 1995. Key large and strategic enterprises remain in state hands, and although the programme has slowed, the government's record and proven commitment to privatise leaves observers confident that the process will continue.

The privatisation of medium and large enterprises began as early as 1994. However, the programme was suspended in May 1997 pending investigations into allegations of price rigging and corruption. The government has resumed the programme and has drawn up a list of about 300 medium and large enterprises to be sold by 2000. About 60 large state enterprises remain state owned, the most important of which will be sold to strategic investors on a case-by-case basis. These include the national airline and mining, power and telecommunication companies.

One issue that must be tackled is the monopoly position of some of the privatised enterprises. In the absence of an anti-monopoly law, these are beginning to exert anti-competitive practices.

*Top: Government building, Bishkek*
*Bottom: Guard at National Palace, Bishkek*

## Land reform

The Kyrgyz Republic has made impressive achievements on ownership of land. More than half of all land has been distributed to the public and in 1997, more than 80 per cent of agricultural output was produced by private farms.

A new law, which was passed by referendum in October 1998 after being repeatedly blocked by parliament, allows state and collective farms to be broken up and leased to farmers. The referendum further allows for outright ownership and gives landowners the right to buy and sell land after a five-year moratorium and to use it as collateral to raise credit. As such, this is a first in the CIS.

# Natural resources

The Kyrgyz Republic has enormous hydroelectric potential afforded by its mountainous landscape. Under Soviet development, it became a net exporter of hydroelectric power and today uses only 10 per cent of the power it produces and exploits only 9 per cent of its installed capacity. The government is considering several projects to increase the installed capacity and expand the distribution network. It needs to reform the sector, in particular pricing, and is seeking energy trading agreements with neighbouring countries.

It renewed a contract to sell electricity to China in 1998 and has renegotiated a regional programme with Uzbekistan and Kazakhstan.

## Minerals

The Kyrgyz Republic has mineral resources, notably gold, antimony, mercury, molybdenum, uranium oxide and large resources of coal. It was ranked the 19th largest gold producer in the world in 1998. There are four major mines – Jerui, Kumtor, Taldy Bulak Levoberezhny and Makmal – which together contain 90 per cent of the country's gold reserves. Jerui, the first gold mine was discovered in 1969. An American–Kyrgyz joint venture formed to exploit the mine did not work out and the government is seeking another partner.

The largest gold deposit is the Kumtor gold mine, with reserves of 514 tonnes. Discovered in 1978, it is located at over 4,000 metres above sea level in an area of constant permafrost and high seismic activity. The Canadian company Cameco entered into a joint venture with the government and formed the Kumtor Operating Company, of which the state-owned company Kyrgyzaltyn owns two-thirds and Cameco a one-third share. The company began production in 1997 with output of 15 tonnes. Annual production from 1998 was expected to be 17 tonnes.

The Kyrgyz Republic has significant resources of coal, but production has suffered from a lack of investment and ageing equipment. The republic also mines antimony and, together with China, dominates the market in the precious metal. The two recently signed an agreement that should coordinate sales of antimony to raise the price and allow the Kyrgyz Republic to produce antimony profitably.

# Finance

## Banking

*The National Bank of the Kyrgyz Republic (NBKR)*

This is the major regulatory body and introduced banking reforms in 1996 and 1997. It has made considerable progress in bank supervision, including the introduction of Basle Capital Adequacy guidelines in 1995 and step-up increases in minimum capital requirements to about US$1 million in January 1999.

It closed two former state-owned banks and is restructuring two others – Elbank and Agropombank – the last state-owned and largest commercial banks. The remaining commercial banks are privately owned. Domestic savings are low, at 2 per cent of GDP. Banks have only just begun to extend long-term loans and investment represents only 14 per cent of GDP.

The NBKR is in the process of modernising the payments system and has been strengthening bank supervision by issuing new regulations on insider lending, foreign exchange exposure, and loan provisioning.

The proportion of bank loans classified as being under monitoring has fallen from 13 per cent to 4 per cent. Three new bank licences were granted in 1997, of which two were to banks with foreign participation.

*Commercial banks*

By the middle of 1998, about 20 banks conformed with the prudential guidelines of the central bank with high solvency ratios and strict limits on related-party lending and foreign currency exposure. The banking system has stabilised considerably after a substantial restructuring of banks in 1996. A Debt Resolution Agency (DEBRA) was setup in 1996 and a Settlements and Savings Corporation (SSC) has been established to provide payments system services and a savings outlet, especially for rural areas.

In April 1997, Promstroi Bank and AKB Bank, two large former state-owned banks, were recapitalised without public funds. In March 1997, the Kyrgyz Agricultural Financial Corporation (KAFC) was launched to take over lending to the agricultural sector.

## The stock exchange

The Kyrgyz Stock Exchange (KSE) was set up in 1994. At first it traded privatisation vouchers and later started trading corporate securities. Activity is still limited on the KSE reflecting the size of the economy. In the first four months of 1998, trading was only US$1.5 million, although the market capitalisation has risen to about 30 per cent of GDP. This is mainly due to the pre-listing of the state-owned energy company Kyrgyzenergo before its privatisation. Only 47 companies are listed and only a few of them are large corporations. Foreign portfolio investment was estimated to be about US$50 million in mid-1998.

In August 1998, the first foreign issuer, the International Business Bank, listed on the KSE. Negotiations have started to establish KSE branch offices throughout the Kyrgyz Republic in an effort to provide local services to investors.

The first pension fund was started in April 1998.

### Treasury bills

The government regularly conducts auctions of three, six and 12-month Treasury bills (T-bills). It had planned to issue a US$200–300 million Eurobond in 1998 or 1999, but has postponed the idea in preference for maintaining the concessionary loans it currently enjoys from international banking institutions such as the World Bank and IMF. The government has also drawn up plans to issue coupon-bearing bonds for two, three and five years, which foreigners will be able to purchase through local brokers.

In February 1999 average yields on sixth issue 12-month T-bills was 56.85 per cent. For six-month paper it was 56.97 per cent and for three-month paper it was 52.57 per cent.

### Foreign exchange

In July 1998, the NBKR discontinued its weekly foreign exchange auctions. In line with IMF recommendations, it now intervenes directly in the interbank market for foreign exchange.

### Pension fund reform

The government plans to reform the pension system in 1999–2000 with the help of the IMF and World Bank. The current system is run on a pay-as-you-go scheme and is part of the Social Fund, which is also undergoing substantial structural change. Pension payments are currently a heavy burden on the Treasury, yet pensioners receive only a small sum and many are living in poverty. The reforms will gradually bring in a voluntary privately funded pension system that will run parallel to the current system. The retirement age will be raised and personal contributions increased.

## Foreign trade

In September 1998, the Kyrgyz Republic became the first FSU republic to join the WTO after the shortest application period in the WTO's history.

The Kyrgyz Republic started to liberalise its trade regime in 1994, with remaining export and import licensing agreements lifted by 1996. It established a customs union with Kazakhstan and Uzbekistan in 1994 and signed a customs union treaty in 1996, the CIS Customs Union, with Russia, Kazakhstan and Belarus. Parliament has not ratified the treaty, however. The Kyrgyz Republic has been running a heavy annual trade deficit, although in 1997 with boosted exports and lowered imports connected to the Kumtor mine, the government reported an improvement in its trade account (see Exhibit 10.7). Russia remains the Kyrgyz Republic's main trading partner, followed closely by Uzbekistan and Kazakhstan. This reliance is weakening and CIS countries accounted for 59 per cent of trade turnover in 1997, down from 80 per cent in 1996. China and India are developing into major trading partners.

The government had set up several free economic zones to boost trade. The zones have, however, increased the imbalance in trade because they provided a favourable climate for imports, which undercut local produce while doing little to improve exports. In November 1998, the government ordered the closure of three of the zones and decreed that the remaining zones restrict imports to 30 per cent of total trade.

## Foreign investment

Investment levels are low (see Exhibit 10.8) and foreign

Exhibit 10.7
**Trade balance, 1994–98**

|  | 1994 | 1995 | 1996 | 1997 | 1998 |
| --- | --- | --- | --- | --- | --- |
| Imports (US$ million) | 459 | 588 | 783 | 646 | 670 |
| Exports (US$ million) | 340 | 409 | 531 | 631 | 630 |
| Trade balance (US$ million) | –119 | –179 | –252 | –15 | –40 |

*Source:* EBRD.

Exhibit 10.8
**Net foreign direct investment (US$ million), 1994–98**

|  | *1994* | *1995* | *1996* | *1997* | *1998* |
|---|---|---|---|---|---|
| Net FDI | 45 | 96 | 46 | 83 | 29 |

*Source:* EBRD.

investors are few, partly because the Kyrgyz Republic lacks high-margin resources such as oil and gas found elsewhere in the region. According to the EBRD, foreign direct investment (FDI) amounted to US$309 million over the period 1993–98, just US$67 per capita, and investment is concentrated in the mining sector. The government set up a State Committee on Foreign Investments and Economic Assistance (Goscominvest) in 1998 to attract investors.

Perhaps the most notable foreign investment so far has been the Kumtor gold mine joint venture, which is one-third owned by a Canadian company and two-thirds owned by the state (see above).

The government has instituted rapid institutional reforms and a reasonable tax regime favouring foreign investment. Its currency has been stable and is freely convertible. The Kyrgyz Civil Code, modelled after the Dutch Civil Code, forms the basis for stable commercial relationships.

Individuals or legal entities can import to and export from the Kyrgyz Republic without limitations. The procedure for registering a foreign company or joint venture with the Ministry of Justice has been simplified. No formal approval of standard investment projects is required, although additional licensing may be required for activities such as securities issuance, investment funds and the exports of arms, explosives, art, specimen plants, or pharmaceutical raw materials.

Goscominvest aims to attract FDI and improve foreign assistance. In 1998, the Foreign Investment Agency was created as the executive body of Goscominvest to:

- Attract foreign investments and economic assistance.
- Increase the effectiveness of foreign investments.
- Prepare and distribute information about investment opportunities and conditions in the Republic.
- Improve the organisation and management of economic assistance.
- Coordinate projects of external economic and technical assistance financed by international financial organisations and institutions and state donors.
- Search for foreign partners to implement investment projects.
- Participate in the resolution of legal issues connected with activities of foreign investors, including support in getting licences, certificates on registration and other documentation.

- Analyse the investment environment and prepare proposals for improving it.

The Foreign Investment Agency incorporates the State Property Fund's Technical Cooperation Agency, its Direct Foreign Investments Agency, its Project Promotion Agency and Goscominvest's consulting agency on international procurement.

Public service-related sectors of the economy currently represent the best long-term prospects for foreign investment. The country is also hoping to develop its agricultural base. The country has the largest number of internet users per capita in the region, helped by an Asian Development Bank US$40 million-loan for education and another US$10-million loan for computers. Main investment priorities are:

- Transport, telecommunications, and energy.
- Public health and education.
- Agriculture and irrigation.

The country also offers opportunities for investment in industry in the following sectors:

- Hydroelectric power.
- Coal, minerals and metal mining.
- Electric engineering and machinery.
- Microelectronics.
- Wool processing and textiles.
- Food processing.
- Tourism.

## International relations

The Kyrgyz Republic is both mountainous and landlocked between Uzbekistan, Kazakhstan and Russia. This makes transport difficult and the country faces high tolls for the passage of goods along major transport routes through neighbouring countries. The Kyrgyz Republic is a member of customs unions (see above), but its small size means it suffers in negotiations on the export of electricity and water and the import of energy.

The country is moving away from its Soviet-era partners and looking south towards China and India. Delhi is the Kyrgyz Republic's nearest large city. China shares a long border with the Kyrgyz Republic and a vibrant trade has sprung up, with shuttle traders buying goods in China and taking them to Siberia. China has also become an important customer for Kyrgyz electricity. In April 1998, President Akayev visited China and signed a trade and economic cooperation accord.

The Kyrgyz Republic is home to over 40,000 Uighurs, who form a majority in the western province of Xinjiang across the border in China. There is a growing separatist movement among Uighurs in Xinjiang and the Kyrgyz law enforcement agencies have cooperated with Chinese authorities, recently arresting alleged separatists who crossed over from China. The Kyrgyz government has also joined an alliance with Russia, Uzbekistan and Tajikistan to fight against alleged Islamic extremists.

Relations with Kazakhstan are more relaxed and were highlighted by a high-level wedding in 1998 when President Akayev's youngest son married the daughter of the President of Kazakhstan, Nursultan Nazarbayev. The wedding took place during a Central Asian summit at Lake Issyk-Kul.

# 11 *Tajikistan*

## History, culture and politics

Tajikistan has been at war for most of the past six years. Although the country is geographically and politically isolated, it was once central to the Silk Route when the Tajik people controlled a strategic crossroads.

Tajikistan shares a 1,030-kilometre mountainous border with Afghanistan, along the Amu Darya river (formerly the Oxus river) and, further east, a 430-kilometre border with China. It suffered heavily from border changes under Stalin, losing the historic and cultural centres of Samarkand and Bukhara to the Uzbeks and rich agricultural land to the Kyrgyz.

Tajikistan was the least developed of the Soviet republics and the most isolated from Moscow. Ethnic Tajiks form 58 per cent of the 5.7 million population, Uzbeks about 23 per cent and ethnic Russians 11 per cent. The Tajiks are Sunni Muslims and speak Farsi, the only Central Asian people who do not speak a Turkic-based language. Some 4 million Tajiks live across the border in Afghanistan (more than in Tajikistan itself) and many Tajiks live in western China and Uzbekistan.

The Tajiks are one of the oldest peoples of Central Asia. They dominated the cities of the region long before the Mongols and the Turkic tribes passed through. Their ancestors were the Sogdians, who lived in the Pamirs before Alexander the Great crossed the Oxus and founded the city of Alexandria-the-farthest, which is today's city of Khodzhent in northern Tajikistan. Timur the Lame (Tamerlane) later ruled the region from Samarkand. The rise of the Uzbeks after Tamerlane signalled a reversal of the Tajik and Persian influence in Central Asia. The Tajiks were ruled by Uzbek khans and then the amirs of Bukhara and Kokand. Russia annexed Tajikistan in the late 19th century and began its rivalry with the British over the region, a battle for influence that became known as the Great Game.

The Russian revolution of 1917 inspired the Tajiks to break from Russian rule. The Bolsheviks retaliated and soon the entire region was at war. The Tajiks were crushed in 1921 but rose again around the Turkish leader Enver Pasha. Pasha was

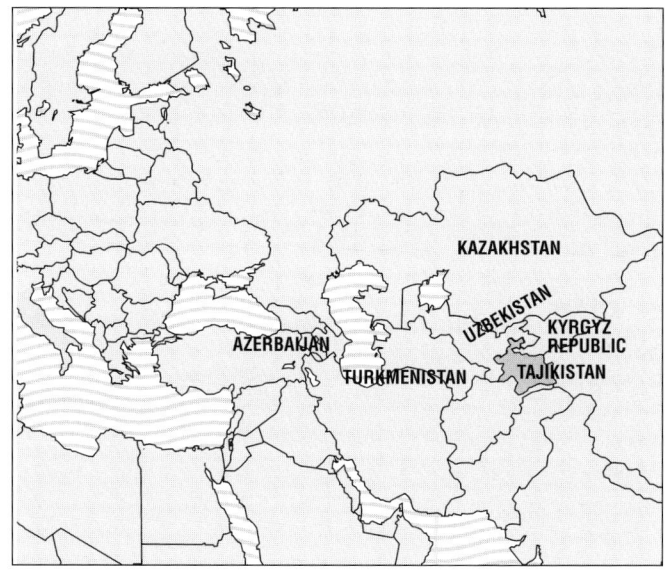

Exhibit 11.1
**Country facts**

| Area | 143,100 square kilometres |
|---|---|
| Population | 5.7 million |
| Capital | Dushanbe |
| Other large cities | Khodzhent, Tursunzade |
| Currency | Rouble (TR) |
| Exchange rate (February 1999) | TR998:US$1 |
| GDP per capita (1997) | US$179 |
| Inflation, annual average % (1998) | 46.3 per cent |

Exhibit 11.2
**Political information**

| President | Imomali Rakhmonov |
|---|---|
| Elected | 5 November 1994 |
| Term | 5 years |
| Percentage of vote | 71.6% (1991: unopposed) |
| Next election | Unknown |

126

killed in 1922 but some Tajiks went on fighting until 1929 at which point the Tajik Soviet Socialist Republic was formed.

The Soviets began massive cotton cultivation and extensive mining of Tajikistan's precious minerals. Nevertheless, Tajikistan remained underdeveloped, with low education levels and high rates of unemployment and infant mortality.

Public unrest broke out in the last days of the Soviet Union with riots in 1990. An Islamic, anti-communist opposition emerged during mass demonstrations in 1991 after the failed Moscow coup. By early 1992, the opposition was granted a share in government and communist leader Rakhmon Nabiyev resigned. Before leaving office, Nabiyev had armed militia groups and fighting had broken out in the south of the country, later moving to the capital, Dushanbe. The coalition government survived only a few months as civil war spread. In December 1992, the Russian airforce and army helped the pro-communist forces – mostly militia from the Kulyab region in southern Tajikistan – to eject the Islamic-democratic opposition from Dushanbe. By March 1993, they had pushed the opposition either back to the eastern province of Badakhshan or out of the country.

In 1993 Imomali Rakhmonov, a former communist chief of the Kulyab region, became the head of the Supreme Soviet. Approximately 20,000 Tajiks had died in the civil war, several hundred thousand had been made homeless and tens of thousands fled into Afghanistan, from where rebel forces continued a six-year fight against Rakhmonov's government.

The opposition parties were banned during the course of the next four years of war. Rakhmonov was elected president unopposed on 5 November 1994 and since 1998 has headed the People's Democratic Party. In 1997, he finally agreed to a peace deal and a power-sharing arrangement with opposition forces. The leaders and their fighters returned from exile to take up 30 per cent of parliamentary seats and a few government posts. The three main parties of the United Tajik Opposition (UTO) are now legalised. These are: the Islamic Renaissance Movement; the Democratic Party; and La'li Badakhshan (Ruby of Badakhshan).

## Political stability and prospects for change

The peace deal between the government and the UTO, which was signed in Moscow in June 1997, is an important achievement for Tajikistan and a turning point in ending the civil war. Because of Russia's close involvement in the civil war, the fact that it presided over the signing is considered important to the agreement's long-term success. Russia retains 20,000 troops in Tajikistan based just 100 yards from the presidential palace in central Dushanbe and also on the border with Afghanistan.

The peace deal allowed the opposition leaders, Said-Abdullo Nuri and Akbar Turajonzoda, to return to Tajikistan along with hundreds of fighters, to take part in a new government of national unity. Nuri, leader of the UTO, was made chairman of the National Reconciliation Commission and Turajonzoda took up the post of first deputy prime minister. Under the peace agreement, the opposition should hold 30 per cent of government posts, but progress is slow. By late 1998, the posts of two deputy prime ministers, the Minister of Economics and the Minister of Labour, were filled by opposition figures, as well as the head of the customs committee and committees on emergencies and agriculture. The opposition should also receive the Ministry of Defence portfolio, but the government has so far refused to endorse its candidate for the top post.

The reintegration of the opposition into political life in Tajikistan has inevitably been difficult and at times violent. In September 1998, the UTO's main secular leader, Otahon Latifi, was assassinated in central Dushanbe.

One problem with the peace agreement is that it omits the ethnic Uzbeks, from the Leninabad region in northern Uzbekistan, from the power-sharing arrangement. In Soviet times, they were the most powerful element in Tajikistan's ruling elite.

A real sign of the durability of the peace and reconciliation process will be Tajikistan's ability to hold parliamentary elections. There is no date set, but if the peace process and the coalition government hold together, elections could be held at the end of 1999.

The peace deal does not answer all issues and requires compromises from both sides. Fighting has broken out frequently, not only in Khodzhent, but in opposition-controlled regions and even in Dushanbe. Neither the president nor the leadership of the UTO wholly control the armed men under them.

Exhibit 11.3
**Inflation (%), 1994–98**

|  | 1994 | 1995 | 1996 | 1997 | 1998 |
|---|---|---|---|---|---|
| Inflation, annual average (%) | 350 | 609 | 418 | 87.8 | 46.3 |
| Inflation, year-end (%) | 1.1 | 2,133 | 40.5 | 163.6 | 10.1 |

*Source:* EBRD.

*Central Bank, Dushanbe*

# Macroeconomic profile

## Economic development

With the signing of the peace agreement in June 1997, the government has embarked on an ambitious reform programme in conjunction with a three-year IMF programme signed in 1998.

## Inflation and currency stability

The government has adhered to a tight monetary policy since the middle of 1997. Inflation was 88 per cent in 1997 and was estimated at around 50 per cent in 1998 (see Exhibit 11.3). The target for 1999 is 12.5 per cent.

The Tajik rouble experienced a sharp depreciation in the first half of 1997 but has shown remarkable stability since the middle of that year when the government tightened monetary control. Further depreciation is expected at a steadier pace. Tajikistan has experienced a trade deficit of varying but manageable levels over recent years. The first nine months of 1998 showed a deficit of US$171 million, aggravated by low aluminium prices. The cotton price has also affected trade figures, showing a dip in exports even though cotton output has increased.

## Price liberalisation

Most prices have now been freed from government control, with the exceptions of water, rents, communal services and transportation. However, electricity costs are still below commercially viable levels.

# The budget deficit

This was estimated at 3.7 per cent of GDP in 1998 and according to the 1999 budget will be 4.8 per cent of GDP. The deficit is largely covered by loans from the IMF and World Bank. However, radically decreased government spending is expected in the wake of the ceasefire. Tax collection remains low at around 13 per cent of GDP in 1997.

## Foreign exchange and trade

The government has pursued a liberal foreign exchange and trade regime. The temporary protectionist measures that were applied in 1996 have now been reversed. A uniform 5 per cent import tariff was applied at the end of 1998 with full de facto current account convertibility. The government is aplying for WTO membership and has completed a customs union, the CIS Customs Union, with Russia, the Kyrgyz Republic, Kazakhstan and Belarus.

## The IMF and World Bank

The IMF approved an Enhanced Structural Adjustment Facility (ESAF) in June 1998 worth US$128 million over three years. Some US$40 million of the disbursements are to be used to ensure currency stability and to build up reserves in 1998. The ESAF aims to combine fiscal restraint and focused expenditure on infrastructure.

The World Bank donor conference in Paris in May 1998 produced conditional pledges for Tajikistan from multilateral and unilateral donors of US$515 million for the years 1998–2000. The World Bank itself pledged US$220 million over three years and immediately agreed a US$50 million credit to facilitate economic reforms. Bilateral donors pledged about US$280 million. The killing of four UN workers in July 1998 has since derailed some of the loan offers, however.

## Foreign debt

Total foreign debt stood at US$874 million at the end of 1997, more than 100 per cent of GDP and nearly 125 per cent of export earnings. It rose to US$922.4 million in 1998 and the government expects it to grow to US$1.5 billion by 2003. The

---

**Exhibit 11.4**
**Economic structure, 1996–98**

|  | 1996 | 1997 | 1998 |
|---|---|---|---|
| GDP at constant prices (% change) | −4.4 | 1.7 | 3.0 |
| Industrial gross output (% change) | −23.9 | −2.8 | na |
| Agricultural gross output (% change) | −17.8 | 1.8 | na |

*Source:* EBRD.

government says, however, that it has renegotiated 90 per cent of its external debts. The International Finance Corporation is helping the government to set up a new system for financial reporting and debt monitoring.

## GDP

Annual per capita income is less than US$200, the lowest in Central Asia. After a drastic decline in GDP in the first half of the decade (30 per cent in 1993 alone) the economy showed modest growth from 1997 (see Exhibit 11.4). Growth is from a low base but impressive given the political instability. Real growth in GDP was 1.7 per cent in 1997 and was forecast to be 3 per cent in 1998. Much of the expansion is attributed to private sector development of agriculture, which is benefiting from peace and land reform. Cotton production, which provides one of Tajikistan's main exports, was expected to record growth in 1998. The 1997 abolition of state procurement and the creation of private cotton marketing companies helped boost production by 15 per cent that year alone. Industrial production was still declining in 1997, but the government reported a sharp turnaround in the first months of 1998.

## Privatisation and industrial restructuring

The government launched a privatisation programme in 1996 that aimed to privatise about 40 per cent of small enterprises and 10 per cent of medium-sized enterprises by the end of 1997 and to make all large enterprises joint stock companies. Vouchers were issued, but only 11 per cent of large companies had undergone any change by the end of 1997. There has been little restructuring or bankruptcies of state enterprises. There are many that owe large debts to workers, while others depend on state credits.

Although privatisation of small enterprises has been swift, Tajikistan is behind on large enterprise privatisation. The private sector represents only 20 to 30 per cent of GDP. Under the new IMF programme, small enterprise privatisation was due to be completed by the spring of 1999, but privatisation of large enterprises has only just begun. In 1998, 120 of the 400 medium and large enterprises were turned into joint stock companies in preparation for their privatisation and 30 enterprises were sold by auction. The government intended to sell all cotton ginneries in international tenders and complete the corporatisation of all assets to be privatised by March 1999.

The government has been more efficient with land reform. In 1996 it approved guidelines on allocating land on leases to farmers or to joint stock companies. A Land Reform Committee was set up to design the programme. Since 1996 there has been a sharp move towards individual leaseholds and there is now discussion of full ownership of land. The

*Presidential Palace, Dushanbe*

number of leaseholds rose from 670 in 1996 to 5,000 (covering 40,000 hectares) in 1997. In June 1997, the EU granted a loan of Ecu8 million (US$10.4 million) to the government to help carry out land reform and privatisation of agro-industrial facilities.

Like much of the Commonwealth of Independent States (CIS), large industrial enterprises are plagued by inter-enterprise arrears and bad debts. Problems at the state electricity company Barki Tajik and the aluminium producer TADAZ have yet to be tackled. In 1996, TADAZ was operating at 40 per cent capacity and paid just 9 per cent of its electricity bill.

As part of a restructuring programme begun in 1998, TADAZ is spinning off its non-core assets.

## Agriculture

### Cotton

Economic recovery has been largely fuelled by an increase in cotton production. Tajikistan like all the Central Asian countries supplied the Soviet Union with cotton and produced 900,000 tonnes a year before 1989. During the war, cotton was left unpicked and production is only just beginning to recover.

Cotton production grew in 1997 and looked set to continue growing in 1998. Approximately 358,000 tonnes of cotton were harvested in 1997, up from 318,000 tonnes in 1996. A harvest of 500,000 tonnes was the official estimate for 1998. The increase in production has been largely thanks to the introduction of futures contracts with western companies. That has led to cotton purchasing firms, including the former state monopoly Glavkhlopkoprom signing pre-financing deals with the large semi-privatised farms. In 1997, futures contracts worth US$50 million were reported with Paul Reinhart of Switzerland alone. Similar deals were made in 1998 with a US$120-million contract with Credit Suisse First Boston. The deal covers 120 collective farms which are expected to produce 230,000 tonnes of raw cotton, equivalent to over half the nation's production. Yields have also shown an improvement, up from 1.4 tonnes per hectare in 1996 to 1.6 tonnes in 1997. In 1998, cotton accounted for 20 per cent of Tajikistan's exports.

Besides cotton, the country offers competitive hydro-electric power and aluminium exports.

## Industry

Industry is concentrated in the north and west of the country as the eastern part of Tajikistan is largely mountainous and rural, although some mining has been developed. Mining began in the Soviet era and by the 1980s Tajikistan was producing coal, zinc, uranium, radium, bismuth, asbestos, mica, lapis lazuli and other minerals. It was also exporting electricity from 80 hydroelectric and oil-fired power stations. It produced some 300,000 tonnes of crude oil in 1989, but by 1990 output had declined to 90,000 tonnes due to a lack of spare parts and the departure of qualified Russian personnel. Aluminium production has been and remains the powerhouse of Tajikistan's industry, even during the war.

### Aluminium

In 1998, aluminium production accounted for 34 per cent of

exports. Production is based around a 20-year-old smelter, one of the largest in the world, at Tursunzade in western Tajikistan. The smelter is in a state of poor repair and the plant is grossly inefficient, reportedly using 40 per cent of the country's total electricity consumption.

Production has fallen consistently since independence and was 187,000 tonnes in 1997, less than half of the 1990 output of 450,000 tonnes. Exports have been hit by the double blow of low world prices and a general decline from ageing equipment. The government reported growth in 1998, however. Output was 158,600 tonnes for the first 10 months of 1998, showing 1.6 per cent growth on the previous year. Aluminium exports for January to April 1998 amounted to US$70.3 million. The government has plans to reorganise the management and enter into a joint venture with a foreign investor to renovate the smelter.

## Energy

Tajikistan produces just 2,000 barrels of oil a day and needs to import almost all its oil and petroleum products from FSU countries. Tajikistan has estimated natural gas reserves of 0.03 trillion cubic metres. However, gas production was minimal in 1993 and Tajikistan relies heavily on imports of natural gas from neighbouring Uzbekistan and Turkmenistan.

In June 1994, gas transmissions to Tajikistan from Uzbekistan were cut by 25 per cent for failure to pay an estimated US$46 million in outstanding gas bills. The government responded by immediately reducing gas supplies to municipal consumers.

Tajikistan's Pamir mountains create ample opportunity for producing hydroelectric energy. In an attempt to develop this energy source, Tajikistan has borrowed heavily from Russia. The terms of the loan require that Tajikistan pledge 50 per cent of the shares of the Nurek hydroelectric power station to Russia.

## Trade

There are no quantitative restrictions on imports, but there is a list of commodities which can only be imported after the Ministry of Economy and Foreign Economic Relations has examined the contract. This list includes trucks, oil and oil products, fertilisers, wheat, flour, rice, tea, sugar and vegetable oil. There is also a list of commodities which need government permission, including natural gas, uranium and other radioactive substances, narcotic and psychotropic substances, weapons and other military equipment, ammunition, cipher equipment and electric power.

# Transport

The civil war led to the decay of the country's transport system. Tajikistan's mountainous landscape adds to the problems in regional communications, which are particularly difficult between the north and the south. In winter, key roads between the two, which are divided by the Pamir mountain range, become impassable.

# Finance

## Banking

Tajik banking is dominated by large specialised banks left over from the FSU state banks. These banks – Agroprombank 'Shark', Tajikorienbank, and Tajikbankbusiness – account for over 96 per cent of bank lending. Sberbank remains the dominant institution in the individual savings market. The National Bank of Tajikistan (NBT) retains a significant role in the sector and the economy as a whole.

Overall, there are 13 banks in Tajikistan in addition to the NBT and Sberbank. Most are partially owned by state enterprises. In addition to these 13, there is a state insurance company and seven new insurance companies. (For a description of the five largest Tajik banks see Chapter 7, Banking and finance.)

Since 1996, the NBT has been implementing prudential regulations, which were revised in 1998. However, only one of the leading banks meets the guidelines and the NBT has insufficient staff to monitor the banking system effectively.

Cash is the dominant method of payment in the economy. Enterprises are not free to cash their bank deposits at will and must use payment orders for the majority of transactions. Cheques are hardly used.

Credit is subject to a variety of controls and has been directed mostly toward sustaining industries and maintaining living standards. Interest rates that are subject to controls are negative in real terms and lower than Russian nominal interest rates. This contributed to an outflow of currency before the collapse of the rouble zone, as arbitrage between Russian and Tajik interest rates took place. Highly negative real rates have also imposed a severe tax on household savings.

The banking sector has been significantly weakened by the loss of key Russian staff. This affects the central bank, commercial banks and the state insurance company.

Several problems stand out in the banking sector and the need to recapitalise the sector as a whole is a large and growing liability for the government. Tajikorienbank, considered one of the country's strongest banks, is estimated to have non-performing loans equal to 30 per cent of its portfolio. There is a continuation of banks' lending relationships with tradition-

*Currency exchange, Dushanbe*

al clients, many of which are nearly insolvent. There is also a lack of arms' length relationship between banks and their shareholders and a lack of effective supervision, particularly in relation to large exposure lending. In addition, hyperinflation has severely affected the capital of solvent banks.

## Bank restructuring

As part of a new bank restructuring programme agreed with the World Bank and IMF in 1998, major state-owned banks will undergo external audits and agree to a timetable for meeting the capital reserve requirements and prudential guidelines. Banks which do not comply will lose their licences. Minimum capital reserves were raised to US$500,000 at the beginning of 1999 and will rise to US$1 million by 2000.

Other financial reforms include the introduction of a Treasury bill market, new laws on banking and collateral effective from June 1998

## Bank laws and regulation

The laws regulating the banking sector are: Law on Banks and Banking Activities in the Republic of Tajikstan, Law on the National Bank in the Republic of Tajikstan, 1991; Resolution No. 778 of the Supreme Soviet of the Republic of Tajikistan Concerning the Basic Thrusts of Monetary Policies for 1993; October, 1991 Gosbank Rules Governing the Regulation of the Activities of Commercial and Cooperative Banks; Insurance Law (Draft); and the Stock Exchange Law.

There are several different legal types of banks: state; state-commercial; joint-stock commercial; commercial; and cooperative. The two state banks are Sberbank, which has a government guarantee on its deposits from households, and Khatlon Reconstruction and Development Bank. Joint-stock banks are able to issue equity to attract capital, in addition to the capital provided by their founders. Commercial and cooperative banks have no ability to issue equity and must rely on their founders for capital. (For a list of banks that have foreign correspondent accounts and are permitted to open hard currency savings accounts see Chapter 7, Banking and finance.)

The government needs to reduce its role by eliminating credit directives and reducing deficit financing.

### The Tajik Interbank Currency Exchange

On 23 May 1995 the first hard currency auction took place since the introduction of the new Tajik currency, the Tajik rouble, on 10 May. The auction was held at the Tajik Interbank Currency Exchange, a closed-stock company established by eight commercial banks, including the NBT. According to government decrees in support of the new currency, these auctions are to be held regularly.

## Foreign investment

Recent steps to improve the investment climate in Tajikistan include a revised bankruptcy law and a law on joint stock companies. Laws on property ownership and foreign investment were under discussion in 1999. The government welcomes foreign investment and Tajikistan offers opportunities for those willing to consider innovative forms of financing and significant risk. The barriers for imports and trade are more a result of geography than government policy. In general, legislation encourages foreign investment but contradictory decrees and a newly expanded tax burden complicate investment. There are still difficulties with repatriation of profits and capital, due to a lack of legislation protecting foreign profits, and problems over the ownership of land.

There were almost 200 registered joint ventures in Tajikistan in 1996, but only a minority of these are currently operational. Seventy per cent of existing joint ventures are involved in production and the rest are mainly in trading and services. The two largest joint ventures are with British mining companies, Zarafshan and Darvoz. There is one Italian joint venture, Giavoni, with Carrera jeans, which started in 1995, and one South Korean cotton processing joint venture, Koobal. There are six registered Tajik-American joint ventures and four American representative offices, but Interfur and Karakum Oil are the most active. There are 73 companies with foreign capital. Due to financial and bureaucratic problems, 229 joint ventures and foreign companies closed in 1996. Most joint ventures are located in areas where raw materials are found and many are in the northern part of the country. At the end of 1998 Coca-Cola announced that it would be investing US$15–20 million in a new plant in Dushanbe.

The Ministry of Economics and Foreign Economic Relations published a set of investment projects, which is designed to attract investors to Tajikistan. Enterprises on the priority list include:

- Several hydroelectric plants.
- A plant producing veterinary medicine.
- An agricultural research and development plant.
- A silkworm egg processing plant.
- A polyethylene bottle producing plant.
- A lemon processing plant.
- A baby food production plant.
- A bitumen processing plant.
- A prosthetic plant.
- A cotton bandage manufacturing plant.
- A bentonite clay processing plant.
- A stone mining plant.

Apart from these specific projects, there is investment potential in the mining sector. Tajikistan possesses large reserves of rare and non-ferrous metals, as well as silver and gold quarries. Western technology is needed to develop these deposits. Tajikistan has made public its desire to seek foreign partners to develop its gold deposits and is courting foreign mining firms. In addition, the government has also made strenuous efforts to attract foreign investment to the hydroelectric energy sector, with some projects already under construction. The country's potential hydroelectric power generation is put at 120 billion Kwh, but the country produced just 15 billion Kwh in 1996.

As part of its effort to attract foreign investment to the mining sector, a September 1995 Presidential decree created the Committee on Precious Metals and Semi-Precious Stones (Tajikdragmetsamotzvety). The goal of this committee is to develop and coordinate state policy on the extraction, processing and use of precious metals and stones.

In the agribusiness sector, there are opportunities in food processing and packaging, particularly in the packaging of tomato paste and dried fruit, as well as the bottling of juices and wine. Currently, about 40–50 per cent of fruits and vegetables that are harvested are wasted due to the lack of preservatives and packaging.

# 12 Turkmenistan

## History, culture and politics

The 19th century Russian imperial expansion met its fiercest resistance from the Turkmens, and Turkmenistan was finally annexed in 1886 after more than 70 years of fighting. Turkmenistan formally became a republic of the Soviet Union in 1925 and endured heavy purges under Stalin that ended the Turkmens' nomadic lifestyle and enforced collectivisation.

Most of the country is covered by the Karakum (Black Sand) desert which stretches from the Amu Darya river in the east to Ashgabat and the Kopet Dagh mountains that form the border with Iran. Huge irrigation projects were launched in Soviet times to turn Turkmenistan into a major cotton producer without regard for the unsuitability of the soil and climate. The 1,100-kilometre Lenin Karakum Canal was begun in the 1950s to bring water from the Amu Darya to Ashgabat and beyond, irrigating new cotton plantations along the way. There are still plans to continue the canal even though it has contributed to the devastating shrinking of the Aral Sea and the attendant environmental problems.

The tribal system in Turkmenistan survived nearly 70 years of communism and villages still adhere to tribal traditions. Turkmens are Sunni muslims, their language is Turkic and close to modern Turkish and Azeri. The Latin alphabet was adopted in 1995. Turkmens have maintained their famous tradition of carpet making, producing some of the finest knotted wool and silk carpets in the world.

The country's president, Saparmurat Niyazov, was elected unopposed with broad popular support as president of the newly declared sovereign Turkmenistan in 1990. He was reconfirmed president under the new Constitution in June 1992 with 99.5 per cent of the vote and his term was extended until 2002 by referendum in January 1994 with 99.9 per cent of the vote. Niyazov also holds the position of prime minister. The Council of Elders is expected to decide on the presidential candidate for the next elections in 2002 at its next session in December 1999. Technically, the president is only per-

Exhibit 12.1
**Country facts**

| Area | 488,000 square kilometres |
| --- | --- |
| Population | 4.4 million |
| Capital | Ashgabat |
| Other large cities | Chardzhou, Mary |
| Currency | Manat |
| Exchange rate (February 1999) | Tm5,200:US$1 |
| GDP per capita (1999) | US$482 |
| Inflation, annual average (1999) | 35.0% |

Exhibit 12.2
**Political information**

| President | Saparmurat Niyazov (born 1940) |
| --- | --- |
| Elected | 21 June 1992 (extended by referendum in 1994) |
| Term | 5 years |
| Percentage of vote: | 99.5% (1994 referendum: 99.9%) |
| Next election | 2002 |

133

Exhibit 12.3
**Inflation (%), 1994–99**

|  | 1994 | 1995 | 1996 | 1997 | 1998 | 1999(p) |
|---|---|---|---|---|---|---|
| Inflation, annual average (%) | 1,748 | 1,005 | 992 | 84 | 40 | 35 |
| Inflation, year-end (%) | 1,328 | 1,262 | 446 | 22 | 28 | na |

(p) projected

*Sources:* EBRD; ABN AMRO.

mitted to serve two terms, but Niyazov may bypass this because his first term was extended by referendum.

The president has widespread powers under the constitution and appoints the Cabinet of Ministers, the five regional governors and the heads of 40 provincial districts. The second highest authority is the Halk Maslahaty, or People's Council, which is a supreme council of executive, legislative and judicial branches. There is also the Majlis, an elected parliament of 50 deputies who pass legislation. Their term is five years and elections are expected to take place in 1999. Niyazov has also created a Council of Elders, based on an old tribal tradition, which like the People's Council, is largely symbolic.

President Niyazov, or Turkmenbashi (Head of the Turkmen) as he is known, dominates political and public life. There is only one registered political party, the Democratic Party, headed by the President. There is little independent political activity or revolutionary Islamic revival inside the country.

Turkmenistan is a member of the Commonwealth of Independent States (CIS), the Islamic Conference Organisation and NATO's Partnership-for-Peace, but President Niyazov has preferred to concentrate on bilateral ties rather than regional organisations. He has built good relations with Iran, and in particular with Turkey. Relations with Azerbaijan and Russia are marred by disputes.

## Macroeconomic profile

### Economic development

Turkmenistan has retained strong state control over the economy with little privatisation. The government has a declared policy of gradual transformation to a market economy but in some sectors there is virtually no progress. The economy is heavily reliant on production of oil, gas and cotton, which have traditionally accounted for over three-quarters of GDP. Turkmenistan is a potentially wealthy country in view of its rich resources and small population of just 4.4 million. Foreign direct investment (FDI) per capita is high (US$118 cumulative from 1989–96). Yet the average monthly wage (US$35 in 1997) remains among the lowest in the CIS and nearly 50 per cent of the population lives below the poverty line.

Developments in the economy up until 1998 were dominated by a contraction in output of gas and cotton, which make up roughly 50 per cent of the country's economic output. GDP declined by 40 per cent between 1993 and 1995 when gas sales to former Soviet countries collapsed. Despite one of the world's largest natural gas reserves, Turkmenistan has been denied access to west European markets through the regional pipeline system and this has largely limited its gas exports to Ukraine and countries of the Caucasus. The supply of hard currency into the economy has, therefore, been thin.

As a result, Turkmenistan stepped up its foreign borrowing and constrained imports by limiting access to foreign exchange in order to sustain gross international reserves at the equivalent of six to nine months of imports. The distortions on the economy associated with the continuation of central controls and the country's monetary policy have contributed to financial instability. Annual average inflation rates were around 1,500 per cent between 1993 and 1995.

In 1996, the government announced an economic reform package to address these growing economic difficulties. This included measures to liberalise the economy and unify the exchange rate and succeeded in reducing inflation from an average of over 900 per cent for that year to 22 per cent by the end of 1997 (see Exhibit 12.3). However, public sector wages doubled in October 1996 against a background of continued payment difficulties in the gas sector and a further decline in GDP due to severe crop failures. Massive wage arrears were incurred, directed credits were resumed on a substantial scale and price pressures intensified as imports continued to fall. In 1997 gas production fell by half and gas exports by 73 per

Exhibit 12.4
**Economic structure, 1997–99**

|  | 1997 | 1998 | 1999(p) |
|---|---|---|---|
| Nominal GDP (US$ billion) | 2.7 | 2.9 | 3.6 |
| Real GDP (% change) | −25.0 | −2.0 | 1.0 |
| Industrial output (% change) | −24.0 | −7.0 | 3.5 |

(p) projected

*Source:* ABN AMRO.

cent when shipments via Russia were suspended in March. Real GDP declined by 25 per cent.

However, some stabilisation has been achieved since then on the back of a construction boom and a sharp rebound in raw cotton and wheat production. The economy is expected to grow in 1999 with both increases in GDP and industrial ouput expected (see Exhibit 12.4).

## The currency and exchange rate

The national currency, the manat, was introduced in 1993 and has held its value well, depreciating by roughly 3 per cent against the dollar between 1996 and 1997. In April 1998, the commercial and official exchange rates were unified as a single rate. Foreign institutions have criticised the screening of access to foreign currency by the State Agency of Foreign Investment, access which is normally tied to import requirements. Surrender requirements remain on export earnings.

## Foreign reserves and the national debt

The build up in foreign reserves, which stood at US$1.2 billion in the fourth quarter of 1998 (see Exhibit 12.5), has been achieved at a cost of a higher debt burden. To ensure the servicing of foreign debt, new regulations were implemented requiring hard currency revenues from three key sectors – oil, gas and agriculture – to be paid directly to the central government.

Exhibit 12.5
**Foreign reserves (US$ million), 1997–99**

|  | 1997 | 1998 | 1999 |
|---|---|---|---|
| Foreign reserves (US$ million) | 1,120 | 1,200 | 1,200 |
| Import cover (months) | 12.5 | 11.1 | 8.7 |
| Total debt/export ratio | 1.0 | 0.7 | 0.6 |

*Source:* ABN AMRO.

## Price liberalisation

The doubling of budgetary wages in early 1997, coupled with the resumption of preferential directed credits on a large scale, still poses a serious threat to price stabilisation. Most food prices have been liberalised, but prices for utility services remain heavily subsidised. The most important cash crops of cotton and wheat are procured by the state at prices far below world levels. Procurement prices for cotton and wheat have been kept at January 1997 levels, a decline of 30 per cent in real terms by mid-1998. Petrol prices doubled in January 1998 to US$0.15 per litre, but this policy was quickly reversed.

*Top: Ashgabat Sports Stadium*
*Bottom: Turkmenbashi Port*

# Privatisation

The economy is still dominated by the state sector. Approximately 81 per cent of registered small enterprises were private by 1997, but their contribution to GDP is estimated at only 25 per cent. Privatisation has so far been largely confined to small enterprises. By 1998, less than half of the small state-owned enterprises had been privatised with virtually no progress in the privatisation of medium- and large-scale state enterprises.

The government made major revisions to the Privatisation Law in 1997, allowing foreign investors to participate in the privatisation process on an equal footing with local entities and allowing for 100 per cent privatisation. However, in the first three months of 1998, only 13 out of 70 enterprises offered for auction were sold.

In January 1998, a new Privatisation Centre was created at the State Agency for Foreign Investment. Its purpose was to privatise 18 large-scale state-owned enterprises through international investment tenders.

At the beginning of 1999, President Niyazov issued a resolution to privatise the agro-industrial sector on a case-by-case basis.

# Agriculture

This is the second most important sector in the economy, accounting for about 10 per cent of GDP and 44 per cent of employment in 1997 despite the fact that only 4 per cent of the country is arable, the rest being desert. The most important cash crops are cotton and wheat. Cotton is exported after processing into cotton fibre, while wheat is consumed domestically.

Turkmenistan also produces livestock, fruits and vegetables for domestic consumption. As with the tightly controlled energy sector, the government continues to exert significant control over the agricultural sector, primarily through state orders.

The government has also turned its attention to wheat production in recent years to ensure that the country is self-sufficient. It has increased the amount of land devoted to wheat growing and spent US$1 billion repairing and upgrading irrigation systems, mills and storage warehouses. The area under cultivation has been increased sharply from 260,000 hectares in 1993 to 452,000 hectares in 1997. The 1998 harvest was a good one and production almost doubled from 600,000 tonnes in 1997 to 1.25 million tonnes. That satisfies domestic demand, which is around 1 million tonnes, although the quality of the wheat remains poor. While farmers now hold land on private leasehold, processing industries remain state owned. Livestock farming is carried out by predominantly private enterprises, and milk and meat are sold free of state controls.

## Land and agricultural reform

Land has been transferred to individual leaseholds in preparation for privatisation, as envisaged under the agricultural reform programme announced at the end of 1996, and the government has made rapid progress in transferring agricultural land to private farmers. Agricultural services and processing industries continued to be state owned.

## Textiles

Turkmenistan traditionally exported its cotton in either a raw state or as cotton yarn. It produced 14 per cent of the Soviet Union's cotton fibre but only 3 per cent of its textiles. Since independence, however, the government has made a concerted effort to develop its own textile manufacturing. The showcase for this programme is the US$90 million Gap–Turkmen textile factory not far from the capital, Ashgabat. The factory employs over 1,000 workers and produces jeans and denim wear for domestic and foreign markets using local cotton. Altogether four textile factories were built in 1997, all were joint ventures with foreign investors.

# Construction

Construction activity is growing. Its share of GDP has more than doubled to reach 24 per cent in 1998. The increase reflects large investment projects. These include: the refurbishment of the Turkmenbashi refinery; the construction of several banks and other large buildings; a new mosque; a presidential palace; the pipeline to Iran; a sports stadium; and the completion of four textile plants. Most of the construction has been undertaken by foreign contractors and financed partly by foreign loans.

# Natural resources

Turkmenistan's gas sector will remain the cornerstone of the economy for the foreseeable future. Following considerable investment in the sector in recent years, production of crude oil also shows signs of substantial increases. Oil production rose by 11 per cent in 1997, largely due to foreign investment projects, and was projected to rise further in 1998 (see below). Investment in the oil and gas sectors was forecast as Tm4.7 trillion in 1999 (approximately US$900,000), more than twice the amount invested in 1998.

Turkmenistan plans to increase its energy output by inviting foreign investment to the country's offshore oil and gas deposits (see below).

## Gas

Turkmenistan is one of the richest countries in terms of natural gas per capita in the world. It also has substantial reserves of oil, both onshore and offshore under the Caspian Sea (see below). Its vast potential prompted ambitions that, with independence, the country would become a new Kuwait. However, unlike Kuwait, Turkmenistan has no easy access to the international market. The exit traditional route for Turkmenistan's gas is through the Russian pipeline system, which, since March 1997, has been closed to Turkmen gas. Turkmenistan's other neighbours are Iran and Afghanistan, neither of which offer Turkmenistan easy access to markets, and Azerbaijan across the Caspian Sea, which presents a physical and geo-political obstacle. Turkmenistan, perhaps more than any other country in the region, has found its energy wealth trapped.

Natural gas reserves are calculated to be 8.1 trillion cubic metres, and potential reserves could be as high as 14 Tcm. Proven gas reserves are 2.9 Tcm. Much of this is concentrated in the Sovetabad and Dauletabad fields in south-eastern Turkmenistan. Gas production peaked in 1989 at almost 90 billion cubic metres (Bcm), but after independence it fell to an average 24 Bcm during 1994–96. Turkmenistan lost access to European markets through the Russian pipeline in 1993 and in 1997 stopped exporting gas via Russia completely.

The underlying problem was that Turkmenistan was not paid the full value for its gas by Armenia, Azerbaijan, Georgia and Ukraine. Turkmenistan became a large-scale creditor and could ill afford to sustain the US$1.2 billion that is was owed by other republics. In 1996, Turkmenistan agreed a deal with the Russian monopoly Gazprom and the trading company Itera to sell gas for US$42 per 1,000 cubic metres. When this deal broke down in March 1997, and Turkmenistan was still unpaid, it stopped exporting via Russia. Since then the government has failed to reach agreement in talks with Gazprom.

Projected figures for gas production in 1999 are 36 Bcm.

### Arrears

By March 1998, the payments crisis in the gas sector had spread across the rest of the economy and overdue payments to suppliers reached 42 per cent of GDP. A netting programme had reduced this amount to 23 per cent by August. However, without an effective bankruptcy law and a developed financial system, the problem of arrears is unlikely to be solved quickly.

## New gas pipeline routes

Turkmenistan has sought other routes for its gas in place of exporting via Russia. So far, it has just one working alternative. In December 1997, Turkmenistan and Iran opened the Korpedzhe–Kurdkui pipeline, the first section of a Turkmenistan–Iran–Turkey–Eruope pipeline. This provides about 2 Bcm of gas a year to the northern part of Iran. Maximum capacity will be 8 Bcm of gas and Turkmenistan will pay for its share of the construction in gas supplies. The demand is limited and there is as yet no onward connection to take the gas further to the international market. This an other planned pipeline routes are complicated by politics. The Turkmenistan–Europe pipeline via Iran is one of two options westwards. The second is across the Caspian Sea to Azerbaijan and through Georgia to Turkey shadowing the proposed main oil pipeline from the Caspian. Feasibility studies are in progress. Each option has difficulties. US sanctions against Iran prevent any US company's involvement in the first pro-

ject, which has been proposed by a consortium of three European companies. The second route is complicated by Turkmenistan's dispute with Azerbaijan over their sea border and over ownership of several offshore oil fields that lie close to the dividing line.

More ambitious plans to pipe gas via Afghanistan to Pakistan are on hold in view of the continued fighting in Afghanistan, although Memoranda of Understanding have been signed with all the countries involved. A plan to pipe gas east to China is proposed but has yet proved economically viable.

## Oil

The government has turned its attention to oil extraction and export. Although Turkmenistan has had an oil industry for a century, it has historically been neglected in favour of gas production and lacks infrastructure and personnel. Oil reserves are estimated to be two to four billion barrels. Oil production has been steadily increasing since 1995. Oil production reached 128,000 barrels a day (bpd) in 1997 up from 88,000 bpd in 1996. During the first half of 1998, oil production reached 130,000 bpd, with plans to reach 140,000 bpd by the end of the year. During the first 11 months of 1998, oil extraction had increased 21 per cent over 1997. Crude oil output in 1997 was 4.7 million tonnes, up from 4.4 million tonnes in 1996. The increase continued with 4.1 million tonnes produced in the first nine months of 1998. The government hopes production will reach 30–40 million tonnes by 2005. Turkmenistan has two oil refineries: one at the Caspian Sea port of Turkmenbashi, which is being upgraded with foreign financing, and one at Chardzhou.

## Foreign participation in the energy sector

The government passed a new Petroleum Law in 1997 that includes a model production sharing agreement (PSA) and has since signed two PSAs with foreign oil companies. Several agreements existed before then, among them a joint venture between the Irish company Dragon Oil and Turkmenneft, the official government agency responsible for oil production, on existing fields in western Turkmenistan. Turkmenistan began exporting crude in 1998 via tanker to Azerbaijan and through a swap deal with Iran, delivering crude to Iran's Caspian Sea coast and swapping it for oil to be exported from the Persian Gulf.

In 1996 Mobil Corporation of the United States has joined Monument Oil of the United Kingdom to develop a large concession at Nebit Dag in western Turkmenistan and signed a PSA in 1998 to develop the adjacent Garashsyzlyk field. Petronas Carigali of Malaysia, which signed the first PSA in Turkmenistan, has begun drilling offshore in the Caspian Sea. In September 1997, the government invited tenders for further offshore exploration, but interest has been limited. Several of

*Memorial to the 1948 earthquake*

Exhibit 12.6
**Trade balance, 1994–99**

|  | 1994 | 1995 | 1996 | 1997 | 1998 | 1999 |
|---|---|---|---|---|---|---|
| Imports (US$ million) | 1,691 | 1,644 | 1,532 | 1,004 | 1,300 | 1,650 |
| Exports (US$ million) | 2,176 | 2,084 | 1,691 | 759 | 1,100 | 1,500 |
| Trade balance (US$ million) | 485 | 441 | 159 | −245 | −200 | −150 |

*Sources:* EBRD; ABN AMRO.

the blocks are contested by Azerbaijan and Iran and, until there is an agreement on the division of the Caspian Sea into sectors, these deals are unlikely to advance. (For details of these and other foreign investments, see Chapter 5, Energy: the key to growth.)

### Other mineral extraction
Turkmenistan has its own mineral and processing plants for its large resources of iodine, sulphur and phosphates. However, many of these are old and in disrepair. The government has announced plans to build new plants, in particular to boost fertiliser production.

## Infrastructure

The government has recently opened infrastructure projects to open tendering after years of closed bilateral contracts. The European Bank for Reconstruction and Development (EBRD) is helping to renovate the road from Ashgabat to Mary and also the port at Turkmenbashi.

## Trade

The government has reoriented trade away from its former Soviet partners. Trade with Russia has fallen from a 54 per cent share of the total to 3 per cent. Trade with Iran and Turkey has grown in comparison and Turkey is now Turkmenistan's leading trading partner, accounting for over US$200 million worth in the first nine months of 1998. The opening of a new 300-kilometre rail link with Iran in late 1996 has also helped to boost trade.

Exhibit 12.6 shows Turkmenistan's trade balance for 1994–99.

## Foreign investment

FDI has declined in Turkmenistan from a peak of US$233 million in 1995 to US$110 million in 1998 (see Exhibit 12.7).

Exhibit 12.7
**Net foreign direct investment (US$ million), 1994–98**

|  | 1994 | 1995 | 1996 | 1997 | 1998 |
|---|---|---|---|---|---|
| Net FDI | 103 | 233 | 129 | 108 | 110 |

*Sources:* EBRD; ABN AMRO.

The government is anxious to attract foreign investment and the Ministry of Foreign Economic Relations has identified priority areas that include gas, communications, telecommunications, transportation, industry, irrigation, agricultural investments, textiles and health. The government has listed 93 key investment projects in these sectors. Additionally, two investment funds were established to make hard currency available for development in the oil and gas, and agriculture sectors.

Turkmenistan is also in the process of announcing international tenders for competitive bids on government projects.

Almost all companies that invest in Turkmenistan form a joint venture with a local company and most include a government partner. German investors have been active and are seeking to increase their investments. At least 10 German firms already operate in Turkmenistan.

## Regulatory environment

Laws on foreign investment, banking, property ownership and intellectual property rights protection passed in 1992 were intended to attract foreign investors. However, Turkmenistan continues to lack sufficient tax, labour, and health and safety laws. This problem could frustrate foreign business ventures. The 1992 Law on Foreign Investment is the principal regulating statute. Foreign investors must register at the Ministry of Foreign Economic Relations and report quarterly to the Ministry on their activities in Turkmenistan.

Most import and export operations, excluding those for cotton, oil and any other government procurement imports, must be conducted through the State Commodities and Raw Materials Exchange (CRME) in Ashgabat. Foreign trading companies and joint ventures must register their transactions with the CRME and pay a 0.2 per cent commission. Additionally, foreign trading companies must receive a licence from the State Agency for Foreign Investment (the Investment Agency) to export products manufactured in Turkmenistan and to import products needed for production. Only the CRME has the authority to issue export-import licences for commercial transactions. These licences are awarded by the CRME through an auction process.

The newly created Investment Agency monitors all foreign investment. It reviews investment proposals and foreign currency credits proposed by government ministries. All ministries and agencies must receive Investment Agency approval before committing to foreign procurement or investment projects. Once the board approves the project, the president normally issues a decree. Preference tends to be given to government priority projects.

The Investment Agency operates within the Turkmen State Bank for Foreign Economic Affairs (Vneshekonombank). Vneshekonombank is a key institution for foreign businessmen, investors and exporters. It is also a fiscal agent for the Turkmen government. Vnesheconombank and the Central Bank of Turkmenistan (CBT) are the only banks that issue sovereign guarantees required for many types of multilateral funding. All state guarantees must be registered with the Investment Agency.

# Finance

## Relations with the supranational agencies

Turkmenistan has never had an agreement with the IMF, although the Fund has a permanent representative in Ashgabat and conducts regular consultations with the government. By the end of June 1998 the EBRD had agreed loans totalling about US$180 million to renovate roads and the port of Turkmenbashi, as well as to assist small businesses.

## Banking

The banking sector consists of 15 commercial banks and the central bank, the CBT. Seven banks are wholly or mostly state owned, four banks are private domestic banks and two are branches of foreign banks. Three state-owned banks dominate the sector and have control over 80 per cent of banking credits. Virtually all of the banks' credits and deposits are from state-owned companies and the use of directed lending at near zero rates is commonplace. The financial sector is not well developed, although banking controls were improved in 1997 with the introduction of loan regulations and capital requirements for banks. However, interference from the government and weak credit appraisal skills have created the problem of non-performing loans, which increased over 40 per cent in the first four months of 1998.

## Treasury bills

As yet there is no securities market in Turkmenistan, although Treasury bills (T-bills) have been issued intermittently since mid-1996. However, these were placed directly with commercial banks and are not tradeable. At the end of 1997, T-bills accounted for less than 1 per cent of GDP.

# Appendix: Fiscal environment

Ernst & Young

## Taxation

The application of Turkmeni tax legislation will depend upon whether or not companies are conducting activities in connection with PSAs for oil companies.

Foreign companies that are not conducting activities under PSAs are subject to tax under the domestic legislation.

## Profits tax

This is payable upon the net income of the entity. Profits tax is only payable by foreign companies operating through branch offices (that is, FLEs) on net income which is sourced in Turkmenistan. The current rate of profits tax is 25 per cent.[1]

It is interesting to note that newly established locally incorporated Turkmen companies (TLEs) with foreign participation are exempt from profits tax during the recoupment period of the initial capital investments, provided that the foreign investor has contributed more than 30 per cent to the charter fund in foreign currency.

The tax base would consist of profit from the sales of goods and services, fixed assets, other property, and income from non-sale operations. Profit is calculated by taking into account costs that are included in the Turkmen Cost of Production Statute,[2] such as material production costs, depreciation (which is stated at low statutory rates), salaries and administrative expenses.

Non-deductible expenses include start-up costs, almost all interest costs (except for interest on supplier credit) and non-compulsory insurance. However, certain costs that have limited deductibility in some other CIS countries are fully deductible in Turkmenistan, such as advertising and representational costs.

The Profits Tax Instruction[3] provides for few additional exemptions and deductions, the most significant of which relate to profit reinvested in social, health, and cultural facilities. None of the following appear to be deductible: loss carryforward/carryback, charitable contributions and capital investments of a production nature.

## Withholding tax

There is no branch remittance tax on payments made by a branch office of an FLE directly to their head office company outside Turkmenistan.

However, any payments that are made by FLEs to foreign companies (other than the head office company) are subject to withholding tax. Tax at a rate of 15 per cent will be withheld on most types of income. It should be noted that a rate of 6 per cent on income earned from international transport and 3 per cent for transport income in Free Economic Zones are assessable.

### Value-added tax (VAT)
FLEs are liable to pay VAT, which is charged on turnover from the sale of goods, works and services in Turkmenistan. Imports and exports are included in the taxable base. The current rate is 20 per cent.

The amount of VAT payable to the Budget is the difference between the VAT received from customers and the VAT paid on inputs.

### Import and export VAT
VAT at a rate of 20 per cent is paid on imported material to the VAT office directly. VAT paid upon the import of goods may not be reimbursed from the Budget. Rather, amounts of tax are included in the cost of the production of goods, and are therefore deductible for profits tax purposes. In addition, exports of goods and services are also subject to VAT.

## Currency issues
### Invoices
According to officials at the Department for Foreign Relations of the Turkmenistan Main State Tax Inspectorate, in order to be permitted to invoice customers and clients in foreign currency, all entities including branch offices of FLEs must obtain a licence from the Central Bank of Turkmenistan and from the president.

According to the officials, a licence is also required in circumstances where an FLE intends to invoice another FLE for goods or services provided in the territory of Turkmenistan.

It is not clear how this requirement is enforced where two FLEs make settlements outside the territory of Turkmenistan for goods or services provided in the country.

### Bank accounts
Companies are permitted to open a local currency account as soon as they receive a certificate of registration from the State Investment Agency. However, companies are not entitled to open a foreign currency account until they have received their final certificate of registration with the tax authorities.

## Personal income tax
### Definition of resident
For the purposes of personal income tax, persons staying in Turkmenistan for more than 183 days in any calendar year are considered to be tax residents.[4] Persons staying in Turkmenistan for more than 183 days in any calendar year, as residents, are subject to Turkmen personal income tax on their worldwide income. For non-residents, only income from sources in Turkmenistan is taxable.[5]

### Tax rate and payments
The personal income tax rates in Turkmenistan are:

| Income (in manats) | Tax rates |
|---|---|
| Less than 200,000 | Exempt |
| Between 200,001 to 400,000 | 8% of amount in excess of 200,000 |
| Between 400,001 to 650,000 | 16,000 + 10% of amount in excess of 400,000 |
| Between 650,001 to 900,000 | 41,000 + 12% of amount in excess of 650,000 |
| Between 900,001 to 1,200,000 | 71,000 + 14% of amount in excess of 900,000 |
| Between 1,200,000 to 1,500,000 | 113,000 + 17% of amount in excess of 1,200,000 |
| Between 1,500,001 to 2,000,000 | 164,000 + 20% of amount in excess of 1,500,000 |
| More than 2,000,000 (approx. US$500) | 264,000 + 25% of amount in excess of 2,000,000 |

Tax residents are required to file preliminary returns, estimate their income, and make advance payments of personal income tax by 15 May, 15 August and 15 November. The final return is due by 1 March of the following year. If foreign employees are paid from the local payroll, income tax must be withheld at source, as with Turkmen citizens.

## Social Fund contributions

In Turkmenistan, there are three types of social security taxes:

- Social Protection Fund – contributions are 30 per cent of employees' salaries (not including salaries paid to foreign employees), and payable by employers.
- Medical Insurance Fund – contributions are 4 per cent of the salaries paid to Turkmeni citizens who have volunteered to join the medical insurance fund, and withheld by employers.

- State Pension Fund – contributions are 1 per cent of salaries paid to Turkmeni citizens (in cash or in kind), and payable by employees (not including salaries to paid foreign employees unless otherwise specified in legislation).

Foreign employees are not subject to Voluntary State Medical Insurance, unless otherwise specified in international treaties or Turkmeni legislation.[6]

Foreign employees do not pay State Pension Fund contributions, unless otherwise specified in international treaties or Turkmeni legislation.[7]

## Excess wages tax
This is one of the most substantial tax burdens facing a company operating in Turkmenistan. This tax is levied at a rate of 50 per cent of any employment remuneration over approximately US$10 per month per employee, and is payable by the employer. The legislation clearly states that taxable representations of FLEs must pay the tax, although it is unclear whether a non-taxable FLE is required to pay it.

## Other taxes
### Assets tax
This tax is payable by representations of FLEs at an annual rate of 1 per cent.

The taxable base includes fixed assets, current assets excluding monetary resources, incomplete construction and transportation facilities. For tax purposes, the average annual net-book value of assets is used. Gross profit for corporate tax purposes is decreased by the amount of assets tax payable.

### Tax on transport facilities
This levy applies to buses, cars and motorbikes. It is payable in foreign currency for transport facilities crossing into the customs territory of Turkmenistan or in transit across Turkmenistan.

The amount of the levy varies in accordance with a vehicle's engine capacity. For vehicles used in the transportation of goods up to 10 tonnes it is US$50, for vehicles with an engine capacity of 10–20 tonnes inclusive it is US$100, for vehicles with an engine capacity over 20 tonnes it is US$150.

## Local taxes
Local administrative bodies are given the right to introduce a number of local taxes, which are listed in Instruction No. 5 of 5 March 1994 of the main state tax inspectorate 'Concerning the Procedure for the Calculation and Payment to the Budget of Local Taxes and Levies'. These taxes are paid from the net profit of legal entities or income of physical persons. The most significant ones are described below.

## Advertising tax

This is payable by FLEs that advertise products. The actual rate is established by the local government agency, but cannot exceed 5 per cent of the cost of advertising.

## Special public services levies

This levy is payable by FLEs, and the rate is set by the local government agency, but cannot exceed 1 per cent of the enterprise's annual wages fund on the basis of the minimum monthly wage.

## Compliance issues

Under the FLE Instruction, each FLE that operates in Turkmenistan must not only register with its local tax office, but also file its own tax returns. A representation (whether or not it is taxable) of an FLE must submit the following:

- An audited tax return by 15 March of the year following the reporting year.
- A statement of activities by 15 March using the established forms.
- Other tax returns for the various taxes to which the FLE is subject (see above).

The tax return may be submitted without being audited, but the FLE must submit an agreement for carrying out an audit by a licensed audit organisation.

## FLEs and TLEs

Below is a summary of the taxation implications for FLEs and TLEs operating in Turkmenistan.

- FLEs have less onerous obligations in relation to registration, reporting and compliance as compared with TLEs. For example, an FLE pays profit tax only once a year in arrears, while a TLE must make twice monthly advance payments.
- FLEs operating in Turkmenistan through a representation are subject to profits tax only on profit earned through that representation, while a TLE is subject to profits tax on its worldwide income.
- Sales of goods and services where title passes outside Turkmenistan and activities that relate to the purchase of goods for re-sale abroad are exempt from profits tax for FLEs.
- Certain activities (such as, collecting and disseminating information, advertising and any activities of a preparatory or auxiliary character) may be exempt from profits tax under Turkmeni domestic legislation or the provisions of a relevant double taxation treaty.
- An FLE can pay its Turkmeni employees in foreign currency from abroad, while a TLE is restricted from doing this.
- A representation of an FLE that is non-profitable may be exempt from the excess wages tax (see above).

## Taxation under PSA arrangements

If a company establishes a branch office to perform work as a contractor to a PSA in Turkmenistan, the taxation rules will be different from the rules established under domestic legislation.

Each PSA contains special rules that govern the taxation of contractors and subcontractors who are conducting operations under that particular PSA. Therefore, in order to determine the exact terms of taxation for a particular PSA, it would be necessary to review the rules under that PSA. In practice, contractors may be able to negotiate terms that vary from those contemplated in the Petroleum Law as described below.

## Contractors

Contractors that are registered and established in Turkmenistan are only liable to profits tax at the rate agreed in the PSA. Certain PSAs provide for a profits tax rate of 25 per cent (equal to the domestic rate).

Contractors to a PSA are not liable to pay VAT, customs duties or other domestic corporate taxes, apart from royalties as provided under the PSA.

Contractors are required to maintain their tax books and records in US dollars, in accordance with international petroleum industry accounting standards.

In addition, employees of contractors are subject to personal income tax in accordance with the domestic legislation. Contractors are also liable to make Social Fund contributions on behalf of Turkmen employees in accordance with the domestic legislation.

A contractor is required within 30 days after the end of each six-calendar month period to provide the government with a list of all Turkmeni and expatriate personnel, together with details of the remuneration paid and the amount of income tax withheld during that six-month period.

In accordance with the Petroleum Law, contractors are required to obtain a licence to conduct hydrocarbon activities in Turkmenistan.

## Subcontractors

Foreign companies that establish a branch office in Turkmenistan to perform work are classified as foreign subcontractors under the PSA.

Based on current PSAs concluded in Turkmenistan, foreign subcontractors that are registered and established in Turkmenistan are only liable to profits tax on taxable profit in the same way as contractor parties to the PSA. This means that foreign subcontractors are taxed at the rates agreed in the PSA (usually 25 per cent).

Foreign subcontractors to a PSA are entitled to the same exemptions as domestic ones and do not have to pay customs duties, VAT or other domestic corporate taxes. Employees of foreign contractors are also subject to personal income tax and Social Fund contributions in accordance with the domestic legislation.

A foreign subcontractor is also required to lodge half yearly reports in relation to all Turkmeni and expatriate personnel. It should also be noted that:

- Foreign subcontractors whose normal place of business is outside Turkmenistan and who are not permanently established in Turkmenistan are only liable to profits tax in accordance with the domestic legislation.
- If foreign subcontractors maintain a permanent establishment in Turkmenistan that also receives income from non-PSA activities, foreign subcontractors are liable to pay taxes on such income in accordance with domestic legislation.
- Employees of foreign subcontractors are subject to personal income tax in accordance with the domestic legislation. Foreign subcontractors are also liable to make Social Fund contributions on behalf of Turkmeni employees.

## Other issues

Contractors and foreign subcontractors may additionally:

- Import foreign exchange and purchase manats from the CBT or other authorised banks or foreign exchange dealers;
- Operate bank accounts in Turkmenistan, in foreign or local currency, provided that the accounts are credited only with foreign currency (or in manats converted from foreign currency) or with proceeds from sale of foreign currency earned from petroleum operations.
- Operate overseas bank accounts that may be credited without restriction, provided that the contractor or subcontractor submits copies of bank statements to the relevant Turkmeni official organisation in accordance with current domestic legislation.
- Purchase foreign currency with previously converted foreign currency, not required for petroleum operations.

1 Article 30 of Instruction 9 on the taxation of foreign legal entities.
2 The Statute 'Concerning the Composition of Expenses to be Included in the Cost of the Production of Goods (Work and Services)', as approved by Decree No. 1676 of the President of Turkmenistan of 1 March 1994
3 Instruction No. 6 of the main State Tax Inspectorate of Turkmenistan of 18 March 1994, 'Concerning the Procedure for the Calculation and Payment to the Budget of Profits Tax'.
4 Article 1 of Edict No. UP-252 of the President of Turkmenistan of 6 January 1992, 'Concerning the Introduction of income Tax on Citizens of Turkmenistan, foreign Citizens, and Stateless Persons'.
5 Edict No. 252 of the President of Turkmenistan of January 6, 1992, as amended by Edict No. 1596 of 31 July 1995
6 Instruction No. 17/46 of 20 October 1995 'Concerning the Procedure for the Calculation and Payment to the State Budget of Payments for State Voluntary Medical Insurance'.
7 Instruction No. 6/477 of 3 July 1995 'Concerning the Procedure for the Calculation and Payment to the Budget of Resources for the State Social Insurance and Pension Funds.

# 13 Uzbekistan

## Introduction

Since its independence in 1991, Uzbekistan has followed its own model of transition to a market economy. State control remains widespread as the government develops what it considers to be the key sectors of the economy. With nearly 24 million people, Uzbekistan is the largest domestic market in Central Asia and offers access to Russia, China and the rest of Asia.

The government's aim is to avoid getting into debt and cites this as the main reason not to resume a programme with the IMF. Other aims include self-sufficiency in energy and grain, and the development and diversification of its industrial base to free the economy from the dependency on raw material and commodity prices.

Uzbekistan's geographic position at the centre of Central Asia and its human and natural resources have attracted some foreign investment, although this remains limited in comparison with the country's potential. Although Uzbekistan emerged from the early years of independence with a relative economic advantage, the government advocates a gradual adoption of market economics, international trade norms and democracy.

## History, culture and politics

Uzbekistan has the largest population in Central Asia, 71 per cent of which are ethnic Uzbeks. With the fabled cities of Bukhara and Samarkand, and the fertile region of the Fergana valley, Uzbekistan is also home to the richest architectural and cultural heritage in the region. It is almost completely land-locked within Central Asia, sharing a border with every other country of Central Asia and also with Afghanistan.

Uzbekistan's history includes the Persian tribes, Alexander the Great, nomadic and then Turkic invaders, and Genghis Khan who devastated the region in 1220. Many of the country's lasting monuments were built in the 14th century by Timur the Lame (Tamerlane), who created a domain that

Exhibit 13.1
**Country facts**

| | |
|---|---|
| Area | 447,400 square kilometres |
| Population (1997) | 23.7 million |
| Capital | Tashkent |
| Other large cities | Samarkand, Namangan |
| Currency | Som (UZS) |
| Exchange rate (February 1999) | UZS112.26:US$1 |
| GDP per capita (1999) | US$483 |
| Inflation, annual average (1998): | 40% |

Exhibit 13.2
**Political information**

| | |
|---|---|
| President | Islam Karimov (born 1938) |
| Elected | 29 December 1991 (extended by referendum in March 1995) |
| Term | 5 years |
| Percentage of vote | 85.9% (1995: 99.6%) |
| Next election | 2000 |

146

stretched from Delhi to Moscow and from Kashgar to the Caucasus.

Uzbeks are descended from Uzbeks Khan, a grandson of Genghis Khan who ruled the territory during the 16th and 17th centuries. By the 18th century the region was split into three Uzbek khanates of Bukhara, Khiva and Kokand. The Russian imperial army arrived in the mid-19th century and by 1873 the khan of Khiva and the emir of Bukhara had signed treaties making their states Russian protectorates. In 1924 the Bolsheviks dissolved the khanates of Bukhara and Khiva and formed the Uzbek Soviet Socialist Republic (SSR). The Fergana valley was divided between the Uzbek, Tajik and Kyrgyz SSRs.

The Soviet era brought the suppression of Islam and enforced modernisation. Literacy of the population increased from 10 per cent to 60 per cent in less than a decade. The republic was forced to grow cotton, at the expense of all else.

The current Uzbek leader, President Islam Karimov, came to power under Mikhail Gorbachev in 1989. He opposed Gorbachev's policy of glasnost, supporting the 1991 attempted coup against him. When the coup collapsed, Karimov quickly declared Uzbekistan's independence and banned the Communist Party. In its place he created the Popular Democratic Party of Uzbekistan, of which he is leader. On 29 December 1991 he organised presidential elections, standing against one opponent. Karimov was declared the winner with 85.9 per cent of the vote. Key opposition figures were not allowed to run, however, and the elections were widely criticised as unfair.

Karimov extended his presidential mandate by a nation-wide referendum in March 1995, confirming another five years' rule until 2000. He received 99.6 per cent of the vote. Although the constitution prohibits the holding of more than two consecutive terms as president, the extension by referendum may allow Karimov to stand again in 2000.

The 1992 Constitution creates a tripartite division of power into president, judiciary and legislative offices, but the overwhelming power lies with the president, who rules mainly by decree. The president appoints and dismisses ministers, the prosecutor general and key members of the judiciary, the head of the central bank, and regional governors or hokims. There are few real opposition parties and there is little independence in the media. The four parties and one social movement that do exist are all seen as government sponsored. Opposition parties Erk and Birlik, which sprang up in the late 1980s in opposition to communism, have been banned. There is little opposition in the parliament, or Oliy Majlis, which authorises the appointments and resolutions of the executive branch. The Majlis consists of 250 deputies. Elections were held in December 1994 with runoffs in early 1995.

Acutely conscious of nearby conflicts in Tajikistan and

*Tashkent Bazaar*

Afghanistan, the leadership has stressed the need to avoid civil unrest. Security forces have a heavy presence in the country and crime is low. There has been little civil unrest since violent ethnic clashes broke out in the Fergana valley in 1989 and 1990. Karimov's regime is secular and represses Islamic militancy. Uzbeks are Sunni muslims, with a strong Sufi tradition.

# Macroeconomic profile

## Economic development

Uzbekistan's economic record since independence has been exceptional when compared with that of most other transition economies in that the decline in GDP between 1991 and 1997 was the lowest of any former Soviet Union (FSU) country. Although it lags behind some of the faster, more agressive reformers, such as the Baltic states, the Kyrgyz Republic and Azerbaijan, Uzbekistan is well ahead of many other countries of the Commonwealth of Independent States (CIS), including Russia and Ukraine, where output is stagnant or in decline. This relative success is particularly striking given the government's hesitancy to engage in rapid market-oriented reforms and instead to pursue reform at a gradual pace. The collapse of the Russian economy has, if anything, confirmed the government's will to reform the economy gradually and avoid the pain of 'shock therapy' experienced in other transition countries.

In the early years of independence, the Soviet-inherited over-reliance on one crop, cotton, left the republic subject to severe fluctuations in foreign currency earnings depending on the world price of cotton. Since its independence in 1991, the republic has begun to develop its considerable mineral wealth. However, liberalisation of the trade and exchange rate regimes

Exhibit 13.3
**Inflation, (%), 1994–98**

| | 1994 | 1995 | 1996 | 1997 | 1998 |
|---|---|---|---|---|---|
| Inflation, annual average (%) | 1,528 | 305 | 54 | 72 | 40 |
| Inflation, end-year (%) | 1,281 | 117 | 64 | 50 | 33 |

*Source:* EBRD.

and the reduction of state control of the banking sector are seen as crucial to economic growth and foreign investment, and reform in these areas has stagnated since 1996.

The private sector share in GDP is estimated to have increased from about 10 per cent in 1990 to approximately 30 per cent in 1995, but probably remained below 50 per cent in 1997, less than most other transition countries during the same period.

The economy managed modest growth in 1996 and 1997. The moderate pace of reform has caused less of the violent upsets in production and sales that have been experienced elsewhere. The country had less industry because it was mostly a supplier of raw materials to the Soviet Union and so its economy was less devastated by the collapse of Soviet industry.

## Currency restrictions

Following the failure of the cotton crop in 1996, which devastated the country's exports (cotton accounted for about 40 per cent of exports), the government reacted by printing money and a few months later introduced currency convertibility restrictions. A black market quickly appeared offering a currency rate 100 per cent higher than the official rate. Since then, the IMF programme (which comprised a Systemic Transformation Facility (STF) and a 15-month standby arrangement which began in 1995) has lapsed without further disbursements. Consultations are continuing, but the programme remains suspended. The main stumbling block is currency convertibility, which is a key condition for resumption of the IMF programme. The government has said that it will introduce convertibility by 2000, but it has taken few steps towards meeting that deadline.

## Price controls

Formal price controls were abolished by 1996 for most foodstuffs, consumer goods and services, but the government still determines the prices of monopoly products and the price at which it buys wheat and cotton from farmers. There are also price controls on energy, rents, communal services, public transport and telecommunications.

## Inflation and fiscal deficits

Uzbekistan did not introduce its own currency, the sum, until

July 1994 and so was late in starting a stabilisation and economic reform programme. The government then brought down the fiscal deficit from 6 per cent in 1994 to 4 per cent in 1995. Inflation was reduced sharply from 1,281 at year-end 1994 to 117 per cent by year-end 1995 (see Exhibit 13.3). In March 1996 the government started issuing Treasury bills and by then had made significant progress in liberalising trade and exchange systems. Yet payments and pension arrears mounted and bad cotton and grain harvests in 1995 and 1996 led the administration to increase spending. Inflation rose and the deficit widened to 7.3 per cent of GDP in 1996. The government reacted by bringing in trade restrictions and curbing access to foreign exchange.

In 1997 the official inflation rate was 50 per cent although there is an acknowledged flaw in the computation. The EBRD figure for the year was 72 per cent. The budget deficit was 2.3 per cent in 1997, a significant improvement on 1996. It is not clear how much the Russian crisis has affected the economy but it has certainly hit exports. There has also been an alarming growth in the difference between the official exchange rate and the black market rate, which climbed steeply in autumn 1998 to triple the official rate.

Exhibit 13.4 shows the government accounts for 1997 to 1999.

## GDP

After a cumulative decline of 17.5 per cent between 1992 and 1995 , real GDP grew by 1.5 per cent in 1996 and 2.4 per cent in 1997 (see Exhibit 13.5). The growth was largely driven by the growth in services in 1996 and a good harvest in 1997. The growth in services was part of a mini-boom when investment increased imports and small businesses and shops sprang up. The private sector share in GDP was estimated to be over 30 per cent in 1997, although this may be misleading given the widespread influence of the state even outside the public sector. The government also managed to stop industrial decline by promoting domestic production of consumer goods with the help of foreign investment and by continuing credits to state-owned enterprises it considered important. This was not always successful, however, and some state-owned factories are still recording falling output despite government credits.

148

Exhibit 13.4
**Government accounts, 1997–99**

|  | 1997 | 1998 | 1999 |
|---|---|---|---|
| Current account (% of GDP) | –4.8 | –6.9 | –8.7 |
| Fiscal balance (% of GDP) | –3.2 | –3.5 | –4.0 |

*Source:* ABN AMRO.

Exhibit 13.5
**Economic structure, 1997–1999**

|  | 1997 | 1998 | 1999 |
|---|---|---|---|
| Nominal GDP (US$ billion) | 14.1 | 11.9 | 12.3 |
| Real GDP (% change) | 2.4 | 1.0 | 0.9 |
| Industrial output (% change) | 4.0 | 1.0 | 2.0 |

*Source:* ABN AMRO.

Exhibit 13.6
**Foreign reserves, 1997–99**

|  | 1997 | 1998 | 1999 |
|---|---|---|---|
| Foreign reserves (US$ million) | 302 | 230 | 280 |
| Import cover (months) | 0.9 | 0.7 | 0.8 |
| Total debt/export ratio | 0.6 | 0.7 | 0.7 |

*Source:* ABN AMRO.

## Foreign exchange reserves

Reserves have been declining steadily, falling by almost US$750 million in 1996 and US$865 billion in 1997 (see Exhibit 13.6). They fell by over US$70 million in 1998 and from six months of imports in 1995 to under one months' worth in 1998. This was partly due to the revaluation of the gold stock.

## Privatisation and the industrial sector

The government is planning to privatise six large enterprises through international tenders. By the fourth quarter of 1998, the government had announced that it would offer 25 per cent of the national aircraft manufacturer and 47 per cent of the Almalyk Metallurgical Factory by the end of the year.

Privatisation began in 1995 but has suffered serious setbacks since mid-1996, proving slower than in most other tran-

sition countries. Having completed the first phase, in which 150 minority stakes were sold to Privatisation Investment Funds (PIFs), the second stage has been delayed. Almost all small-scale enterprises have been privatised, but far less progress has been made on the privatisation of medium- and large-sized enterprises. Official estimates put the share of the non-state sector in GDP and employment at over 70 per cent, but this is misleading. Even in businesses partially privatised or reorganised, the state remains directly or indirectly in control. There are many cases where the government has simply transferred a 49 per cent stake to other state-owned enterprises. Independent economists put the private sector at between 30 and 45 per cent of GDP in 1997. The state also controls the private sector by channelling direct and indirect subsidies, for example, access to privileged foreign exchange rates. This makes it hard for the private sector to compete and grow.

Virtually all housing has been handed over to residents and 94 per cent of small businesses are now private, mostly in the form of workers collectives. About 25 per cent of agricultural land had been transferred by the end of 1996, often in leasehold form to family farmers. In contrast, less than 20 per cent of the nearly 12,000 medium- and large-sized enterprises had been privatised by the same date and those often only partially. The government announced plans to partially privatise another 1,000 in 1997, in a mass-privatisation programme based on PIFs, with support from the World Bank. Monthly auctions of companies began in December 1996 and, by April 1997, 55 enterprises had been sold, raising about US$4 million. There are about 50 PIFs and 60 management companies active in the privatisation process, through which individuals can buy shares. PIFs can acquire more shares on the stock exchange but are limited to holding 10 per cent of shares in any one company.

Ownership of privatised companies is typically restricted to a maximum 49 per cent for the general public, including foreign investors. The State Property Company (SPC) typically retains 25 per cent, while 26 per cent is usually sold to workers' collectives. In many cases large parts of the 49 per cent for the general public are sold off to other state concerns including ministries, state-owned banks or the SPC itself. There has been little restructuring of companies, even when privatised. Companies still receive soft credits from the state, face little competition within their sector and are susceptible to intervention from the state. There has been a bankruptcy law and a special commission introduced since 1996, but few large companies have come under scrutiny.

Industry has been based around the oil and gas sector, mining and engineering, and machine building. During World War II a large section of the Soviet military industry was moved beyond the Urals into Central Asia to be safe from the Nazi invasion. Much of the industry remained after the War and

*Kalan Mosque
and Minaret,
Bukhara*

151

Uzbekistan became an important producer of aircraft, motors, cranes and elevators. After independence Uzbekistan began a programme of converting military plants to civilian use with the help of grants from the United States.

The Tashkent Aircraft Manufacturing Amalgamation has been manufacturing Ilyushin cargo jets – among them the Ilyushin-76 and Antonov cargo and passenger planes – for over 50 years. Since 1992 the plant has also produced the Ilyushin-114, a smaller passenger plane. It also produces wings for the heavy lift Antonov freighter, which is the largest plane in the world, and carries out operations to increase the cargo capacity of Ilyushins. The company, known by its acronym Tapoich, has four plants in Tashkent, Fergana and Andijan. It is the largest and most important aircraft assembly plant in Central Asia.

Following independence Uzbekistan aimed to diversify its industrial base. It has launched several new projects with foreign investors in the car and farm machinery sectors. It also held the first hard-currency privatisation in Central Asia when British American Tobacco (BAT) bought three tobacco companies in Tashkent, Samarkand and Ozgut with the plan to grow tobacco and produce 20 billion cigarettes a year.

It has also tried to turn attention to using its raw materials at home in local manufacturing rather than exporting them. It has started to develop its textile industry, in particular silk processing, cotton and wool weaving, and carpet making.

Uzbekistan achieved growth in the industrial sector in 1996 and 1997, although consistent growth in future years is not yet assured. Much of the growth is due to several large projects started with foreign investment, which produce consumer goods such as cars, television sets and video machines. Yet some of the foreign joint ventures have been hurt by currency convertibility restrictions and the effects of the Asian and Russian crises in 1998.

# Agriculture

Agriculture accounts for nearly 30 per cent of GDP, but there has been little reform in the sector. State orders remain in effect for cotton and grain and farmers have to sell their crops to the cotton monopoly, at prices well below world prices. There are still bans and tariffs imposed on several agricultural export products and all exports have been effectively centralised in four state trade agencies. In Soviet times Uzbekistan imported three-quarters of its grain requirement. Since independence the government has been determined to boost grain production to become self-sufficient. Grain production reached 3.8 million tonnes in 1997, up from 1.9 million tonnes in 1992, and by 1995 the government had managed to halve what it spends on grain imports.

## Cotton

Uzbekistan is blessed with the warmest climate in the FSU and it has become the world's fifth largest cotton producer and second largest cotton exporter. In 1997–98 the republic produced 6 per cent of the world's cotton and its share of world cotton exports was 16 per cent (936,000 metric tonnes). The World Bank is running a programme to modernise cotton farming. Approximately 95 per cent of the land needs to be irrigated and farms rely on ageing irrigation systems.

Uzbek cotton export earnings peaked in 1995 at US$1.54 billion, boosted by high world market prices. These earnings fell to US$1.39 billion in 1997, reflecting lower world prices and a poor harvest (3.7 million tonnes). In 1998 the harvest rose to 4.16 million tonnes, although still below a high in Soviet times of 9 million tonnes.

Although cotton's share of total exports is declining, it still remains Uzbekistan's number one export.

# Natural resources

## Oil and gas

Although Uzbekistan does not directly border the Caspian Sea, it shares several of the region's hydrocarbon basins and will benefit from proposed oil and gas export routes shared with other Caspian countries. Uzbekistan has considerable mineral wealth, particularly natural gas and gold. It is among the world's ten largest gold producers and has substantial reserves of natural gas (1.9 trillion cubic metres) and oil (0.6 billion barrels). While its reserves do not match those of neighbouring Turkmenistan and Kazakhstan, it has quickly become not only self-sufficient in energy but a net exporter. It also has substantial deposits of coal, silver, copper, lead, zinc, wolfram, uranium and tungsten, among others minerals. Most minerals are based in the south of the country, in the Fergana valley and around Samarkand and Bukhara. The western part of the country, lying on the edge of the Caspian basin, contains natural gas.

The gas industry is the strongest sector in Uzbekistan and accounts for two-thirds of energy production. The country is among the ten largest suppliers of gas in the world. Most of its gas lies along the Turkmen border and around Bukhara, with more in the Fergana valley. To its credit, Uzbekistan started developing new fields as old fields declined and was the only FSU country not to suffer a decline in production after independence. By 1995, Uzbekistan was exporting 4.2 billion cubic metres (Bcm) of gas to Kazakhstan, Tajikistan, the Kyrgyz Republic and Afghanistan. Production in 1997 was 51.7 Bcm of gas and 7.9 million tonnes of oil and condensate, the latter showing particularly strong growth since 1990 production of only 2.8 million tonnes. But the strong growth in domestic demand for gas has reduced the volume of gas Uzbekistan is able to export.

Energy production has been a priority of the government and the sector has attracted foreign investment. Uzbekistan is the only FSU republic to have substantially increased its oil production since becoming independent, with total production increasing from 66,000 barrels a day in 1992 to 165,000 barrels a day in 1998. As a result, Uzbekistan is no longer a net importer of petroleum, although it has had to import some refined products because its oil has tended to be too high in sulphur content for its refineries. As well as gas and oil exploration and production, the government has constructed and rehabilitated two refineries in Bukhara and Fergana and is currently planning a large new chemical complex at the big gas field of Shartan. The country became self-sufficient in oil for the first time in 1995 and may well become an oil exporting country, pipelines permitting (see Chapter 6, Energy transport and pipeline politics). Only ten of the country's 30 or so proven oilfields have been developed. (For details of new oil and gas fields to be developed, see Chapter 5, Energy: the key to growth.)

## Minerals

Gold reserves are estimated at 2,500–3,000 tonnes, copper 1.4 million tonnes, lead 1.1 million tonnes, zinc 750,000 tonnes and molybdenum 20,000 tonnes. Mining has been developed extensively. Gold exports netted nearly US$1 billion for the government in 1996, and US$738 million in 1997, reflecting the fall in world gold prices. Copper is another large resource, concentrated in three large deposits. Approximately 85 per cent of the country's output comes from the Kalamakyl open pit mine at Almalyk, south of Tashkent. Copper production has declined significantly but the government aims to boost production. Almalyk is a major industrial centre where there is also a large zinc refinery that used to process Russian and Kazakh concentrates. Uzbekistan's main steel plant, at Bekabad on the Tajikistan border, is being modernised. Coal production has halved since 1991 but is still a significant resource in Uzbekistan. Production was 2.9 million tonnes in 1997, up from the previous year. In 1991 production was 5.9 million tonnes. Reserves are large, mostly brown coal based in two large deposits at Angren and Baisun, but the country is a long way from meeting domestic demand, which is 8.5 million tonnes a year.

# Finance

## The stock exchange

Uzbekistan has a securities commission and a stock exchange, founded in 1994, but activity has been limited. At the end of 1996 the Tashkent Republic Stock Exchange had listed stocks in 400 enterprises. Sales rose quickly at first but are still low as a ratio of GDP. Trading is limited to a handful of companies and banks.

Trading has almost stopped since the government prohibited managers from buying shares in their own companies in early 1998. According to the 1998 EBRD report: 'The lack of convertibility and occasional violations of shareholders rights have discouraged foreign investors'. Many of the shares on the stock market have been bought by state-owned or state controlled entities. (For further details on the capital markets, see Chapter 7, Banking and finance.)

## Banking

Uzbekistan's banking system, like those of many of the FSU countries, originates from the Soviet era. In 1998, the USSR's monobank, Gosbank, was elevated to the role of regulator and five specialist banks were created to deal with different areas of the economy. Following independence, Uzbekistan gained control of the local operations of these banks.

Since then, progress has been slow. According to Thomson BankWatch: 'The banking system in Uzbekistan has been characterised by a slow pace of reform, a relatively low number of banks, a high level of concentration, and state ownership of nearly the entire banking system'. The pace of reform may increase following the advice of a group of consultants who are working with the government under the auspices of the World Bank and Barentes Group.

There are 31 commercial banks in Uzbekistan, including four joint ventures with foreign capital participation and one subsidiary of a foreign bank. Most banks are directly owned by the state or controlled through intermediaries. Foreign partners in the banking sector include: Daewoo, ABN AMRO, MeesPierson, the EBRD, MFK-Unexim (Russia) and Ziraat Bankasi (Turkey). At the beginning of February 1999, the gov-

Exhibit 13.7
**Ten largest banks by total assets, year-end 1996**

|  | US$ million | Ownership |
|---|---|---|
| National Bank of Uzbekistan | 3,427 | State controlled |
| Nadrodniy Bank | 872 | State controlled |
| Promstroybank | 654 | State controlled |
| Pakhta Bank | 574 | State controlled |
| Asaka Bank | 299 | State controlled |
| Uzprivatbank | 165 | Joint-venture |
| Galla-bank | 112 | State controlled |
| Uzsavdogarbank | 80 | State controlled |
| Tadbirkorbank | 55 | State controlled |
| Uzzhilsberbank | 35 | State controlled |

*Source:* Thomson BankWatch.

ernment announced that it was planning to set up a development bank with authorised capital of US$100 million. Likely founders include the EBRD, Asian Development Bank, International Finance Corporation, Kreditanstalt fur Wideraufbau and National Foreign Economic Bank,

Banks act as tax collectors for the state and have a strong hold on their non-government clients as it is hard to change accounts. Domestic companies are allowed bank accounts with no more than one bank for reasons of tax administration. Local accounting standards are broadly in line with International Accounting Standards, but many banks have weaknesses in their reporting standards according to Thomson BankWatch.

The state-owned National Bank of Uzbekistan, the largest bank, dominates the sector and accounts for roughly 60 per cent of the assets in the banking system (see Exhibit 13.7). It conducts a wide range of businesses and is the main conduit for foreign exchange transactions. In 1997, it accounted for nearly 70 percent of total commercial bank loans and about 70–80 percent of all transactions in foreign currency. In the second tier, Narodniy Bank, Promstroybank, Pakhta Bank and Asaka Bank are trying to become more universal in the businesses they conduct. Narodniy Bank operates the branches of the former state savings banks and controls around 90 per cent of the country's 6,000 branches.

## Central bank regulation
The Central Bank of Uzbekistan (CBU) has been working on a set of prudential regulations similar to those required under EU directives. Particular attention has been paid to related-party lending. Regulation of the banking sector is expected to develop further.

The CBU relies on compulsory reserve requirements and a set of specified ratios, against which banks are evaluated once a month.

## Uzbekistan Banking Association
With the encouragement and financial help of the government, the Uzbekistan Banking Association has been formed to foster the development of the industry and act as a lobby group for the interest of the country's banks. The Association has also worked with the Finance Academy of the Republic of Uzbekistan.

## Transport and trade
Uzbekistan has set itself the goal of recreating the country as the trade and commerce hub of Central Asia. Russia is still the country's main trading partner, accounting for 57 per cent of total trade in 1997. Kazakhstan and Ukraine are other major trade partners. But Uzbekistan has been developing trade with Europe and Asia, especially in cotton and gold exports. Its major concern now is to develop quick and cheap access to other international markets and in particular to a sea port.

The government has several projects in hand. In 1996 a railway line between Iran and Turkmenistan opened, providing the shortest route from Central Asia to the Persian Gulf. For Uzbekistan, the most desirable trade route would be south through Afghanistan to the Pakistani port of Karachi. Continued conflict in Afghanistan has, however, kept the border closed and development of the project has been postponed.

## External relations
As a geo-political power, Uzbekistan is considered the heavyweight of the region. With large communities of ethnic Uzbeks living in all the neighbouring countries, Uzbekistan has an interest in its neighbours affairs. The issue is sensitive in Tajikistan, where ethnic Uzbeks are now pitted against the coalition government and have been accused by the Tajik government of receiving support from the Uzbek government. Uzbekistan has also shown strong support for the Uzbek leaders in the north of Afghanistan who were pitted against the Taliban forces. The Taliban are now in control of most of the country and make uncomfortable neighbours for Uzbekistan. Russia has until now been the dominant military force in the region but is gradually handing over border guard duties to the CIS force. There may come a time when Uzbekistan, which has the largest army in the region, becomes the major force in Central Asia.

## Environmental problems and the Aral Sea
Uzbekistan's central position in Central Asia places it at the heart of one of the world's worst environmental disasters, the shrinking of the Aral Sea. For the past 30 years the Aral Sea, fed by the region's two great rivers, the Amu Darya and Syr Darya, has been shrinking with appalling ecological and socio-economic consequences. Fishing villages are now sand-bound in the desert, several kilometres from the sea, and the entire region is suffering from the pollution of pesticides and salts blown up by winds across the new desert lands. The problem, shared with Kazakhstan which also borders the Aral Sea, involves all the countries of Central Asia because it concerns water resources used by the whole region. The solution is by no means clear, but regional cooperation will be essential.

## Foreign trade
New trade restrictions introduced in 1996 undid much of the progress that had been made towards liberalisation. The average import tariff rose from 12 per cent to 17 per cent and new excise taxes were introduced on imports of a number of con-

sumer goods and cars. Excise taxes on exports also expanded. Since October 1996, an import-licensing system has been in place whereby import contracts must be registered. High import restrictions were placed on non-essential consumer goods and all imports were checked for quality, prices and compliance with foreign exchange regulations. This has complicated the import of equipment and other necessary goods for many foreign companies working in Uzbekistan.

There was some liberalisation of exports in 1997 and early 1998, but this was balanced by a further tightening on imports. All cotton and gold exports, accounting for almost 60 per cent of total exports in 1997, must go through official marketing structures. Since February 1998, all imports have had to be prepaid in hard currency. Export licences have now been abolished on most goods, but the state has a monopoly in the export of gold and cotton, which constitute its main foreign exchange reserves. Four categories remain for export licences: uranium, gold, military and nuclear materials. Overall, import tariffs were again raised significantly from 1997–98 and excise taxes were extended to cover a wider range of goods, while the state's involvement in import procurement has grown.

Exhibit 13.8 shows Uzbekistan's trade balance between 1994 and 1999.

## Liberalisation of the exchange rate regime

Currency convertibility remains the main problem for foreign investors. The government's balance of payments difficulties led it to introduce a multiple exchange regime. An official rate is used for accounting and customs purposes and for export proceeds under an obligatory surrender requirement. There are still multiple exchange rates, ranging from the highly overvalued auction rate and commercial bank rate which are used to convert export revenues under the obligatory surrender regime, to the widely used (but illegal) black market rates, which were half as high as the formal rates in mid-1998.

There is a separate auction rate for importers and for investment goods of high priority companies, and a commer-

Top: Textile factory
Bottom: Hotel construction, Tashkent

cial rate for some consumer goods. There is also a cash market and a much-expanded black market operating at a difference of some 200 per cent in late 1998.

At the end of 1996, an IMF stand-by-credit expired pending commitments from the government to unify the exchange rate and move towards full current account convertibility.

## Foreign investment

Accurate foreign direct investment (FDI) figures for Uzbekistan are difficult to obtain. Official statistics indicate a steadily rising dollar amount of foreign investment.

Foreign investment has slowed. In 1996, FDI was just US$2

Exhibit 13.8
**Trade balance, 1994–99**

|  | 1994 | 1995 | 1996 | 1997 | 1998 | 1999 |
|---|---|---|---|---|---|---|
| Imports (US$ million) | 2,727 | 3,238 | 4,240 | 3,767 | 4,160 | 4,370 |
| Exports (US$ million) | 2,940 | 3,475 | 3,534 | 3,695 | 3,900 | 4,050 |
| Trade balance (US$ million) | 214 | 237 | –706 | –72 | –260 | –320 |

*Sources:* EBRD; ABN AMRO.

per capita, the lowest of the entire FSU, along with Tajikistan, which was still at war. Cumulative inflows between 1989 and 1996 were just US$7 per capita. According to the EBRD, actual FDI in 1996 was US$90 million; in 1995 it was negative (US$–24 million) and in 1994 US$73 million (see Exhibit 13.9).

Uzbekistan has formed a Ministry of Foreign Economic Relations designed to work with foreign investors. But so far, inward foreign investment has been slowed by tight restrictions on foreign currency conversion (see above). There are some major joint ventures in tobacco, gold mining and the automotive sector, and the government has granted tax holidays and the duty-free import of capital goods to foreign investors following the May 1998 laws on foreign investment. Although the government has been party to membership negotiations with the WTO and a Cooperation Agreement with the EU, little progress has been made on the issues of foreign exchange convertibility and trade liberalisation.

The main difficulty foreign investors face is access to foreign exchange to buy the necessary imports for their operations. The repatriation of dividends is permitted under the law.

The main foreign investments are:

- Lonhro UK's US$25-million offer for a gold field development project.
- BAT's US$200 million tobacco industry rehabilitation project.
- Daewoo Corporation's US$100 million investment in the Andizhan automobile plant.
- Newmont Mining's US$225 million investment in the Newmont Mining gold processing joint venture.

Uzbekistan's flagship investment project has been the investment by the South Korean firm Daewoo Corporation to construct the first car assembly plant in Central Asia. Daewoo has invested US$100 million in the car manufacturing factory (in addition to a further US$45 in a television parts factory). Together, Daewoo and its Uzbek partner, Uzavtosanoat, created the joint venture UzDAEWOOavto, with the plan to produce 200,000 world standard cars a year in the town of Asaka, in the southern Andijan region. Of those 100,000 will be saloon cars, 50,000 Damas micro-buses and 50,000 compact Tico cars. Worth about US$661 million, the project

Exhibit 13.9
**Net direct foreign investment (US$ million), 1994-99**

|  | 1994 | 1995 | 1996 | 1997 | 1998 | 1999 |
|---|---|---|---|---|---|---|
| Net FDI | 73 | –24 | 90 | 167 | 60 | 70 |

*Sources:* EBRD; ABN AMRO.

began in 1993 and exported its first cars abroad, to Russia, in August 1996. Some 11,000 cars were sold in the CIS in the first year of export. In 1997 the company exhibited its cars at a trade and industry fair in Ürümqi, China. The company plans that by 2000, 70 per cent of cars will be made locally.

In May 1997, Uzavtosanoat and a Turkish company began construction of another factory in Samarkand to make cars and trucks. Domestic demand for buses and medium-sized trucks is expected to reach about 18,500 a year. Russia is seen as the main market for the company, with other CIS countries following. In view of the Russia crisis in 1998, however, which is likely to affect sales, Uzavtosanoat is looking to export further abroad, to China, Syria, Romania, Poland and Saudi Arabia.

Newmont Mining of the United States was the first foreign company to set up a mining joint venture with the government of Uzbekistan, establishing Zarafshan-Newmont, a 50:50 partnership in 1992 with the local Navoi Mining and Metallurgic Combine. The company extracts and processes gold at the Muruntau open pit gold mine, one of the largest open pit gold mines in the world, situated in the Kyzylkum desert region in central Uzbekistan. Muruntau mine started production in the 1960s and became the largest gold producer in the Soviet Union, accounting for approximately 30 per cent of Soviet gold production. The US$225-million project plus a US$135 million-loan from the EBRD aims to treat about 2 billion tonnes of stockpiled low-grade oxide ore.

Bullion is refined locally for international export. The operation produces over 400,000 ounces of gold a year and Zarafshan-Newmont plans to recover 5 million ounces over 17 years at the mine. The joint venture has reserves of 220 million tonnes of ore, containing 5.6 million ounces of recoverable gold. The Muruntau mine is just one of several gold mining projects planned by the Uzbek government.

Lonhro UK also established a joint venture with Navoi in 1995 in the Amantaytau gold mines with a loan commitment from the IFC. In total, US$100 million will be invested and output is projected to be 145 tonnes after four years. German industrial concerns have also invested in Uzbekistan. There are 14 joint enterprises involving German capital operating in Uzbekistan and 13 German firms have established representative offices in Tashkent.

More than 20 Turkish companies have offices in Tashkent and a total of 172 joint projects operate in the republic's textile, food, building and automobile industries.

An Uzbek–German joint venture with Mercedes Benz is manufacturing buses, while French company Alcatel is re-equipping the national telecommunications network. Thomson is modernising Uzbekistan's air traffic control system, Biomed has started operations in pharmaceuticals and there are other French ventures in non-financial services. The Turkish group Koç Holding is building a bus and trailer factory near Samarkand. The Uzbek textiles sector, in particular, has attracted joint ventures. Silk ribbons are produced with an Italian firm in Namangan, cotton yarn and cloth is produced with a Korean firm in Tashkent, and shirts and bed-linen, with a Turkish firm in Andijan. A Malaysian firm, Probadi is redeveloping the Karaktai oil and gas deposit.

The official Uzbekistan Business Guide lists 166 offices of foreign companies in Tashkent, Andijan, Namangan, Samarkand and Termez. IBM has set up in Tashkent to serve Azerbaijan, Tajikistan and Turkmenistan. There are also a large number of medium- and large-sized German firms, including Schering, Hoechst, Siemens and Deutsche Bank, plus nearly 20 French companies such as Louis Reihart, Olivier, Rhône Poulenc, and Delaplanque, as well as Japan's Tomen Corporation.

## Prospects

Uzbekistan remains a conundrum for foreign investors. The government is in many ways leading a commendably cautious programme. It is determined not to get into debt and gives this as the main reason not to resume its programme with the IMF. It is determined to become self-sufficient in energy and grain and to develop and diversify its industry rather than rely on raw materials and commodities prices. Its critics say it could achieve this faster with external assistance. That may be so, but Uzbekistan has been determined to avoid the drastic dislocations of 'shock therapy.' External economists tend to warn against delaying change, but Russia's example has, if anything confirmed the Uzbek government's resolve. Progress in economic reform is, therefore, expected to remain slow in the immediate future, but the opportunities remain and many will be watching Uzbekistan's development keenly.

[1] Thomson BankWatch report on Uzbekistan, 1998.

# Appendix: Fiscal environment

Ernst & Young

## Accounting and auditing

Accounting in Uzbekistan is undergoing fundamental changes as the country slowly moves towards a market economy.

Under the old planned economic system, the main function of accounting was the collection and processing of information for government authorities. A company was merely a linking device for the management of state-owned property, with accounting the tool for providing the information on how well this property was managed.

With the appearance of investors and non-government owners, financial information and the functions of accounting have become more applicable. The regulations 'On accounting and financial reporting' issued in 1994, 'On the composition of costs' issued in 1995, and the law 'On accounting' issued in 1996, along with numerous supporting instructions and clarification letters, have introduced certain changes, for example, classification of costs, basic accounting principles and reporting guidelines, which more closely resemble International Accounting Standards (IAS). However, they still do not provide sufficiently detailed information on certain issues, for example, the revaluation of liabilities.

In 1998 Uzbekistan started adopting new accounting standards (NSBU) which are generally in line with IAS.

It is likely, however, that the determination of accounting policies available to management under IAS will be limited by existing legislative provisions other than NSBU, such as the statute on accounting and reporting, instructions on preparation of annual financial statements, the statutory chart of accounts, and various letters from the Ministry of Finance. Most companies and representatives of authorities are likely to struggle with the application of the new methodologies. Interpretation of the NSBU's requirements is also unknown territory and will evolve as the country develops a sufficient number of qualified accountants.

IAS were created to meet the expectations of users of financial statements to have more transparent and understandable financial information on which decisions can be made. These users include investors, shareholders, banks, other creditors, customers and suppliers, management, employees, government agencies and the general public. In formerly state-managed economies' such as Uzbekistan, users were primarily defined as management and the state (including tax authorities). At the current stage of development of Uzbek capital markets, it is premature to expect that compliance of locally issued financial statements with IAS will be of such impor-

tance as to put companies under substantial pressure to produce high-quality IAS-compliant financial statements. However, the new standards will certainly ease preparation of such financial statements for those companies that are willing or obliged to do so by or for the sake of foreign investors. In addition, they provide leverage for the users to initiate gradual moves towards better-quality financial statements.

Unfortunately, in the preparation of the NSBU, much of the background material and implementation guidance of IAS has been omitted. The omitted parts are useful to better understand the requirements of the standards and to apply them in particular situations. The omission of background material from the NSBU, the exclusion of the differentiation between benchmark and allowed alternative treatment, and the ambivalence in the wording of these standards leave many blank spaces within the NSBU that only practice will help complete.

To date nine Uzbek standards have been issued, covering the following topics:

- Accounting policies and financial statements.
- Revenues from operations.
- Income statement.
- Inventories.
- Non-current assets.
- Accounting for leases.
- Intangible assets.
- Cash flow statement.
- Accounting for and disclosure of government subsidies.

The listing of legislative acts presented to the Ministry of Justice for approval shows that 12 other accounting standards have been prepared and are likely to be published in the near future.

## Auditing

Uzbek legislation provides for the following two types of audit conducted in Uzbekistan:

- The audit of commercial banks for compliance with IAS.
- The audit of other legal entities for compliance with statutory accounting requirements.

The Ministry of Finance of the Republic of Uzbekistan is the primary government body regulating the audit of all companies, apart from commercial banks. The audit of commercial banks is regulated by the CBU.

The law 'Concerning Audit', issued in 1992, provided the legislative basis for the audit of all companies, including commercial banks. In 1993 a resolution of the cabinet of ministers introduced the basis for establishing the Chamber of Auditors, which is the primary non-government agency for the promotion of the development of audit in Uzbekistan. In 1996 the CBU issued regulations concerning its specific requirements for the audit of commercial banks.

Uzbek audit standards have not yet been issued, however, draft versions are available that are based on International Standards of Auditing. The Ministry of Finance, which is authorised to develop the procedure for conducting audits, has not yet fully realised the authority with which it has been empowered. The CBU is more active in this respect and has introduced a number of statutes stipulating the requirements for conducting an audit of commercial banks. However, there is still a general lack of audit procedures in existence and auditors have been forced to rely on the provisions of either International Auditing Standards or specific in-house guidelines. For this reason, the Chamber of Auditors is expected to play an important role and take over the functions of the above government agencies.

Uzbek legislation provides that the following types of companies should be subject to audit:

- Banks.
- Insurance companies.
- Commodity and stock exchanges.
- Companies with foreign equity capital investment.
- Investment and financial institutions (that is, the agents on stock exchanges).
- Companies with shares quoted on the stock exchange.
- Companies, whose legal form implies the limitation of the founders' liability.

# Taxation

## Sources of law

Taxation in Uzbekistan is primarily regulated by the Tax Code, which identifies the taxes that may be assessed in Uzbekistan and defines the following:

- Taxpayers.
- Taxable bases.
- Tax reliefs and exemptions.
- Violations and penalties.
- The appeals process related to taxation.

In addition to this fundamental law, the tax system includes:

- Instructions, issued by the State Tax Committee jointly with the Ministry of Finance in support of the Tax Code, providing the details on assessment, computation and payment of specific taxes.
- Clarification letters, issued by the above authorities and generally aimed at addressing specific issues identified and raised by certain taxpayers and/or local tax authorities in the course of practical implementation of the provisions of the Tax Code and Instructions.
- Presidential edicts and resolutions of the cabinet of ministers that further govern such areas as the provision of incentives to certain groups of taxpayers or the introduction of certain tax-related requirements.

As the body of Uzbek legislation is relatively small in its volume and coverage, it leaves many issues open to interpretation. Uzbekistan's reliance on a civil law system based on statutes that does not recognise case precedents can, therefore, make interpretation of tax legislation rather challenging.

## Tax system

The Tax Code comprises national and local taxes, as summarised below:

| National taxes | Local taxes | Corporate income profits/gross margin tax |
|---|---|---|
| Personal income tax | Property tax | Additionally, the following mandatory payments, contributions and levies to non-budgetary funds are imposed on all corporate taxpayers: |
| VAT | Land tax | |
| | Advertising tax | |
| Excise tax | Tax on re-sale of transport vehicles | |
| Subsurface usage tax | Merchandising fee | |
| Ecology tax | Registration fee for legal entities, and for entrepreneurial activity of individuals | pension fund (based on payroll and gross sales) |
| Tax for the use of water resources | | Employment fund (based on payroll) |
| Single tax (alternatively applied instead of all other taxes) | Parking fee | Trade union fund (based on payroll) |
| | Public works fee | Road fund (based on gross sales) |

## Taxation of corporate income

Depending on the nature of the company's operations, one of the following three taxes on corporate income would apply.

159

| Taxpayers | Taxes | Tax rate |
|-----------|-------|----------|
| Banks, insurance companies, enterprises engaged in video or audio rentals, auctions, casinos, lotteries | Income tax | 35% |
| Merchandising and catering companies | Gross margin tax | Variable |
| Other companies | Profit tax | 35% |

Foreign legal entities with a permanent establishment in Uzbekistan are subject to the same rates as stated above. An additional 10 per cent withholding tax also applies on repatriation of a foreign legal entity's profit from Uzbekistan.

## Taxable base

Taxable base for profits tax purposes, equals profit determined in accordance with Uzbek statutory accounting rules and adjusted for certain expenditures, deduction of which is limited by Uzbek tax legislation, including the following:

- Advertising and entertainment (which are limited based on gross sales).
- Business trip expenses in excess of statutory limits.
- Voluntary insurance (the legislation specifies compulsory insurance for companies by industry).

Companies subject to income tax calculate their taxable base on substantially the same basis as used by profits tax payers, with modifications for the add-back of certain expenses, primarily labour costs.

## Gross margin tax

Merchandising and catering enterprises are subject to gross margin tax at progressive rates varying between 14 and 50 per cent. The taxable base for gross margin tax equals the difference between the selling and purchase price of goods, adjusted for non-operational gains and losses.

## Single tax

This can be applied to certain qualified 'small companies' (that is, with personnel between five and 50 people, depending on the nature of business). Where applicable, this tax applies instead of all national and local taxes discussed above.

## Value-added tax (VAT)

VAT applies at a rate of 20 per cent on sales of goods, works and services in Uzbekistan other than sales of exempted items, including services related to monetary settlements and the issue of loans. From 1998, VAT also applies to the customs value (including customs duties and excise tax) of imported goods, works, and services.

Exported goods, works, and services incur no VAT unless exported to countries that impose VAT on exports to Uzbekistan (for example, certain CIS member states).

## Road fund contributions

Road tax applies to net sales (gross sales net of VAT and excise taxes) within Uzbekistan at a rate of 0.5 per cent by merchandising companies and 1.4 per cent by all other legal entities.

## Ecology tax

This applies at a rate of 1 per cent on the total cost of sales of all legal entities producing goods, works and services in Uzbekistan (selling, general and administrative expenses for merchandising enterprises).

## Property tax

This is assessed at a rate of 4 per cent on the average annual cost of fixed assets (ignoring depreciation), including freehold assets and assets acquired under capital leases and intangibles.

## Customs duties

All goods, works and services imported into Uzbekistan are subject to import duties based on their customs value and the country from which they originate.

Generally, the default customs duty rate of 3 per cent applies to items imported from countries with a 'favoured nation' status. However, Uzbek legislation provides for higher customs duties on certain items, including computers, soft drinks, alcohol and cars.

For goods, works and services originating from countries with a 'free-trade' status (primarily CIS member states) no import duties are applied.

For goods, works and services originating from countries with neither 'favoured-nation' nor 'free-trade' status, the import duty rates discussed above are doubled.

## Excise duty

These are imposed upon the import, production and export of certain goods, including natural resources, alcoholic beverages, tobacco products and motor vehicles. The rates are subject to frequent changes, with the highest rate applied on imported alcohol products at 90 per cent inclusive of excise duty.

## Withholding tax

This applies at a rate of 15 per cent on the distribution of interest and dividends to Uzbek residents, both legal entities and individuals.

Withholding tax also applies to income paid to non-residents at the rates shown below:

| Type of income | Rate (%) |
| --- | --- |
| Dividends and interest | 15% |
| Insurance premiums | 10% |
| Telecommunication and transport (freight) | 6% |
| Royalties, rent, consulting, management fees, other income | 20% |

However, many tax treaties provide for lower withholding tax rates on payments to foreign entities.

## Personal income tax

This applies at progressive rates varying from 15 to 45 per cent. Monthly income of an individual derived in Uzbekistan and exceeding the amount of 15 times the minimum monthly salary, that is UZS19,800 (that is, equivalent to US$180 at the beginning of 1999), would be subject to a marginal tax rate of 45 per cent.

*The co-publishers*

# Specialised state joint-stock commercial bank Asaka

Since it was first established in January 1996, Asaka Bank has quickly become one of the leading private banks in Uzbekistan. Among the original founders were the Ministry of Finance, UzAutoSanoat Association, the National Bank of Foreign Economic Activity, and the People's Bank of Uzbekistan. Asaka Bank's basic range of services includes cash and payment clearing; deposit taking; international payments; lending to retail and corporate borrowers; correspondent banking accounts; operations on international money markets, the domestic securities market and advice on banking and financial operations.

Being a specialised institution, Asaka has concentrated most heavily on financing of the automotive industry and its infrastructure. At the same time Asaka has continued to develop its corporate loan portfolio through a policy of diversification in order to guarantee a stable and progressive liquidity as well as maintaining its strong position among the largest and most stable banks in Uzbekistan. According to Akhbor-rating, the interbank rating agency of the Association of Banks of Uzbekistan, Asaka ranks second. As of 1 January 1999, the bank's own capital increased by 1.3 times to reach more than 15 billion sums. Asaka's assets are 33 billion sums while its income in 1998 increased by 1.5 times compared to 1997 to reach 3.24 billion sums.

In the securities markets, the bank trades state short-term T-bills and corporate securities. Over the last two years, Asaka's trading volume of T-bills increased by over five times and its client base increased 300 per cent. In the equity market, according to the Uzbek Securities Market Co-ordination and Control Centre, Asaka ranked fifth among 250 brokers.

The bank manages it's own proprietary portfolio holding shares such as Uzbekneftegaz, Minenergo and Optbirgetorg. Several of the shares have produced a total return of over 130 per cent per annum. By carefully monitoring its own portfolio Asaka is able to constantly investigate new investment opportunities, particularly in shares in the rapidly developing insurance and financial sectors.

Development of the bank's corporate loan portfolio is undertaken with prudent conservatism. Lending decisions are based on meticulous research of a borrower's financial statements and credit history. By virtue of its expertise in the automotive sector, the bank has strongly supported UzDaewooAuto Limited, Uzautotechchizmat Company and UzAutoSanoat Service Limited. The increase of credit operations has been carried out on the basis of diversification of borrowers as well as maturities. Financing activity has also been increased in the retail market to support private borrowers purchasing UzDaewooAuto cars. Because of the trend towards diversification, as well as a firm policy framework under which all lending decisions are made, by early 1999, the proportion of non-performing loans was less than 0.8 per cent.

To better serve the business community as a whole and develop new client relations, the bank has implemented a Program of Small and Medium-Sized Business Development in partnership with the European Bank of Reconstruction and Development. The EBRD extended a total credit in two tranches of US$30 million in order to support this programme.

Asaka's client base, served by 18 branch offices throughout the country, is characterised by large and financially stable enterprises as well as a considerable number of small business account holders, giving the bank a reliable asset base. Over the last year, Asaka achieved several key goals in the development of its retail operations:

- the expansion and increased quality of banking services
- a more detailed approach to retail service
- use of state-of-the-art information technology
- creation of a user-friendly environment for consumers

- constant monitoring of financial markets, which allowed the bank to offer the most competitive interest and conversion rates.

The strengthened public confidence in Asaka is best demonstrated by the significant increase in all sectors of its client base. At the beginning of 1999, the bank had over 18,000 clients. Over the last year, the total number of clients has more than doubled. Asaka's clients include promising institutions in the automotive industry and oil and gas sector, as well as retail businesses, storage and distribution enterprises, among others.

The most important clients of the bank remain in the automotive sector. Among these clients are UzDaewooAvto and other enterprises producing spare parts for cars. Taking into consideration the importance of these key accounts, a special division was created at Asaka to serve corporate clients. Senior managers are made responsible for individual clients, and make regular visits to their businesses to improve understanding of their banking needs.

The installation of a new dealing room has substantially increased productivity and efficiency at the heart of Asaka, thus strengthening its position on the international currency market. The bank now has the most up-to-date Reuters Dealing 2000 system, which has considerably facilitated management of the bank's liquidity and currency positions. Asaka is an active participant in all internal and most major international currency markets. The types of transactions carried out include spot and forward currency conversions, futures, options, and money market operations. Free consultation is provided to all of the banks' clients regarding currency legislation, customs regulations, and foreign trade transactions. A wide network of 29 correspondent banks across the globe, including Chase Manhattan Bank, Bank of New York, ABN AMRO, Deutsche Bank, Berliner Bank, Credit Suisse, Barclays Bank, Korea First Bank, Korea Exchange Bank and Bank Brussels Lambert, enables Asaka to offer its clients a broad spectrum of international financial services, such as bank transfers, letters of credit, bank guarantees and trade finance. Asaka can also conduct placements of deposits with all of its correspondent banks. Forex lines have been established with Deutsche Bank, Chase Manhattan Bank, Union Bank of Switzerland and AIG Financial Group.

The basis of the dynamic development of Asaka Bank is the efficiency and professionalism of its highly skilled staff of specialists. The total staff size has increased reaching 1,200, with over half of these under the age of 30. More than 700

employees of the Head Office and local branches have been put through rigorous training at the Regional Banking Training Center and the Banking Academy. Forty-three specialists were trained abroad in Hungary, Japan, Germany, the United States, the United Kingdom, Turkey and Egypt among other countries. As part of an ongoing professional development programme, the bank closely cooperates with Tashkent State Economic University and Tashkent Finance Institute. More than 150 bank employees are training part time at these institutions to perfect their banking skills.

Asaka continues to develop and strengthen its position as one of the largest and most reliable financial institutions in Uzbekistan. To maintain such high standards and to compete globally, Asaka Bank is committed to achieving the following goals:

- increasing the efficiency of the bank's activity through a sound credit and investment policy
- improving the quality of retail services on the basis of strengthening client relationships
- expanding the bank's branch network and improving management systems and financial monitoring
- the introduction of payment cards
- developing and implementing the bank's social programme.

For further information, please contact:

R. Adilov, Chairman of the Board
Asaka Bank
Nukus Str. 67
70015 Tashkent
Uzbekistan
tel: (998-71) 120-8111, 120-8112
fax: (998-71) 254 06 59

Ernst & Young is one of the world's leading professional services firm dedicated to helping companies and investors identify and capitalise on global business opportunities. Worldwide, our team numbers nearly 82,000 people in more than 670 offices located in over 130 countries.

Our practice areas include accounting and auditing, tax and legal services, management consulting, corporate finance, restructuring and reorganisation, capital markets, benefits and compensation consulting, cash management, and business valuations. Our varied client base includes multinational corporations, owner-managed companies, state agencies, and non-profit institutions throughout the developed and emerging markets of the world.

In the CIS, we have been helping our clients invest and grow since 1989. Our offices and representatives, staffed by over 500 local and expatriate experts, are located in Moscow, St. Petersburg, Almaty, Astana, Kyiv, Baku, Ashgabat, Tashkent and Tbilisi.

We operate as a single globally integrated firm consistently ensuring high-quality, value-added service to our clients. Our international resources enable us to deliver a uniform level of quality from one country to another. All our offices and people work under common professional, ethical and independent work standards and are linked by state-of-the art information technology that enables instantaneous transfer of knowledge and data.

The CIS practice is especially focused on several key sectors: energy, telecom, financial services, and industrial/consumer goods. The vast amount of foreign investment over the past several years has been concentrated these key areas. Using our experience and knowledge gained from other emerging markets, we have assisted both domestic and international companies to successfully establish market-based enterprises in one of world's most difficult and challenging commercial environments.

In the energy sector, Ernst & Young's expertise has been recognised and confirmed by the *Petroleum Economist,* the oil industry's leading trade publication. In 1997 and 1998, the *Petroleum Economist* named Ernst & Young 'the international accounting firm that has the best knowledge of energy in central and eastern Europe (including the former Soviet Union)'. We have been mandated by the World Bank and the European Union to conduct major studies on restructuring vital aspects of the CIS energy industry.

We advise many international and local energy companies that are operating or evaluating joint ventures in the CIS. Our recent clients include AGIP, BP Amoco, Anglo-Suisse, BHP, Caspian Pipeline Consortium, Chevron Azerbaijan, Conoco, Deminex, Elf Aquitaine, Gulf Canada, KazakhOil, Mobil, Neste OY, Occidental, Shell, Statoil, Tengizchevroil and others. We know from first-hand experience the major issues and concerns of energy investors. Our CIS Energy Industry Tax and Financial Working Group attracts participants from nearly 40 exploration and production companies with interests in this market. Our activity extends throughout the former Soviet Union and throughout Central Asia: Kazakhstan, Azerbaijan, Uzbekistan, Turkmenistan, Kyrgyzstan and Georgia. We have advised the government of the Russian Federation on the privatisation and valuation of its state-owned energy firms. We have also consulted with the Russian federal and Sakhalin regional governments on international practices regarding the valuation of oil and gas deposit tenders. Ernst & Young's leading oil and gas joint venture experts have advised clients in Kazakhstan and conducted privatisation seminars for the government of Kazakhstan. We have also organised seminars for the Republic of Kazakhstan in accounting, privatisation, energy and market transition.

The fast-paced changes in the region will continue in the near future, creating investment opportunities for organisations that anticipate, rather than react to, developments in this dynamic environment. As a firm that thoroughly understands the Caspian region and Central Asian markets, Ernst & Young offers high-quality, proactive business advice and service to all our clients.

Our global perspective benefits our clients, who have come

to depend on our value-added approach and business insight. Our newly opened offices in Astana and Ashgabat increase our presence and ability to serve clients in the region. Our key strength is our knowledge of the energy sector. Our growing client base includes Aktobe Preussag Munai, Amerada Hess, Atyrau Refinery, BP Amoco Azerbaijan, BP Amoco Kazakhstan, Caspian Pipeline Consortium-K, Chevron Azerbaijan, Embamiunaigaz, Georgian International Operating Company, Karakuduk Munai, KazakhOil, Mobil in Azerbaijan, Kazakhstan and Turkmenistan, Munai Impex, Statoil Azerbaijan, TengizChevroil, Tengizmunaigas, Uzenmunaigas, Veba Oil, and a number of production enterprises and refineries in Kazakhstan and Kyrgyzstan.

## Audit

At Ernst & Young, our people are our most valuable asset. We blend our expertise in local rules and regulations with an experienced international outlook. Our regional and expatriate professional staff is well-trained in local and international auditing and accounting principles and is able to advise both local and multinational clients on the unique and challenging business environment prevailing in the CIS. We have also established an invaluable network of contacts within the local business communities throughout the CIS as well as regional and federal governments.

Ernst & Young has built a strong reputation performing value-added audits, designed to accommodate the unique disclosure requirements of CIS regulatory authorities and the corporate reporting requirements of large local and multinational corporations. More specifically, our audit services include the following:

*Accounting.* Accounting consultation and preparation of financial statements in accordance with Generally Accepted Accounting Principles (GAAP), International Accounting Standards (IAS) and local requirements.

*Advisory services.* Advice on the implications of differences in accounting principles and reporting requirements.

*Audit.* Full or limited-scope audit procedures for corporate, local statutory and international financial reporting.

*Internal controls review.* Identification of relevant controls, determination of effective controls and advice on establishing controls that are missing or needed.

*Financial analyses.* Analyses may include interpretation of statutory Russian accounts in order to provide greater understanding to a foreign reader.

*Accounting due diligence.* Procedures may include restatement of accounts to International Accounting Standards; investigation of debts, liabilities and ownership; and produce cost analyses.

## Tax

One of the most significant factors in any business venture is the tax burden the operator must bear. The constantly changing tax regime in the CIS makes strategic planning even more challenging. Ernst & Young tax professionals are knowledgeable, innovative and responsive specialists and advise our clients on the complex tax issues facing business entities in the CIS. More importantly, our approach is adapted to each client's specific business objectives. Our foremost concern is ensuring that our clients' tax situations in the CIS are consistent with their objectives.

Ernst & Young has the reputation as the market leader in technical analysis and planning for business operations in the CIS. Our services include:

*Corporate tax planning.* We focus on establishing a tax-efficient structure under existing law, often the most critical phase of any venture in the CIS. Whether setting up a Representative Office or a local or foreign legal entity, our clients receive accurate, proactive advice.

*Indirect taxes.* Customs duties and VAT in the CIS have a uniquely complicated structure compared with the rest of the world. Our specialists provide advice on the options available to businesses regarding import and export of goods into and from the CIS in the most efficient manner.

*Registration.* Our start-up services include assistance in registering new businesses with the necessary local, regional and national tax authorities as well as with appropriate payroll and social funds throughout the CIS.

*Personal tax.* The tax system presents a formidable challenge. Our experienced staff assists our clients in complying with personal tax laws. In addition, we have special expertise in US expatriate taxes and are ready to assist our clients with any US personal tax filings.

*Payroll services.* The demands on a new company to comply with local tax reporting can be overwhelming. Our personal tax group provides a special service helping clients with all local tax registrations and filings of payroll declarations.

*Legal services.* In addition to the aforementioned registration assistance, our Moscow-based legal services include accreditation, commercial contract drafting and review, basic due diligence procedures and advice concerning currency, labour and financing issues.

## Corporate finance

Companies operating in the CIS need specialised, independent assistance with their investment transactions. Both CIS companies and multinational investors rely on Ernst & Young

Corporate Finance Services (CFS) to help them achieve their business objectives.

We initiate and execute acquisition, joint venture, strategic alliance, divestiture and financing transactions on behalf of CIS and foreign companies. Our corporate finance services are characterised by high value-added potential, strong ties to capital sources and investor networks, in-depth structuring skills and strict quality control. Our knowledge of the CIS markets, our extensive international network of business contacts, understanding of cultural issues and our reputation for quality have proved critical to our clients' success.

*Financing feasibility studies.* Often, before an investment project is even considered, a feasibility study is performed to ensure that the investment concept can support an attractive return. CFS consultants can evaluate the soundness of an investment proposal from the perspectives of markets, operations, strategy and financial returns.

*Due diligence.* CFS consultants perform services for investors and major trading partners, providing detailed analyses of the financial, operational and commercial aspects of a potential partner or investment target. Services can range from a brief enterprise assessment to a full-fledged due diligence assignment, in which our consultants assess management capabilities, restate accounts to International Accounting Standards and investigate debts, liabilities, ownership and financial liquidity.

*Valuation services.* CFS valuation specialists have extensive experience in assessing the fair market value of business holdings and fixed assets throughout the CIS. Using proven in-house methodologies that blend Ernst & Young international valuation techniques with CIS business realities, we perform valuations for potential foreign investors, international financial institutions and domestic corporations.

*Business/strategic plan preparation.* This is the first step on the path to securing financing, yet many CIS enterprises try to approach potential investors without a well-written, thoroughly thought-out business plan. CFS brings years of experience in preparing business and strategic plans and knows how to prepare them for the emerging market investor.

*Market studies.* Our comprehensive knowledge of the market and our numerous contacts in domestic and multinational companies throughout the CIS enable Ernst & Young to prepare detailed market studies providing answers to the most critical questions for a potential investor: Is there a market and what are its prospects? Who are the main players in the targeted market? What is the best market entry strategy?

*International investor/partner search.* Our Moscow-based professionals provide an insider's knowledge of the CIS for inward investors and offer the same insight into foreign financial markets to CIS clients looking to attract investors/ partners. We help our clients identify and screen candidates to determine a strategic fit. By leveraging Ernst & Young's international Mergers & Acquisitions network, as well as our world-wide client base, CFS consultants also assist CIS enterprises to find the financing they need, whether from a strategic or financial investor.

## Management consulting

Ernst & Young offers a wide range of consulting services that help our clients meet the challenges of doing business in the CIS. Our team of professionals understands the different issues faced by clients ranging from joint ventures seeking to bring together diverse cultures and management styles to locally owned companies seeking to compete in international markets. Our local and expatriate staff is experienced in developing Management Information Systems and assisting clients with their Information Technology requirements.

*Financial procedures and controls implementation.* One of the most important issues facing clients is financial control. Our specialists review, define and establish accounting and finance processes and controls that provide better measures of an organisation's progress.

*Software specification and selection.* We assess existing or planned computer-based systems to determine how well they meet our clients' business needs. Our experts use tested methodologies that document the compatibility of various software packages to our clients' specific criteria. We detail software and hardware specifications and help our clients select integrated dual accounting (local statutory and IAS) MIS systems. Project Management, our structured system of implementation control, is designed to ensure that the software our clients purchase is implemented properly and the experience gained by their staff helps reduce future hidden costs associated with ongoing system support.

*Performance improvement.* Ernst & Young performance improvement assignments focus on and measure specific business processes in terms of cost, time, output quality and customer satisfaction. We combine our performance improvement methodologies with business expertise to develop projects that bring manifold benefits to our clients' organisations. Our approach has been successfully applied to a wide range of problems including cost management at major enterprises, reducing raw material reserve requirements, redesigning organisational structure, and reducing staffing requirements.

*Enterprise development.* Major organisational change requires people to modify their behaviour, knowledge, beliefs, and expectations. We use proven Organisational Change Management methodologies to help our clients manage the human aspects of change, maximise the effectiveness of their initiatives and accurately plan the resources and time required.

*Technology.* We are experienced in all major networking platforms and specialise in integrating them into our clients' businesses. Our local and wide area networking team plans, designs, and provides purchase support and implementation of LAN and WAN networks both in Moscow and across the CIS. For our clients in the CIS, we plan and implement comprehensive Lotus Notes systems, train users, and integrate Notes databases into their businesses.

*Communications.* The quality of telecommunications is one of the largest and most expensive challenges facing businesses in the CIS. Our telecommunications specialists identify and analyse options to help our clients find the most economical solution.

*"We are **creative catalysts** who **join forces** with our clients to do all it takes — **from thought to finish** — to achieve **positive, significant change.**"*

**ERNST & YOUNG**

*FROM THOUGHT TO FINISH.*™

**HSBK**

**HALYK SAVINGS BANK
OF KAZAKHSTAN**

## History

Halyk Savings Bank of Kazakhstan is the most influential financial institution in Kazakhstan and maintains a truly unique position within the financial services sector by virtue of a number of the bank's operating and ownership characteristics.

Halyk Savings Bank of Kazakhstan is a majority state-owned national savings bank with a 65 per cent share of the retail deposit market in 15 million accounts in 1,385 outlets throughout the country.

The bank was established in 1936 as a branch of the Soviet Sberbank (savings bank of the former Soviet Union) and was, historically, the only one of the Soviet banks that dealt exclusively in the retail banking market. Halyk inherited a widespread network of district branches and retail outlets that

*Karim Massimov*
*Chairman of the Board*

enhance its deposit collection capability. In 1992, the bank became a separate legal entity wholly owned by the Republic of Kazakhstan. In 1995, the bank was re-incorporated as a closed joint stock bank.

In line with the government's programme, the privatisation of the bank started in February 1998 with the re-incorporation of the bank into an open joint stock company. Through auctions 17.6 per cent of the equity were sold to the bank's depositors; this increased the number of shareholders to over 44,000. In accordance with legislation, a joint stock company (JSC) with more than 500 shareholders must be registered as an open JSC. Privatisation continued with the sale of 10 per cent of the equity to private investors.

Currently the ownership structure is: the government of Kazakhstan (80 per cent), over 44,000 depositors of the bank (10 per cent), and private investors (10 per cent). Further tranches, each involving 10 to 15 per cent of the bank's equity held by the government, will be sold throughout the years 1999–2001.

The bank's shares are listed on the Kazakhstan Stock Exchange in the highest category 'A'.

In 1997, the bank was assigned foreign currencies long-term credit ratings of Ba3 by Moody's Investors Service Inc. and B+ by Standard & Poor's Ratings Group. In October 1998, Standard & Poor's downgraded the bank's long-term credit rating to B due to a change in sovereign credit rating from BB− to B+. The outlook was changed by both rating agencies from stable to negative.

In February 1999, Moody's downgraded the foreign currency deposit rating from B1 to B2 due to a change in sovereign rating.

In December 1998 Thomson Bank Watch confirmed its assigned ratings of Intra-Country Issuer IC-B/C and short-term (local currency) LC-1. According to the rating agency the ratings of Halyk Bank are the highest in the CIS countries currently assigned by Thomson Bank Watch.

In December 1997 the bank made its debut in the inter-

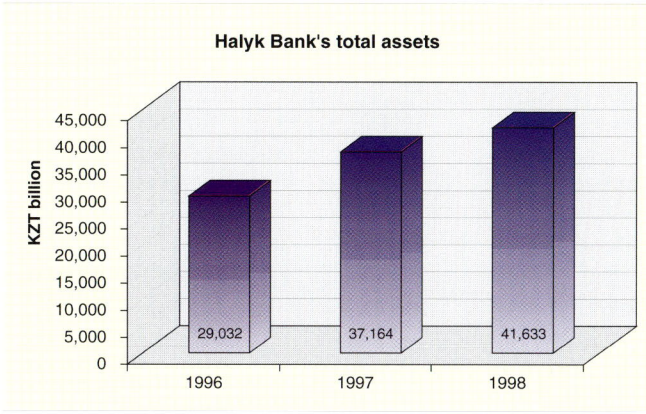

Halyk Bank's total assets

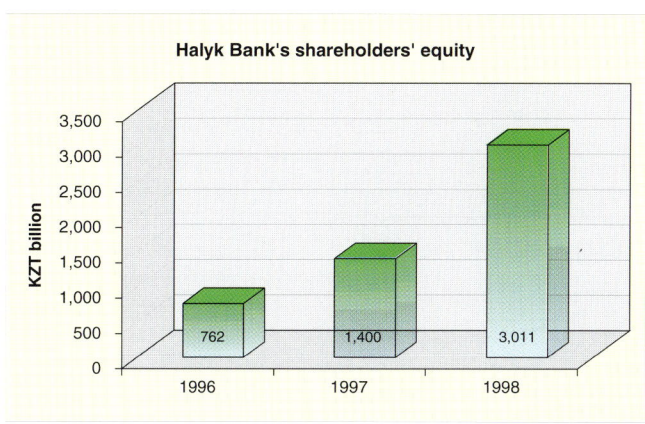

Halyk Bank's shareholders' equity

national financial markets with its first syndicated loan, raising US$40 million, which was successfully repaid in October 1998.

## Financial highlights

Halyk Savings Bank is the largest financial institution in Kazakhstan in terms of total retail deposits, which amounted to KZT20,806 million and which, according to statistics published by the National Bank of Kazakhstan (NBK), represented 66 per cent of the total market share as of 31 December 1998. The market share has steadily increased from 40 per cent since separation from Sberbank in 1994 as a result of banking sector consolidation and flight to quality. Halyk is viewed by depositors as a safe and stable bank. The bank is also the second largest bank in Kazakhstan, according to statistics published by the NBK, based on total assets of KZT39,734 million at 31 December 1998. The bank's net income for 1998 was KZT553 million, representing a 94 per cent increase compared to 1997.

The bank has strengthened its capital base through the privatisation process with an increase of capital by KZT1.6 billion in 1998, reaching KZT3 billion as of 1 January 1999. With further privatisation of the bank, capital is expected to increase accordingly.

## Business operations

The bank's core business is focused on consumer and corporate banking and acting as the principal paying and collection agent for the government and various government agencies.

Currently the bank is authorised to provide the following services:
• taking deposits from individual and corporate clients;
• operating correspondent and other accounts for banks and corporate clients;

• cash, transfer and inventory operations for individual and corporate clients;
• lending;
• transfer payments for individual and corporate clients, including transfers for correspondent banks on their correspondent accounts;
• clearing, custody and lombard services;
• issuance of credit cards;
• cash collection and transportation, currency exchange;
• trading precious metals;
• issuance of depository certificates and bank guarantees;
• issuance of the bank's securities (except for shares);
• leasing;
• factoring and forfaiting operations;
• broker/dealer operations, custodial and clearing services in the securities market; and
• other banking activities that do not contravene Kazakhstan's banking legislation.

These activities are conducted by Halyk under licence from the Central Bank and under any special regulations covering these types of activities.

### Retail banking

With the most extensive retail distribution network in Kazakhstan, the bank is able to service its customers through 1,385 retail outlets, including regional and district branches in 14 regions throughout Kazakhstan, which as of 31 December 1998 were staffed by 11,489 employees. The bank's retail banking operations include branch banking, deposit taking activities, credit and debit card services and, to a lesser extent, consumer lending.

Total deposits including demand and time deposits totalled KZT32,794 million and accounted for approximately 94 per cent of Halyk's funding base. Outstanding retail account balances have increased by 5.5 per cent in 1998. Currently the bank offers its customers 12 types of deposit accounts.

To grow its retail banking business further, the bank has

*Halyk Bank's plastic cards*

increased its credit card operations. In the first quarter of 1997, the bank launched a national debit card, Altyn, which is targeted at the middle income market. In 1996, the bank also became a member of Visa, Mastercard and American Express, and began marketing these cards in the second quarter of 1997. To date, the bank has issued a total of approximately 300,000 credit and debit cards, including 170,000 Altyn cards. This represents an increase of over 60 per cent since end-1997. The bank has also recently established and ATM network, and currently has 119 ATM units in operation and over 1,621 terminals accepting its cards. In this area Halyk Bank, with its capability to offer credit card services to clients of other financial institutions, is an acknowledged leader in Kazakhstan.

## Corporate banking

The corporate banking business provides a range of wholesale banking products and services to local and multinational customers, financial institutions and government entities. The bank provides commercial banking products and services to over 37,000 small, medium- and large-sized businesses in Kazakhstan. Products and services include Tenge and foreign currency-denominated loans, guarantees, export financings, documentary credits (principally letters of credit), capital markets and investment banking products, custody, deposit taking and advisory services.

As of 31 December 1998 total loans to customers and loans and advances to banks in the amount of KZT18,843 million accounted for 47.4 per cent of total assets. Halyk's total credit exposure, which includes loans to customers, loans and advances to banks, receivables and off-balance sheet credit exposure, totalled KZT21,836 million at 31 December 1998.

A number of strategically important and large companies in the economy of Kazakhstan, such as Kazakoil, KazTransOil, Kazakhmys, KazAtomProm, KazPhosphor, Mangustaymunaigas and Tengizmunaigas, are corporate clients of the bank.

## Other banking and financial services

Due to its unique branch network, Halyk carries out many tasks assigned by the government. Some of the tasks, such as pension and government salary distribution, cannot be performed by any other financial institution in the country. Currently the bank serves 3 million pensioners with pension payments distributed from 3,892 locations.

Moreover, one of the important tasks of the bank is the collection of tax and utilities payments from the public.

In addition to providing personal and corporate banking services, Halyk Savings Bank is also a leading participant in the fixed-income securities market and the foreign currency market in Kazakhstan. The bank is a primary dealer in both Treasury bills and short-term notes of the National Bank of Kazakhstan. Most of the bank's foreign exchange activity is undertaken on behalf of customers. In 1996, the bank was issued a licence to engage in certain precious metal transactions in Kazakhstan and abroad.

Halyk Bank is a founder member of the Kazakhstan Stock Exchange (KASE), the Almaty Financial Instruments Exchange (AFINEX) and the Central Depository. It is also an active member of the Association of Banks and Brokers/Dealers of Kazakhstan.

## Strategy

The bank's principal objective is to remain the pre-eminent financial services provider in the retail and corporate banking sectors throughout Kazakhstan. The bank intends to achieve this by strengthening the balance sheet through improved asset quality and raising capital, while lowering risk through diversification of assets, enhancing shareholder value by identifying additional revenues sources, improving cost efficiencies and expanding its existing banking businesses.

In the retail banking sector, the bank intends to consolidate its position as a leading savings institution in Kazakhstan. The principal objective is to capitalise on the bank's widespread branch network to grow its traditional range of retail products, such as deposit taking, consumer lending and credit cards.

In corporate banking, the bank aims to focus on building a clearly defined customer base in strategically important sectors of the economy such as oil and gas, transportation and mining. The bank intends to maintain its leading position as the government's principal paying and collection agent and to increase the products and services offered to its customers, such as electronic banking services and trade finance products. Other potential new revenue sources include investment banking and advisory services. With the evolving securities markets in Kazakhstan, management believes there are significant opportunities to develop its investment banking business.

The bank will continue to invest in information technology, thus improving security, intra-bank communication systems, the credit and debit card system, etc. The bank is also aiming to implement same-day payments and settlements, linking all branches with real-time systems.

# Subsidiaries

Under the pension reform now taking place in Kazakhstan, Halyk Savings Bank has established the Pension Fund of Halyk Savings Bank of Kazakhstan, which is the largest private pension fund in the country and has over 50 per cent of the private pension fund market with over 365,000 customers as of 1 January 1999. To manage the pension fund assets the bank has established the Asset Management Company of Halyk Savings Bank.

### *HALYK SAVINGS BANK OF KAZAKHSTAN*

**Almaty Office**
97 Rozybakieva street
Almaty 480046
Kazakhstan
Telephone: 7 (3272) 509 991
Fax: 7 (3272) 540 241
Telex: 251531.KRONA SU

**Astana Office**
30/1 Molodezhnaya district
Astana 473040
Kazakhstan
Telephone/Fax: 7 (3172) 393 593

# The International Bank of Azerbaijan – a pillar of strength

## History

Founded in 1990 as the Azerbaijan branch of the former Soviet Vneshcombank, the International Bank of Azerbaijan (IBA) became a joint-stock company in 1992. The majority of shares are still held by the state, although there are plans to sell these shares to long-term strategic investors. The first few years have been challenging for IBA, but key accomplishments were made. In 1993, IBA became a founding member of the Baku Interbank Stock Exchange, and in 1994 a full member of Europay International. In 1995, IBA became a member of SWIFT and in 1997 joined VISA International.

In 1998, IBA finally achieved its long-term goal of stability, efficiency and profitability. The results of IBA's activity over the last four years, which have been fully audited by Price Waterhouse in accordance with IAS standards, demonstrate exactly how stable development has been. In those years, equity, assets and revenue have grown continuously.

Even in the face of a significant decline in interest rates, 1997 was the most successful year, ending with a profit of Am34,852 million. Post-tax profits totalled Am27,892 million, a 61.3 per cent increase over the year before. The bank's assets also increased by 10.6 per cent to Am1,356,069 million. The size of the corporate loan portfolio has increased considerably. Along with the increase in loans, the reserve requirement for bad debt has been decreased substantially as a result of improved credit control and generally increased corporate profits. Foreign trade operations have also been on the increase.

IBA offers all services related to foreign trade including letters of credit, confirmations and guarantees. Stabilisation and growth in the national economy, a stable currency, and low inflation have certainly provided an ideal environment for these improved results.

The image of strength, security and reliability – for which IBA has worked long and hard – has brought about an increase in customers' deposits. The main principle of IBA's management policy has always been that the bank works in the customers' interests and protects their deposits as if they

Fuad Akhundov,
Chairman of the
Board and Chief
Executive Officer

were its own. National confidence is such that today, more than 50 per cent of the total deposits held within the Azeri banking sector are on deposit with IBA. Most major foreign corporates active in Azerbaijan rely on IBA, including British Petroleum, Mobil, Lukoil, the Hyatt Regency, Exxon, Shell, Total, Turkish Petroleum and the Azerbaijan International Operating Consortium, as well as local companies State Oil Company of the Republic of Azerbaijan and Caspian Shipping Company.

IBA's current position is the result of a remarkable turnaround story. Three years ago, the bank was nearly insolvent as the result of inheriting a weak, volatile loan portfolio. This turn-around was largely due to the new management's commitment to follow a number of strategies, including the:

- Transformation of IBA into a universal bank offering a wide range of banking services. These included extending the range of retail services offered to current clients and increasing the volume of operations to these clients.
- Increase in the scale of banking services offered to consortiums and joint ventures that are investing in the development, operation and transportation of oil.

- Provision of consulting services to clients.
- Focus on the interbank cash, forex and stock market operations and their participants to ensure IBA takes timely measures to prevent any negative affects from any resulting financial problems on the bank's assets or clients.
- Increase in the bank's assets and interest raised from them.

## Services

IBA is constantly implementing substantial measures to meet the demands of its customers. A number of new banking services have been launched recently. IBA was the first Azeri bank to issue international travellers cheques and first to become a fully authorised issuer in the EuroCard-MasterCard and Visa International networks. IBA was also the first bank to develop a nationwide network of automatic teller machines.

In forex and capital market operations, IBA has been increasing its lead. Because of its growing transaction volume, IBA has become the most active bank in the Azeri currency markets.

IBA is particularly keen to expand its branch network. To date, 27 branches have been opened in Baku and other regions of the country providing extensive nationwide coverage. An IBA representative office has been established in Moscow to offer clients advice and the ability to carry out banking transactions in Russia.

## Project finance

The bank's stable development, strong market activity and respected image as a reliable partner have led to a much greater presence within the international banking industry. An example of this is IBA's lead management, in conjunction with major foreign banks, in the project financing of the construction of Baku airport terminal. The airport project involved agreements with the UK Export Credit Guarantee Department (ECGD), HSBC Investment Bank and Turkeximbank, among others. The total amount of the financing involved was US$60 million. Participation in this project will earn IBA over US$2 million in fees. In a number of syndicated financing transactions involving major foreign banks, the presence of IBA on the syndicate has often been specially requested.

Another major project has been the recent financing of the refurbishment of a large ethylene-polyethylene plant producing one of the most important by-products of the oil industry. IBA is also financing a compressor station in the Bahar oil field as well as tyre plants in Baku and Sumgayit.

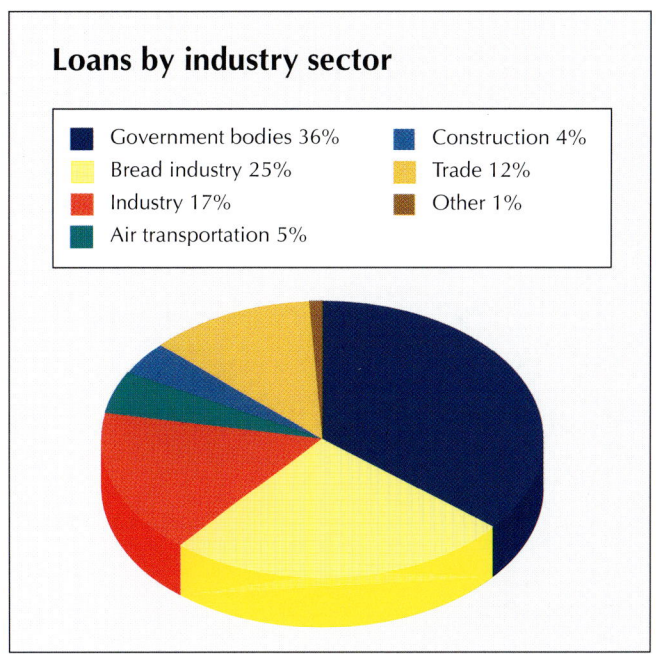

**Loans by industry sector**

- Government bodies 36%
- Bread industry 25%
- Industry 17%
- Air transportation 5%
- Construction 4%
- Trade 12%
- Other 1%

With the goal of playing a dominant role in financing the country's small and medium-sized enterprises, an agreement was reached on establishing a direct credit line between the IBA and the European Bank for Reconstruction and Development without government guarantee. A programme has been developed to increase the efficiency of utilising new credit lines. The programme will target ways to finance for a profit small start-up businesses and better manage overall risk. In addition, discussions are under way with the German Export Insurance Corporation to establish a new direct credit line.

## Human resources

All these achievements have been possible because IBA's professional staff is a highly trained, talented and motivated group committed to the bank's long-term development and strength. There are currently 501 staff including 185 at the head office.

Recognising the vital importance of human resource development, the EU TACIS Project joined IBA in financing an Ecu2 million twinning programme. This programme involves training staff with the close cooperation of Crédit Commercial de France and Arthur Andersen. Thirty-eight employees participated in various training programmes in the United States, Austria, Germany, Belgium, the Netherlands, Switzerland, Turkey, the

**Key financial indicators, 1995–97**

| | 1995 | | 1996 | | 1997 | |
|---|---|---|---|---|---|---|
| | *manat m* | *US$ m* | *manat m* | *US$ m* | *manat m* | *US$ m* |
| Assets | 1,333,243 | 300.3 | 1,225,550 | 299.1 | 1,356,069 | 348.8 |
| *including:* | | | | | | |
| Loans | 517,002 | 116.4 | 646,192 | 157.7 | 697,181 | 179.3 |
| Deposits | 222,032 | 50.0 | 213,782 | 52.1 | 251,899 | 64.8 |
| Equity | (39,556) | (8.9) | 1,475 | 0.4 | 18,323 | 4.7 |
| *including:* | | | | | | |
| Statutory capital | 3,000 | 0.7 | 11,372 | 2.8 | 11,393 | 2.9 |
| Income | 60,516 | 13.6 | 83,374 | 20.3 | 81,168 | 20.9 |
| *including:* | | | | | | |
| Interest received | 45,226 | 10.2 | 51,213 | 12.5 | 50,034 | 12.9 |
| Commission | 13,448 | 3.0 | 18,120 | 4.4 | 24,682 | 6.3 |
| Expenditures | 66,171 | 14.9 | 56,688 | 13.8 | 46,316 | 11.9 |
| Profit | (5,655) | (1.3) | 26,686 | 6.5 | 34,852 | 9.0 |
| *including:* | | | | | | |
| Net income | | | | | | |
| after taxation | (28,754) | (6.5) | 17,295 | 4.2 | 27,893 | 7.2 |
| Deposits attracted | 213,798 | 48.2 | 361,556 | 88.2 | 453,546 | 116.7 |

United Kingdom, Hungary, Russia and Israel, among other countries. Staff training with regularly scheduled weekly seminars is part of the bank's ongoing development activities.

## Advanced technology

IBA will continue to be at the cutting edge of implementing the most advanced, robust information technology system. The bank's main computers already have the capacity to process more than 30 million transactions a day using the MIDAS system software.

This system includes communication modules linked in real time to accounting, crediting, dealing, fund transfer, SWIFT and telex. MIDAS allows payment orders to be processed quickly and reliably and also facilitates the calculation of interest rates and commissions. Another key advantage of MIDAS is that since all branches are linked in the network, accounting and financial control functions can be standardised and monitored on a real time basis.

A Reuters Dealing 2000 IT system allows IBA to carry out operations in the world foreign exchange markets. Having entered into correspondent relations with 150 foreign banks in 40 countries, IBA is by far the most internationally well-connected bank in Azerbaijan.

An IBA subsidiary, *Business-Rabite* – an official partner of *Global One* – plays an active role in integrating Azeri banks into the international payment and forex system. *Business-Rabite* is the only company in Azerbaijan with the expertise needed to implement SWIFT and Reuters Dealing 2000 systems.

In 1997 IBA together with Most-Bank Azerbaijan invested over US$1 million in the establishment of the AzeriCard Processing Centre. Today IBA is granted MSP (Member Service Provider) status by Europay International and is completely certified by Visa International. In 1999 IBA intends to issue 35,000 cards, increase by 2.5 times the number of transactions per day and service banks such as ABN AMRO and the British Bank of Middle East through the AzeriCard Processing Centre.

## The future

The next two years will be a decisive period for IBA's further restructuring. The final stages of privatisation will be completed and shareholders' interest will become even more paramount. The management have a long-term strategic goal of turning IBA into a modern, fully universal bank offering a complete range of banking services well above and beyond the import-export operations that have been the main area of business in the past. This transformation will involve strengthening contacts with international financial institutions and constantly improving the quality of service.

As Azerbaijan's macroeconomic environment and growing oil industry become increasingly attractive to foreign investors, a stable, reliable, well-connected local banking partner is essential for success in Azerbaijan. Whether for corporate commercial, capital market or advisory services, IBA, after its remarkable turnaround and solid position as the leader of the Azeri banking sector, is the essential banking partner for operating in Baku and throughout the entire country.

### The International Bank of Azerbaijan
**Balance sheet at 31 December 1998 and 1997 (manat m)**

| | 1998 | 1997 | | 1998 | 1997 |
|---|---|---|---|---|---|
| **Assets** | | | **Liabilities** | | |
| Cash and short-term funds | 96,951 | 224,604 | Deposits from banks | 329,947 | 519,246 |
| Loans and advances to banks | 103,971 | 251,899 | Customer accounts | 366,884 | 453,546 |
| Loans and advances to customers | 641,575 | 697,181 | Other borrowed funds | 255,105 | 290,889 |
| Investment securities | 10,685 | 1,870 | Accrued interest expense | 39,197 | 675 |
| Investments | 5,573 | 2,011 | Other liabilities | 44,545 | 70,908 |
| Accrued interest income | 51,393 | 13,225 | Deferred tax liability | – | 2,482 |
| Other assets | 74,886 | 83,358 | **Total liabilities** | 1,035,678 | 1,337,746 |
| Premises and equipment | 91,206 | 81,921 | | | |
| Deferred tax asset | 10,156 | – | | | |
| **Total assets** | 1,086,396 | 1,356,069 | | | |
| | | | | | |
| **Shareholders' equity** | | | Total interest income | 48,719 | 50,275 |
| Paid-in capital | 11,466 | 11,393 | Operating income | 54,089 | 57,474 |
| Revaluation reserve for premises | | | Profit before taxation | 21,983 | 34,852 |
| and equipment | 32,028 | 20,628 | Net profit | 29,457 | 27,893 |
| Retained earnings | 7,224 | (13,698) | | | |
| **Total shareholders' equity** | 50,718 | 18,323 | | | |
| **Total liabilities and shareholders equity** | 1,086,396 | 1,356,069 | | | |

# ◼️● KAZKOMMERTSBANK – *leading*
## *Kazakhstan's financial sector*

*Nurzhan Subkhanberdin*
*Chairman of the Board*

First established in 1990 as Medeu Bank, Kazkommertsbank (KKB) registered its present name in 1993, and a year later merged with Astana Holding Bank. KKB was instrumental in launching the Kazakh state promissory note programme from 1995 to 1996 and was one of the first banks in the region to join the EBRD twinning programme in March 1997, being partnered with Crédit Commercial de France (CCF). CCF, one of the most dynamic French banks, provided an advisory team which contributed substantially to upgrading KKB's credit procedures, asset and liability management, information technology and payment systems.

During its brief history, KKB has established itself as the leading financial institution not only in Kazakhstan, but has also become one of the leading banks in Central Asia as a whole. Pursuing its strategy to become a truly international financial institution and the dominant provider of corporate and retail banking services in Kazakhstan, KKB took a major step in broadly expanding its shareholder base. In July 1997,

the bank completed an international share offering in the form of American Depository Receipts (ADRs) and raised US$50 million, effectively doubling its capital. Authorised share capital was increased by 28.7 per cent to a total of 283 million shares. The issue price exceeded the highest expectations: a premium of 1.7 times book value. The ADRs were purchased mainly by institutional investors in Western Europe and the United States. Presently, 33.22 per cent of shareholders are foreign investors. The ADR issue made KKB, already the largest private sector bank in terms of assets, the country's largest bank in terms of equity. Market capitalisation was over US$230 million as of February 1998.

### Key financial indicators, 30.09.1998

| | |
|---|---|
| Total assets | US$638.2 million |
| Deposits | US$160.0 million |
| Shareholders' equity | US$123.3 million |
| Loans to customers | US$432.3 million |
| Net profit | US$17.5 million |

KKB is a universal bank providing a wide range of corporate and retail banking services through 18 branches in key industrial regions. It issues VISA, MasterCard, AMEX, Cirrus and Maestro cards. KKB also advises a large number of major Kazakh corporates on raising finance and attracting foreign partners. The bank enjoys access to long-term inexpensive credit lines available from the EBRD, IFC, ADB, DEG, FMO, and other multilateral financial institutions.

## Loan portfolio

The corporate loan market is one of the most active areas of business for KKB, making it one of the most important sources of finance for Kazakh industry as well as giving the bank a wide network of strategic relations throughout the entire economy.

The wide distribution of KKB's loan portfolio demonstrates its extremely diverse asset base and at the same time reflects the diverse nature of the Kazakh economy. KKB has made great efforts to incorporate the most sophisticated risk management

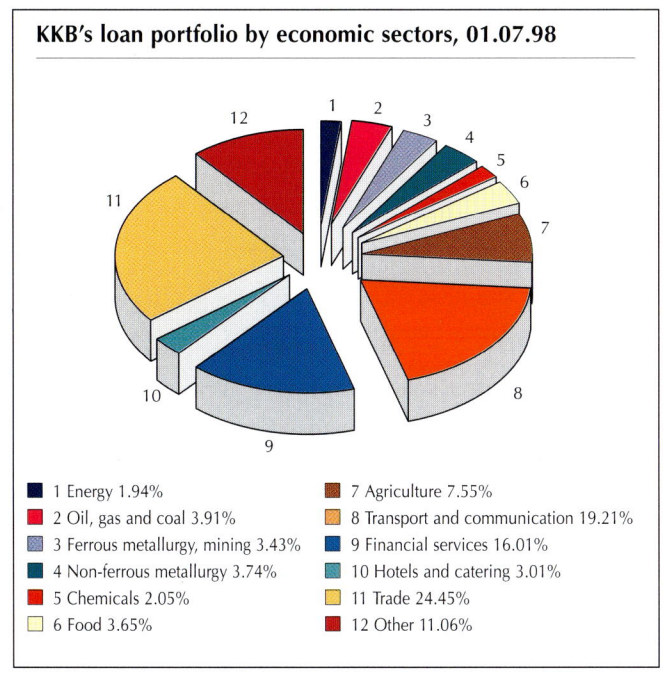

**KKB's loan portfolio by economic sectors, 01.07.98**

- 1 Energy 1.94%
- 2 Oil, gas and coal 3.91%
- 3 Ferrous metallurgy, mining 3.43%
- 4 Non-ferrous metallurgy 3.74%
- 5 Chemicals 2.05%
- 6 Food 3.65%
- 7 Agriculture 7.55%
- 8 Transport and communication 19.21%
- 9 Financial services 16.01%
- 10 Hotels and catering 3.01%
- 11 Trade 24.45%
- 12 Other 11.06%

practices based on those of Western lending institutions. Credit decisions are carefully made with regard to industry sector, cash flow, quality of management and quality of volatility of a potential borrower's account receivables. While problematic cash flow and bad debt have been issues plaguing all of the nascent private industry in the former Soviet Union, KKB has effectively managed to deal with these problems and develop a highly profitable and reliable lending business.

**Market share, 30.09.1998 (%)**

| | |
|---|---|
| Net assets | 26.99 |
| Deposits | 26.82 |
| Loans to customers | 34.30 |
| Securities | 28.14 |
| Interbank loans | 64.53 |

## International debuts

In August 1997, KKB became the first Kazakh company to be listed abroad when its Global Depository Receipts (GDRs) were admitted for trading on the parallel market of the Istanbul Stock Exchange. At the same time, the GDRs were quoted on the OTC market on both the Frankfurt and the Berlin Stock Exchanges. Several months later, KKB's common shares were listed on the Kazakh Stock Exchange (KASE). KKB thus became the first and so far the only Kazakh company to be listed in the A category.

At almost the same time, KKB made another important debut, this time as a creditworthy borrower on the international capital markets. In July 1997, KKB took out the first internationally syndicated loan to be granted to the Kazakh banking sector. This US$30 million general corporate-purpose syndicated facility for an initial six-month maturity, and three subsequent roll-over options, was arranged by Bankers Trust. Building on this success, KKB simultaneously launched two more international borrowing programmes aimed at strengthening its lending base. One was a syndicated loan, which proved to be highly successful despite the decline in international bond and equity markets. Priced at 300 basis points over Libor, this loan was jointly arranged by ING Barings and Commerzbank AG and was 2.5 times oversubscribed. The loan agreement was signed in Frankfurt in November 1997 with a final amount of US$50 million, increased from US$20 million.

In April 1998 Kazkommertsbank tapped the syndicated loans market for a US$35 million 12-month term loan which was priced at 375 basis points over Libor and was arranged by ING Barings and Commerzbank.

In November 1998 Kazkommertsbank received another syndicated loan of US$20 million for six months with one roll-over option, thus proving to be the only borrower in the former Soviet Union to have been able to tap the market since the Russian crisis last year. The deal was self arranged and was provided by Citibank, ABN AMRO Bank Kazakhstan, Commerzbank, ING Barings and American Express Bank.

Kazkommertsbank has participated in several bilateral trade facilities programmes and structured trade finance deals.

By now KKB has a positive trace record with international investors and lenders. During the Russian crisis, KKB was punctually meeting all its international obligations and by December 1998 had repaid about US$100 million borrowed in the international capital markets. This had a very positive impact on KKB in particular and Kazakhstan in general.

**Kazkommertsbank's affiliated companies**

| Name | Share (%) | Name | Share (%) |
|---|---|---|---|
| ABN AMRO Asset Management | 28.00 | Kazakh Telekom | 1.07 |
| ABN AMRO Bank Kazakhstan | 29.00 | Kazenergoprom Bank | 25.13 |
| Almaty Financial Instruments Exchange | 2.22 | Kazkommerts Capital B.V. | 100.00 |
| Central Asia Leasing | 30.00 | Kazkommerts Finance B.V. | 100.00 |
| Central Depositary | 3.45 | Kazkommerts International B.V. | 100.00 |
| Global Kazkommerts Bank | 100.00 | Kazkommerts Securities | 100.00 |
| Kazakhstan Interbank Financial House | 6.25 | Kazkommerts-Ziraat International Bank | 35.00 |
| Kazakhstan Stock Exchange | 4.76 | ShNOS (Shymkent Oil Refinery) | 15.00 |
| Kazakhstan Telecommunications | 16.00 | Umit Pension Fund | 25.00 |

# Credit ratings

In January 1997, KKB became the first bank in Kazakhstan to receive an international credit rating when it was assigned a B– long-term debt rating by Thomson BankWatch, which represented the Kazakh sovereign ceiling at the time.

**KKB's credit ratings**

| | Previous | Current |
|---|---|---|
| **Standard & Poor's** | | |
| Long-term | B+ | B− |
| Short-term | B | C |
| Rating opinion | Stable | Negative |
| | | |
| **IBCA** | | |
| Short-term | B | B |
| Long-term | B+ | B+ |
| Individual | D | D |
| Legal | 4T | 4T |
| | | |
| **Thomson BankWatch** | | |
| Intra-country issuer | IC-C | IC-C |
| Short-term (local currency) | LC-2 | LC-2 |
| Unsecured debt (long-term) | B | B |
| | | |
| **Moody's** | | |
| Financial strength | E+ | E+ |
| Short-term | B2 | B2 |
| Long-term | Not prime | Not prime |

In October 1997, KKB decided to tap the Eurobond market, which had already responded favourably to two consecutive sovereign Eurobond issues by Kazakhstan and at that time was showing substantial appetite for emerging market corporate paper. The unfortunate timing – which coincided with the start of the Asian crisis – forced the deal to be postponed. Eventually, in May 1998, KKB succeeded in launching the first Kazakh corporate Eurobond issue. An additional US$100 million three-year Euronote issue is planned for completion as soon as market conditions stabilise. KKB is already one of the major Kazakh recipients of multilateral finance, with a US$40 million term loan granted by the EBRD and US$30 million credit facility from the IFC. The IFC financing was finalised at the end of a long process that required KKB to meet a series of demanding requirements, notably the improvement of its capital adequacy ratio and the quality of its loan portfolio.

# Trade finance

KKB is active in international and domestic trade finance. The improved capital base and transparency of KKB were reflected in the substantial increase in confirmed credit lines extended to the bank by foreign correspondent and partner institutions. As of December 1997, the total amount of trade-related credit facilities reached US$62.5 million, representing a 33 per cent increase over 1996.

KKB continues to act as the EBRD's servicing agent in its loan programme aimed at supporting small and medium-sized businesses in Kazakhstan. In 1997, the programme provided US$142 million in loan finance. The bank is also successfully collaborating with the Asian Development Bank in utilising a US$20 million facility to finance the purchase of technology and equipment for agricultural production.

KKB was accepted as a certified borrower by the German state-owned export credit insurance agency Hermes. Prior to this acceptance, Hermes had only accepted the Kazakh central government as a borrower and extended its cover only to projects covered by sovereign guarantees. The recognition of the financial standing of KKB by Hermes represented not only a major achievement for KKB itself, but also a step forward for the entire Kazakh private banking sector.

## Privatisation

With large-scale privatisation still not completed, KKB will play a leading role in the restructuring of the Kazakh economy. The bank will act as adviser to the government in the sale of major oil and gas companies. It has also provided advisory services in the privatisation of the mining, metals, telecommunications, transport and power sectors. KKB acted as financial operator for Kazakh National Railways, trust manager for the Air Kazakhstan National Air Company, and as lead banker for the state-owned monopoly producer of uranium, Kazatomprom. These activities helped to further strengthen KKB's considerable client base among both domestic and foreign corporate clients.

Kazakhstan represents one of the most exciting investment opportunities in the former Soviet Union. Yet, at the same time, the economy can prove to be one of the harshest commercial environments in all the emerging markets. Reliable, professional and in-depth financial services are essential for any financial or direct investor. KKB is committed to providing such a service and enabling foreign institutions to take advantage of Kazakhstan's restructuring.

Please contact us for further information:
Kazkommertsbank
Head Office
135 ZH, Gagarina Street
Almaty, 480060
Republic of Kazakhstan
Tel:  7 3272 505 101, 505 113
Fax: 7 3272 505 100, 505 281

## Our vision

Change is an unavoidable characteristic of every growing economy. It could be argued that, in today's world, change imbues every possible aspect of our life – not necessarily economic and not necessarily in an emerging market. What distinguishes the atmosphere of growing economies, however, is that this change is persistent and requires constant and careful monitoring of trends, and immediate reaction. Moreover, the countries that have not yet fully integrated into the global economy adapt the trends inherent in that economy to their local operations.

The need for careful monitoring and constant adjustment of global trends to local conditions emphasises the importance of local companies capable of serving as efficient facilitators in the flow of capital among emerging markets.

Kazkommerts Securities is itself a product of this dynamic environment. The systematic changes in Kazakhstan started in 1991, which led to the country's independence and transition to market economy, opened boundless investment opportunities for both domestic and international investors. The traditional hospitality of the Kazakh people enhances the welcoming investment climate. Most of the investors soon realised that investing in an unfamiliar economy with sophisticated traditions, although promising positive prospects, could be a long and uneasy adventure without the right partner.

Kazkommerts Securities has proven itself a partner that has been helping investors to establish trade and investment links with local businesses, and helped local companies increase their efficiency through the introduction of new technologies and management practices.

The team at the core of Kazkommerts Securities was established in 1991 to take advantage of the new economy and soon evolved into the leading securities company in Central Asia. Kazkommerts Securities has participated in most of the region's successful investment projects and is working on the further integration of Central Asia into the global economy. We understand Central Asia and its people because we are a part of them.

Our vision is a company that provides world-class financial services on a regional level. We see increasing growth opportunities in the Central Asian market as the region achieves higher integration in the global economy.

## Our mission

Kazkommerts Securities' mission is to create value for our clients, shareholders and partners by providing high-quality financial services, and through sharing its understanding of the local environment. Kazkommerts Securities concentrates on providing advisory to foreign investors operating in

Central Asia by exploiting its leadership in analysis, its ability to design and carry out complex transactions, and its established links with the region's banking and financial sector and major industrial enterprises.

Kazkommerts Securities continues to provide Central Asian companies and governments with access to leading-edge technologies and management techniques. We also enhance the region's integration into the international financial markets. Kazkommerts Securities participated in the debut corporate Eurobond issue for Kazkommertsbank. Kazkommerts Securities also participated in arranging American and Global Depository Receipts programmes for Kazakh issuers including Shymkent Oil Refinery, Kazkommertsbank and Kazakhtelecom.

## Our values

### Focusing on customers

Customers remain our highest priority. We value our clients and structure our services to provide them with efficiency and quality of service.

Our trading team offers customer-tailored settlement procedures with the minimum possible formalities. Kazkommerts Securities is an active member of the Kazakhstan Stock Exchange (KASE). It is also the most influential participant in the OTC market with a market share of over 50 per cent of the total transaction volume in Kazakhstan.

Our research team covers all major domestic companies and industrial sectors, and carries out analysis of the political and economic environment in Kazakhstan and adjacent countries. We share with our clients first-hand experience and insightful analysis of core events and changes in the complex environment of the growing Kazakh economy. Kazkommerts Securities' professionals also provide clients with regular updates on the region's major political news and events.

Our corporate finance team provides a wide range of services, including advice on debt and equity markets services, mergers and acquisitions, project finance and corporate restructuring.

### Building a team

Essential for our current and future success is the team of professionals who devote themselves to constant professional

growth and continuous improvement of our customer service. The major advantage of our professional team is its ability to combine conservatism and dynamism. Our staff include experienced professionals who have years of experience working for major Kazakh enterprises and government bodies. They provide important insights to trends and processes in the political and economic environment of Kazakhstan and help our clients to establish ties with regional businesses and government bodies, and to better understand traditions and cultures in Central Asia.

Our team harmoniously complements this team of more experienced professionals with young and energetic staff. In such a dynamic environment as Central Asia, it is important to keep a hand on the region's pulse, continuously seeking new opportunities, adjusting and developing our existing range of services to best fit clients' needs. This constantly challenging atmosphere requires a continuously innovative approach, which we derive from our younger colleagues.

## Emphasising excellence

We are consistently striving to achieve excellence in the quality and range of services we provide to our customers.

Leading local and international publications have recognised our excellence in providing quality customer service. Kazkommerts Securities was awarded the 'Best securities firm in Kazakhstan' by *Euromoney* in 1998. This award recognises the role that the company plays in the region's economy and financial system. *Global Investor* ranked our research team the best in Central Asia in 1997.

Numerous regional publications and independent agencies rank our traders as the best in Kazakhstan. *Global Investor* has also ranked us the best execution team in Central Asia in 1997. The company acts as an exclusive adviser to a range of major Central Asian corporations, most notably Kazakhtelecom, the monopoly telecommunications operator in Kazakhstan; Kazkommertsbank, the largest private sector bank in Central Asia; energy sector companies and other corporations. Kazkommerts Securities in the consortium with other international investment companies has been recently awarded exclusive mandates by the government of Kazakhstan to advise it on the sale of state-owned shares in Aktobemunaigas, the third largest oil and gas producer in Kazakhstan, and Ust-Kamenogorsk Titanium and Magnesium Plant.

Please contact Kazkommerts Securities for further information:

65 Furmanov Street

480004 Almaty

Kazakhstan

Tel: + 7 3272 50 90 60

Fax: + 7 3275 81 14 98

E-mail: enquiry@kazks.kz

# ONE LAW FIRM AROUND THE WORLD

Founded in New York in 1901, White & Case is a global law firm with more than 900 lawyers in offices in the United States, Latin America, Europe, the Middle East, Africa and Asia.

Our clients include many of the largest international corporations and organizations in the world, investment and financial institutions, as well as governments and government agencies.

White & Case lawyers have been advising on matters involving Kazakhstan, Uzbekistan, Turkmenistan, Kyrgyzstan, Ukraine, Russia and other CIS States for many years.

We advise on all facets of investment in Central Asia and the Caspian from simple trading transactions and joint ventures to complex financing arrangements and acquisitions of controlling blocks in enterprises. We have extensive experience of advising on privatization, oil and gas, telecommunications, minerals, real estate, banking, capital markets and securities transactions as well as litigation and intellectual property matters arising in this region.

White & Case has a critical mass of US, English and international lawyers with unmatched experience in providing legal advisory services to and in developing or emerging countries. The qualifications of our CIS lawyers also permit us to render legal opinions on questions of various local laws.

*For more information about the legal services we provide in this region, please contact:*

**YURIY MALTSEV (PARTNER)**
WHITE & CASE LLC
64 AMANGELDY STREET
ALMATY 480012, KAZAKHSTAN
TELEPHONE: (7-3272) 50-7491/2
FACSIMILE: (7-3272) 50-7493
E-MAIL: MALTSYU@ALMATY.WHITECASE.COM

**HUGH VERRIER (PARTNER)**
WHITE & CASE LLC
4 ROMANOV PEREULOK
MOSCOW 103875, RUSSIA
TELEPHONE: (7-095) 787-3000
FACSIMILE: (7-095) 787-3001
E-MAIL: VERRIHU@MOSCOW.WHITECASE.COM

**WHITE & CASE**

LIMITED LIABILITY PARTNERSHIP

*Specific transactions we have been involved with in Central Asia and the Caspian include:*

We advised the Republic of Kazakhstan in its debut and second issuance of Eurobonds for the amount of $200 million and $350 million, respectively;

We acted a underwriter's counsel in the issuance of ADRs/GDRs by Kazkommertsbank, the first international offering of Kazakhstan equity;

**INTERNATIONAL DEBT AND EQUITY OFFERINGS**

We advised EBRD and IFC in connection with the $450 million financing of Ispat-Karmet's $1.3 billion investment program for its steel plant in Karaganda (Kazakhstan);

We advised the borrower in the first syndicated loan to the banking sector in Kazakhstan in the amount of $30 million and represented the lenders in a number of other syndicated loans;

We advised Crédit Lyonnais and ING Bank in a secured US$120 million syndicated copper pre-purchase financing;

**SYNDICATED LOANS AND PRE-EXPORT TRADE FINANCING**

We advised a major European bank in establishing the first wholly foreign owned banking subsidiary in Kazakhstan;

We advise a number of Western investment banks in connection with various securities transactions in Kazakhstan;

**BANKING AND SECURITIES**

We represented the purchaser of the Shymkent Oil Refinery as well as investors in the privatization of various other industries;

We are currently advising the government of Kazakhstan and Kazkommertsbank in relation to the sale of a major interest in Kazakhtelecom, the national telecommunications operator;

**PRIVATIZATION**

We advised a major oil company in the purchase from the government of Kazakhstan of a 25% interest in Tengizchevroil;

We advised a group of foreign investors in obtaining several licenses for the exploration and development of the Tasbulat, Aktas and Turkmenoy oil fields;

**OIL AND GAS**

We have advised on a wide range of corporate and commercial transactions including domestic and cross-border mergers and acquisitions as well as joint venture arrangements for numerous European, U.S. and Asian companies investing in the region.

**CORPORATE AND COMMERCIAL**